EDITORS' NOTE

The Atlas of Tumor Pathology has a long and distinguished history. It was first conceived at a Cancer Research Meeting held in St. Louis in September 1947 as an attempt to standardize the nomenclature of neoplastic diseases. The first series was sponsored by the National Academy of Sciences-National Research Council. The organization of this Sisyphean effort was entrusted to the Subcommittee on Oncology of the Committee on Pathology, and Dr. Arthur Purdy Stout was the first editor-in-chief. Many of the illustrations were provided by the Medical Illustration Service of the Armed Forces Institute of Pathology, the type was set by the Government Printing Office, and the final printing was done at the Armed Forces Institute of Pathology (hence the colloquial appellation "AFIP Fascicles"). The American Registry of Pathology purchased the Fascicles from the Government Printing Office and sold them virtually at cost. Over a period of 20 years, approximately 15,000 copies each of nearly 40 Fascicles were produced. The worldwide impact that these publications have had over the years has largely surpassed the original goal. They quickly became among the most influential publications on tumor pathology ever written, primarily because of their overall high quality but also because their low cost made them easily accessible to pathologists and other students of oncology the world over.

Upon completion of the first series, the National Academy of Sciences-National Research Council handed further pursuit of the project over to the newly created Universities Associated for Research and Education in Pathology (UAREP). A second series was started, generously supported by grants from the AFIP, the National Cancer Institute, and the American Cancer Society. Dr. Harlan I. Firminger became the editor-in-chief and was succeeded by Dr. William H. Hartmann. The second series Fascicles were produced as bound volumes instead of loose leaflets. They featured a more comprehensive coverage of the subjects, to the extent that the Fascicles could no longer be regarded as "atlases" but rather as monographs describing and illustrating in detail the tumors and tumor-like conditions of the various organs and systems.

Once the second series was completed, with a success that matched that of the first, UAREP and AFIP decided to embark on a third series. A new editor-in-chief and an associate editor were selected, and a distinguished editorial board was appointed. The mandate for the third series remains the same as for the previous ones, i.e., to oversee the production of an eminently practical publication with surgical pathologists as its primary audience, but also aimed at other workers in oncology. The main purposes of this series are to promote a consistent, unified, and biologically sound nomenclature; to guide the surgical pathologist in the diagnosis of the various tumors and tumor-like lesions; and to provide relevant histogenetic, pathogenetic, and clinicopathologic information on these entities. Just as the second series included data obtained from ultrastructural (and, in the more recent Fascicles, immunohistochemical) examination, the third series will, in addition, incorporate pertinent information obtained with the newer molecular biology techniques. As in the past, a continuous attempt will be made to correlate, whenever possible, the nomenclature used in the Fascicles with that proposed by the World Health Organization's International Histological Classification of Tumors. The format of the third series has been changed in order to incorporate additional items and to ensure a consistency of style throughout. Close cooperation between the various authors and their respective liaisons from the editorial board will be emphasized to minimize unnecessary repetition and discrepancies.

To its everlasting credit, the participation and commitment of the AFIP to this venture is even more substantial and encompassing than in previous series. It now extends to virtually all scientific, technical, and financial aspects of the production.

The task confronting the organizations and individuals involved in the third series is even more daunting than in the preceding efforts because of the ever-increasing complexity of the matter at hand. It is hoped that this combined effort—of which, needless to say, that represented by the authors is first and foremost—will result in a series worthy of its two illustrious predecessors and will be a suitable introduction to the tumor pathology of the twenty-first century.

Juan Rosai, M.D.
Leslie H. Sobin, M.D.

ACKNOWLEDGMENTS

The classification of uterine corporeal tumors and gestational trophoblastic disease presented in this text was developed between 1985 and 1988 by two subcommittees of the Classification and Nomenclature Committee of the International Society of Gynecological Pathologists, chaired by Dr. Robert E. Scully, in conjunction with the World Health Organization. The chairman for the subcommittee for the uterine corpus tumors was Dr. Steven G. Silverberg, who is responsible for the discussion of that subject in the text. Dr. Robert J. Kurman chaired the gestational trophoblastic disease subcommittee and is responsible for those sections of the Fascicle. The other members of the uterine corpus subcommittee were Drs. Gisela Dallenbach-Hellweg, Alexander Ferenczy, Harold Fox, Claude Gompel, Richard L. Kempson, Frederick T. Kraus, Robert J. Kurman, Alexander W. Miller, and Ichiro Taki. Drs. Shirley Driscoll, Harold Fox, Donald P. Goldstein, Michael T. Mazur, William B. Ober, Kazuyosha Yamaguchi, A. E. Szulman, and Leo B. Twiggs were the members of the gestational trophoblastic disease subcommittee. All of the individual members of these subcommittees contributed not only their expertise but in many instances also cases and photographs that will appear in the World Health Organization publication detailing the classification and in some instances appear in this Fascicle as well.

Most of the photographs in the uterine corpus section of this Fascicle were taken by Barbara Neuburger from cases originating either from the surgical pathology files of the George Washington University Medical Center or the pathology repository of the Gynecologic Oncology Group. Some of the color photographs were contributed by our colleague at the George Washington University, Dr. Lucien Nochomovitz. The photomicrographs in the gestational trophoblastic disease section were taken by Mr. Luther Duckett at the Armed Forces Institute of Pathology and Mr. Raymond Lund from the Johns Hopkins Hospital. The material that was utilized was from the Armed Forces Institute of Pathology, made available by Dr. Henry J. Norris, and from consultation material that was sent to one of us (RJK). The electron micrographs used in the gestational trophoblastic disease section were contributed by Dr. Michael T. Mazur. Ms. Dorothy Molero played a key role in organizing the work of the original uterine subcommittee and also typed the manuscript of that section of this text. Ms. Sue Skierkowski provided excellent secretarial assistance for the gestational trophoblastic disease section. Other colleagues, as well as our wives Kiyoe and Carole, were understanding and patient as work on this project took us away from other responsibilities. Equal patience, as well as useful advice, came from the Editor of this Third Series, Dr. Juan Rosai, and my editorial consultant, Dr. Leslie Sobin. Dr. Robert E. Scully deserves special mention for his critical review of the gestational trophoblastic disease section.

Finally, we are all the products of our personal and professional experience, and we wish to thank our mentors, colleagues, and students over the years, all of whom have contributed to the development of the experience and confidence that have enabled us to undertake and complete a project of this magnitude.

Steven G. Silverberg, M.D.
Robert J. Kurman, M.D.

Permission to use copyrighted illustrations has been granted by:

Chicago Lying-In Hospital:
    J Reprod Med 29:788–91, 1984. For figures 291 and 292.

JB Lippincott Company:
    Cancer 37:1853–65, 1976. For figures 153 and 156.
    Cancer 38:1214–26, 1976. For figures 341, 342, 345, and 348.

John Wiley & Sons:
    Surgical Pathology of the Uterus, 1977. For figure 1.

Raven Press:
    Am J Surg Pathol 14:415–38, 1990. For figure 131.
    Diagnostic Surgical Pathology, vol. 2, 1989. For Table 6.
    Int J Gynecol Pathol 3:101–21, 1984. For Table 13 and figures 290 and 309.
    Int J Gynecol Pathol 6:213–29, 1987. For Table 12.

Springer-Verlag New York, Inc.:
    Blaustein's Pathology of the Female Genital Tract, 3rd ed., 1987. For Tables 7, 10, 11, and 15
        and figures 293, 303, 304, 312, 319, 321, 322, 331, 340, and 347.
    Gestational Trophoblastic Disease, 1987. For Table 9.

WB Saunders Company:
    Hum Pathol 20:370–81, 1989. For figures 333 and 351.
    Placenta 5:349–70, 1984. For figures 275, 277, 278, 284, 285, 287,and 288.
    Semin Diagn Pathol 5:135–53, 1988. For figures 16 and 56.

Williams & Wilkins Company:
    The Pathology of Reproductive Failure, 1991. For figures 271, 279, and 289.

TUMORS OF THE UTERINE CORPUS

Contents

Contents

GESTATIONAL TROPHOBLASTIC DISEASE

TUMORS OF THE UTERINE CORPUS

EMBRYOLOGY, GROSS ANATOMY, AND HISTOLOGY

The embryology, gross anatomy, and normal histology of the uterine corpus represent a complex topic that has been the subject of several long chapters and books to which I refer the reader interested in an in-depth discussion (1–3,5,6). I discuss this subject only briefly so that I can devote more space to uterine neoplasms and tumor-like lesions.

EMBRYOLOGY

The müllerian or paramesonephric ducts appear in the human embryo at about 40 days of gestation. They are initially observed as thickenings and subsequent invaginations of the coelomic epithelium on the lateral aspect of the intermediate mesoderm, at the cephalic end of the mesonephros. The ducts are initially solid cords of cells, and they extend caudally in close association with the mesonephric ducts. The two müllerian ducts subsequently develop central lumina and fuse caudally within the urorectal septum. At 63 days, the fused müllerian ducts are identifiable as the uterus and are beginning to be divided into the corpus and the cervix by a constriction arising between them. The cervix comprises the inferior two-thirds of the fetal uterus and the corpus the superior one-third.

The corpus begins to differentiate into layers of mucosa (endometrium), muscle (myometrium), and serosa by the nineteenth week of gestation, and glands begin to form in the endometrium about a week later. Both the endometrium and myometrium continue to develop during the remainder of intrauterine life. At birth, the appearance of the endometrium is influenced by the maternal hormonal milieu and may be either proliferative or secretory. Approximately 1 month after delivery, this functional activity ceases and is replaced by a state of atrophy that persists until puberty.

GROSS ANATOMY

The human adult uterus is a thick-walled hollow organ situated in the pelvic cavity between the urinary bladder anteriorly and the rectum posteriorly. In the adult, the uterine corpus comprises the superior two-thirds and the cervix the inferior one-third of the entire length of the uterus, which averages about 7.5 cm. The corpus and cervix are in continuity with each other through the internal os.

The corpus forms a pyramid, the apex of which is bent toward the base. Its exact position is quite variable because it is a mobile organ. However, the long axis of the uterus usually meets the long axis of the vagina at approximately a right angle. The size of the normal uterine corpus is generally given as about 5.0 cm in height (length), 5.0 cm in width, and 2.5 cm in anteroposterior thickness, with a weight ranging from 40 to 100 g. However, all reported measurements and weights have derived from either hospital autopsy series or surgically removed uteri, neither of which are likely to be representative of all normal uteri in healthy women. Multigravid uteri are considerably larger than nulligravid ones, so that the upper limits of size and weight of a normal multigravid uterus are probably considerably above those quoted above.

The lumen of the uterine corpus communicates with the fallopian tubes and the cervix. The portion of the corpus above the level of communication with the tubes is the fundus, which is the widest segment of the uterus. The lowermost portion, which gradually merges with the cervix through the internal os, is the isthmus or lower uterine segment. The remainder of the organ is the corpus proper.

The anterior (vesical) surface of the uterine corpus is covered by peritoneum down to the level at which the peritoneum is reflected forward onto the upper surface of the bladder. The peritoneal covering of the posterior (rectal) surface extends further inferiorly before being reflected onto the rectosigmoid. Thus, the anterior and posterior surfaces can be distinguished in an isolated uterine specimen by the lower extension of peritoneum posteriorly (fig. 1). This distinction is also facilitated because the fallopian

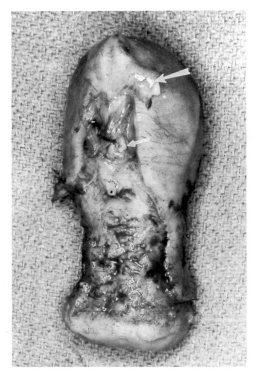

Figure 1
LEFT LATERAL VIEW
OF HYSTERECTOMY SPECIMEN
The anterior surface is to the left in the illustration. Note the more caudal extension of peritoneum on the posterior surface (right) and the stump of fallopian tube (long arrow) posterior to and above that of the round ligament (short arrow). (Fig. 4-1 from Silverberg SG. Surgical pathology of the uterus. New York: John Wiley & Sons, 1977.)

tubes are attached to the uterus posterior to and above the round ligaments.

The anterior and posterior peritoneal coverings of the uterine corpus meet laterally and form the broad ligaments, which extend to the pelvic side walls and include the fallopian tubes and the round and ovarian ligaments. The round ligaments help to maintain the uterus in its normal anteverted position, whereas the ovarian ligaments stabilize the ovaries.

The uterus is nourished by the uterine arteries, which arise from the internal iliac arteries. The veins of the corpus, as well as those of the cervix and vagina, drain to the uterovaginal venous plexus in the base of the broad ligament. The uterine veins ultimately open into the internal iliac veins. Uterine lymphatics drain from a subserosal uterine plexus into the pelvic and periaortic lymph nodes; a few lymphatics from the fundus accompany the round ligament of the uterus and drain into the superficial inguinal nodes.

The myometrium has a rich autonomic innervation that appears to be predominantly, if not exclusively, sympathetic. The exact function of the innervation is unknown.

HISTOLOGY

From external to internal surface, the uterine corpus is composed of 1) the serosa or visceral peritoneum, which is composed of mesothelial cells; 2) the myometrium or muscular layer, which is divided into an external zone of longitudinal fibers, a middle zone of interdigitating fibers coursing in all directions, and an internal zone of circular fibers; and 3) a mucosa or endometrium, which consists of a surface epithelium underlaid by a network of glands and stroma. The endometrium itself is generally divided into three layers: 1) the superficial layer or compacta, which consists of the surface epithelium and immediately underlying gland necks and stroma and which shows less pronounced cyclic variations than the middle layer; 2) the middle layer, or spongiosa or functionalis, which occupies most of the thickness of the endometrium and reacts intensely to hormonal stimulation; and 3) the deep layer or basalis, which generally reacts feebly to estrogenic stimulation and not at all to progestational stimulation. The basalis is nourished exclusively by the basal arteries, whereas the remainder of the endometrium is nourished by the spiral arteries. The latter vessels extend upward to the mucosal surface and undergo marked cyclic modifications, with markedly increased tortuosity during the secretory phase of the menstrual cycle.

The Menstrual Cycle. The endometrial glandular epithelium and stroma, particularly of the spongiosa or functionalis, vary markedly during the course of the menstrual cycle. These cyclic variations have been described in great detail at the routine light-microscopic, histochemical, ultrastructural, and functional (including hormone receptor) levels, and only a brief summary of the changes evident by routine light-microscopic examination are presented here. The menstrual cycle is divided by convention into 28 days, although individual cycles in different patients may be considerably longer or shorter. By convention, day 1 is generally assigned to the first day of menses, although some authors fix day 1 as the day on which ovulation takes place. If day 1 is assigned as the first day of menstrual flow, then day 14 represents the day of ovulation in the typical menstrual cycle, and the proliferative phase constitutes days 4–14. This phase is characterized by proliferation of gland cells, stromal cells, and vascular endothelial cells, leading to an increase of the endometrial volume under the predominant influence of estrogen. Early in the proliferative phase (figs. 2, 3), the total thickness of the endometrium is between 1 and 2 mm, the glands are small, round, and regular, and the stroma is dense and composed of small cells with nuclei that are round to oval. Mitoses are present in both glandular epithelium and stromal cells, and glandular epithelial pseudostratification is present but not prominent.

Later in the proliferative phase (fig. 4), the mucosa becomes thicker and the glands more tortuous. Despite this tortuosity, the glands are all oriented essentially parallel to one another and perpendicular to the surface. The stroma is abundant and edematous. Mitotic activity is increased in both glandular epithelium and stroma, as is gland cell pseudostratification. Clear and ciliated cells are most prominent as normal constituents of the glandular epithelium during this part of the cycle. When they become so numerous that they constitute the predominant lining cell of one or more glands, the term *ciliary change* is appropriate (see Tumor-Like Lesions).

Between 1 and 2 days after ovulation, the endometrium begins to show evidence of a response to progesterone at the light-microscopic level and is said to enter the secretory (luteal, progestational) phase. This part of the cycle is conveniently divided into early, mid-, and late secretory and premenstrual phases because the changes are more dramatic after ovulation than before. During the early secretory phase (days 16–18), the first and most prominent manifestation that ovulation has taken place is the development of subnuclear glycogen vacuoles (figs. 5, 6). The glands remain tortuous, and some mitotic activity and nuclear

pseudostratification may still be present, but these rapidly disappear over the next few days. The nuclei are pushed toward the apical surfaces of the cells by the subnuclear vacuoles, where they form a single orderly layer (fig. 6). In the midsecretory phase (days 19–20), the secretory vacuoles begin to migrate from subnuclear to supranuclear position (fig. 7). The nuclei of the endometrial glandular cells thus return to a more basal position. The general appearance of the glands remains essentially the same, but glandular mitoses have mostly disappeared. The stroma again begins to become markedly edematous.

In the late secretory phase (days 21–25), the glands begin to show regressive phenomena, manifested by irregularly collapsed contours, with gradually increasing numbers of papillary projections into the lumina. The intraglandular secretions are now mostly luminal rather than intracellular (fig. 8). However, the most rapidly changing aspect of endometrial morphology at this time is stromal rather than glandular. The stroma becomes markedly edematous, and coiling of spiral arterioles becomes prominent around day 23. Within another day, the spiral arterioles become surrounded by a mantle of predecidual stroma (fig. 8), and by day 25 the stroma of the compacta or superficial layer of the endometrium is extensively predecidualized (fig. 9). Predecidua (fig. 10) is characterized by an admixture of large polygonal cells with eosinophilic cytoplasm and small round cells resembling lymphocytes but with a small amount of cytoplasm containing eosinophilic and phloxinophilic granules, the so-called endometrial granulocytes. The latter cells are currently thought by most researchers to be true lymphoid cells derived from bone marrow, although their exact function is unknown.

During the premenstrual phase (days 26–28), endometrial glands show pronounced shrinkage, the spread of predecidual change throughout the stroma continues, and inflammatory cells, particularly neutrophils, begin to make their appearance both in the stroma and subsequently within gland lumina. Small hemorrhagic foci also appear at this time.

Finally, the menstrual phase (days 1–3) is characterized by massive hemorrhage and necrosis, with only small detached fragments of endometrial tissue visible in a curettage

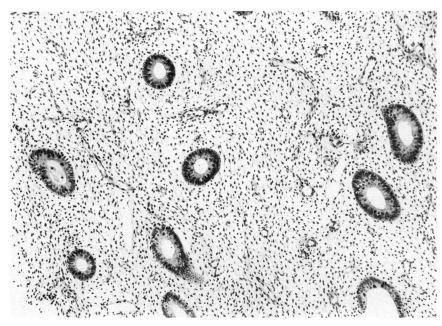

Figure 2
(Figures 2 and 3 are from the same patient)
ENDOMETRIUM, EARLY PROLIFERATIVE PHASE
Small, round, regular glands are widely separated by a stroma without edema, which contains small, regularly distributed blood vessels.

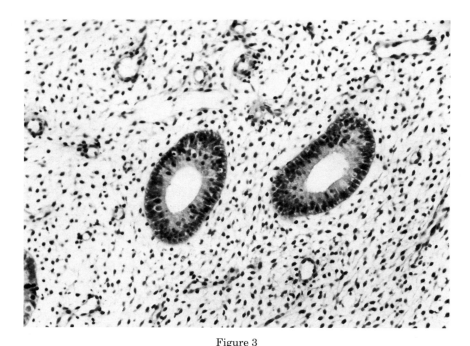

Figure 3
ENDOMETRIUM, EARLY PROLIFERATIVE PHASE
Higher magnification of the endometrium seen in figure 2 shows glands with slight pseudostratification, occasional mitotic figures, and a few clear cells. The stromal cells are uniform and small, with round-to-ovoid nuclei and occasional mitotic figures.

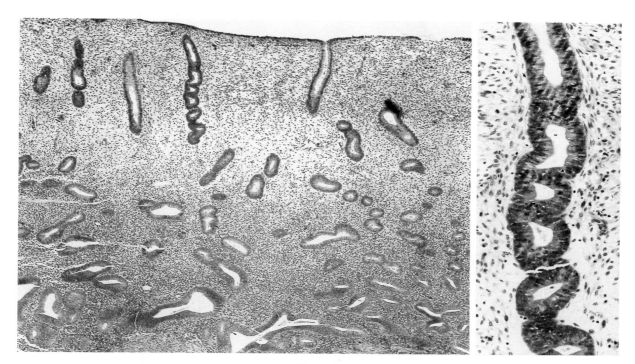

Figure 4
ENDOMETRIUM, LATE PROLIFERATIVE PHASE
This endometrium from day 10–12 shows glands that are more tortuous and crowded than those in figure 2. Intraglandular nuclear pseudostratification and mitotic activity are more prominent (see inset), and the stroma is edematous and mitotically active.

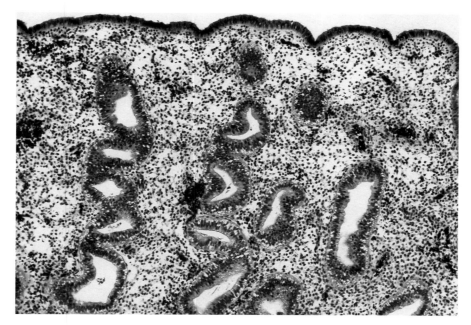

Figure 5
ENDOMETRIUM, EARLY SECRETORY PHASE
In this illustration, the glands exhibit a regular tortuosity and are clearly oriented from the base to the surface of the endometrium. Subnuclear glycogen vacuoles are clearly visible at this magnification.

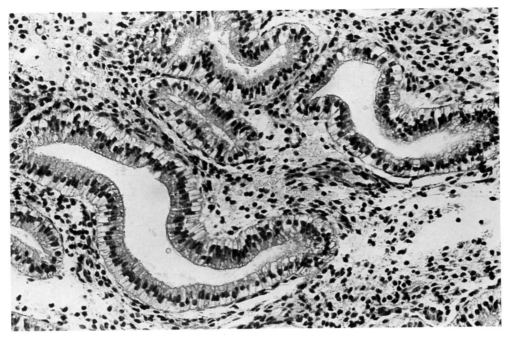

Figure 6
ENDOMETRIUM, EARLY SECRETORY PHASE
The glands of this day-17 endometrium contain prominent subnuclear glycogen vacuoles underlying a single row of nuclei in the endometrial glands.

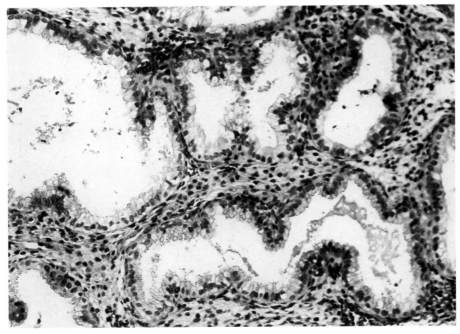

Figure 7
ENDOMETRIUM, MIDSECRETORY PHASE
These regularly tortuous glands in this day-20 endometrium contain secretions that are largely intracellular, apical, and partially intraluminal.

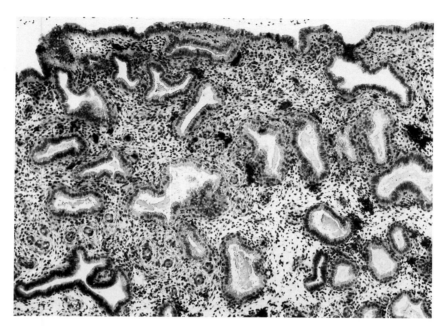

Figure 8
ENDOMETRIUM, LATE SECRETORY PHASE
In this endometrium from day 23–24, the glands are beginning to show regressive changes. Spiral arterioles are present and are most prominent in the lower left portion of the illustration. They are beginning to be surrounded by cuffs of predecidua. Predecidual stromal change is not yet apparent in the superficial compacta.

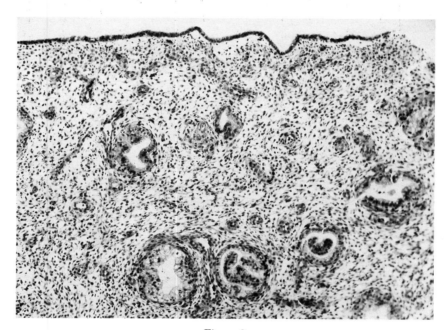

Figure 9
ENDOMETRIUM, LATE SECRETORY PHASE
The glands of this day-25 endometrium are markedly regressed, and the superficial compacta has a diffusely predecidualized stroma.

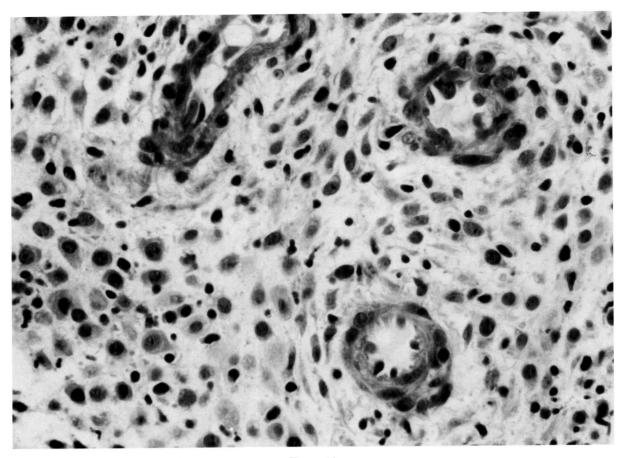

Figure 10
ENDOMETRIUM, LATE SECRETORY PHASE
This high-power photomicrograph of a day-25 endometrium shows a spiral arteriole cut in multiple profiles and surrounded by predecidual stroma. Note the admixture in the stroma of large decidualized cells and smaller endometrial granulocytes.

specimen (figs. 11, 12). Because of the fragmented nature of the endometrium at this time, as well as the loss of contiguity between epithelium and stroma, a mistaken diagnosis of hyperplasia or even carcinoma may be suggested. However, cytologic atypia is minimal, evidence of stromal invasion is not present, and some residual predecidual stroma may be seen beneath the surface epithelium to indicate that the endometrium had reached the premenstrual level of development before bleeding began. In addition, the fragmented glandular epithelium may show persistent progestational changes.

Lymphoid tissue is a normal constituent of cycling endometrium, and its presence, even in large nodular aggregates (fig. 13), should not lead to confusion with either chronic endometritis or malignant lymphoma (see Miscella-

neous and Secondary Tumors and Tumor-Like Lesions). T lymphocytes and macrophages are said to constitute about 5 percent each of the endometrial stromal cell population throughout the menstrual cycle and are seen in basal aggregates, scattered through the stroma, between glandular epithelial cells, and in gland lumina (4). B lymphocytes are rare except in basal aggregates.

Noncycling Endometrium. After this description of normally cycling endometrium, it is pertinent to add that many clinical situations are accompanied by noncycling or abnormally cycling endometrium. Some of the situations in which an endometrial biopsy specimen cannot be dated or phased are listed in Table 1. There is an additional group of conditions (such as anovulatory bleeding and luteal-phase defects) in which the endometrial morphology is

Figure 11
MENSTRUAL ENDOMETRIUM
This low-power photomicrograph shows the typical fragmentation, stromal collapse, and the bloody necrotic background of a menstrual specimen.

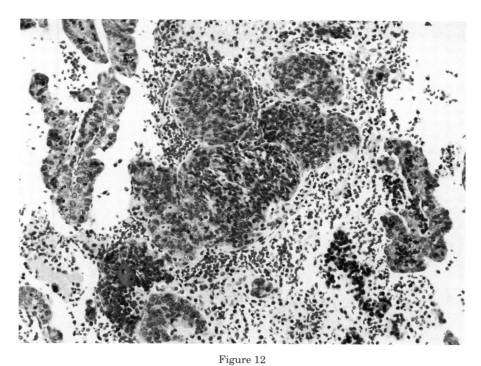

Figure 12
MENSTRUAL ENDOMETRIUM
This photomicrograph shows the balls of endometrial stroma that, taken out of context, are occasionally mistaken for endometrial carcinoma or sarcoma.

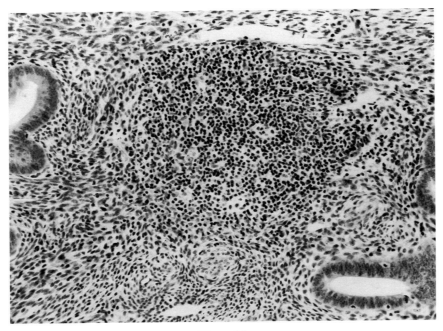

Figure 13
LYMPHOID AGGREGATE IN PROLIFERATIVE ENDOMETRIUM
This is a normal finding and should not be interpreted as evidence of endometritis.

Table 1

COMMON SITUATIONS PRECLUDING ENDOMETRIAL DATING

Specimen Inadequate
- No tissue
- Improper fixation or processing
- Artifactual distortion
- Endocervix
- Lower uterine segment

Patient Not Cycling (Physiologic)
- Prepubertal
- Postmenopausal
- Pregnant
- Postpartum

Patient Not Cycling (Pathologic)
- Atrophy (premature ovarian failure, hypopituitarism, etc.)
- Cycle disturbances (anovulation, luteal phase defect, etc.)
- Metaplasia
- Hyperplasia
- Cancer

Patient Cycling by Induction or Not Cycling Iatrogenically
- Oral contraceptives
- Estrogens ± progestins
- Other hormones/drugs

Patient Cycling but Endometrium Unresponsive
- Endometritis
- Polyps
- Iatrogenic (IUD)

inappropriate to the date of the cycle, and these conditions are usually associated with either infertility or habitual abortion or both. Finally, there are endometrial appearances that are totally outside the menstrual cycle, the most common of which are infantile, pubertal, gestational, postpartum, and postmenopausal endometrium. Atrophic endometrium (figs. 14, 15) in particular can be seen normally in the prepubertal or postmenopausal period, as well as abnormally due to pituitary or ovarian failure or treatment with various iatrogenic agents. The pattern of cystic atrophy (fig. 15) is particularly important because it may be confused with either simple hyperplasia or endometrial polyps (see Endometrial Polyps and Hyperplasias). Gestational changes (particularly those described by Arias-Stella) may also be confusing; these are discussed in more detail in the chapter on Tumor-Like Lesions.

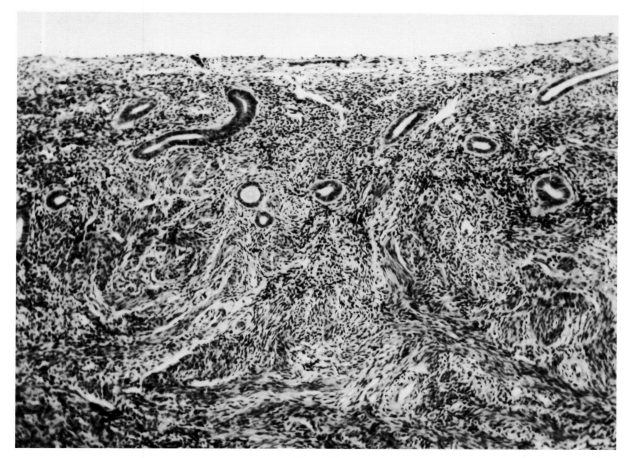

Figure 14
SIMPLE ATROPHY OF ENDOMETRIUM
This hysterectomy specimen from a postmenopausal woman contains a thin endometrium with only a few residual glands surrounded by an atrophic, somewhat fibrotic stroma. The junction between endometrium and myometrium is not sharply defined, and the underlying myometrium also appears atrophic.

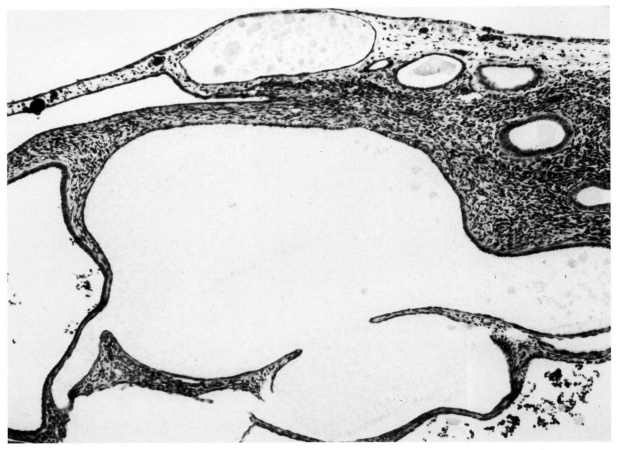

Figure 15
CYSTIC ATROPHY OF ENDOMETRIUM
This photomicrograph shows most of the specimen obtained at curettage from a postmenopausal woman who presented with vaginal bleeding. The glands vary from small to cystically dilated, but all are lined by a single layer of epithelial cells that are cuboidal to flattened (cf. illustrations of simple hyperplasia without atypia in Endometrial Polyps and Hyperplasias).

REFERENCES

1. Dallenbach-Hellweg G. Histopathology of the endometrium. 4th ed. Berlin: Springer-Verlag, 1987.
2. Ferenczy A. Anatomy and histology of the uterine corpus. In: Kurman RJ, ed. Blaustein's pathology of the female genital tract. 3rd ed. New York: Springer-Verlag, 1987:257–91.
3. Gompel C, Silverberg SG. The corpus uteri. In: Gompel C, Silverberg SG, eds. Pathology in gynecology and obstetrics. 3rd ed. Philadelphia: JB Lippincott, 1985:149–277.
4. Marshall RJ, Jones DB. An immunohistochemical study of lymphoid tissue in human endometrium. Int J Gynecol Pathol 1988;7:225–35.
5. McLean JM. Embryology and anatomy of the female genital tract and ovaries. In: Fox H, ed. Haines and Taylor obstetrical and gynaecological pathology. 3rd ed. Edinburgh: Churchill Livingstone, 1987:1–50.
6. Wynn RM, Jollie WP. Biology of the uterus. 2nd ed. New York: Plenum Medical Book, 1989.

TUMOR CLASSIFICATION

The classification and nomenclature used in this text is the one recently developed by a committee of pathologists from six countries (see Acknowledgments) under the auspices of the International Society of Gynecological Pathologists and subsequently approved by that society and pending approval by the World Health Organization. The classification is to be published by the World Health Organization after the present text. As chairman of the committee that developed the classification, I fully anticipate that it will continue to be modified and improved after its publication, but it is presented at this time as the most current and, I hope, most widely accepted classification available.

HISTOLOGIC CLASSIFICATION OF TUMORS AND RELATED LESIONS OF THE UTERINE CORPUS

1. Epithelial Tumors and Related Lesions

1.1. Endometrial hyperplasia

1.1.1. Simple
1.1.2. Complex (adenomatous)

1.2. Atypical endometrial hyperplasia

1.2.1. Simple
1.2.2. Complex (adenomatous with atypia)

1.3. Endometrial polyp

1.4. Endometrial carcinoma

1.4.1. Endometrioid

1.4.1.1. Adenocarcinoma

Variants

1.4.1.1.1. Secretory
1.4.1.1.2. Ciliated cell

1.4.1.2. Adenocarcinoma with squamous differentiation

1.4.1.2.1. Adenocarcinoma with squamous metaplasia (adenoacanthoma)
1.4.1.2.2. Adenosquamous carcinoma

1.4.2. Serous adenocarcinoma
1.4.3. Clear cell adenocarcinoma
1.4.4. Mucinous adenocarcinoma
1.4.5. Squamous cell carcinoma
1.4.6. Mixed carcinoma
1.4.7. Undifferentiated carcinoma

2. Nonepithelial Tumors and Related Lesions

2.1. Endometrial stromal tumors

2.1.1. Stromal nodule
2.1.2. Low-grade stromal sarcoma
2.1.3. High-grade stromal sarcoma

2.2. Smooth muscle tumors

2.2.1. Leiomyoma

Variants

2.2.1.1. Cellular
2.2.1.2. Epithelioid
2.2.1.3. Bizarre (symplastic, pleomorphic)
2.2.1.4. Lipoleiomyoma

2.2.2. Smooth muscle tumor of uncertain malignant potential
2.2.3. Leiomyosarcoma

Variants

2.2.3.1. Epithelioid
2.2.3.2. Myxoid

2.2.4. Other smooth muscle tumors

2.2.4.1. Metastasizing leiomyoma
2.2.4.2. Intravenous leiomyomatosis
2.2.4.3. Diffuse leiomyomatosis

2.3. Mixed endometrial stromal and smooth muscle tumors

2.4. Adenomatoid tumor

2.5. Other soft tissue tumors (benign and malignant)

2.5.1. Homologous
2.5.2. Heterologous

3. Mixed Epithelial-Nonepithelial Tumors

3.1. Benign

   3.1.1. Adenofibroma
   3.1.2. Adenomyoma

Variant

     3.1.2.1. Atypical polypoid adenomyoma

3.2. Malignant

   3.2.1. Adenosarcoma

     3.2.1.1. Homologous
     3.2.1.2. Heterologous

   3.2.2. Carcinosarcoma (malignant mixed mesodermal tumor; malignant mixed müllerian tumor)

     3.2.2.1. Homologous
     3.2.2.2. Heterologous

4. Miscellaneous Tumors

4.1. Sex cord-like tumors

4.2. Tumors of germ cell type

4.3. Neuroectodermal tumors

4.4. Lymphomas

4.5. Others

5. Secondary Tumors

6. Unclassified Tumors

7. Tumor-Like Lesions

7.1. Epithelial metaplastic and related changes

   7.1.1. Squamous metaplasia and morules
   7.1.2. Mucinous metaplasia (including intestinal)
   7.1.3. Ciliary change
   7.1.4. Hobnail change
   7.1.5. Clear cell change
   7.1.6. Eosinophilic cell change (including oncocytic)
   7.1.7. Surface syncytial change
   7.1.8. Papillary proliferation
   7.1.9. Arias-Stella change

7.2. Nonepithelial metaplastic and related changes

   7.2.1. Smooth muscle metaplasia
   7.2.2. Osseous metaplasia
   7.2.3. Cartilaginous metaplasia
   7.2.4. Fatty change
   7.2.5. Glial tissue
   7.2.6. Foam cell change
   7.2.7. Retained fetal products

7.3. Adenomyosis

7.4. Epithelial cysts of myometrium

7.5. Chronic endometritis

7.6. Lymphoma-like lesions

7.7. Inflammatory pseudotumor

7.8. Others

❖❖❖

ENDOMETRIAL POLYPS AND HYPERPLASIAS

ENDOMETRIAL POLYP

Definition. Endometrial polyps are benign nodular protrusions above the endometrial surface, consisting of irregularly distributed endometrial glands and stroma.

Although endometrial polyps are among the most common pathologic lesions of the uterine corpus, it is surprising how little is known about their pathogenesis. They are generally assumed to arise in and from the endometrial basalis and to result, at least in part, from estrogenic stimulation (4). The latter part of this hypothesis is supported by the recent observation of unusually large and proliferative endometrial polyps in postmenopausal women receiving tamoxifen, a substance with both estrogenic and anti-estrogenic activities (3).

The prevalence of endometrial polyps is not established, but gross polyps are frequently seen in uteri removed for other reasons, and microscopic polyps are even more common in curettage specimens.

Clinical Features and Gross Findings. Most endometrial polyps are probably asymptomatic, although they are seen most frequently in specimens from curettages performed for abnormal uterine bleeding. They are most commonly encountered in perimenopausal women but are also seen earlier during the reproductive years and after the menopause. They have been reported as a cause of infertility (2).

When a polyp is large enough to be seen at the gross level, it may be either sessile or pedunculated and may occur anywhere within the endometrial cavity, including the lower uterine segment. In rare instances, polyps may fill the entire endometrial cavity and may even extend down through the external cervical os. The surface of the polyp is usually smooth, tan, and glistening, but there may be granular erosions and foci of hemorrhage and necrosis. Grossly visible polyps are usually solitary but can be multiple; microscopic polyps are frequently multiple.

Microscopic Findings. Ideally, endometrial polyps should be recognized by their projection above the endometrial surface; their smooth-surfaced polypoid configuration, with surface epithelium covering three sides; and their difference from nonpolypoid endometrium in the same specimen, which tends to be more fragmented and often is in a different phase of the menstrual cycle (figs. 16–20). However, in many curettage specimens, polyps may be fragmented, and their recognition then depends on a constellation of findings involving the internal aspect. These include glands that are often sparse, irregularly distributed, at least focally dilated, and generally lined by atrophic, inactive, or proliferative epithelium; stroma that is either focally or diffusely fibrotic; and, most characteristically, thick-walled, usually dilated blood vessels (figs. 21–23).

Variations from the classic appearance may occur, and it should be noted that any physiologic or pathologic appearance encountered in the endometrium may be seen within a polyp. Secretory changes may occur, although they are usually poorly developed (fig. 20). Gestational changes may also be seen (fig. 24), as may the entire spectrum of metaplastic and related changes (figs. 25, 26). Hyperplasias (fig. 26), carcinomas (fig. 27), sarcomas, and mixed tumors (fig. 28) may also be seen, although malignant tumors within otherwise benign polyps are rare.

Variable amounts of smooth muscle may be seen within the stroma of endometrial polyps. When the stroma is composed predominantly of smooth muscle, the lesion should be classified as adenomyoma. Alarming degrees of stromal atypia are also occasionally encountered within endometrial polyps (figs. 29, 30). Polyps of this sort are considered to be analogous to those encountered more frequently in the vagina and vulva. If they lack hypercellularity, mitotic activity, and periglandular cuffing, they may be considered benign.

Differential Diagnosis. A benign endometrial polyp, particularly if it is large, can be confused with a polypoid carcinoma or sarcoma on gross examination. However, the external surfaces of malignant tumors are usually more irregular, and the cut surfaces show foci of hemorrhage and necrosis, which are unusual in benign polyps. Microscopic examination should lead to the correct diagnosis.

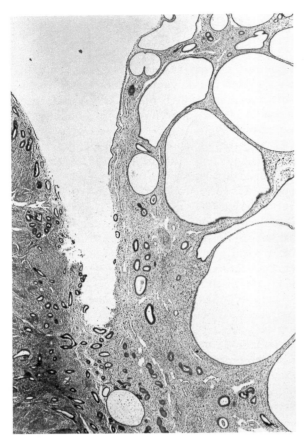

Figure 16
ENDOMETRIAL POLYP
This low-power photomicrograph shows the polyp attached by a broad base to underlying endometrium and myometrium. Compared with adjacent proliferative endometrium, the polyp has a fibrotic stroma, cystically dilated glands, and dilated, thick-walled blood vessels. (Fig. 4 from Silverberg SG. Hyperplasia and carcinoma of the endometrium. Semin Diagn Pathol 1988;5:135–53.)

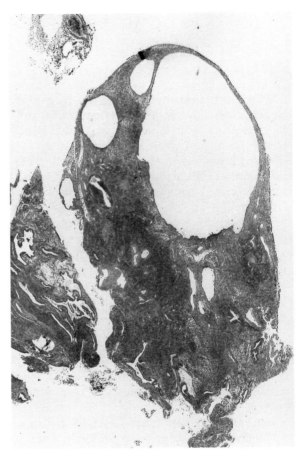

Figure 17
(Figures 17 and 23 are from the same patient)
ENDOMETRIAL POLYP
This low-power photomicrograph of a curettage specimen shows the intact nature of the polypoid tissue fragment, in which dilated glands, fibrotic stroma, and dilated, thick-walled vessels may be seen. (Figure 23 shows a higher magnification of the vessels seen near the center of this polyp.)

At the microscopic level, the most perplexing differential diagnoses are with atrophic or proliferative endometrium or endometrial hyperplasia. Fibrotic stroma containing cystically dilated glands lined by atrophic endometrial epithelium may be encountered in cystic atrophy. However, neither a polypoid configuration nor the typical blood vessels of a polyp should be present in this lesion, and the picture should be uniform throughout the endometrium available in the specimen. The nonpolypoid endometrium accompanying a polyp, on the other hand, usually differs in appearance from that of the endometrium within the polyp.

When a polyp contains actively proliferating endometrium, the lesion may be missed and interpreted as normal proliferative endometrium. Again, if nonpolypoid endometrium is present in the specimen, the difference between the polypoid and nonpolypoid fragments should alert the observer to the correct diagnosis. Also, proliferative endometrial glands tend to be oriented with their long axes perpendicular to the surface. Because the surface covers most aspects of an endometrial polyp, the architecture of the glands is generally distorted, in contradistinction to the regular architecture of a normal proliferative endometrium.

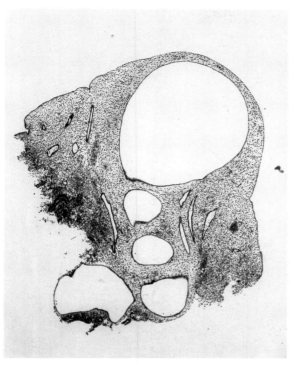

Figure 18
ENDOMETRIAL POLYP
Another small polyp found in a curettage specimen demonstrates the same microscopic features noted in figures 16 and 17.

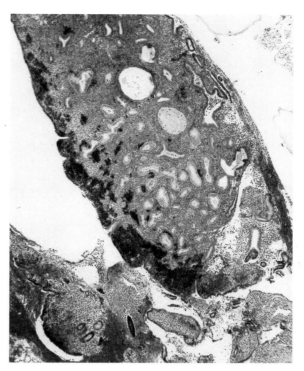

Figure 19
ENDOMETRIAL POLYP
In this illustration, the difference in appearance at scanning magnification between the polyp in the upper part of the field and the adjacent nonpolypoid endometrium in the lower part is apparent.

Because one of the characteristics of endometrial hyperplasia is glandular disarray, it is easy to envision the difficulty encountered in differentiating between hyperplasia and polyps. Indeed, in the series of Winkler and colleagues (7), polyps represented the most common lesion misinterpreted as endometrial hyperplasia. These authors commented that "the key to the recognition of endometrial polyps is their dense fibrotic stroma and thick-walled vessels," which is in agreement with my own views. Winkler and colleagues also noted that polyps may contain foci of hyperplasia (fig. 26). It is probably worthwhile in this context to distinguish between hyperplasia in a polyp and polypoid hyperplasia. In the former lesion, the hyperplasia is limited to a polyp, and the accompanying nonpolypoid endometrium is not hyperplastic, whereas in polypoid hyperplasia the endometrium is entirely or largely hyperplastic, and the hyperplastic endometrium forms multiple small polyps. Although follow-up studies in which these two entities are distinguished have not been reported, I assume that the premalignant potential of a diffuse polypoid hyperplasia would be greater than that of a focal hyperplasia in a polyp that has been removed by curettage.

Additional differential diagnosis of endometrial polyps includes polypoid adenomyomas, adenofibromas, and adenosarcomas. A polypoid lesion in which the stroma consists largely or exclusively of smooth muscle should be designated adenomyoma. In adenofibroma, the surface is papillary, and epithelium penetrates in long clefts into the underlying stroma, which is diffusely fibrotic; these lesions are as rare as endometrial polyps are common. In adenosarcoma, a papillary configuration and cleft-like spaces are also common; the stroma, at least focally, is hypercellular, atypical, and mitotically active and tends to form cuffs of dense stromal cellularity around the glands. Additionally, the

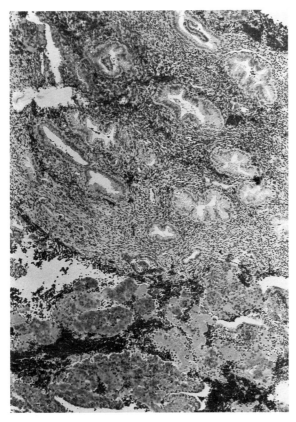

Figure 20
ENDOMETRIAL POLYP
This polyp was identified in a curettage specimen from a menstruating patient. The intact nature of the polyp (above) compared with the fragmented menstrual endometrium below, is indicative of the manner in which polyps are often first recognized in a curettage specimen. In this polyp, the endometrial glands show secretory changes, which, however, are retarded relative to the phase of the menstrual cycle.

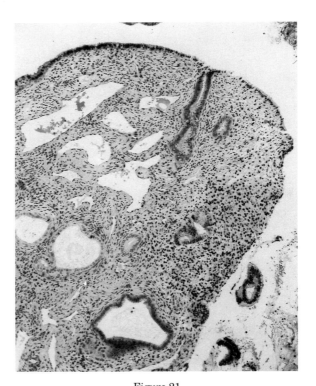

Figure 21
ENDOMETRIAL POLYP
This polyp is composed of relatively few glands, fibrotic stroma, and dilated, thick-walled blood vessels.

glands of an adenosarcoma have a more proliferative appearance than those of most endometrial polyps.

For malignant tumors arising within endometrial polyps, the differential diagnosis is that of the specific malignant tumor involved. If the tumor is believed to have arisen in a polyp, this should be stated in the pathology report, because cancers limited to a polyp usually have a more favorable prognosis than those that are more widespread (5,6).

Treatment and Prognosis. Polyps have usually been adequately treated by the time they are diagnosed by the pathologist. Endometrial curettage usually cures abnormal bleeding associated with small polyps, and hysterectomy certainly cures large polyps.

The relationship of polyps to endometrial carcinoma is unclear. Although carcinoma is only rarely found within endometrial polyps (4), polyps have been reported to occur in 12 to 34 percent of uteri containing endometrial carcinoma (4,5). Armenia (1) reported that endometrial carcinoma developed subsequent to the diagnosis of a polyp in 3.5 percent of the cases, but many of these women had been treated with intracavitary radium. Nuovo and colleagues (3) noted carcinoma within three of seven endometrial polyps developing in postmenopausal patients receiving tamoxifen, suggesting a high risk of malignant transformation in this clinical situation.

ENDOMETRIAL HYPERPLASIA

Definition. In the new International Society of Gynecological Pathologists classification,

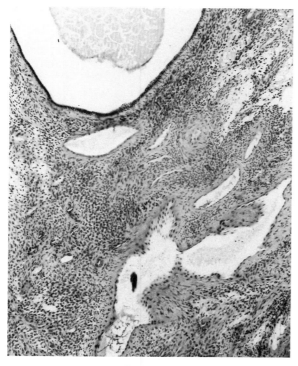

Figure 22
ENDOMETRIAL POLYP
In this illustration, dilated, thick-walled vessels are seen adjacent to a cystically dilated gland (top) lined by a single layer of flattened epithelium.

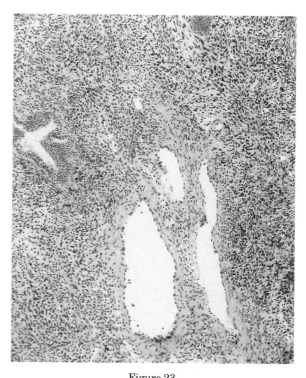

Figure 23
(Figures 23 and 17 are from the same patient)
ENDOMETRIAL POLYP
These dilated, thick-walled vessels are a higher magnification of those seen in figure 17.

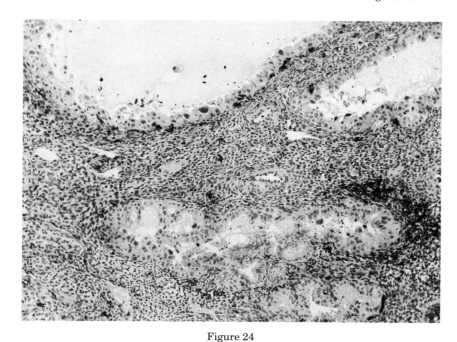

Figure 24
ENDOMETRIAL POLYP
This polyp, seen in a pregnant patient, contains some endometrial glands that show gestational changes, with Arias-Stella phenomenon but without decidual change of the stroma.

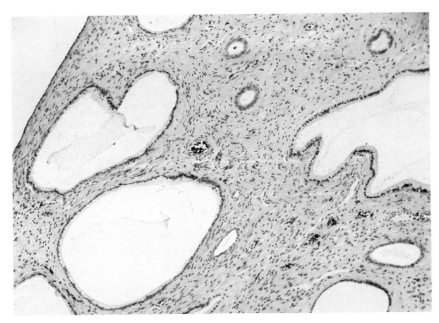

Figure 25
ENDOMETRIAL POLYP
The glands illustrated here show endocervical-type mucinous metaplasia. The stroma is diffusely fibrotic. More typical endometrial glands were seen elsewhere in this large polyp.

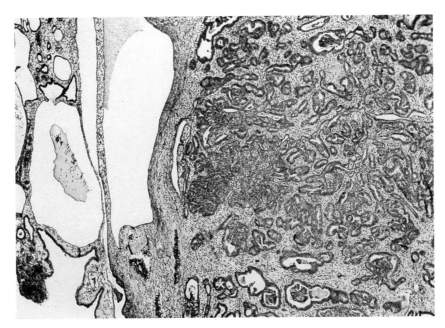

Figure 26
ENDOMETRIAL POLYP
This polyp contains complex hyperplasia with morular metaplasia. The left side of the illustration shows a more typical endometrial polyp without hyperplasia or metaplasia.

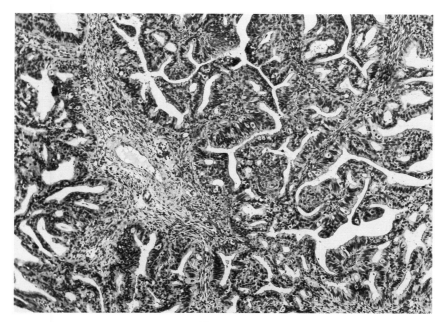

Figure 27
ENDOMETRIAL POLYP
This polyp contains well-differentiated endometrioid adenocarcinoma. Only the dilated, thick-walled blood vessel to the left of center suggests that this carcinoma arose in a polyp, but elsewhere in the lesion, the typical histologic findings of a benign endometrial polyp were noted.

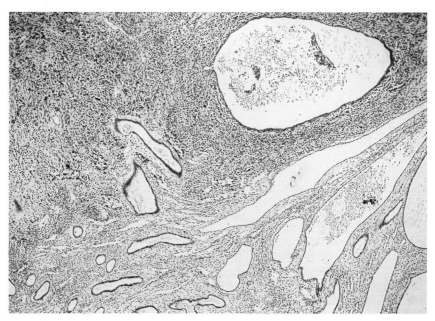

Figure 28
ENDOMETRIAL STROMAL SARCOMA
ARISING IN AN ENDOMETRIAL POLYP
The upper half of the illustration shows the sarcomatous stroma infiltrating between benign glands of the polyp. Numerous mitotic figures are present.

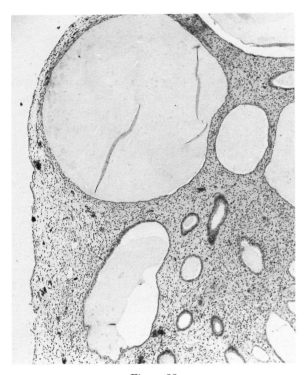

Figure 29
(Figures 29 and 30 are from the same patient)
ENDOMETRIAL POLYP WITH
PSEUDOSARCOMATOUS STROMAL ATYPIA
At this magnification, the polypoid nature of the lesion can be seen, as well as a suggestion of scattered enlarged and hyperchromatic nuclei. See figure 30 for higher magnification.

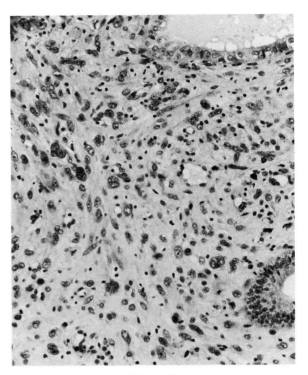

Figure 30
ENDOMETRIAL POLYP WITH
PSEUDOSARCOMATOUS STROMAL ATYPIA
Higher magnification of the polyp illustrated in figure 29 shows large, often multinucleate cells with large hyperchromatic nuclei. These findings were limited to this polyp in a hysterectomy specimen, and mitotic figures were absent. The lesion never became more cellular than it is in this field. No densely cellular cuffs were noted around endometrial glands.

hyperplasias of the endometrium are separated into endometrial hyperplasia and atypical endometrial hyperplasia. Endometrial hyperplasia is a benign proliferation characterized by increased density of morphologically abnormal endometrial glands without cytologic atypia. Atypical endometrial hyperplasia is a benign proliferation characterized by increased density of morphologically abnormal endometrial glands with cytologic atypia. Each of these entities is further subdivided into simple and complex, with *adenomatous* listed as an acceptable but less preferred synonym for *complex*.

Endometrial hyperplasias have historically been considered to represent a continuous spectrum of proliferative disease that gradually increases in morphologic and clinical severity as one progresses from simple to complex hyperplasia without atypia to atypical hyperplasia (25,32). Most authors have assumed that there

is an equally gradual transition from severe hyperplasia to early or focal well-differentiated adenocarcinoma of endometrioid type, with the differential diagnosis between these entities being difficult (but possible) to make in most cases. Some authors have recommended the interposition of a diagnostic category of *adenocarcinoma in situ* between atypical hyperplasia and well-differentiated adenocarcinoma, but the definitions of adenocarcinoma in situ in the literature have been so variable that it is currently recommended that this term not be used (25,32). Fox (15) probably had the last word on this diagnostic term when he said that a "a true adenocarcinoma in situ of the endometrium is one in which the glands have undergone neoplastic change but in which there is no invasion of the endometrial stroma. It is doubtful if an adenocarcinoma of this type exists or if it could be recognized even if it did exist."

An alternative approach has been the use of the term *endometrial intraepithelial neoplasia* to encompass both atypical hyperplasia and early carcinoma (16,31). This concept has some theoretical justification because several cytokinetic and immunohistochemical studies have suggested that if there is a natural breakpoint in the spectrum of hyperplasias and carcinoma, it may be between hyperplasias with and without atypia rather than between hyperplasias with atypia and carcinoma (13,26,33,35). The main problem with the endometrial intraepithelial neoplasia terminology, however, is that the intraepithelial element is still difficult, if not impossible, to define in a biopsy or curettage specimen. Therefore, invasive carcinomas with deep myometrial penetration could be underdiagnosed as endometrial intraepithelial neoplasia.

The present recommended nomenclature, which separates endometrial hyperplasia and atypical hyperplasia, clearly indicates a fundamental difference between these two entities but continues to support the concept that the distinction between endometrial hyperplasia (including atypical hyperplasia) and carcinoma is both feasible and important.

General Features. Very few epidemiologic studies of endometrial hyperplasia and atypical hyperplasia have been reported (30), but it is generally assumed that the population distribution and epidemiologic relationships for the endometrial hyperplasias are similar to those reported in numerous studies for endometrial carcinoma (see Endometrial Carcinoma). Thus, endometrial hyperplasias are associated with such factors as obesity (and a Western diet), nulliparity, diabetes mellitus, hypertension, functioning ovarian tumors and stromal proliferations, and exogenous estrogen administration. It is not clear whether endometrial hyperplasias are less prevalent in populations with relatively low rates of endometrial carcinoma. The comparative epidemiology and geographic distribution of endometrial hyperplasia versus atypical hyperplasia, as defined above, is completely unknown.

Clinical Features. Both endometrial hyperplasia and atypical hyperplasia usually present with abnormal uterine bleeding, whether in the premenopausal or postmenopausal years. Endometrial hyperplasias are uncommon in asymptomatic women, with a reported prevalence of slightly over eight cases per thousand screened postmenopausal women (22). The uterus is frequently but not always enlarged, and curettage yields copious amounts of endometrial tissue the gross appearance of which is unremarkable.

The successful detection rate of endometrial hyperplasia varies with the sampling technique used, the universally accepted standard being formal curettage. Techniques exist for both histologic and cytologic sampling of the endometrial cavity. Classic cytologic techniques have relied on the finding of endometrial cells at an abnormal time (after the tenth day of a menstrual cycle or after the menopause), frequently in association with a background suggesting estrogenic stimulation, in a scrape of the lateral vaginal wall, or in a vaginal pool aspiration. Techniques for direct sampling of material from the endometrial cavity for cytologic examination now exist, but a review of the literature noted that even these techniques were able to detect only between 20 and 70 percent of endometrial hyperplasias, and false-positive diagnoses of carcinoma frequently occurred (36). The author of this study and the authors of other studies published subsequently (9,17) have agreed that sampling techniques that obtain histologic material are preferable to those that yield only material suitable for cytologic examination.

Gross Findings. The gross appearances of endometrial hyperplasia and atypical hyperplasia are not distinctive. Usually, the endometrium is increased in volume, as noted in either a curettage or hysterectomy specimen (pl. I). This is not apparent in endometrium obtained by a more limited sampling technique, and if hyperplasia is focal, it may not be detectable on gross examination, even in a hysterectomy specimen. When hyperplasia is grossly visible, it may be either diffuse or polypoid, and the hyperplastic endometrium is generally soft and velvety, often with no significant difference from that of a normal secretory phase.

Microscopic Findings. The diagnosis of the different forms of endometrial hyperplasia depends on the nomenclature and classification system chosen, and these have varied considerably

PLATE I

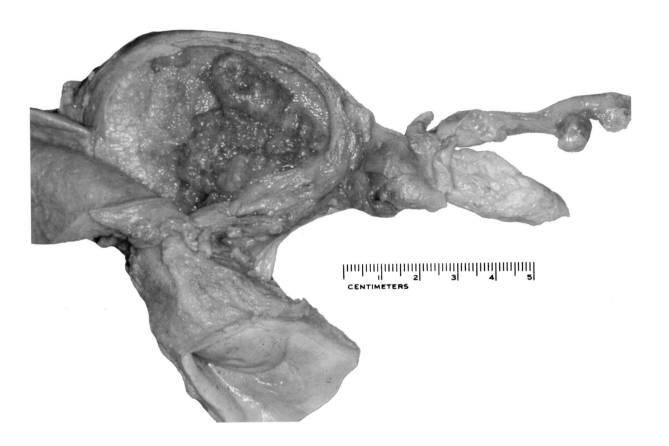

ENDOMETRIAL HYPERPLASIA

This hysterectomy specimen shows a voluminous soft, velvety endometrium with numerous polypoid projections. There is no hemorrhage or necrosis, and the myometrium is uninvolved.

in the literature, as discussed previously. The International Society of Gynecological Pathologists classification has adopted most of the thinking of Kurman and Norris and their colleagues on this subject, as expounded in a series of publications (23–25,28,29), and this is the format that is followed in this discussion.

In simple hyperplasia, there is an increase in the volume of both the glandular and stromal compartments, and although the number of glands relative to the stroma is increased, the glands are not markedly crowded (figs. 31, 32). In most examples, at least some of the glands are cystically dilated, and these cystic glands may be either perfectly rounded or display focal outpouchings (figs. 31–34). The nondilated glands are round to slightly tortuous but lack the complex angularity of complex hyperplasia. The glands are lined by proliferative-type endometrial epithelium lacking nuclear atypia, and the stroma is cellular and well vascularized, with uniform round-to-ovoid stromal cells that are more densely packed than those in normal proliferative endometrium (fig. 35). Mitotic activity is generally not significantly increased in either the glandular or the stromal component.

In complex hyperplasia, the glands are more closely packed, with a concomitant loss of the intervening stroma (figs. 36–41). They also acquire an increased architectural complexity, with numerous lateral buds and a random distribution. Within the hyperplastic glands, there is generally more cellular stratification than in simple hyperplasia, but the nuclei are still uniform in size and shape and show normal polarity, with their axes uniformly perpendicular to the basement membrane (fig. 37). Mitotic activity is variable, and nucleoli tend to be inconspicuous. The stromal component is far less prominent than in simple hyperplasia, and stromal cells often show considerable spindling, perhaps as the result of compression between adjacent glands. However, they are still easily recognizable as endometrial stromal cells; fibrosis and necrosis, which are important features in the differential diagnosis from well-differentiated adenocarcinoma, are absent.

Because the two main features distinguishing complex from simple hyperplasia are increased glandular complexity and increased glandular crowding, cases are occasionally encountered in which one but not both of these

features may be present. For example, in figure 38, glands are more closely crowded together than in simple hyperplasia but mostly lack architectural complexity, whereas in figure 39, the glands are relatively complex but are not tightly crowded. I would classify both of these examples as complex hyperplasia, but other observers might prefer to place one or both into the category of simple hyperplasia.

In atypical hyperplasia, the features of either simple or complex hyperplasia are present, but in addition, some or all of the hyperplastic endometrial glands are lined by epithelium displaying cytologic atypia. The atypia is usually focal, with atypical glands found immediately adjacent to hyperplastic glands lacking cytologic atypia (figs. 41–43). The cells of atypical hyperplastic glands are enlarged and show loss of polarity (figs. 40–45). The nuclear/cytoplasmic ratio is increased, and nuclei are large and variable in size and shape, many being more rounded than cigar shaped. Nuclear outlines are irregular, there is hyperchromatism and a thickened nuclear membrane, and nucleoli are prominent. Cellular stratification is usually present but often is no more marked than in complex hyperplasia without atypia. Mitotic activity is also variable and is not a reliable diagnostic criterion. The appearance of the stroma varies with the type of atypical hyperplasia (simple or complex), as described above, but there are no stromal findings specific for atypical hyperplasia. Papillary infoldings of some glands may be present (fig. 45), but a cribriform or confluent pattern is absent. Any of the hyperplasias may be accompanied by metaplastic and related changes. By far the most common change encountered in this situation is squamous metaplasia, particularly its morular variant (fig. 46). Extensive morular metaplasia should not lead to a diagnosis of adenocarcinoma with squamous metaplasia unless the glandular component shows the usual features of adenocarcinoma. Similarly, as discussed more extensively in the chapter on Epithelial Metaplastic and Related Changes, other epithelial metaplasias in endometrial hyperplasia should not provoke an erroneous diagnosis of atypical hyperplasia or adenocarcinoma.

Differential Diagnosis. The differential diagnosis of the various forms of endometrial hyperplasia can be conveniently grouped into

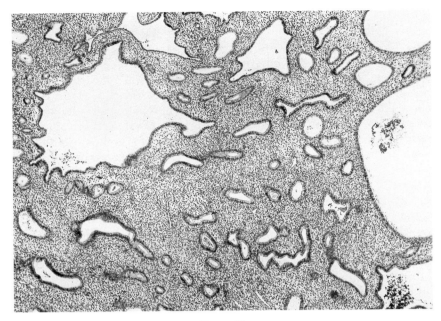

Figure 31
SIMPLE HYPERPLASIA
The endometrial glands in this lesion are irregularly distributed but widely separated by stroma, which is also hyperplastic. The glands are mostly round or tubular, with only a few irregular angularities encountered.

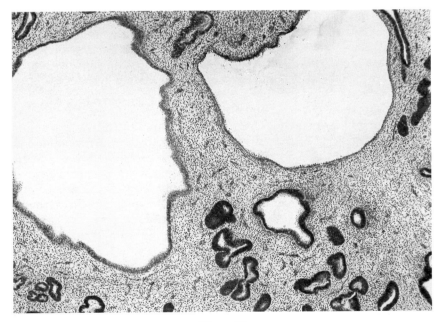

Figure 32
SIMPLE HYPERPLASIA
Another low-power view shows irregularly distributed proliferative-type glands widely separated by active cellular stroma with numerous small, regularly distributed blood vessels.

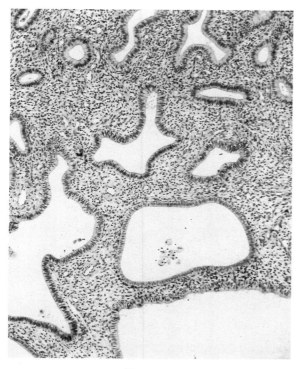

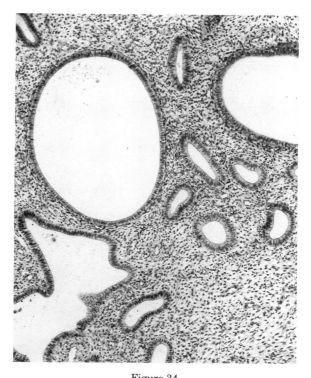

Figure 33
SIMPLE HYPERPLASIA
Small and large glands are lined by proliferative-type endometrial epithelium and are widely separated by cellular endometrial stroma.

Figure 34
SIMPLE HYPERPLASIA
Another case at the same magnification as figure 33 shows essentially the same features.

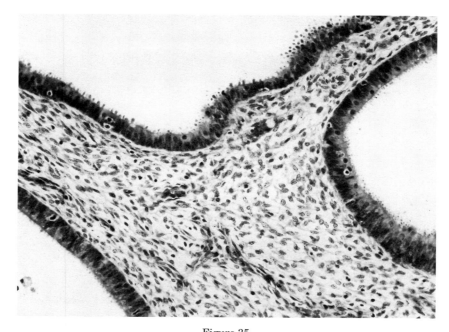

Figure 35
SIMPLE HYPERPLASIA
Higher magnification shows three cystic glands lined by proliferative-type endometrial epithelium without atypia and separated by cellular stroma.

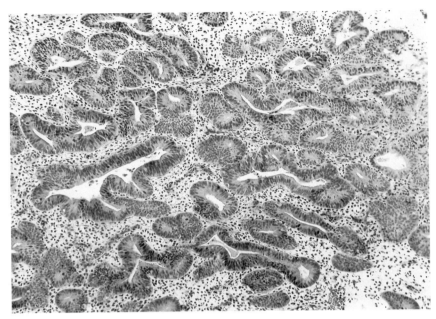

Figure 36
COMPLEX HYPERPLASIA
The endometrial glands in this illustration are more closely packed than those in the illustrations of simple hyperplasia and have more architectural irregularity, with numerous bud-like projections. Stroma is present between all glands.

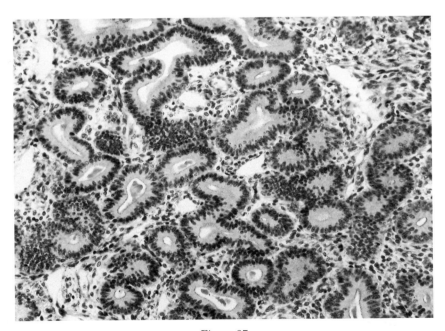

Figure 37
COMPLEX HYPERPLASIA
The nuclei in these glands are uniform in size and shape and show normal polarity, with their axes perpendicular to the basement membrane. All glands are separated by stromal cells.

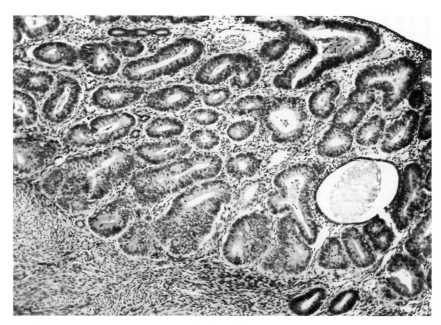

Figure 38
COMPLEX HYPERPLASIA
These glands are more closely crowded together than in simple hyperplasia but lack architectural complexity. This case is probably borderline between simple and complex hyperplasia.

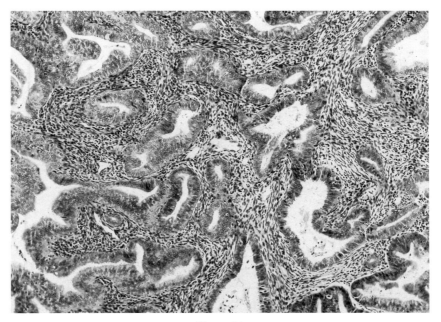

Figure 39
COMPLEX HYPERPLASIA
In this case, the glands are fairly widely separated by stroma (as in simple hyperplasia) but show considerable architectural complexity. Cytologic atypia is absent. Some observers might prefer to classify this lesion as simple hyperplasia.

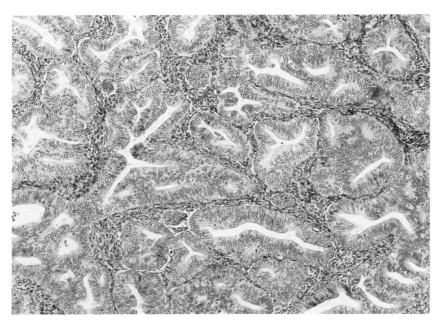

Figure 40
(Figures 40 and 41 are from the same patient)
ATYPICAL HYPERPLASIA (COMPLEX)
The irregularly shaped glands in this case are very closely packed but are still separated by residual endometrial stroma. See figure 41 for cytologic detail.

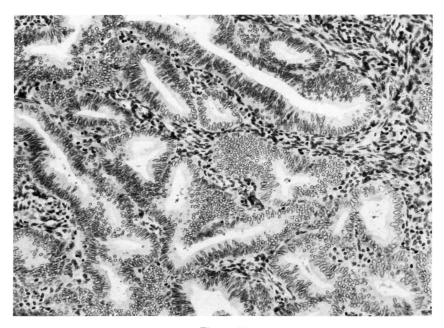

Figure 41
ATYPICAL HYPERPLASIA (COMPLEX)
Higher magnification of another field from figure 40 demonstrates mild cytologic atypia at the lower right, characterized by increased nuclear roundness, clearing of nuclear chromatin, and occasional prominent nucleoli.

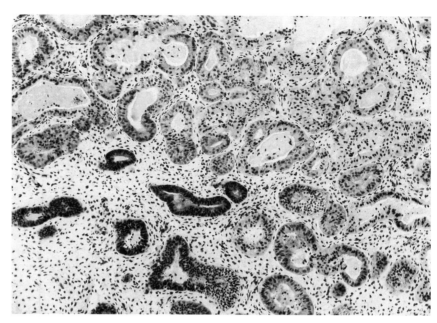

Figure 42
(Figures 42 and 43 are from the same patient)
ATYPICAL HYPERPLASIA (SIMPLE)
The lower left quadrant of this illustration shows simple hyperplasia without atypia, whereas the remainder of the field is occupied by glands with more eosinophilic cytoplasm and irregularly stratified nuclei. See figure 43 for detail of the cytologic atypia in this case.

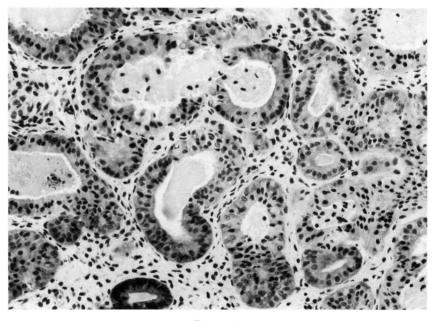

Figure 43
ATYPICAL HYPERPLASIA
Higher magnification of the upper left-hand portion of figure 42 shows glands lined by cells with eosinophilic cytoplasm and dyspolaric, stratified nuclei with moderate anisonucleosis and hyperchromatism. Prominent nucleoli are seen in many of the nuclei. Necrotic debris is present in some gland lumina.

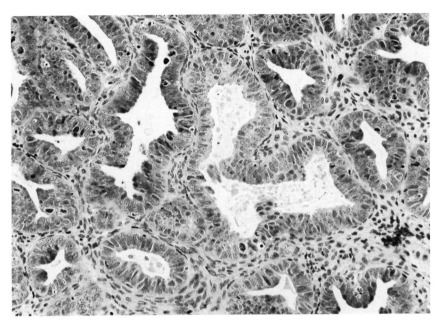

Figure 44
ATYPICAL HYPERPLASIA (COMPLEX)
The glandular epithelium here is extremely atypical, but residual endometrial stroma separates all glands in this field. Because of the severity of the atypia, a specimen such as this should be examined thoroughly to rule out the concomitant presence of carcinoma.

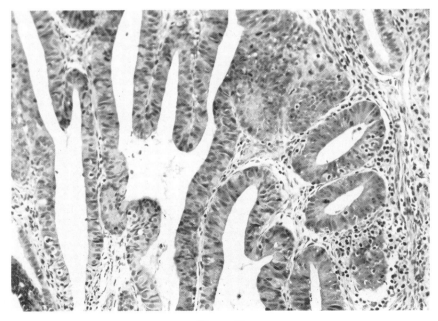

Figure 45
ATYPICAL HYPERPLASIA (COMPLEX)
In addition to dyspolarity, stratification, and nuclear atypia, there are also papillary infoldings (top) into a large endometrial gland in this illustration.

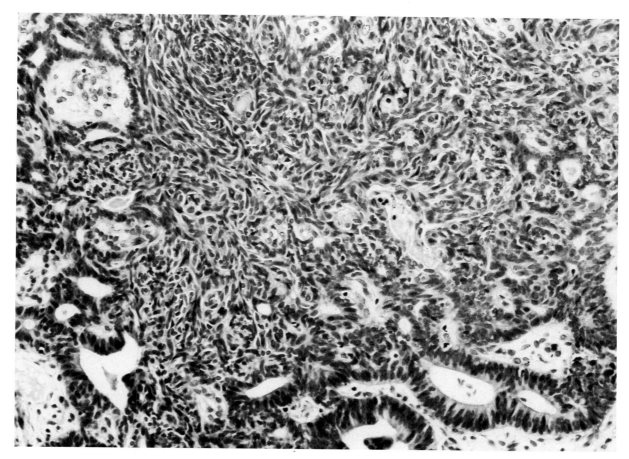

Figure 46
COMPLEX HYPERPLASIA WITH MORULAR METAPLASIA
This specimen from a 28-year-old woman with clinical features of the Stein-Leventhal syndrome shows complex hyperplasia with extensive morular metaplasia. The glands around the periphery of this large focus of spindle-celled morular metaplasia lack cytologic atypia and are separated by at least thin wisps of residual endometrial stroma.

three categories: 1) differential diagnosis among the different types (discussed previously), 2) differential diagnosis from other benign lesions, and 3) differential diagnosis from endometrial adenocarcinoma.

Other Benign Lesions

Although most of the discussion in the literature about the differential diagnosis of endometrial hyperplasia concerns its distinction from adenocarcinoma, other benign conditions actually represent a more frequent problem. Winkler and colleagues (7) reviewed 100 consecutive cases referred to them with a diagnosis of endometrial hyperplasia and found that their consultation diagnosis was identical to the referral diagnosis in only 24 cases. The diagnosis was changed and upgraded to well-differentiated adenocarcinoma in only 3 cases, but the change was a downgrading in 69 cases. The most common downgraded diagnoses were normal proliferative or secretory endometrium (17 cases) and endometrial polyps (27 cases). Endometrial metaplasias were also present in 9 cases. In an additional 16 cases, the presence of hyperplasia was confirmed, but the diagnosis was downgraded to a less severe variant.

Further confirmation of the tendency to overdiagnose endometrial hyperplasias was provided by the report of Huang and colleagues (19) in which 38 of 96 endometrial specimens with an initial diagnosis of hyperplasia were found on review to demonstrate only persistent proliferative endometrium.

Careful observance of the criteria listed above for the diagnoses of endometrial hyperplasia and atypical hyperplasia should prevent the overdiagnosis of lesser degrees of abnormality as hyperplastic. Proliferative endometrium, whether sampled during an ovulatory or an anovulatory cycle, should show a regularity that is absent in cases of hyperplasia (fig. 47). The glands, even if tortuous, are tortuous in a uniform manner and proliferate in a uniform direction from base to surface of the endometrium, unlike the anarchic proliferation in either a simple or complex hyperplasia. The stromal proliferation of simple hyperplasia is not seen in normal proliferative endometria, although the stromal compression of complex hyperplasia also should not be seen. Certain cases in which glands appear tightly compressed usually represent artifact (fig. 47) and can be recognized as such by the very focal nature of the glandular crowding, usually involving no more than five or six glands. In addition, the artifactually compressed glands may be fragmented or telescoped (with double-barreled lumina or glands within glands), and erythrocytes are commonly found between the glands.

The microscopic appearance of endometrial polyps is discussed earlier in this chapter. As indicated previously, the presence of a diffusely or focally fibrotic stroma and of dilated, thick-walled blood vessels should be diagnostic of a polyp or polyps. Hyperplasia can, as previously stated, occur within polyps, and diffuse hyperplasia can be a polypoid process; these two lesions should be distinguished from one another. Atypical polypoid adenomyoma also enters into the differential diagnosis and is usually recognized by the presence of interlacing fascicles of benign smooth muscle between the endometrial glands (see Mixed Epithelial-Nonepithelial Tumors).

Other types of benign processes can be confused with hyperplasia as well, with the differential diagnosis usually dependent on the specific variant of hyperplasia involved. Thus, simple hyperplasia may be confused with cystic atrophy, in which cystically dilated glands are also found. However, in cystic atrophy the volume of endometrium is less, the stromal component is also atrophic (usually with small, shrunken cells), and the glands are lined by a single layer of epithelium that is flattened to cuboidal (fig. 15).

Endometritis also enters into the differential diagnosis of complex hyperplasia because the glands in endometritis may be crowded, architecturally complex, and even focally atypical (fig. 48). However, the presence of an inflammatory cell infiltrate is distinctly unusual in endometrial hyperplasia, whereas it is required for a diagnosis of endometritis.

Foci of atypical hyperplasia may be confused with endometrial epithelial metaplastic and related changes, specifically papillary proliferation and ciliary, eosinophilic cell, and surface syncytial changes. These should only pose a problem when they occur in a hyperplastic endometrium and thus might erroneously raise the diagnosis from hyperplasia to atypical hyperplasia. More complete descriptions of these entities are presented in the chapter on Tumor-Like Lesions.

Adenocarcinoma

The differential diagnosis of endometrial hyperplasias from adenocarcinomas is a subject that has already been discussed briefly in the initial remarks of this section. The ground rule for the subsequent discussion is that this differential diagnosis both can and should be made at the routine light-microscopic level. It also should be understood that diagnostic problems only arise with the distinction of complex hyperplasia and atypical hyperplasia from well-differentiated adenocarcinoma of endometrioid type. Neither simple hyperplasia without atypia nor more poorly differentiated or nonendometrioid carcinomas should present any problem in differential diagnosis.

This subject has been discussed and reviewed in many publications (15,16,18,24,25,28,29, 31,32,34), most of which list criteria that are somewhat divergent and often subjective but depend mostly on the evaluation of the presence or absence of stromal invasion (Table 2). Thus, in the diagnostic scheme currently favored by most authors, atypical endometrial proliferations in which the glands have not invaded their own stroma are classified as hyperplasias,

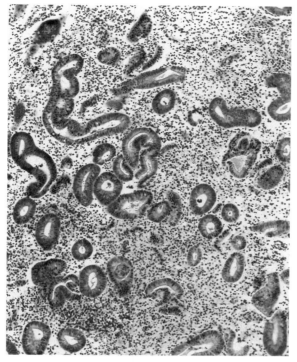

Figure 47
PROLIFERATIVE ENDOMETRIUM
This is an example of a proliferative endometrium with artifactual changes secondary to curettage, which was misinterpreted as endometrial hyperplasia. The glands in this field are neither architecturally irregular nor cystically dilated. The ratio of glands to stroma is about normal for a midproliferative endometrium, and a general orientation of the glands from upper left to lower right is noteworthy.

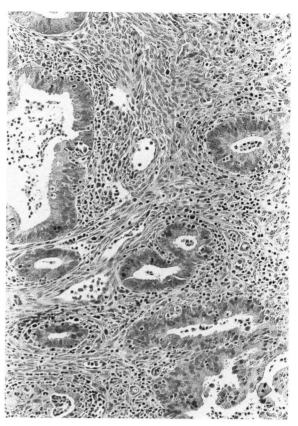

Figure 48
CHRONIC ENDOMETRITIS WITH REACTIVE GLANDULAR PROLIFERATION
The spindled stroma contains a massive lymphoplasmacytic infiltrate. Endometrial glands are irregularly distributed and variable in size and shape but are also infiltrated by the inflammatory cells.

whereas those in which stromal invasion has occurred are classified as adenocarcinomas. Proliferations that totally lack atypia are, of course, hyperplasias or a lesser condition. The problem then becomes one of recognizing the morphologic criteria for the presence of stromal invasion in an atypical proliferation.

As mentioned earlier, even the most marked complex hyperplasia with or without atypia should have some residual endometrial stromal cells between adjacent glands. I believe that when those stromal cells disappear completely, invasion has occurred and the lesion is an adenocarcinoma. The three most common manifestations of disappearance of normal stroma are 1) total absence of stroma between glands (glandular confluence), 2) fibrosis of stroma between

glands, and 3) necrosis of stroma between glands. These may occur either separately or together and either focally in a hyperplastic endometrium (figs. 49, 50) or diffusely.

In the case of glandular confluence, stromal cells cannot be demonstrated between adjacent glands (figs. 50–53). In some cases, the nuclei of stromal cells cannot be identified between glands, but a small amount of acellular space still seems to be present (fig. 54). Such cases are probably best diagnosed as complex hyperplasias or borderline lesions, but in many of them, obvious carcinoma will be seen in adjacent microscopic fields (fig. 55).

Stromal fibrosis is generally the easiest (although not universally present) indicator of stromal invasion to recognize at low magnification

Table 2

COMPARISON OF PUBLISHED CRITERIA FOR HISTOPATHOLOGIC DIAGNOSIS OF WELL-DIFFERENTIATED ENDOMETRIOID ADENOCARCINOMA

Tavassoli and Kraus (34)	Kurman and Norris (24)	Hendrickson et al. (18)
Cytologic patterns malignant • Nuclei large, variable size • Nuclear outlines irregular • Nuclear membranes irregular • Nucleoli large, irregular, spiculated • Cytoplasm scant, pale, amphophilic	Infiltrating glands producing a fibrous, desmoplastic stromal reaction	Confluent complex glands with little intervening stroma
	Confluent glandular bridges and aggregates of glands lacking intervening stroma	Gland-within-gland pattern with papillary infoldings and bridges (complex filigree pattern)
Loss of nuclear polarity	Branching, complex papillary epithelial-lined processes	Cellular stratification (nucleomegaly, chromatin clearing, prominent nucleoli, mitotic figures)
Extensive intraglandular proliferation with cribriform pattern	Squamous cell proliferations replacing glands and forming solid sheets	
Intraglandular gland cell bridging without stromal support (persistent in multiple levels)	The previous three patterns must occupy half of a low-power field (2.1 mm) unless frank cytologic features of malignancy are present	
Gland profiles irregular		
Gland size variable		
Mitoses variable		

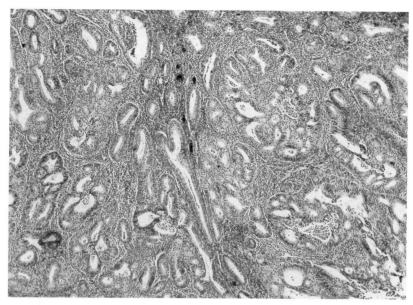

Figure 49
(Figures 49 and 50 are from the same patient)
COMPLEX HYPERPLASIA WITH FOCAL WELL-DIFFERENTIATED
ENDOMETRIOID ADENOCARCINOMA

The endometrioid adenocarcinoma takes the form of several ovoid masses consisting of a number of confluent endometrial glands, some with a cribriform pattern. Many other glands are separated by unremarkable endometrial stroma. See figure 50 for higher magnification.

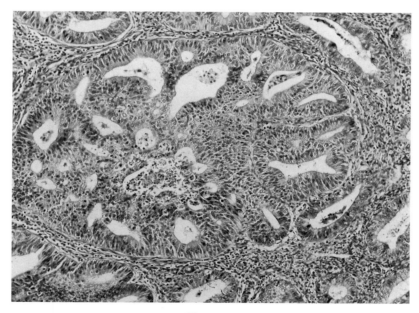

Figure 50
COMPLEX HYPERPLASIA WITH FOCAL WELL-DIFFERENTIATED
ENDOMETRIOID ADENOCARCINOMA

This is a detail of one of the microscopic foci of endometrial carcinoma seen in figure 49. This type of lesion would not be expected to invade the myometrium (as exemplified by these photomicrographs, which were taken from a hysterectomy specimen).

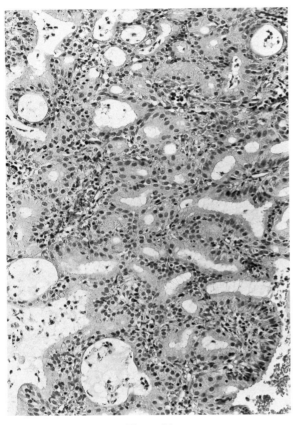

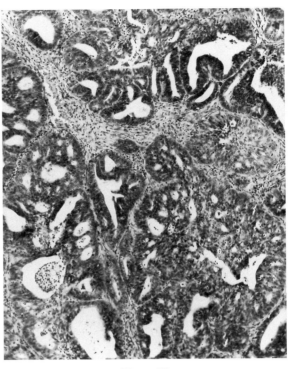

Figure 52
WELL-DIFFERENTIATED ENDOMETRIOID
ADENOCARCINOMA
In this illustration, several large masses of glands show
a confluent or cribriform pattern, whereas others are sepa-
rated by a desmoplastic stroma.

Figure 51
WELL-DIFFERENTIATED ENDOMETRIOID
ADENOCARCINOMA
The glands illustrated here lack cytologic atypia but are
confluent, with no intervening stroma.

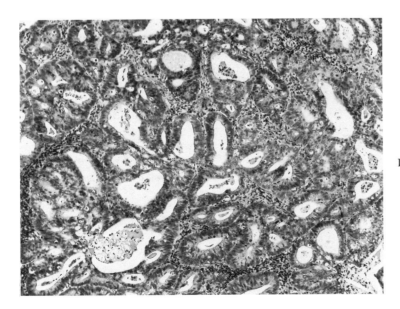

Figure 53
WELL-DIFFERENTIATED
ENDOMETRIOID ADENOCARCINOMA
This illustration shows a confluent glandu-
lar pattern.

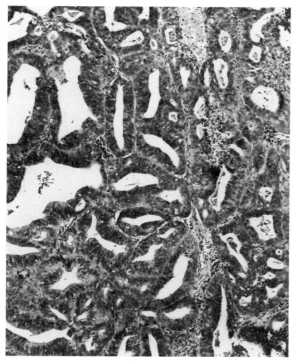

Figure 54
(Figures 54 and 55 are from the same patient)
WELL-DIFFERENTIATED ENDOMETRIOID
ADENOCARCINOMA VERSUS ATYPICAL
(COMPLEX) HYPERPLASIA
The glands in this field show both architectural and cytologic atypia but are still separated by thin wisps of mostly acellular stroma. Obvious carcinoma was seen in an adjacent microscopic field (see figure 55).

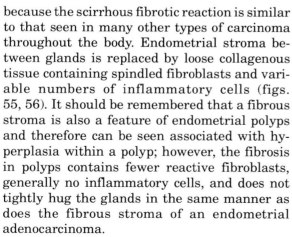

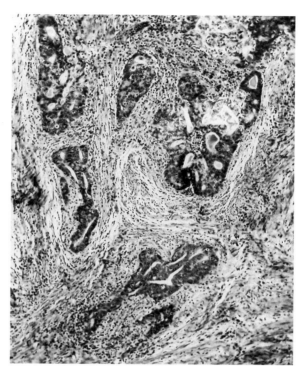

Figure 55
WELL-DIFFERENTIATED ENDOMETRIOID
ADENOCARCINOMA
This microscopic field, a few millimeters away from the field seen in figure 54, shows the desmoplastic or scirrhous stromal response of invasive carcinoma. Focal stromal necrosis is also present.

because the scirrhous fibrotic reaction is similar to that seen in many other types of carcinoma throughout the body. Endometrial stroma between glands is replaced by loose collagenous tissue containing spindled fibroblasts and variable numbers of inflammatory cells (figs. 55, 56). It should be remembered that a fibrous stroma is also a feature of endometrial polyps and therefore can be seen associated with hyperplasia within a polyp; however, the fibrosis in polyps contains fewer reactive fibroblasts, generally no inflammatory cells, and does not tightly hug the glands in the same manner as does the fibrous stroma of an endometrial adenocarcinoma.

Stromal necrosis is the least common pattern seen in well-differentiated endometrial adenocarcinoma and is usually associated with one or more of the other patterns of stromal invasion (figs. 55, 57). In this pattern, stromal cells between glands disappear and are replaced by neutrophils, with or without necrotic acellular debris. It should be noted that disappearance and replacement of stroma is mandatory for the application of this criterion because neutrophils are seen infiltrating within stroma in endometritis and in normal menstrual endometrium; in either of these situations, cytologic atypia should be absent as well. Although endometrial carcinomas may develop extensive necrosis after radiation therapy, it is unusual for a tumor to be so necrotic that a diagnosis cannot be made before therapy on a biopsy or curettage specimen (fig. 58).

A final stromal appearance that may be seen in endometrial adenocarcinoma is the presence

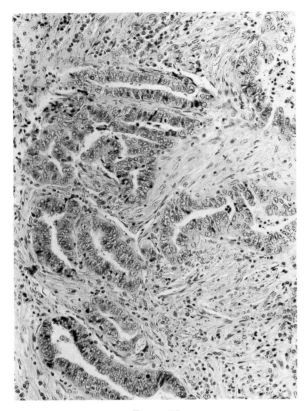

Figure 56
WELL-DIFFERENTIATED ENDOMETRIOID
ADENOCARCINOMA
A marked desmoplastic stromal pattern is seen in this illustration. (Fig. 13 from Silverberg SG. Hyperplasia and carcinoma of the endometrium. Semin Diagn Pathol 1988;5:135–53.)

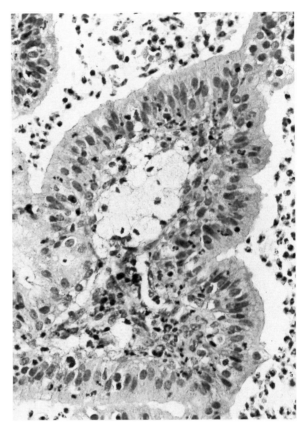

Figure 57
WELL-DIFFERENTIATED ENDOMETRIOID
ADENOCARCINOMA
A group of foam cells is seen at the center of this illustration. The remainder of the stroma in this field is replaced by neutrophils (stromal necrosis).

of endometrial stromal foam cells (figs. 57, 59). This change is not considered diagnostic of adenocarcinoma because stromal cells (albeit altered ones) are still present separating glands, and stromal foam cells have also been reported in endometrial hyperplasias and polyps (10). I believe, however, that they are much more common in carcinomas and that the possibility of carcinoma should be considered whenever they are encountered in a biopsy.

The question may be raised as to whether there is a threshold amount of stromal invasion that must be seen before the diagnosis of adenocarcinoma is made. Kurman and Norris (24) have recommended that stromal invasion manifested by any histologic pattern other than fibrosis be required to occupy at least one-half of a low-power (4.2 mm in diameter) microscopic

field before it can be accepted as evidence of invasive adenocarcinoma. For these authors, this additional criterion seemed to provide a good distinction between lesions that did or did not invade the myometrium at subsequent hysterectomy, but other authors (20) have not had a similar degree of success in applying this criterion. Thus, I prefer to diagnose as invasive adenocarcinoma any lesion in which stromal invasion is clearly present and to indicate the size of the focus or foci of tumor in a separate note in the surgical pathology report. It is clear that myometrial invasion, as well as extension beyond the uterine corpus, will be rare in cases in which the tumor is both well differentiated and minute.

It should be noted that the diagnosis of complex or atypical hyperplasia in a biopsy or curettage

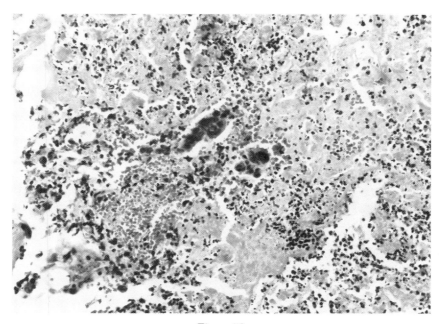

Figure 58
NECROTIC ENDOMETRIAL CARCINOMA
In this pretherapy curettage specimen, only rare neoplastic cells (center) were seen in voluminous necrotic debris. Better microscopic evidence must be sought before making a definitive diagnosis of carcinoma.

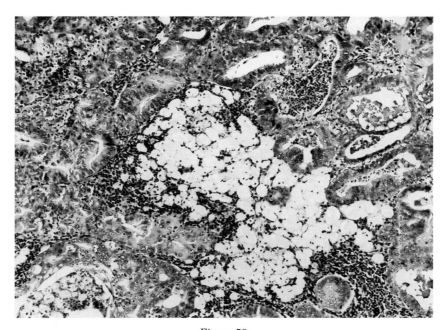

Figure 59
ENDOMETRIAL ADENOCARCINOMA
Note the large numbers of stromal foam cells in this illustration.

specimen does not guarantee the absence of adenocarcinoma in a subsequent hysterectomy specimen. Indeed, carcinoma has been reported in the uterus in 17 percent and 25 percent of cases after an initial diagnosis of atypical hyperplasia (24,34). Rarely, however, did these tumors deeply invade the myometrium. These prevalence rates of concurrent carcinomas are not markedly different from some of the incidence rates reported for subsequent carcinomas in an intact uterus after a diagnosis of atypical hyperplasia (25), suggesting that the tumors that developed in these cases progressed very slowly or merely persisted after incomplete removal by curettage.

Special Techniques. As mentioned above, numerous techniques other than conventional light microscopy have been used over the years to attempt to distinguish between endometrial hyperplasia and carcinoma or between those hyperplasias with low and high risks of progression to carcinoma. These have included studies of the ultrastructure (12,21), morphometry (8,27), steroid hormone receptors (11), proliferative indexes (13), and immunohistochemistry (26,33,35) of different types of hyperplasias and carcinomas. All of these studies can be summarized by stating that 1) thus far there is no technique demonstrated to be superior to conventional light microscopy in distinguishing between hyperplasia and carcinoma, and 2) those techniques that demonstrate that some hyperplasias are more like carcinomas than others (and thus presumably more likely to progress to carcinoma) invariably identify the atypical hyperplasias as being closer in their reaction patterns to carcinoma than to hyperplasia without atypia.

Treatment and Prognosis. The treatment of endometrial hyperplasia has basically two goals: the cessation of abnormal uterine bleeding and the prevention of endometrial carcinoma. The first of these goals is usually accomplished by curettage, which usually leads to a diagnosis. Refractory bleeding after curettage can be treated either hormonally (usually with progestins alone or in combination with estrogens) or by hysterectomy.

Treatment directed at the prevention of endometrial carcinoma is more controversial because our knowledge of the risk of development of carcinoma from endometrial hyperplasia is still far from definitive. Numerous published reports have attempted to document the likelihood of endometrial hyperplasia untreated by hysterectomy progressing to carcinoma, with highly variable results. This variability has been the result of numerous factors, including different histopathologic criteria for the diagnosis of the different types of hyperplasia (and of carcinoma as well), different follow-up intervals between the initial curettage and eventual hysterectomy, and different intervening nonoperative treatments, including various hormonal manipulations and radiation therapy. In any event, there is general agreement that simple hyperplasia without atypia carries a minimal risk of progression to carcinoma; that complex atypical hyperplasia carries a significant risk (although the exact magnitude may be anywhere between 25 and 80 percent); and that complex hyperplasia without atypia and simple atypical hyperplasia occur somewhere in between these two extremes (15–17,19,23, 25,28,31,32,37). As mentioned, newer techniques have thus far not proved superior to conventional histologic examination in predicting the outcome in a given case of hyperplasia.

Complex hyperplasia without atypia is a particularly vexing problem. Although these lesions are almost invariably diploid, so are most adenocarcinomas of the endometrium, and some well-differentiated adenocarcinomas show little or no more cytologic atypia than do most complex hyperplasias. Thus, because the only difference between the diagnosis of complex hyperplasia and that of some very well-differentiated adenocarcinomas lies in the disappearance of a few wisps of stroma between adjacent glands, it would seem logical that complex hyperplasia without atypia should have an appreciable risk of progression to carcinoma. However, among recent prospective studies, only that of Sherman and Brown (31) has demonstrated frequent progression (22 percent), whereas several others have all noted a progression rate of less than 10 percent (14,19,23).

Finally, many factors other than histopathology probably affect the premalignant potential of an endometrial hyperplasia. These include, among others, patient age, the presence or absence of underlying ovarian or other endocrine pathology, and exogenous hormone administration both before and after the diagnosis of hyperplasia. It is possible that the extent of the hyperplastic process within the endometrium, or the degree of cytologic atypia within the hyperplasia, also influences the risk of progression, although this has not been demonstrated. Because endometrial carcinoma can be found in a specimen from a hysterectomy performed immediately after the diagnosis of hyperplasia almost as frequently as in that from a hysterectomy delayed 1 or more years (25,32,34), it is possible that many examples of "progression" may merely represent persistence of an adenocarcinoma that was not sampled by the curettage.

If a patient with hyperplasia is treated nonoperatively, the pathologist will usually be asked to evaluate a repeat biopsy or curettage for evidence of response to hormonal therapy. Because the agent used will generally be progestational, a comment should always be made comparing the current specimen with the pre-treatment specimen with respect to both persistence of hyperplasia (and atypia, if initially present) and development of gland atrophy and stromal decidualization, which are the usual manifestations of progestational therapy (figs. 60–62). If hyperplasia persists after an adequate trial of hormonal therapy, the next step may be hysterectomy.

In examining a hysterectomy specimen from a patient with known endometrial hyperplasia, the main concern should be the detection of a previously unsuspected carcinoma. This finding has been reported in 17 percent and 25 percent of uteri removed after an initial diagnosis of atypical hyperplasia of the endometrium (24,34). Thus, it is important to submit multiple (usually at least 10–12) sections of the endometrium and underlying myometrium from these specimens.

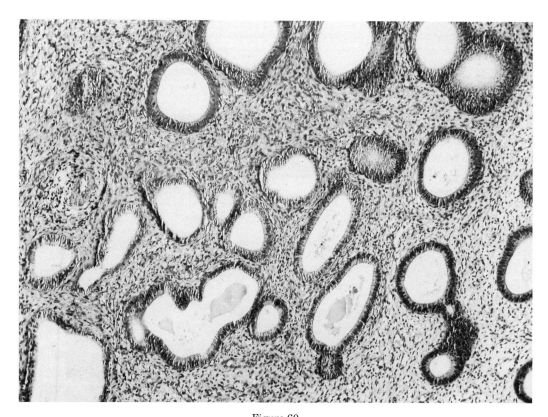

Figure 60
(Figures 60–62 are from the same patient)
SIMPLE HYPERPLASIA OF THE ENDOMETRIUM AT INITIAL CURETTAGE
Compare with figures 61 and 62, which represent repeat curettage from the same patient after 1 year of progestin therapy.

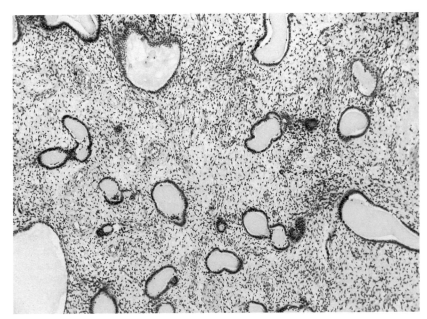

Figure 61
PARTIAL RESPONSE OF SIMPLE HYPERPLASIA
TO PROGESTIN THERAPY
These glands differ from those seen at the same magnification in figure 60 (before hormonal therapy) in that they are slightly smaller, less crowded, and are lined by a single layer of cells rather than the proliferative-type epithelium seen in figure 60. This pattern may be characterized as regressed hyperplasia.

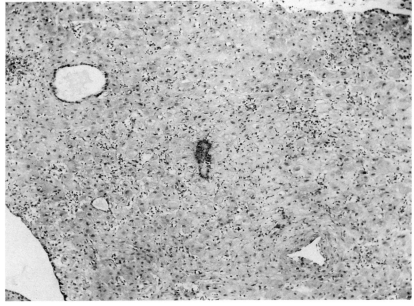

Figure 62
COMPLETE RESPONSE OF SIMPLE HYPERPLASIA
TO PROGESTIN THERAPY
Another field of the same specimen shows inactive glands in a decidualized stroma. This pattern is characteristic of the response to progestational agents, but the preexisting condition (simple hyperplasia in this case) can no longer be specified by an examination of material such as this.

REFERENCES

Polyps

1. Armenia CS. Sequential relationship between endometrial polyps and carcinoma of the endometrium. Obstet Gynecol 1967;30:524–9.
2. Foss BA, Horne HW Jr, Hertig AT. The endometrium and sterility. Fertil Steril 1958;9:193–206.
3. Nuovo MA, Nuovo GJ, McCaffrey RM, Levine RU, Barron B, Winkler B. Endometrial polyps in postmenopausal patients receiving tamoxifen. Int J Gynecol Pathol 1989;8:125–31.
4. Peterson WF, Novak ER. Endometrial polyps. Obstet Gynecol 1956;8:40–9.
5. Salm R. The incidence and significance of early carcinoma in endometrial polyps. J Pathol 1972;108:47–53.
6. Silverberg SG, Major FJ, Blessing JA, et al. Carcinosarcoma (malignant mixed mesodermal tumor) of the uterus: a Gynecologic Oncology Group pathologic study of 203 cases. Int J Gynecol Pathol 1990;9:1–19.
7. Winkler B, Alvarez S, Richart RM, Crum CP. Pitfalls in the diagnosis of endometrial neoplasia. Obstet Gynecol 1984;64:185–94.

Hyperplasia and Atypical Hyperplasia

8. Baak JP. The use and disuse of morphometry in the diagnosis of endometrial hyperplasia and carcinoma. Pathol Res Pract 1984;179:20–3.
9. Bibbo M, Kluskens L, Azizi F, et al. Accuracy of three sampling techniques for the diagnosis of endometrial cancer and hyperplasias. J Reprod Med 1982;27:622–6.
10. Dawagne MP, Silverberg SG. Foam cells in endometrial carcinoma. Gynecol Oncol 1982;13:67–75.
11. Ehrlich CE, Young PC, Cleary RE. Cytoplasmic progesterone and estradiol receptors in normal, hyperplastic, and carcinomatous endometria: therapeutic implications. Am J Obstet Gynecol 1981;141:539–46.
12. Ferenczy A. Cytodynamics of endometrial hyperplasia and carcinoma. Prog Surg Pathol 1982;4:95–113.
13. _____ . Cytodynamics of endometrial hyperplasia and neoplasia, Part II: in vitro DNA histoautoradiography. Hum Pathol 1983;14:77–82.
14. _____ , Gelfand MM. Hyperplasia vs neoplasia: two tracks for the endometrium? Contemp Obstet Gynecol 1986;28:79–96.
15. Fox H. The endometrial hyperplasias. Obstet Gynecol Annu 1984;13:197–209.
16. _____ , Buckley CH. The endometrial hyperplasias and their relationship to endometrial neoplasia. Histopathology 1982;6:493–510.
17. Gusberg SB, Milano C. Detection of endometrial cancer and its precursors. Cancer 1981;47(Suppl 5):1173–5.
18. Hendrickson MR, Ross JC, Kempson RL. Toward the development of morphologic criteria for well-differentiated adenocarcinoma of the endometrium. Am J Surg Pathol 1983;7:819–38.
19. Huang SJ, Amparo EG, Fu YS. Endometrial hyperplasia. Surg Pathol 1988;1:215–29.
20. King A, Seraj IM, Wagner RJ. Stromal invasion in endometrial adenocarcinoma. Am J Obstet Gyencol 1984;149:10–4.
21. Klemi PJ, Gronroos M, Rauramo L, Punnonen R. Ultrastructural features of endometrial atypical adenomatous hyperplasia and adenocarcinomas and the plasma level of estrogens. Gynecol Oncol 1980;9:162–9.
22. Koss LG, Schreiber K, Oberlander SG, Moussouris HF, Lesser M. Detection of endometrial carcinoma and hyperplasia in asymptomatic women. Obstet Gynecol 1984;64:1–11.
23. Kurman RJ, Kaminski PF, Norris HJ. The behavior of endometrial hyperplasia. A long-term study of "untreated" hyperplasia in 170 patients. Cancer 1985;56:403–12.
24. _____ , Norris HJ. Evaluation of criteria for distinguishing atypical endometrial hyperplasia from well-differentiated carcinoma. Cancer 1982;49:2547–59.
25. _____ , Norris HJ. Endometrial hyperplasia and metaplasia. In: Kurman RJ, ed. Blaustein's pathology of the female genital tract. 3rd ed. New York: Springer-Verlag, 1987:322–37.
26. Morris WP, Griffin NR, Wells M. Patterns of reactivity with the monoclonal antibodies HMFG1 and HMFG2 in normal endometrium, endometrial hyperplasia and adenocarcinoma. Histopathology 1989;15:179–86.
27. Norris HJ, Becker RL, Mikel UV. A comparative morphometric and cytophotometric study of endometrial hyperplasia, atypical hyperplasia, and endometrial carcinoma. Hum Pathol 1989;20:219–23.
28. _____ , Connor MP, Kurman RJ. Preinvasive lesions of the endometrium. Clin Obstet Gynaecol 1986;13:725–38.
29. _____ , Tavassoli FA, Kurman RJ. Endometrial hyperplasia and carcinoma. Diagnostic considerations. Am J Surg Pathol 1983;7:839–47.
30. Schiff I, Sela HK, Cramer D, Tulchinsky D, Ryan KJ. Endometrial hyperplasia in women on cyclic or continuous estrogen regimens. Fertil Steril 1982;37:79–82.
31. Sherman AI, Brown S. The precursors of endometrial carcinoma. Am J Obstet Gynecol 1979;135:947–56.
32. Silverberg SG. Hyperplasia and carcinoma of the endometrium. Semin Diagn Pathol 1988;5:135–53.
33. Söderström KO. Lectin binding to human endometrial hyperplasias and adenocarcinoma. Int J Gynecol Pathol 1987;6:356–65.
34. Tavassoli F, Kraus FT. Endometrial lesions in uteri resected for atypical endometrial hyperplasia. Am J Clin Pathol 1978;70:770–9.
35. Thor A, Viglione MJ, Muraro R, Ohuchi N, Schlom J, Gorstein F. Monoclonal antibody B72.3 reactivity with human endometrium. Int J Gynecol Pathol 1987;6:235–47.
36. Vuopala S. Diagnostic accuracy and clinical applicability of cytological and histological methods for investigating endometrial carcinoma. Acta Obstet Gynecol Scand Suppl 1977;70:1–72.
37. Wentz WB. Progestin therapy in endometrial hyperplasia. Gynecol Oncol 1974;2:362–7.

ENDOMETRIAL CARCINOMA

Definition. Endometrial carcinoma is a malignant epithelial tumor arising from the endometrium. Most endometrial carcinomas are adenocarcinomas; the most common type is endometrioid adenocarcinoma.

General Features. In the United States, endometrial carcinoma is the most frequent invasive malignant tumor of the female genital tract and one of the most common cancers in women. Similar incidence rates are seen elsewhere in North America and Northern Europe, but endometrial carcinoma is a relatively uncommon disease in Asia and Africa (38), although recent increases in incidence rates in these areas have also been reported (45). The incidence of endometrial carcinoma increased rapidly in the United States during the early 1970s and then fell equally rapidly. Both instances apparently were related to changing patterns in the usage of unopposed exogenous estrogen by postmenopausal women (4).

Various studies have cited numerous factors in addition to exogenous estrogens that have been associated with increased risk of development of endometrial carcinoma (38). The best documented of these are obesity, nulliparity, and late menopause. Other factors that are considered less well documented include diabetes mellitus, hypertension, family history, and a high-fat diet. Endometrial carcinoma has been reported to follow large doses of therapeutic radiation for other cancers (24). Combination-type oral contraceptives in which progestin influence is dominant have been reported to decrease the risk for endometrial carcinoma (38), as has cigarette smoking (40).

Because exogenous estrogens have been associated with endometrial carcinoma, it is not surprising that ovarian lesions associated with increased estrogen production have also been associated with endometrial carcinoma; these include polycystic ovaries, stromal hyperplasia, and hyperthecosis (56,68). Indeed, it is considered that the roles of most of the factors mentioned above are mediated through endogenous hyperestrinism.

These observations on the relationship of estrogens to endometrial carcinoma, supplemented by similar observations about endometrial hyperplasia, have led to the assumption that endometrial carcinoma could be prevented by the early detection and treatment of endometrial hyperplasia (30). However, several recent reports have emphasized that a subset of endometrial carcinomas, including the more aggressive variants, appears to be unassociated with endometrial hyperplasia (6,16). In a screening study of asymptomatic women, Koss and colleagues (39) reported essentially equal frequencies of endometrial carcinoma and hyperplasia, suggesting that many carcinomas are not preceded by hyperplasia. Thus, not only does the rate at which the various forms of hyperplasia progress to carcinoma remain controversial (as discussed in Endometrial Polyps and Hyperplasias), but also the proportion of carcinomas that have gone through a stage of hyperplasia remains to be determined.

Although the endometrioid type of endometrial carcinoma is the most common type in all major published series, prognostically unfavorable types appear to be relatively more frequent in low-risk populations such as the Japanese (64) and among black women in the United States (38). Thus, the relative frequencies of the various subtypes depend not only on the diagnostic criteria applied but also on the population of women being studied. Nevertheless, it can be assumed that general statements concerning endometrial carcinoma in both these and other references apply predominantly (although not necessarily exclusively) to the endometrioid subtype.

Clinical Features. Although endometrial carcinoma can occur at virtually any age, most cases occur in perimenopausal and postmenopausal women. Many of the patients have one or more of the associated clinical findings mentioned above (obesity, nulliparity, late menopause, diabetes mellitus, hypertension, history of exogenous estrogen administration, etc.). The initial manifestation of endometrial carcinoma in almost all patients is abnormal vaginal bleeding, with pain appearing only late in the course of the disease. Occasionally, a patient may be asymptomatic (67).

Although various radiologic and sonographic techniques may indicate the diagnosis, and even the extent of tumor within the uterus (8,83), definitive diagnosis still requires microscopic confirmation. Cervicovaginal cytology is generally conceded to have an unacceptably high rate of false negativity (60), and even direct endometrial sampling for cytologic examination is not as accurate as histopathologic study (58,80). The type of histopathologic sampling that is best suited to the detection and correct diagnosis of endometrial carcinoma is still debatable. Office biopsy procedures are probably best for screening purposes, but they often must be followed by a formal dilatation and curettage. Even this procedure may show significant discrepancies when compared with subsequent hysterectomy specimens (70).

Gross Findings. Endometrial carcinoma usually arises in the corpus proper, but some cases appear to originate in the lower uterine segment (31). Almost all of the histologic subtypes are similar in gross appearance, with the probable exception of the rare verrucous carcinoma. The uterus is usually slightly to moderately enlarged but may be of normal size or even small. On gross examination, carcinoma usually presents as a single dominant mass (pl. II) but may be seen as two or more separate masses or as diffuse thickening of much of the endometrial surface. Most tumors are at least partially exophytic and are seen more frequently on the posterior than on the anterior wall.

The typical carcinoma has a shaggy, often focally ulcerated surface, beneath which is a friable mass of soft white-gray tissue. An increasing volume of tumor projecting into the endometrial cavity is usually associated with a greater possibility of myometrial invasion, which may display either pushing or infiltrating borders on cut section through the uterine wall. Deep myometrial invasion indicates more advanced disease, as does extension into the lower uterine segment and cervix. Advanced tumor may also penetrate through the full thickness of the myometrium into the surrounding parametrium.

Microscopic Findings. Endometrioid adenocarcinoma is the prototypical carcinoma of the endometrium and is by far the most common type encountered. The tumor is basically a glandular one, with tumor grading dependent mostly on the extent of gland formation by the neoplastic cells. As discussed in the chapter on Endometrial Polyps and Hyperplasias, the main

criterion for the distinction of well-differentiated endometrioid adenocarcinoma from complex or atypical hyperplasia is the presence of stromal invasion. This may be manifested by glandular confluence (disappearance of endometrial stroma between adjacent glands), stromal fibrosis, or stromal necrosis. These changes are illustrated in figures 51–59.

The glands of most endometrioid carcinomas are small, round, and fairly uniform (figs. 63–66). Each gland is usually easily distinguishable from adjacent glands, and multiple lumina or slit-like lumina within glands are relatively uncommon. However, some tumors may have a focal or extensive cribriform pattern.

The cells lining the glands of a well-differentiated endometrioid carcinoma are usually fairly uniform in size, shape, and tinctorial properties. In these cytologically well-differentiated tumors, the nuclei may be in a single row (fig. 67) or moderately stratified (see fig. 72) and range from oval to round. When oval, their long axes are perpendicular to the basement membrane. Mitotic activity is variable but generally is not much more impressive than in benign proliferative or hyperplastic endometria. Nucleoli are generally present, occasionally prominent, and rarely gigantic.

In some tumors, there is increased nuclear atypia, manifested by increasingly rounded nuclei, increased hyperchromatism, anisonucleosis, nuclear clearing with clumping of chromatin along the nuclear membrane (fig. 68), or a combination of these features.

A variation of well-differentiated endometrioid carcinoma is the papillary or villoglandular type (figs. 69–72). In this variant, the cells line papillae that are characteristically short and blunt. The lining cells are similar to those lining glands of other endometrioid carcinomas, and indeed, glands and papillae often grow side by side. The tumor lacks the marked nuclear pleomorphism, cellular stratification and buds, desquamating cells, necrosis, and psammoma bodies that characterize serous carcinoma (10). Indeed, the main reason to recognize the papillary or villoglandular type of endometrioid carcinoma is to avoid confusing it with serous carcinoma, which has a much poorer prognosis (10).

Grading. In general, as the cells of an endometrial carcinoma diverge from a glandular

PLATE II
ADENOCARCINOMA OF THE ENDOMETRIUM

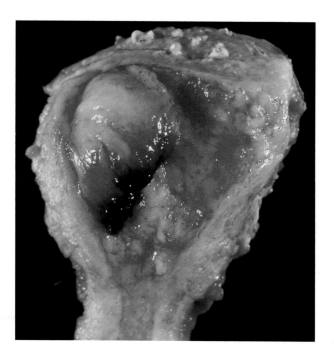

A

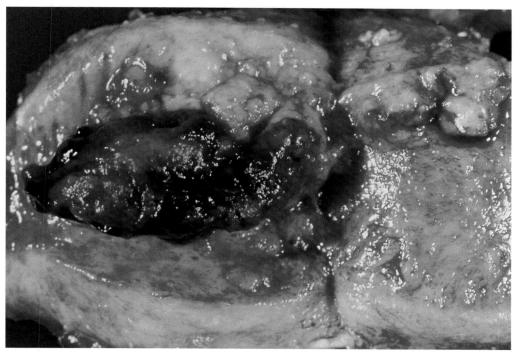

B

This tumor, which occupies a small uterine cavity, grows primarily as a firm polypoid mass and does not invade the myometrium (A) (Courtesy of Dr. Lucien Nochomovitz, Washington, D.C.). This tumor fills the entire endometrial cavity and infiltrates the myometrium (B).

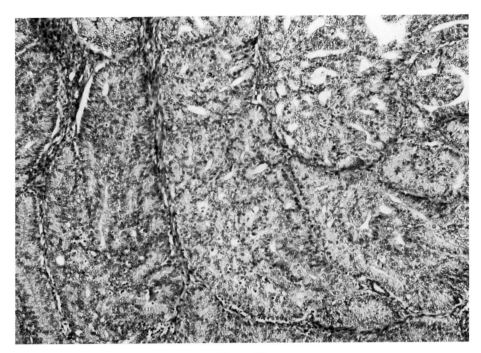

Figure 63
WELL-DIFFERENTIATED ENDOMETRIOID ADENOCARCINOMA (GRADE I)
This illustration shows small, round, regular glands growing in a confluent pattern.

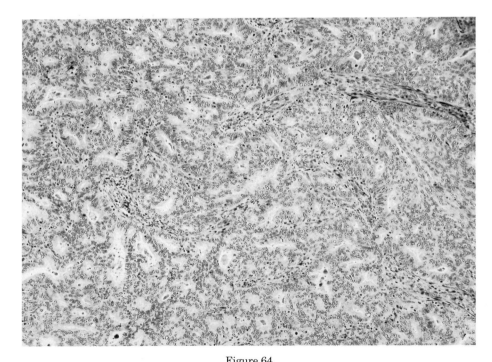

Figure 64
(Figures 64 and 65 are from the same patient)
WELL-DIFFERENTIATED ENDOMETRIOID ADENOCARCINOMA
This illustration is photographed at the same magnification as figure 63 but is from a different case. The findings are essentially identical.

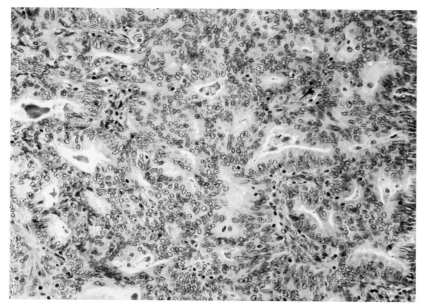

Figure 65
(Figures 65 and 64 are from the same patient)
WELL-DIFFERENTIATED ENDOMETRIOID ADENOCARCINOMA
At higher magnification, the tumor is composed of confluent glands lined by slightly stratified cells with uniform but somewhat rounded nuclei, many with single prominent nucleoli.

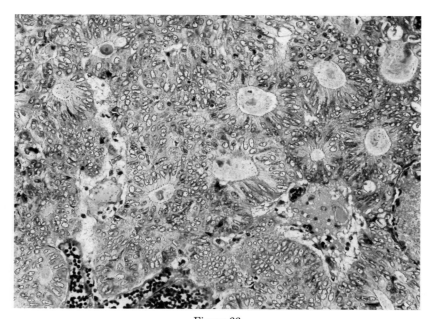

Figure 66
(Figures 66 and 68 are from the same patient)
MODERATELY DIFFERENTIATED ENDOMETRIOID ADENOCARCINOMA
(GRADE II)
In this case, some solid sheets of tumor cells are seen in addition to glands, and the nuclei are more variable in size and shape and show more irregularity of nuclear chromatin than those seen in either figure 65 or figure 67. Because a few solid foci might be the result of tangential sectioning of glands, the nuclear atypia helps to characterize this tumor as moderately differentiated.

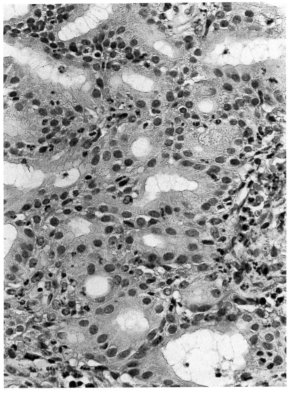

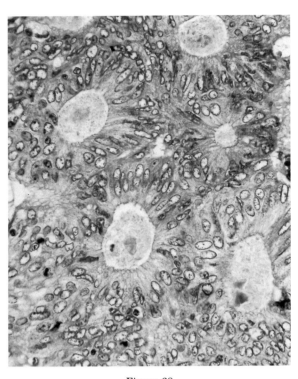

Figure 68
(Figures 68 and 66 are from the same patient)
MODERATELY DIFFERENTIATED ENDOMETRIOID
ADENOCARCINOMA
Another field of the same tumor illustrated in figure 66 shows anisonucleosis, prominent nucleoli in some nuclei, and nuclear clearing with clumping of chromatin along the nuclear membrane.

Figure 67
WELL-DIFFERENTIATED ENDOMETRIOID
ADENOCARCINOMA
Visible in this illustration are confluent glands lined predominantly by a single row of cells with large, round, normochromatic nuclei that are somewhat variable in size and irregularly distributed.

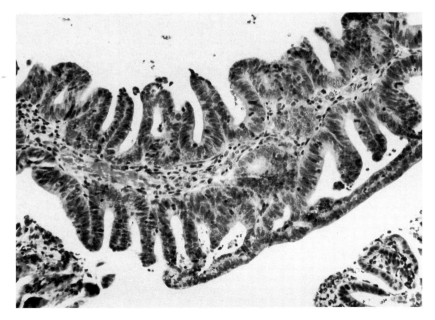

Figure 69
(Figures 69 and 70
are from the same patient)
WELL-DIFFERENTIATED
ENDOMETRIOID ADENO-
CARCINOMA (PAPILLARY
OR VILLOGLANDULAR TYPE)
The tumor cells are well differentiated but grow in a papillary rather than a glandular pattern. Compare this and the next three figures with figures 89–94, which illustrate serous carcinomas growing in papillary patterns.

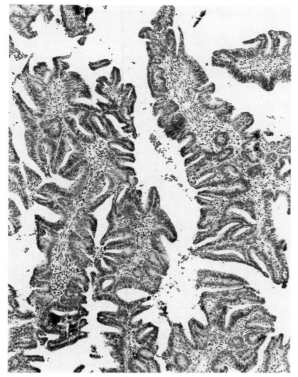

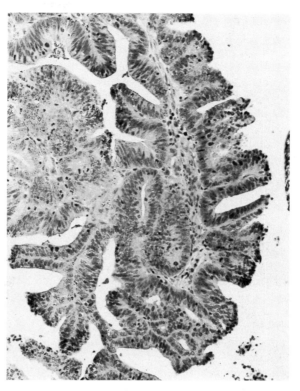

Figure 70
(Figures 70 and 69 are from the same patient)
WELL-DIFFERENTIATED ENDOMETRIOID
ADENOCARCINOMA (PAPILLARY OR
VILLOGLANDULAR TYPE)
Low magnification shows the growth pattern of this
tumor. Cellular detail is illustrated in figure 69.

Figure 71
(Figures 71 and 72 are from the same patient)
WELL-DIFFERENTIATED ENDOMETRIOID
ADENOCARCINOMA (PAPILLARY OR
VILLOGLANDULAR TYPE)
This is another case illustrating the villoglandular
architecture. See figure 72 for cellular detail.

Figure 72
WELL-DIFFERENTIATED
ENDOMETRIOID ADENO-
CARCINOMA (PAPILLARY
OR VILLOGLANDULAR TYPE)
Higher magnification of figure 71
shows typical features of serous papillary adenocarcinomas: relatively uniform nuclei and a lack of prominent
mitotic activity, marked cellular stratification, cellular buds, and exfoliation
of groups of cells into lumina.

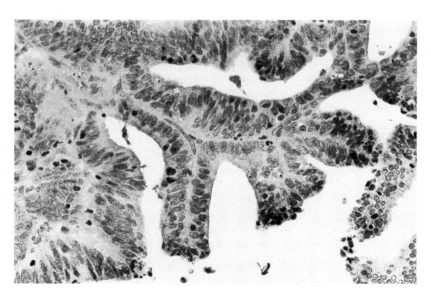

or papillary pattern to form solid sheets of cells (figs. 73, 74), the tumor is considered more poorly differentiated at the architectural level. Grading of the glandular component of all endometrioid carcinomas is performed as follows. In grade I adenocarcinoma, there is 5 percent or less of a nonsquamous nonmorular solid growth pattern. In grade II, from 6 to 50 percent of the tumor has such a solid pattern, and more than 50 percent of a nonsquamous nonmorular solid growth pattern is seen in grade III tumors. Notable nuclear atypia, inappropriate for the architectural grade, raises the grade of a grade I or grade II tumor by one. Note that this grading system varies in some of the nonendometrioid adenocarcinomas. In serous, clear cell, and squamous cell carcinomas, only nuclear grading is used. Adenocarcinomas with squamous differentiation are graded according to the grade of the glandular component only.

The benign endometrium adjacent to an endometrioid adenocarcinoma is usually hyperplastic, proliferative, or atrophic, although endometrial carcinomas have been reported to arise in secretory endometrium (53) or even in association with intrauterine pregnancy (72). Examination of the surrounding endometrium is important because the presence of hyperplasia is associated with a more favorable prognosis, with other factors being equal (6,16).

Variants of Endometrioid Carcinoma. In addition to the papillary or villoglandular type discussed above, two other variants of endometrioid adenocarcinoma are currently recognized. In *secretory adenocarcinoma*, the tumor is composed of well-differentiated glands that resemble those of early to midsecretory endometrium (figs. 75, 76). The entire tumor may be of this appearance, or foci of secretory differentiation may be seen within otherwise typical endometrioid adenocarcinomas. This tumor type appears to be associated with a favorable prognosis (76). The other variant, *ciliated carcinoma*, is an endometrioid adenocarcinoma in which the tumor is composed predominantly of ciliated cells (figs. 77, 78) (35). Although these tumors can extensively invade the myometrium, the ultimate clinical outcome of the few reported cases has been relatively favorable. Because most ciliated endometrial proliferations are benign, it is important that all of the criteria for the diagnosis of carcinoma be met before this entity is diagnosed.

Endometrioid adenocarcinomas may be associated with various metaplastic changes, but this should not change the underlying diagnosis. Both epithelial and stromal metaplastic and related changes may be present, with the former far more common. The presence of benign heterologous tissues within an endometrial carcinoma should not be confused with heterologous differentiation in a carcinosarcoma (49).

A sertoliform pattern (21), trophoblastic differentiation (fig. 74) (59), and tumor cell argyrophilia (2,5,57) have also been noted in endometrial carcinoma. Argyrophilia can be demonstrated in a high proportion of endometrial carcinomas, ranging up to 56 percent in some series. In some cases, the argyrophilia is related to argyrophilic mucin or glycogen granules, whereas in other cases it appears to be due to neuroendocrine cells containing serotonin or other hormones (2). Most authors believe that the presence of argyrophilia is of no clinical significance (2,5).

On the other hand, a variant of endometrioid adenocarcinoma that has a debatable clinical significance is *adenocarcinoma with squamous differentiation*. In this variant, small or large foci of squamous (including morular) differentiation are present. Because ordinary endometrioid adenocarcinomas may contain significant areas of solid growth, standardized criteria for squamous differentiation must be applied to make this diagnosis (figs. 79–86). By the International Society of Gynecological Pathologists criteria, a solid focus of tumor in an endometrioid-type carcinoma should be considered glandular unless at least one of the following criteria suggesting squamous differentiation is present:

- keratinization demonstrated with standard staining techniques
- intercellular bridges
- three or more of the following four criteria:
    sheet-like growth without gland formation or palisading
    sharp cell margins
    eosinophilic and thick or glassy cytoplasm
    a decreased nuclear/cytoplasmic ratio (compared with foci elsewhere in the same tumor).

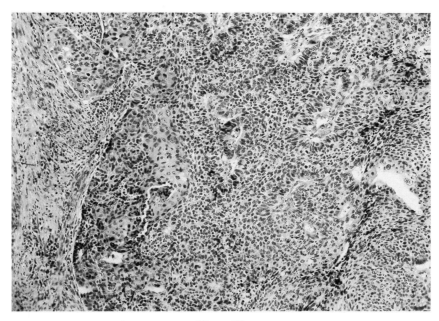

Figure 73
POORLY DIFFERENTIATED ENDOMETRIOID ADENOCARCINOMA
(GRADE III)
Only a few small round glands remain in this field to identify this tumor as adeno-
carcinoma of endometrioid type. Most of the tumor grows in solid sheets of anaplastic
cells.

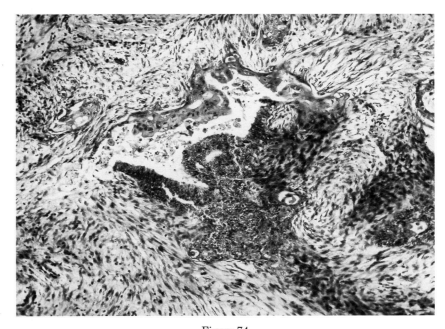

Figure 74
POORLY DIFFERENTIATED ENDOMETRIOID ADENOCARCINOMA
This field shows a few malignant glands at the center from which solid sheets of
anaplastic tumor cells stream into a reactive spindled stroma. At the top of the large lumen
in the center of the field, some of the lining cells resemble syncytiotrophoblastic cells.

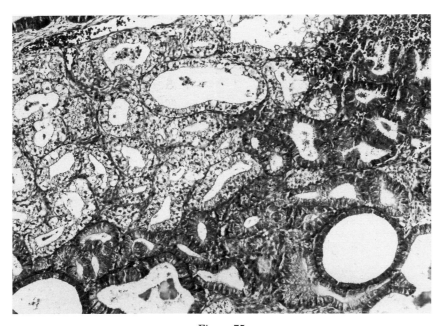

Figure 75
(Figures 75 and 76 are from the same patient)
WELL-DIFFERENTIATED ENDOMETRIOID ADENOCARCINOMA
(SECRETORY VARIANT)
The glands at the upper left of this illustration demonstrate clear cytoplasm due to
accumulation of glycogen.

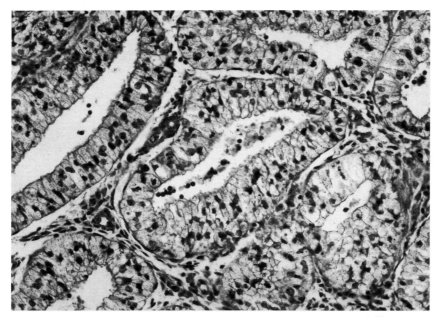

Figure 76
WELL-DIFFERENTIATED ENDOMETRIOID ADENOCARCINOMA
(SECRETORY VARIANT)
A higher magnification of the secretory element of figure 75 reveals small, regular
nuclei and abundant vacuolated cytoplasm.

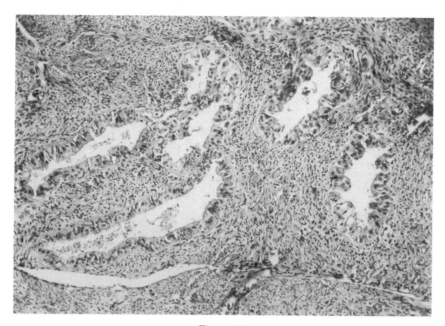

Figure 77
(Figures 77 and 78 are from the same patient)
WELL-DIFFERENTIATED ENDOMETRIOID ADENOCARCINOMA
(CILIATED VARIANT)
Irregular glands invading deeply in the myometrium are lined predominantly by
ciliated cells (see figure 78 for detail).

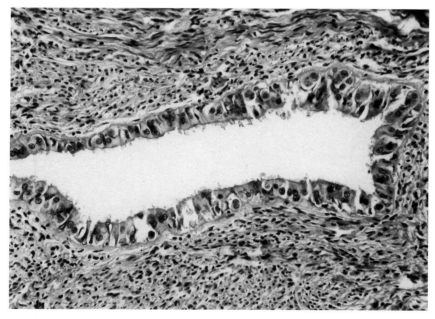

Figure 78
WELL-DIFFERENTIATED ENDOMETRIOID ADENOCARCINOMA
(CILIATED VARIANT)
One of the invading glands from the tumor illustrated in figure 77 is lined predominantly by ciliated cells. In the absence of myometrial invasion or other clear-cut
evidence of malignancy, most proliferations of this sort would be difficult to diagnose
as carcinoma.

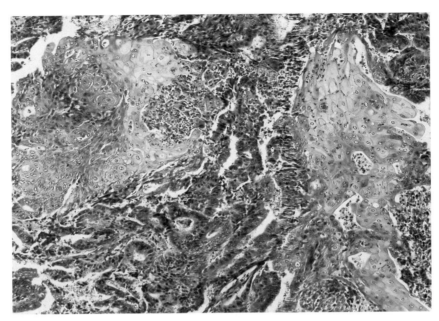

Figure 79
ENDOMETRIOID ADENOCARCINOMA WITH
SQUAMOUS DIFFERENTIATION

This well-differentiated adenocarcinoma contains large foci of benign-appearing squamous epithelium (adenocarcinoma with squamous metaplasia or adenoacanthoma).

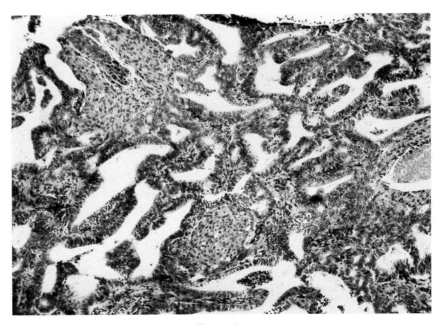

Figure 80
(Figures 80–82 are from the same patient)
ENDOMETRIOID ADENOCARCINOMA WITH
SQUAMOUS DIFFERENTIATION

Several morules appear in this well-differentiated adenocarcinoma. Note that the glandular component of this case is malignant by the usual criteria. Figures 81 and 82 show details of the morules in this case.

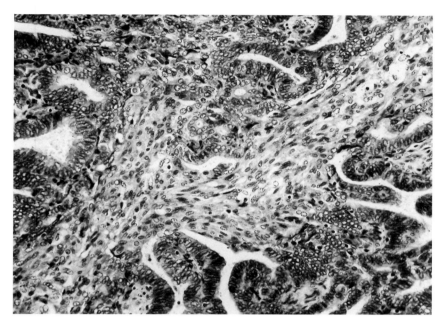

Figure 81
ENDOMETRIOID ADENOCARCINOMA WITH
SQUAMOUS DIFFERENTIATION

This morule from the case illustrated in figure 80 is surrounded by malignant but well-differentiated glands. The cells of the morule do not show keratinization or intracellular bridges but do demonstrate sheet-like growth, eosinophilic and glassy cytoplasm, and a decreased nuclear/cytoplasmic ratio compared with the immediately adjacent glandular cells. Most of them are spindle shaped. This tumor may be designated adenocarcinoma with squamous or morular metaplasia or adenoacanthoma, but most importantly, the glandular component is well differentiated or grade I.

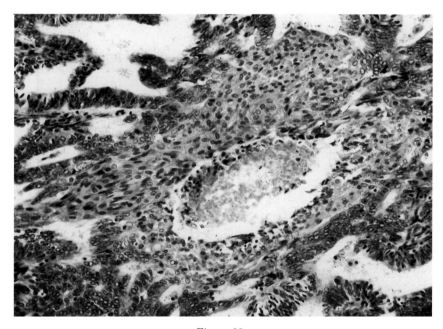

Figure 82
ENDOMETRIOID ADENOCARCINOMA WITH
SQUAMOUS DIFFERENTIATION

This is a detail of another morule from the same case illustrated in figures 80 and 81. Note the central necrosis, which does not imply malignant squamous differentiation.

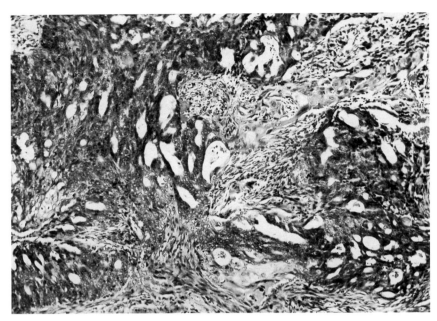

Figure 83
ENDOMETRIOID ADENOCARCINOMA WITH
SQUAMOUS DIFFERENTIATION
In this tumor, the glandular component is poorly differentiated, and the non-keratinizing squamous component is cytologically malignant, focally spindled, and invades at the top center and bottom center into the surrounding reactive stroma. This tumor may also be designated adenosquamous carcinoma.

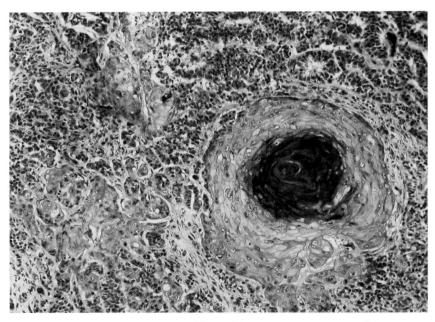

Figure 84
ENDOMETRIOID ADENOCARCINOMA WITH
SQUAMOUS DIFFERENTIATION
In this adenosquamous carcinoma, the glandular component is poorly differentiated, and the squamous element is histologically malignant, keratinizing, and invasive.

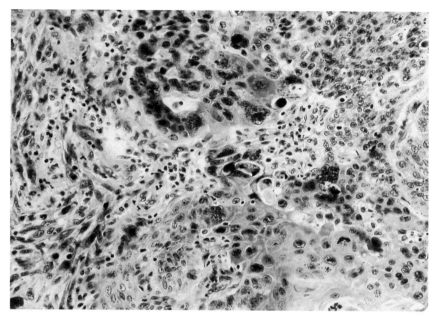

Figure 85
ENDOMETRIOID ADENOCARCINOMA WITH
SQUAMOUS DIFFERENTIATION
This adenosquamous carcinoma shows mostly the squamous component, except for
a single malignant gland located slightly above and to the left of center. The squamous
component is judged malignant by the usual cytologic criteria, as well as by mitotic
activity and destructive stromal invasion. More importantly, the glandular component
of this tumor was poorly differentiated.

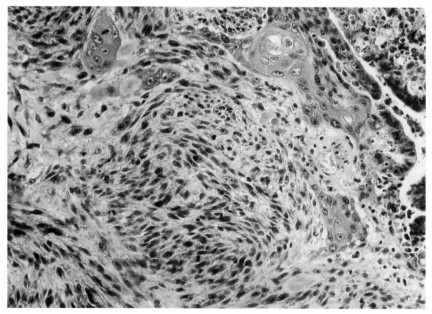

Figure 86
ENDOMETRIOID ADENOCARCINOMA WITH
SQUAMOUS DIFFERENTIATION
In this case, the squamous elements are cytologically malignant (adenosquamous
carcinoma). Some of the squamous cells appear to drop off into the surrounding stroma
to create a pseudosarcomatous pattern.

Once squamous differentiation is identified by the above criteria, the squamous cells may be classified as histologically malignant (adenosquamous carcinoma) as opposed to histologically benign (adenocarcinoma with squamous metaplasia or adenoacanthoma) if they satisfy one or more of the following criteria:

• standard cytologic criteria of malignancy
• mitoses in the indisputably squamous component
• destructive stromal infiltration by the squamous elements.

Malignant squamous elements in adenosquamous carcinomas do not need to be graded or characterized further, but the glandular component of all of these tumors should be graded as described above for endometrioid adenocarcinoma.

Figures 79–86 show some of the variations of endometrioid adenocarcinoma with squamous differentiation. In figures 79–82, the squamous (fig. 79) or morular (figs. 80–82) metaplastic component appears histologically and cytologically benign. These appearances resemble, respectively, squamous metaplasia or reserve cell hyperplasia of the cervix. Nuclear atypia and mitotic activity are absent, and the metaplastic cells show no tendency to invade into the stroma. The accompanying glandular component in these illustrations, as in almost all of these cases, is well differentiated.

On the other hand, the squamous element in figures 83–86 appears malignant, and thus these tumors can be referred to as adenosquamous carcinoma. In these lesions, the squamous component resembles squamous carcinoma of the cervix, including keratinizing (fig. 84), bizarre (fig. 85), and spindled (fig. 86) patterns. The squamous elements usually invade into the stroma, and the glandular component is usually moderately to poorly differentiated. Indeed, as suggested by the elaborate criteria listed above, the distinction between foci of high-grade adenocarcinoma and foci of a malignant squamous component may be extremely difficult. If there is any doubt whether such a focus is squamous, the appropriate diagnosis is poorly differentiated adenocarcinoma.

A number of issues related to adenocarcinoma with squamous differentiation remain unresolved. Most of these have been discussed in reviews by Silverberg (63) and Zaino and Kurman (84). The first of these issues is the true frequency of adenocarcinoma with squamous differentiation as a proportion of all endometrial carcinomas. After initial speculation that this frequency has been increasing, it now appears to be stable, but the actual proportion of adenosquamous carcinomas, for example, has varied in different series from 5 to 41 percent of all endometrial carcinomas (63). Part of this difference seems to be related to differences in diagnostic criteria, but part is probably real, reflecting a tendency for more poorly differentiated carcinomas to occur in certain populations such as Japanese and American black women (38).

A more important unresolved question concerns the prognostic significance of these histologic patterns. There seems to be little question that, considered as a group, adenocarcinomas with squamous differentiation behave no differently than endometrioid adenocarcinomas without squamous differentiation. There is also little question that adenosquamous carcinomas are associated with a poorer prognosis than are adenocarcinomas with squamous metaplasia (adenoacanthomas). However, this difference is probably due largely, if not entirely, to the usual difference in differentiation of the glandular elements in these two tumor types. In my experience, adenosquamous carcinomas, although prognostically unfavorable, are no more so than other poorly differentiated adenocarcinomas. On the other hand, adenocarcinomas with squamous metaplasia seem to have a more favorable prognosis than even comparably well-differentiated adenocarcinomas. The validity of these results needs to be confirmed in large series.

Immunohistochemical and Ultrastructural Findings. Immunohistochemical study of endometrial carcinoma has revealed many findings of interest but few of diagnostic utility. One of the more interesting findings is that many endometrial carcinomas coexpress cytokeratins and vimentin (14,52). This may be of diagnostic utility in distinguishing primary endometrial carcinoma from endocervical carcinoma, which appears not to express vimentin, and metastatic endometrial carcinoma from other metastatic adenocarcinomas that do not express vimentin. Immunohistochemical studies of the squamous epithelium in various adenocarcinomas with squamous differentiation have also been of interest because studies of keratin and involucrin localization have suggested that there is no fundamental difference between the two subtypes (adenosquamous carcinoma and adenocarcinoma with squamous metaplasia) (81). Other studies with commercially available antibodies have attempted to distinguish either between endometrial carcinoma and hyperplasia (48,69,74) or between endometrial and endocervical adenocarcinoma (42). Studies of the first type have generally demonstrated that atypical hyperplasia bears more resemblance to adenocarcinoma than to the other hyperplasias, and thus immunohistochemistry is not useful in distinguishing between endometrial atypical hyperplasia and well-differentiated adenocarcinoma. The attempts to distinguish between endometrial and endocervical origin of adenocarcinomas by the use of carcinoembryonic antigen have also been unsuccessful because in most studies comparable proportions of both tumor types are positive for this antigen. A newly described antigen, MSN-1, appears to be fairly specific for endometrioid versus serous or intestinal differentiation but also does not distinguish endometrial from endocervical adenocarcinoma (51).

Another immunohistochemical determination that is both interesting and potentially useful is the immunohistochemical localization of estrogen and progesterone receptors (61). The prognostic value of biochemical determination of these steroid hormone receptor levels in endometrial carcinoma tissue is discussed below, but it is worthwhile at this point to note that immunohistochemical evaluation can be more precise because both benign endometrial and myometrial elements may contain receptors and thus give a false-positive biochemical assay if the tissue submitted does not consist entirely of carcinoma.

As with immunohistochemistry, ultrastructural findings in endometrial carcinoma are not specific either for malignancy or for the endometrial origin of the tumor (20,23,25). In general, the ultrastructural findings become more divergent from those of normal and hyperplastic endometrium with decreasing differentiation of the tumor (figs. 87, 88). Nuclear pleomorphism is, as expected, prominent, and mitochondria are often pleomorphic as well. Surface and junctional structures such as microvilli, cilia, and desmosomes are usually decreased in number. Lysosomes, glycogen, and lipid may be unusually prominent but are often decreased. Some structures, such as cilia, primary lysosomes, and intracytoplasmic lumina, are predictive of hormone receptor positivity but no more so than are histologic and nuclear grade as judged by light microscopy (25).

Other Special Techniques. As mentioned previously, the analysis of sex-steroid hormone receptors is important in the study of endometrial carcinoma. Receptor levels are generally higher in well-differentiated tumors, with high receptor levels being positively correlated both with favorable prognosis and therapeutic response of metastatic disease to progestins in most reports (9,25,26,50,61). The relationship of receptor levels to survival has been reported both to be (9,50) and not to be (25) an independent prognostic variable when subjected to multivariate statistical analysis.

Quantitative techniques that attempt to more reproducibly assess the differentiation or proliferative capacity of a tumor have also been demonstrated to bear a significant relationship to prognosis (75,78,85). These include both morphometric and flow-cytometric studies. What still remains to be determined is whether these sophisticated and expensive studies can add significant information to a careful light-microscopic assessment of architectural and nuclear grade. It has also been noted that these techniques seem to be no more successful than routine histologic examination for separating endometrial hyperplasias from well-differentiated carcinomas.

Other Microscopic Types. In addition to the variants of endometrioid adenocarcinoma discussed above, there are several other histologic types of endometrial carcinoma recognized in the International Society of Gynecological Pathologists classification. These types are serous, clear cell, and mucinous adenocarcinomas; squamous cell carcinoma; mixed carcinoma; and undifferentiated carcinoma.

The most common of these subtypes is *serous carcinoma*, which in most large series comprises between 5 and 10 percent of all endometrial carcinomas (12,19,36,55,62). Serous carcinoma is also important because it is a particularly aggressive form of endometrial carcinoma, with

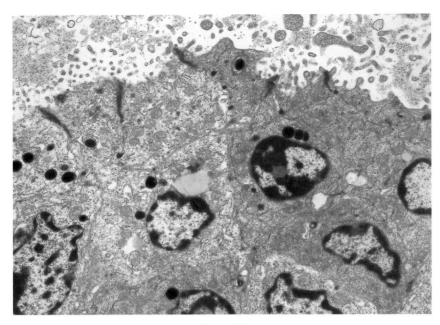

Figure 87
ENDOMETRIOID ADENOCARCINOMA
This was a well-differentiated tumor at the light-microscopic level, but in this electron micrograph the nuclei are fairly pleomorphic. Note the numerous short microvilli at the luminal surface (right), as well as well-formed junctional complexes, numerous mitochondria, and lysosomes. X3774.

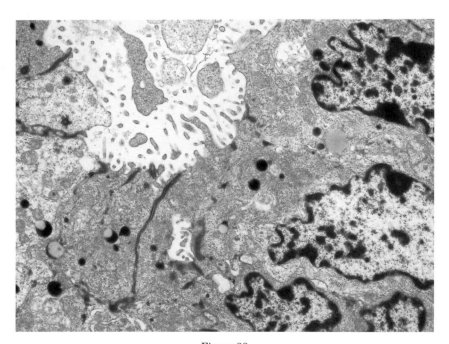

Figure 88
ENDOMETRIOID ADENOCARCINOMA
In this electron micrograph, the tumor has somewhat more irregular nuclei than the case illustrated in figure 87, but microvilli and junctional complexes are somewhat better formed. Lysosomes are also numerous in this case, free ribosomes are prominent, and some lipid vacuoles are present. X3330.

a tendency for myometrial invasion (often in the form of extensive lymphatic/vascular space permeation) and early dissemination beyond the uterus, typically involving peritoneal surfaces. In gross appearance, serous carcinoma resembles other endometrial carcinomas, but it has a characteristic microscopic appearance. The tumor tends to grow in complex papillary fronds that are broad to fine, with central fibrovascular connective tissue cores (fig. 89). Smaller, purely epithelial papillae and buds (fig. 90) are also common, as is a complex papilloglandular pattern in which the lumina are reduced to irregular slit-like spaces (figs. 91, 92). Psammoma bodies (fig. 93) are encountered in about 30 percent of these tumors, and foci of necrosis are common. The tumor is composed of relatively small cells with round, usually pleomorphic nuclei and frequent mitotic figures (fig. 94). Macronucleoli and bizarre multinucleate tumor cells are often present. Exfoliation of single cells and small clusters of cells from the papillary processes into the lumina is a characteristic feature. As mentioned previously, the tumor has a strong propensity to invade lymphatic or vascular channels (figs. 93, 95), which probably accounts largely for its unfavorable prognosis. However, even tumors limited to the endometrium often recur in the peritoneum, indicating that the endometrial carcinoma may represent one aspect of a multicentric neoplasm (62). Serous carcinomas also differ from endometrioid carcinomas by often demonstrating aneuploidy, c-*myc* proto-oncogene amplification, and biochemical absence of estrogen and progesterone receptors (55).

Clear cell adenocarcinoma comprises about 4 percent of all endometrial carcinomas documented in most large published series (11,19, 82). It occurs predominantly in postmenopausal women, and neither the clinical presentation nor the gross features differ significantly from those of other endometrial carcinomas. However, it is often associated with higher stage disease and thus with a poorer prognosis. Microscopically, the characteristic feature is the presence of large tumor cells with clear cytoplasm on routine hematoxylin and eosin staining (figs. 96–101). Special stains such as periodic acid-Schiff or Best's carmine, as well as ultrastructural examination, demonstrate the clear appearance of the cytoplasm to be the result of

massive accumulations of glycogen. Hobnail cells (individual cells projecting like hobnails into lumina) may also be prominent, to the extent that they may be more numerous than the clear cells for which the tumor is named. A dense hyalinized stroma (fig. 98) and extracellular (rarely intracellular) mucin may be prominent features. The characteristic cell types may grow in solid (fig. 96), papillary (fig. 97), tubular (fig. 98), or mixed (fig. 99) architectural patterns, but the architecture is not used to grade these neoplasms. Nuclear grade should be used exclusively, and typically these are tumors with large, extremely pleomorphic nuclei (figs. 100, 101) that often cause the tumor cells to resemble those of the benign Arias-Stella change (fig. 101). These tumors may be difficult to differentiate histologically from serous carcinomas, and in one report (36), clear cell and serous differentiation often coexisted in the same tumor.

Mucinous adenocarcinoma is, in most published series and in my own experience, a rare variant of endometrial carcinoma. However, in the series of Ross and colleagues, it comprised 9 percent of all cases of surgical stage I endometrial carcinoma (46,54). The lesion is a primary adenocarcinoma of the endometrium in which most of the tumor cells contain prominent intracytoplasmic mucin (figs. 102, 103). Otherwise most of these tumors resemble typical endometrioid carcinomas and are usually well differentiated. Mucin can be demonstrated with a mucicarmine stain, and carcinoembryonic antigen is usually present within the cells. The prognosis appears to be similar to that of other low-grade adenocarcinomas of the endometrium. The differential diagnosis includes otherwise typical endometrioid carcinomas with minor foci of mucinous differentiation, which were present in 38 percent of the tumors in one series (54). The term *mucinous carcinoma* should not be used to refer to otherwise typical endometrioid carcinomas with abundant extracellular (luminal) mucin but an absence of intracellular mucin.

Squamous cell carcinoma is a rare primary carcinoma of the endometrium, with fewer than 30 well-documented cases reported (65). Because squamous cell carcinoma of the cervix is so much more common, squamous cell carcinoma of the endometrium should be diagnosed only in the absence of a cervical squamous

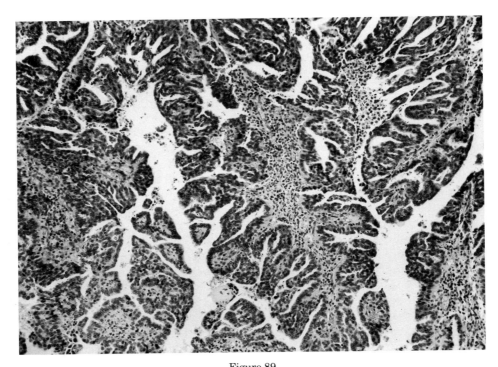

Figure 89
SEROUS CARCINOMA
This low-power photomicrograph shows the typical broad fibrovascular cores lined by stratified cells, forming secondary papillae and cellular buds.

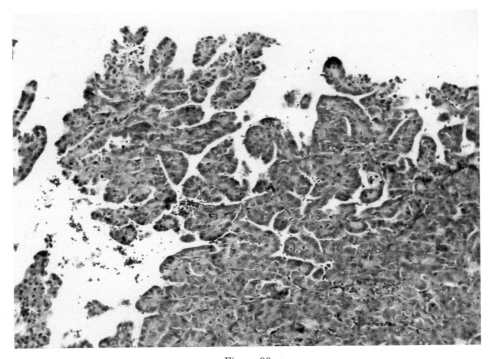

Figure 90
SEROUS CARCINOMA
In this field, the papillae are small and complex, and the cells are poorly differentiated.

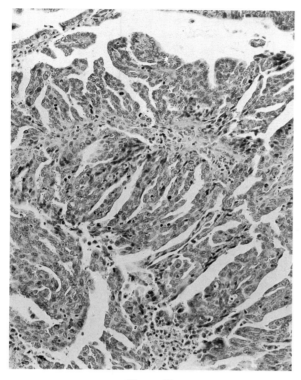

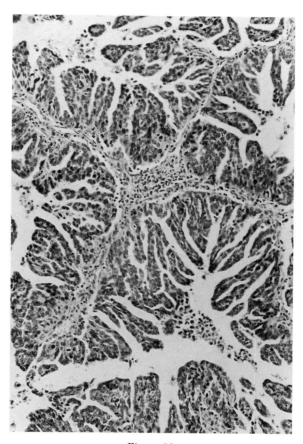

Figure 91
SEROUS CARCINOMA
This field shows a complex papilloglandular pattern with slit-like lumina, as opposed to the round lumina of endometrioid carcinoma.

Figure 92
SEROUS CARCINOMA
This is another field with a complex papilloglandular pattern. Note the exfoliation of small groups of cells into the lumina.

Figure 93
SEROUS CARCINOMA
This illustration shows invasion of myometrial lymphatics. Note the psammoma bodies within the papillary nests of tumor cells.

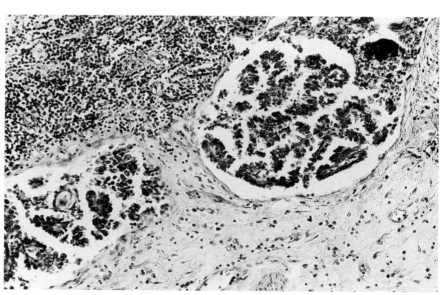

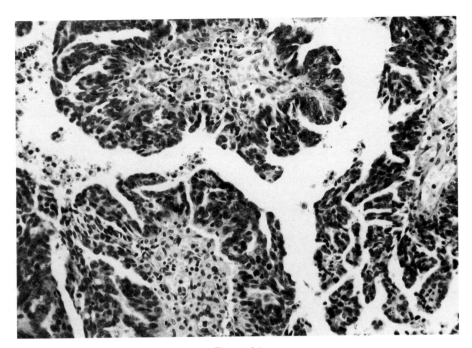

Figure 94
SEROUS CARCINOMA
This high magnification shows the small but very round and very hyperchromatic nuclei that are typical of these poorly differentiated tumors. Necrotic debris and exfoliated tumor cells in the lumina are also characteristic. The fibrovascular stromal cores of the papillae are infiltrated by lymphocytes.

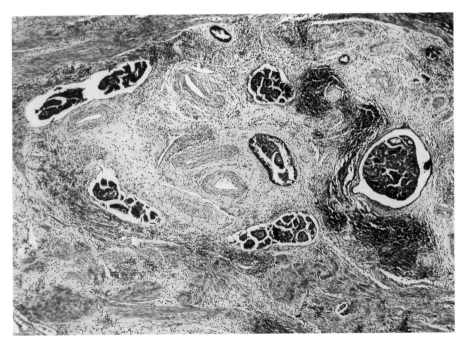

Figure 95
SEROUS CARCINOMA
Extensive invasion of myometrial lymphatics is evident in this illustration. A moderate host lymphocytic response is also present.

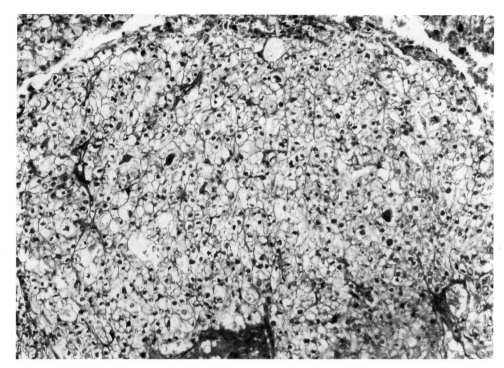

Figure 96
CLEAR CELL ADENOCARCINOMA
A solid sheet of tumor cells with voluminous clear cytoplasm characterizes this tumor focus.

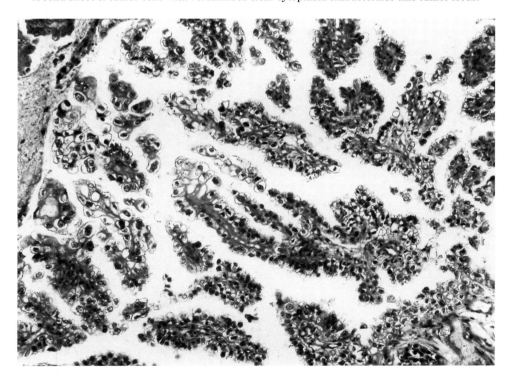

Figure 97
CLEAR CELL ADENOCARCINOMA
The tumor in this field shows a predominantly papillary growth pattern.

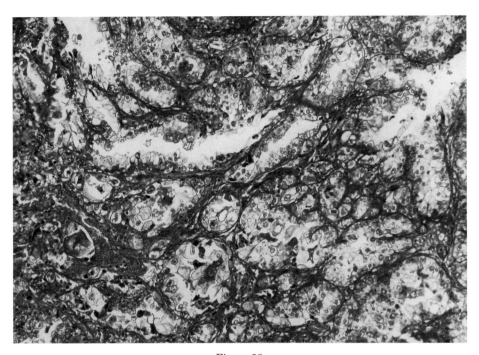

Figure 98
CLEAR CELL ADENOCARCINOMA
The growth pattern in this field is tubuloglandular. Nuclear pleomorphism is apparent. Both clear and hobnail cells are present.

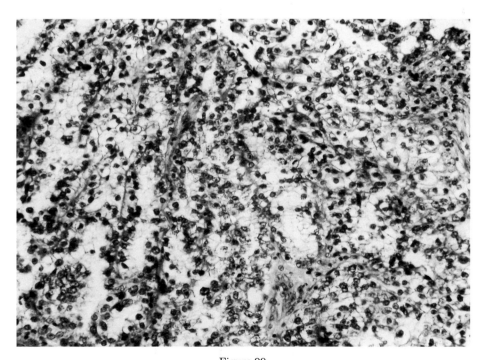

Figure 99
CLEAR CELL ADENOCARCINOMA
The tubuloglandular growth pattern on the left in this field blends with a more solid pattern on the right.

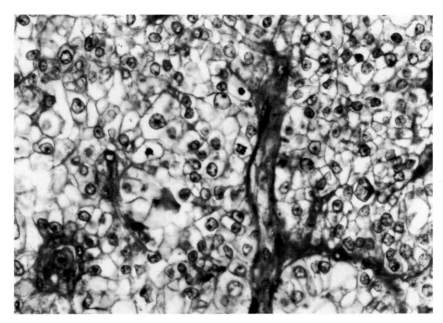

Figure 100
CLEAR CELL ADENOCARCINOMA
In this example, a solid focus of tumor is composed of cells with pleomorphic, hyperchromatic nuclei, each with one or more prominent nucleoli. Voluminous clear cytoplasm is present.

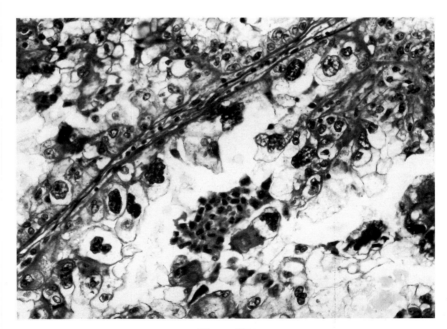

Figure 101
CLEAR CELL ADENOCARCINOMA
This field shows cellular stratification, voluminous clear cytoplasm, and bizarre, occasionally multiple, nuclei resembling Arias-Stella change. However, at lower magnification, this was an obviously invasive malignant tumor.

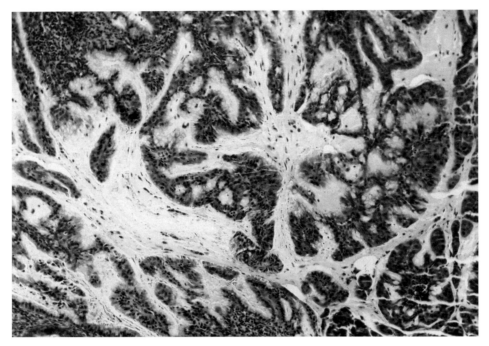

Figure 102
MUCINOUS ADENOCARCINOMA
This invasive adenocarcinoma contains abundant mucin both within lumina and in the cytoplasm of the glandular cells.

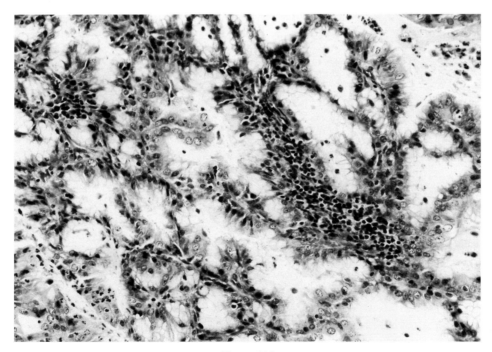

Figure 103
MUCINOUS ADENOCARCINOMA
In this illustration, irregular, confluent malignant glands are lined by well-differentiated cells containing intracytoplasmic mucin.

cancer. A thorough sampling of the tumor should also be performed to rule out the possibility of an adenosquamous carcinoma in which the squamous component has become dominant. The prognosis of primary squamous cell carcinoma of the endometrium appears to be extremely poor. Microscopically, this tumor resembles squamous cell carcinomas found in other sites. When the tumor cells become spindled (fig. 104) or develop clear cytoplasm (fig. 105), the differential diagnosis with a sarcoma or clear cell adenocarcinoma may be difficult. A variant of squamous cell carcinoma that is particularly rare in the endometrium is verrucous carcinoma (37). This tumor is characterized by a papillary architecture, bland cytologic features, and invasion on a broad pushing front. As with verrucous carcinomas elsewhere, it is best treated surgically and has a favorable prognosis.

Mixed carcinoma of the endometrium is a carcinoma containing more than one of the cell types described above. For the tumor to be characterized as mixed, the second type must comprise at least 10 percent of the total volume of the tumor, as estimated from the examination of multiple sections. The types of tumor encountered and their relative proportions should be specified in the pathology report. The prognostic implications of mixed carcinomas in which the subordinate type is less favorable have thus far been poorly characterized.

Undifferentiated carcinoma of the endometrium is relatively uncommon but can show a variety of patterns. Some of these tumors are of small cell type (fig. 106) and exhibit the usual markers of neuroendocrine differentiation (44). Other undifferentiated carcinomas are of giant cell (fig. 107) or spindle cell type.

Scattered case reports of other types of carcinoma, particularly those more commonly encountered in the uterine cervix, have appeared in the literature. These include glassy cell carcinoma (32) and possibly adenoid cystic carcinoma (27). I have no doubt that other rare types will continue to be reported, and their clinical significance will remain unknown until larger numbers of cases have been seen.

Differential Diagnosis. The major differential diagnosis of endometrioid carcinoma and its variants is with endometrial hyperplasia and atypical hyperplasia, and this has been discussed in detail in the chapter on Endometrial Polyps and Hyperplasias. As mentioned in that section, many more hyperplasias are overdiagnosed as carcinomas than carcinomas underdiagnosed as hyperplasias. This differential diagnostic problem usually only involves well-differentiated adenocarcinomas and adenocarcinomas with squamous differentiation and thus should not impact on the diagnosis of either grade II and III carcinomas or on the diagnosis of carcinomas of nonendometrioid type.

Other benign lesions occasionally entering into the differential diagnosis of endometrial carcinoma include normal menstrual endometrium, various reactive glandular atypias, and endometrial epithelial metaplastic and related changes. *Menstrual endometrium* can be a problem because of the fragmented nature of the specimen in which glands and stroma are typically dissociated, crowded together, and admixed with blood and necrotic debris. Tissue specimens of this sort are illustrated in the chapter on Embryology, Gross Anatomy, and Histology of the Uterine Corpus. In a premenopausal patient, the diagnosis of endometrial carcinoma should be made only on the basis of an adequate specimen in which well-preserved and clearly malignant glands are present.

Reactive glandular atypias are seen in several clinical circumstances, the most common of which is *endometritis*. In the atypias accompanying acute or chronic endometritis, glandular proliferation and architectural anomalies are frequently noted, but the involved glands are permeated by neutrophils or plasma cells (or separated by granulomas in the case of granulomatous endometritis), and nuclear atypia is absent or minimal. In the reactive atypias after *curettage* or *radiation therapy*, the opposite situation is true in that the endometrial epithelium is generally cytologically atypical but lacks the architectural features of malignancy. The clinical history should be helpful in making the correct diagnosis. The endometrial *epithelial metaplastic and related changes* represent one of the most difficult problems in the differential diagnosis of virtually all of the types of endometrial carcinoma (for further discussion, see the chapter on Tumor-Like Lesions). Most of these changes, if they occur in benign endometrium, lack the architectural features (stromal disappearance, stromal fibrosis, or stromal necrosis) of invasion that are necessary for the

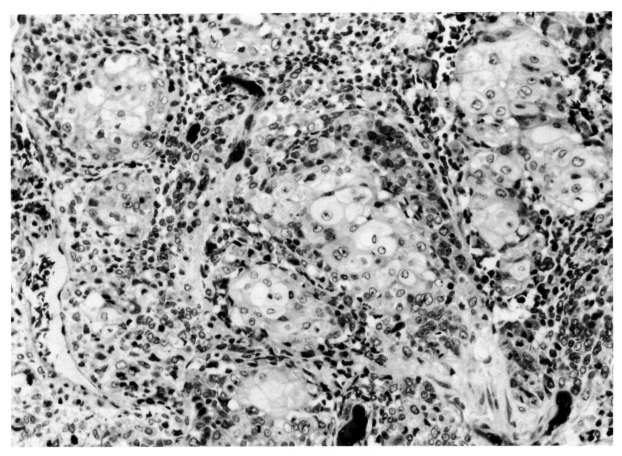

Figure 104
SQUAMOUS CELL CARCINOMA
No glandular component was seen in this tumor, and no involvement of the cervix was present.

diagnosis of endometrial carcinoma. These same metaplastic and related changes can occur in malignant epithelium, but in this case the architectural features of carcinoma should be present.

The differential diagnosis of higher grade endometrioid carcinomas is related mostly to the correct identification of the solid elements in these tumors. The question of when to characterize the solid component of an endometrioid carcinoma as squamous has been discussed in detail above. This problem is probably not a crucial one in high-grade tumors because the clinical behavior and treatment of high-grade endometrioid carcinoma with and without squamous differentiation are similar (63,84). However, in a low-grade tumor, if squamous (including morular) metaplasia is misinterpreted as

solid adenocarcinoma, the grade of the tumor will be raised inappropriately and the patient may receive unnecessary treatment.

When the solid portion of a poorly differentiated adenocarcinoma consists of spindled cells, the differential diagnosis with *carcinosarcoma* (if a malignant glandular component is present) or *endometrial stromal sarcoma* (if malignant glands cannot be identified) becomes important. One of the easiest ways to differentiate at least some carcinomas with spindle cell or sarcomatoid foci from carcinosarcomas is to observe in the former a gradual transition from malignant glandular or squamous epithelium to malignant spindle cells, with no intervening basement membrane or connective tissue visible at the light-microscopic level. Cases in which the malignant epithelial component is more

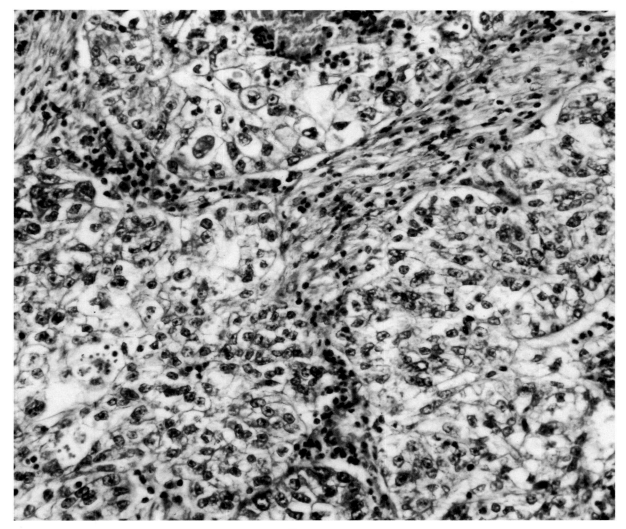

Figure 105
SQUAMOUS CELL CARCINOMA
The tumor cells in this field contain clear cytoplasm and might be mistaken for those of a clear cell adenocarcinoma.
However, elsewhere in this tumor, keratinization and other evidence of squamous differentiation were present.

sharply demarcated from the malignant spindled stromal cells should be designated as carcinosarcomas, although ultrastructural, immunohistochemical, and clinical evidence indicates that many of these cases are metaplastic carcinomas as well (see Mixed Epithelial-Nonepithelial Tumors). Because otherwise typical carcinosarcomas frequently demonstrate both ultrastructural and immunohistochemical markers of epithelial differentiation in their stromal component (15), these studies should not be used in the differential diagnosis

of carcinoma with spindle cell metaplasia from carcinosarcoma.

Another important differential diagnosis involving a tumor of mixed epithelial-nonepithelial type is the distinction of *atypical polypoid adenomyoma* from low-grade endometrioid carcinoma with myometrial invasion. This may be particularly difficult in a curettage specimen because the former lesion, which is benign, is characterized by an intimate admixture of atypical glands, often with extensive morular metaplasia, and interlacing fascicles

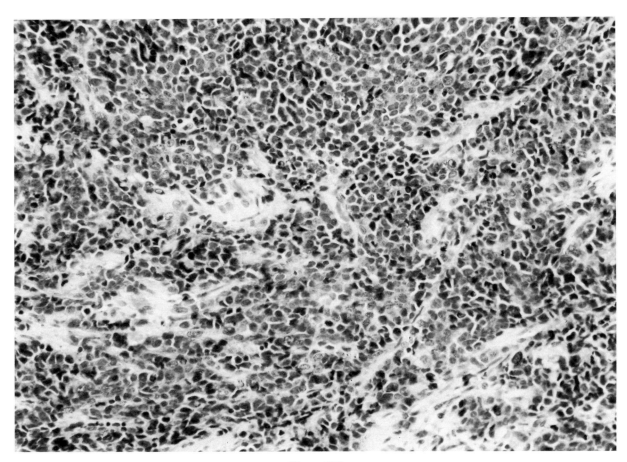

Figure 106
UNDIFFERENTIATED CARCINOMA (SMALL CELL NEUROENDOCRINE TYPE)
The resemblance to a small cell carcinoma of the lung is evident in this illustration.

of smooth muscle (see Mixed Epithelial-Nonepithelial Tumors). It is important to remember that atypical polypoid adenomyoma usually occurs in younger women than does endometrial carcinoma, contains a fascicular pattern of smooth muscle that would be unusual in normal myometrium, and lacks a stromal desmoplastic response like that seen in the event of invasive carcinoma. In addition, curettage specimens in cases of endometrial carcinoma rarely yield fragments of myometrium.

Another important differential diagnosis of the various types of endometrial carcinoma is their distinction from each other. First, none of the variants should be diagnosed as pure unless it constitutes more than 90 percent of a tumor in sections available for examination; if a secondary type constitutes more than 10 percent of the tumor, the preferred diagnosis is mixed

carcinoma. Second, the term *adenocarcinoma with squamous differentiation* does not imply benign or malignant differentiation of the squamous component; if the pathologist wishes to separate these into adenocarcinoma with squamous metaplasia (adenoacanthoma) and adenosquamous carcinoma, the criteria have already been listed in detail. Third, adenocarcinomas that grow predominantly in a papillary pattern may be of endometrioid, serous, or clear cell type; the important feature for prognosis and treatment is the cell type, not the papillary (as opposed to glandular) growth pattern, and the criteria for making this distinction have been discussed. Fourth, the distinction between clear cell adenocarcinoma and the secretory variant of endometrioid adenocarcinoma is important because both are characterized by clear cells containing large quantities of

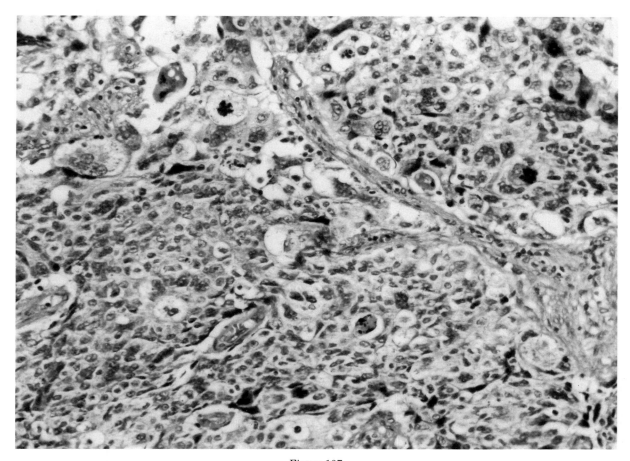

Figure 107
UNDIFFERENTIATED CARCINOMA (GIANT CELL TYPE)
A single gland is present in this field, but most of the tumor grows as solid sheets of anaplastic cells, many of which are multinucleate.

intracytoplasmic glycogen; however, secretory carcinomas are composed of glands resembling normal early secretory endometrium, with columnar cells and minimal nuclear atypia, whereas clear cell adenocarcinomas are composed of polygonal cells that grow in tubular, papillary, and solid patterns, usually contain admixed hobnail cells, and invariably demonstrate nuclear grade II or III. Fifth, the distinction between a pure squamous cell carcinoma and an adenosquamous carcinoma has also already been discussed. A malignant glandular component should be searched for carefully in every putative case of pure squamous cell carcinoma of the endometrium.

Finally, each type of endometrial carcinoma has its own unique differential diagnosis with other benign and malignant lesions. Although the distinction between an endometrial and endocervical adenocarcinoma is often difficult in a biopsy or curettage specimen, the problem becomes particularly acute in the case of mucinous adenocarcinoma of the endometrium because the carcinoma essentially shows endocervical differentiation. Thus, such special techniques as staining for carcinoembryonic antigen (which have been recommended with variable enthusiasm) are useless in this situation because the reaction will show an endocervical pattern. It is important in this situation to note the type of stroma associated with the carcinoma because the presence of endometrial stroma indicates that the tumor is in the endometrium, even if it is not necessarily of the endometrium. Mucinous carcinoma also has its own specific metaplasia differential diagnosis, with both architectural and nuclear features being useful in distinguishing this tumor from benign mucinous metaplasia.

Other specific carcinoma versus metaplasia differential diagnoses include 1) secretory endometrioid adenocarcinoma versus clear cell change, 2) ciliated cell endometrioid carcinoma versus ciliary change, 3) adenocarcinoma with squamous metaplasia versus squamous metaplasia and morules in a proliferative or hyperplastic endometrium, 4) serous adenocarcinoma versus surface syncytial change and papillary proliferation, 5) clear cell adenocarcinoma versus Arias-Stella change. In each of these instances, the finding of a glandular component invading its own stroma is diagnostic of adenocarcinoma, and in most cases the presence of nuclear atypia in adenocarcinoma is important as well. The latter feature is particularly important in the differential diagnosis of serous adenocarcinoma from surface syncytial change and papillary proliferation because these benign diagnoses should be made only in the absence of nuclear atypia and mitotic activity, whereas serous carcinomas are usually of high nuclear grade.

Finally, any type of endometrial carcinoma must occasionally be distinguished from a *metastatic adenocarcinoma* in the endometrium. Metastatic carcinomas are usually recognized, or at least suspected, because they do not fit neatly into the classification listed and discussed previously and because they tend to preserve benign endometrial glands within large masses of tumor. Prominent involvement of endometrial lymphatics should also raise the possibility of metastatic tumor. However, remember that metastases to the endometrium are extremely rare and usually occur on the background of a known primary carcinoma elsewhere.

Intraoperative Consultation. Intraoperative consultations (frozen sections and cytologic techniques) are usually performed in cases of endometrial carcinoma in one of two clinical circumstances. First, a curettage may be performed in the operating room immediately before simple hysterectomy for supposed benign disease to rule out the presence of a carcinoma (71). In most instances, the diagnosis is benign, but occasionally a carcinoma is identified. The criteria for the diagnosis of endometrial carcinoma at frozen section are the same as those already discussed for permanent sections, with the additional observation that smears or imprints of the fresh tissue submitted can be a very useful adjunct (1). As in permanent sections, the differential diagnosis between a severe hyperplasia and a well-differentiated endometrioid adenocarcinoma may be a problem, but both of these will probably be treated by simple hysterectomy in any event, with radical hysterectomy being reserved for those more poorly differentiated tumors that are easier to diagnose by frozen section examination.

Intraoperative consultation in cases of endometrial carcinoma is also used to estimate the extent of spread of a known endometrial carcinoma. This may involve either the examination of pelvic or paraortic lymph nodes before the performance of a radical hysterectomy or the examination of the hysterectomy specimen itself before the performance of a lymph node dissection. In the former case, preoperative evaluation has already indicated the need for a radical procedure, but metastatic disease in a paraortic lymph node might obviate that procedure. Abrams and Silverberg (1) indicate that cytologic techniques are generally superior to frozen sections for the evaluation of a group of lymph nodes for metastatic disease because they can examine more tissue rapidly and thus have a greater chance of detecting tumor foci unsuspected on gross examination.

The opposite situation occurs when an intraoperative evaluation of prognostic factors such as depth of myometrial invasion and involvement of the cervix and lower uterine segment will determine whether a simple hysterectomy for carcinoma will be converted into a radical one with a lymph node dissection. Two recent studies (17,43) have indicated that an excellent ability to provide an intraoperative evaluation of these factors can be obtained by careful gross examination combined with frozen sections as appropriate.

Cytology. In general, cervicovaginal cytology has an unacceptably low sensitivity, and even direct endometrial sampling may be associated with both false-positive and false-negative diagnoses. In the best of circumstances, however, one should be able to diagnose endometrial carcinoma cytologically when the cells are present in the specimen submitted. In a vaginal smear, the tumor cells may resemble benign endometrial cells, but their presence in a postmenopausal woman, particularly on the background of an estrogenic-type smear, is highly suspect (fig. 108), although many such women are not found to have carcinoma. In specimens obtained by direct endometrial sampling, the carcinoma cells are usually better preserved and thus easier to diagnose. The cells of even well-differentiated adenocarcinomas are enlarged, have increased nuclear/cytoplasmic ratios, and demonstrate such nuclear features of malignancy such as anisonucleosis, hyperchromatism, chromatin clumping, and prominent nucleoli (fig. 109). These features become even more prominent in poorly differentiated carcinomas (fig. 110), and additional features such as a prominent papillary growth pattern, cells with voluminous clear cytoplasm, or foci of squamous differentiation (fig. 111) may indicate a specific cell type.

An additional issue in any discussion of cytology of endometrial carcinoma is the prognostic significance of the cytology of peritoneal fluid obtained at the time of hysterectomy. It is generally agreed that patients with a positive peritoneal fluid cytology have a poorer prognosis, but whether this is an independent prognostic indicator remains to be determined; some studies (77) find that it is, whereas others (29,41) state that, when other risk factors are equalized, positive peritoneal cytology alone does not indicate a worse prognosis.

Spread and Metastases. Endometrial carcinoma invades into the myometrium, where it can then invade lymphatic and vascular channels and metastasize to distant sites (13,34). The grade and histologic type of the tumor (as seen in a biopsy or curettage specimen) and the extent of myometrial invasion (established in a hysterectomy specimen) can be used to predict the probability of distant metastatic spread (3,13,34). Extension into the cervix is considered stage II disease and is also predictive of an increased risk of distant metastasis.

Tumor can also extend locally, laterally through the serosa into the parametria and anteriorly or posteriorly (as a late event) into the urinary bladder or rectum, respectively. Initial lymph nodal metastases are to the pelvic and, subsequently, paraortic nodes. Visceral metastases in the pelvis most frequently involve the vagina and ovaries, and pelvic and abdominal peritoneum are colonized less frequently than in cases of ovarian carcinoma (except in

endometrial serous carcinoma, which frequently involves the peritoneum). Distant metastases are most commonly pulmonary and usually occur as a late event.

Staging. The usual staging system used for endometrial carcinoma (and presumably applicable to other malignant tumors of the uterine corpus as well) is that of the International Federation of Gynecology and Obstetrics (FIGO), which was most recently revised in 1988 (3). This staging system is presented in Table 3. According to this system, endometrial carcinoma is now surgically staged, and procedures previously used for determination of stages are therefore no longer applicable. It is also noted in the announcement of the 1988 revision of FIGO stages that for those few patients who are treated by primary radiation therapy without undergoing hysterectomy, the 1971 FIGO clinical staging system would still apply, but designation of that staging system would be noted. Additionally, it is mentioned that "ideally, width of the myometrium should be measured along with the width of tumor invasion." Finally, the "G123" portion of the staging system refers to grades I, II, and III, as defined earlier under Microscopic Findings in this chapter.

With this new staging system, the pathologist becomes the key figure in the staging of endometrial carcinoma. Thus, it is extremely important to be sure that a carcinoma and the uterus containing it are adequately sampled for microscopic examination. In my own laboratory, this usually means histologic examination of the entire tumor, unless the tumor is so large that representative sampling seems more appropriate, or deep invasion is obvious from gross examination and requires only a few sections to confirm it. However, extensive sampling is important, not only to demonstrate the deepest point of invasion of the myometrium but also to demonstrate such prognostically significant features as the tumor grade (which depends on the proportion of solid versus glandular growth in a well-sampled specimen), the tumor extent longitudinally (i.e., involvement of the lower uterine segment or cervix), and the presence of lymphatic or vascular space invasion (66).

Several points are important in reference to the evaluation of the depth of myometrial invasion. First, sections should be submitted, if possible, through tumor and adjacent benign

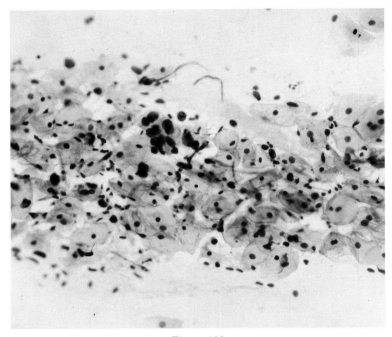

Figure 108
ENDOMETRIAL CARCINOMA (VAGINAL SMEAR)
This vaginal smear from a postmenopausal woman shows a cluster of small adenocarcinoma cells on the background of numerous superficial cells, indicating estrogenic activity.

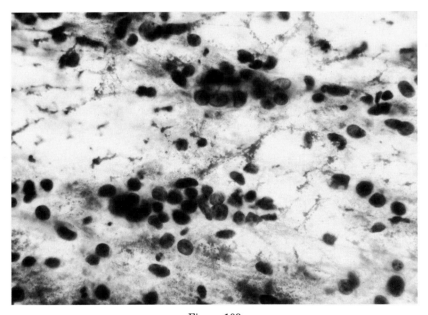

Figure 109
WELL-DIFFERENTIATED ENDOMETRIAL ADENOCARCINOMA
(ENDOMETRIAL ASPIRATE)
This field shows clustered and single small tumor cells in a necrotic background. The small and relatively uniform cells show some anisonucleosis, irregular chromatin clumping, and prominent nucleoli in some of the nuclei. Compare with figure 110 (poorly differentiated adenocarcinoma of the endometrium, photographed at the same magnification).

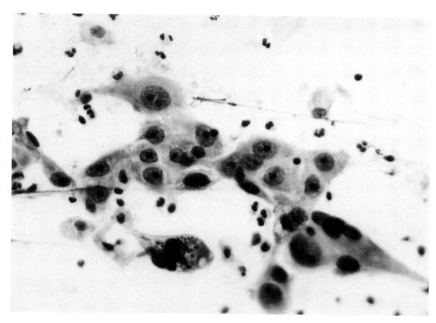

Figure 110
POORLY DIFFERENTIATED ENDOMETRIAL ADENOCARCINOMA
(ENDOMETRIAL ASPIRATE)
This photomicrograph shows large tumor cells with marked anisonucleosis, hyperchromatism, chromatin clumping, and huge prominent nucleoli. Compare the size of the tumor cells with those in figure 109 (photographed at the same magnification).

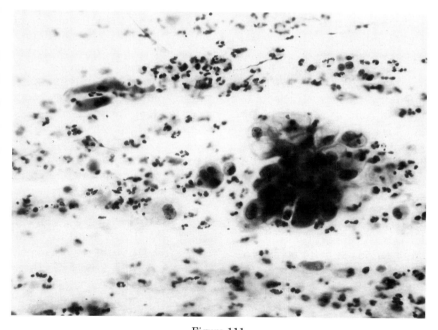

Figure 111
ADENOCARCINOMA WITH SQUAMOUS DIFFERENTIATION
(ENDOMETRIAL ASPIRATE)
The clumped tumor cells toward the center of the illustration represent adenocarcinoma, but the two spindled cells with eosinophilic cytoplasm at the upper left indicate a squamous component.

Table 3

CORPUS CANCER STAGING (FIGO 1988) (3)

Stage		Definition
IA	G123	Tumor limited to endometrium
IB	G123	Invasion to < 1/2 myometrium
IC	G123	Invasion to > 1/2 myometrium
IIA	G123	Endocervical glandular involvement only
IIB	G123	Cervical stromal invasion
IIIA	G123	Tumor invades serosa and/or adnexae and/or positive peritoneal cytology
IIIB	G123	Vaginal metastases
IIIC	G123	Metastases to pelvic and/or paraortic lymph nodes
IVA	G123	Tumor invasion of bladder and/or bowel mucosa
IVB		Distant metastases including intra-abdominal and/or inguinal lymph nodes

endometrium and myometrium, so that the maximal depth of tumor invasion can be compared with the distance from the endometrial-myometrial junction to the serosa in the same section. In the case of an extremely thick uterine wall or an extremely bulky tumor, such sectioning may not be possible, but a comment or diagram should always indicate exactly how the sections were taken in these cases.

Second, endometrial carcinoma can demonstrate several different patterns of invasion. In the bulky or pushing pattern (fig. 112), the junction between tumor and subjacent myometrium is well demarcated. It is essential in such a case to have adjacent endometrial-myometrial junction available for comparison because without it not only is it impossible to measure the depth of invasion, but it may even be impossible to determine whether any invasion is present.

In the second pattern, which fortunately is the most common because it is the easiest to identify, the invading glands or solid masses of carcinoma are separated from myometrial smooth muscle fibers by a stromal response consisting of loose edematous fibrous tissue containing inflammatory cells (fig. 113). In the third pattern, this cuff of reactive stroma is absent, and individual glands penetrate through the myometrium with no surrounding reaction whatsoever (fig. 114). If the carcinoma is particularly well differentiated but invades

only superficially, it may be extremely difficult to identify this as myometrial invasion, but usually this pattern penetrates deeply into the myometrium and poses no diagnostic problem. Occasionally, foci of invasive carcinoma undergo complete necrosis, particularly after radiation therapy, and their former presence is marked only by necrotic debris or foamy macrophages.

In contrast to these examples of myometrial invasion, there are cases in which malignant glands or small groups of glands penetrate into the myometrium in preexisting tongues of benign endometrium (fig. 115). If these tongues penetrate deeply, the diagnosis is carcinoma in adenomyosis. These nests of tumor are characteristically rounded and well demarcated from the surrounding myometrium, are not surrounded by a fibrosing or inflammatory response, and may show foci of benign endometrial glands or stroma within the same nests as the tumor. It is important to distinguish these signs from those of true myometrial invasion because the former do not carry the same unfavorable prognostic implications as the latter (33).

Other problems in pathologic staging involve both stages II and III. In the former, although cervical involvement should now be evaluated on the basis of a hysterectomy specimen, endocervical curettage specimens will no doubt continue to be presented for the purpose of evaluating the presence or absence of cervical

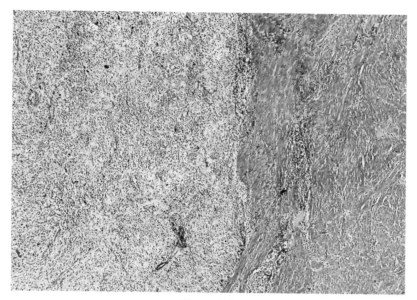

Figure 112
ENDOMETRIAL ADENOCARCINOMA WITH BULKY OR PUSHING
PATTERN OF MYOMETRIAL INVASION
This is an example of the bulky or pushing pattern of myometrial invasion. This
tumor (left) invades deeply into the myometrium (right), but the junction between
tumor and subjacent myometrium is well demarcated. It is difficult to determine
the depth of myometrial invasion without adjacent endometrial-myometrial junction available on the same slide for comparison.

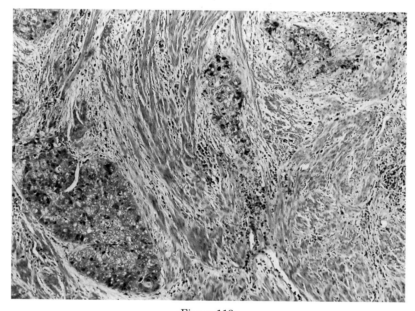

Figure 113
ENDOMETRIAL ADENOCARCINOMA INVADING MYOMETRIUM
This poorly differentiated tumor stimulates a marked stromal response of loose
edematous or myxoid tissue with fibroblastic proliferation, which separates the
nests of carcinoma from the surrounding myometrium. This is the most common
pattern of myometrial invasion by carcinoma.

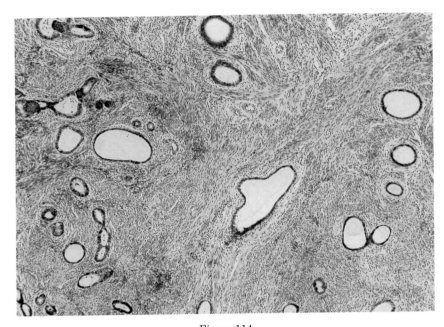

Figure 114
ENDOMETRIAL CARCINOMA INVADING MYOMETRIUM
In this illustration, well-differentiated endometrial glands infiltrate singly through
the myometrium, with minimal surrounding reactive stroma.

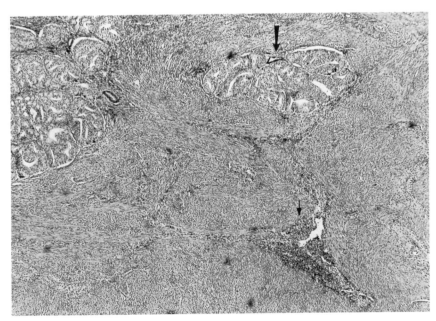

Figure 115
ENDOMETRIAL CARCINOMA EXTENDING INTO MYOMETRIUM
IN ADENOMYOSIS
This pattern should not be confused with true myometrial invasion, with its atten-
dant unfavorable prognostic implications. The focus of carcinoma in adenomyosis (long
arrow) is characterized by its sharply defined rounded border, the lack of a stromal
response around it, and the persistence of a benign gland at the arrow. A focus of
adenomyosis without carcinoma is present deeper in the myometrium (short arrow).

involvement by endometrial carcinoma. The variations in appearance of these specimens and their clinical implications have been discussed in detail by Frauenhoffer and colleagues (22). In general, the most useful pattern seen in endocervical curettage specimens is either total absence of carcinoma, which is highly predictive of absence of cervical involvement by endometrial carcinoma, or tumor within endocervical tissue (fig. 116), which is a good predictor of cervical involvement by tumor. The presence of carcinoma in the specimen but not in cervical tissue is of little clinical relevance because cervical involvement can be neither ruled in nor out on the basis of this finding.

Ovarian tumor involvement in patients with endometrial carcinoma is also a clinicopathologic problem. Although the new FIGO staging system classifies ovarian tumor involvement as stage IIIA, it has been noted in several reports (18,47) that simultaneous endometrioid carcinomas of the endometrium and one or both ovaries often represent separate primary tumors rather than an endometrial carcinoma with ovarian metastasis. In situations where the patient is young, both tumors are well differentiated, and the endometrial carcinoma does not invade the myometrium, the clinical behavior and prognosis are those of primary ovarian carcinoma, and the patient should be treated accordingly.

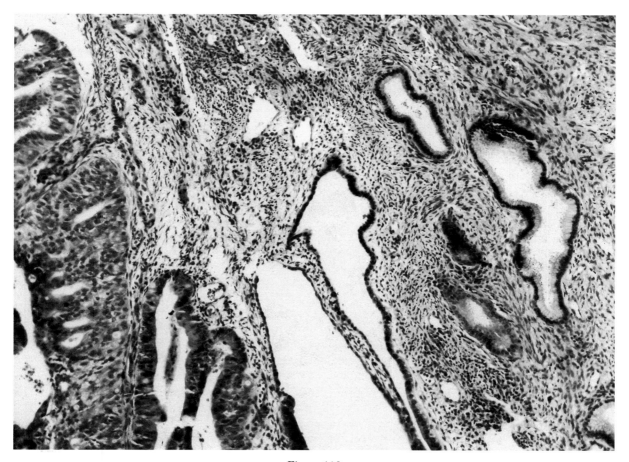

Figure 116
ENDOMETRIAL CARCINOMA WITH INVASION OF ENDOCERVIX
This photomicrograph shows carcinoma invading endocervical stroma, a feature necessary for the diagnosis of true cervical invasion.

Treatment and Prognosis. Both the treatment and the prognosis of endometrial carcinoma are strongly related to the stage of the disease (7,28). Over 80 percent of all patients with endometrial carcinoma present with clinical stage I disease, although some of these are found to have higher stage disease at the time of exploratory laparotomy (28). Patients with stage I endometrial carcinoma currently can expect a 5-year survival rate in the range of 82 to 95 percent (7,28). This survival rate falls to 50 to 60 percent for patients with stage II tumors, 15 to 25 percent for clinical stage III disease (but considerably higher for patients with pathologic stage III tumors that were thought preoperatively to be in stage I), and even lower for those few unfortunate patients whose tumors are initially found to be in stage IV (7,28). Standard treatment for patients with early-stage disease is surgery with or without adjuvant radiation therapy, but occasional patients with inoperable disease are treated with radiation therapy alone (73).

It is still debatable whether all patients operated on for endometrial carcinoma should undergo exploratory laparotomy with pelvic and paraortic lymph node dissection or whether this treatment should be reserved for patients with high risk factors such as high tumor grade, deep myometrial invasion, and extension to the lower segment or cervix (13). As mentioned earlier, these factors may have to be evaluated by gross and frozen-section examination of a hysterectomy specimen (17,43).

First-line chemotherapy for endometrial carcinoma consists of progestational agents (79). Unfortunately, the tumors that respond best to these agents are those that contain progesterone receptors and are of low grade (9,25,26,50), and these are exactly the tumors that are least likely to recur and require subsequent treatment. The role of adjuvant progestagen therapy in low-stage endometrial cancer remains to be determined (79). Nonhormonal chemotherapy in advanced or recurrent disease is beginning to show promise (7).

Although the prognosis of endometrial cancer is clearly related to stage, the fact that most patients have stage I disease indicates that other factors are important in the evaluation of this group of cases. Most of these rely on the pathologist either for direct histologic examination or for submission of fresh tumor tissue for appropriate additional studies. The main microscopic features of prognostic significance include 1) tumor grade (now part of the new staging system); 2) histologic type (with serous, clear cell, squamous cell, and undifferentiated carcinomas appearing to have an innately poorer prognosis); 3) presence or absence and depth of myometrial invasion (also part of the new staging system); 4) involvement of the lower uterine segment (13,31); 5) myometrial lymphatic/vascular space invasion (66); and 6) the presence of hyperplasia in the benign endometrium accompanying the tumor, which confers a favorable prognosis (6,16).

Nonmicroscopic analyses reported to supply important prognostic information include 1) estrogen and progesterone receptor determinations (positivity for one or both of these has been reported to be associated with a favorable prognosis in numerous studies) (9,25,50,78); 2) ploidy and proliferative indexes, as measured by flow cytometry (25,75,78); and 3) quantitative morphometric analysis of tumor cells (actually a microscopic determination but one requiring considerably more sophisticated study than the light-microscopic determinations listed in the preceding paragraph) (78,85). The relative values of these sophisticated and often expensive studies, especially compared with standard thorough light-microscopic examination of a curettage or hysterectomy specimen, remain to be determined. At the present time, it is certainly obligatory for the pathologist to provide as much of the information listed in the preceding paragraph as the specimen allows and to save tumor tissue (if enough is available) for hormone receptor and flow cytometric analyses if these are requested.

86

REFERENCES

1. Abrams J, Silverberg SG. The role of intraoperative cytology in the evaluation of gynecologic disease. Pathol Annu 1989;24:167–87.
2. Aguirre P, Scully RE, Wolfe HJ, DeLellis RA. Endometrial carcinoma with argyrophil cells. Hum Pathol 1984;15:210–7.
3. Anonymous. Announcements. FIGO stages—1988 revision. Gynecol Oncol 1989;35:125–7.
4. Austin DF, Roe KM. The decreasing incidence of endometrial cancer: public health implications. Am J Public Health 1982;72:65–8.
5. Bannatyne P, Russell P, Wills EJ. Argyrophilia and endometrial carcinoma. Int J Gynecol Pathol 1983; 2:235–54.
6. Beckner ME, Mori T, Silverberg SG. Endometrial carcinoma: nontumor factors in prognosis. Int J Gynecol Pathol 1985;4:131–45.
7. Berek JS, Hacker NF, Hatch KD, Young RC. Uterine corpus and cervical cancer. Curr Probl Cancer 1988; 12:61–131.
8. Cacciatore B, Lehtovirta P, Wahlström T, Ylostalo P. Preoperative sonographic evaluation of endometrial cancer. Am J Obstet Gynecol 1989;160:133–7.
9. Chambers JT, MacLusky N, Eisenfield A, Kohorn EI, Lawrence R, Schwartz PE. Estrogen and progestin receptor levels as prognosticators for survival in endometrial cancer. Gynecol Oncol 1988;31:65–81.
10. Chen JL, Trost DC, Wilkinson EJ. Endometrial papillary adenocarcinomas: two clinicopathological types. Int J Gynecol Pathol 1985;4:279–88.
11. Christopherson WM, Alberhasky RC, Connelly PJ. Carcinoma of the endometrium: I. A clinicopathologic study of clear-cell carcinoma and secretory carcinoma. Cancer 1982; 49:1511–23.
12. _____ , Connelly PJ, Alberhasky RC. Carcinoma of the endometrium. V. An analysis of prognosticators in patients with favorable subtypes and stage I disease. Cancer 1983;51:1705–9.
13. Creasman WT, Morrow CP, Bundy BN, Homesley HD, Graham JE, Heller PB. Surgical pathologic spread patterns of endometrial cancer. A Gynecologic Oncology Group study. Cancer 1987;60(Suppl 8):2035–41.
14. Dabbs DJ, Geisinger KR, Norris HT. Intermediate filaments in endometrial and endocervical carcinomas. Am J Surg Pathol 1986;10:568–76.
15. de Brito PA, Orenstein JM, Silverberg SG. Carcinosarcoma of the female genital tract. Immunohistochemical and ultrastructural analysis of 28 cases. Hum Pathol, in press.
16. Deligdisch L, Cohen CJ. Histologic correlates and virulence implications of endometrial carcinoma associated with adenomatous hyperplasia. Cancer 1985; 56:1452–5.
17. Doering DL, Barnhill DR, Weiser EB, Burke TW, Woodward JE, Park RC. Intraoperative evaluation of depth of myometrial invasion in stage I endometrial adenocarcinoma. Obstet Gynecol 1989;74:930–3.
18. Eifel P, Hendrickson M, Ross R, Ballon S, Martinez A, Kempson R. Simultaneous presentation of carcinoma involving the ovary and the uterine corpus. Cancer 1982;50:163–70.
19. Fanning J, Evans MC, Peters AJ, Samuel M, Harmon ER, Bates JS. Endometrial adenocarcinoma histologic subtypes: clinical and pathologic profile. Gynecol Oncol 1989;32:288–91.
20. Ferenczy A. The ultrastructural dynamics of endometrial hyperplasia and neoplasia. In: Koss LG, Coleman DV, eds. Advances in clinical cytology. London: Butterworth, 1980:1–43.
21. Fox H, Brander WL. A sertoliform endometrioid adenocarcinoma of the endometrium. Histopathology 1988; 13:584–6.
22. Frauenhoffer EE, Zaino RJ, Wolff TV, Whitney CE. Value of endocervical curettage in the staging of endometrial carcinoma. Int J Gynecol Pathol 1987;6:195–202.
23. Fu YS, Parks PJ, Reagan JW, et al. The ultrastructure and factors relating to survival of endometrial cancers. Am J Diagn Gynecol Obstet 1979;1:55–72.
24. Gallion HH, van Nagell JR Jr, Donaldson ES, Powell DE. Endometrial cancer following radiation therapy for cervical cancer. Gynecol Oncol 1987;27:76–83.
25. Geisinger KR, Homesley HD, Morgan TM, Kute TE, Marshall RB. Endometrial adenocarcinoma. A multiparameter clinicopathologic analysis including the DNA profile and the sex steroid hormone receptors. Cancer 1986;58:1518–25.
26. _____ , Marshall RB, Kute TE, Homesley HD. Correlation of female sex steroid hormone receptors with histologic and ultrastructural differentiation in adenocarcinoma of the endometrium. Cancer 1986; 58:1506–17.
27. Gernow A, Ahrentsen OD. Adenoid cystic carcinoma of the endometrium. Histopathology 1989;15:197–8.
28. Grigsby PW, Perez CA, Kuske RR, Kao MS, Galakatos AE. Results of therapy, analysis of failures, and prognostic factors for clinical and pathologic stage III adenocarcinoma of the endometrium. Gynecol Oncol 1987; 27:44–57.
29. Grimshaw RN, Tupper WC, Fraser RC, Tompkins MG, Jeffrey JF. Prognostic value of peritoneal cytology in endometrial carcinoma. Gynecol Oncol 1990;36:97–100.
30. Gusberg SB. Detection and prevention of uterine cancer. Cancer 1988;62(Suppl 8):1784–6.
31. Hachisuga T, Kaku T, Enjoji M. Carcinoma of the lower uterine segment. Int J Gynecol Pathol 1989;8:26–35.
32. _____ , Sugimori H, Kaku T, Matsukuma K, Tsukamoto N, Nakano H. Glassy cell carcinoma of the endometrium. Gynecol Oncol 1990;36:134–8.
33. Hall JB, Young RH, Nelson JH Jr. The prognostic significance of adenomyosis in endometrial carcinoma. Gynecol Oncol 1984;17:32–40.
34. Henriksen E. The lymphatic spread of carcinoma of the cervix and of the body of the uterus. Am J Obstet Gynecol 1949;58:924–42.
35. Hendrickson MR, Kempson RL. Ciliated carcinoma—a variant of endometrial adenocarcinoma: a report of 10 cases. Int J Gynecol Pathol 1983;2:1–12.
36. _____ , Ross J, Eifel P, Martinez A, Kempson R. Uterine papillary serous carcinoma: a highly malignant form of endometrial adenocarcinoma. Am J Surg Pathol 1982;6:93–108.

37. Hussain SF. Verrucous carcinoma of the endometrium. A case report. APMIS 1988;96:1075–8.

38. Kelsey JL, Hildreth NG. Breast and gynecologic cancer epidemiology. Boca Raton, Florida: CRC Press, 1983: 71–92.

39. Koss LG, Schreiber K, Oberlander SG, Moussouris HF, Lesser M. Detection of endometrial carcinoma and hyperplasia in asymptomatic women. Obstet Gynecol 1984; 64:1–11.

40. Lawrence C, Tessaro I, Durgerian S, et al. Smoking, body weight, and early-stage endometrial cancer. Cancer 1987;59:1665–6.

41. Lurain JR, Rumsey NK, Schink JC, Wallemark CB, Chmiel JS. Prognostic significance of positive peritoneal cytology in clinical stage I adenocarcinoma of the endometrium. Obstet Gynecol 1989;74:175–9.

42. Maes G, Fleuren GJ, Bara J, Nap M. The distribution of mucins, carcinoembryonic antigen, and mucus-associated antigens in endocervical and endometrial adenocarcinomas. Int J Gynecol Pathol 1988;7:112–22.

43. Malviya VK, Deppe G, Malone JM Jr, Sundareson AS, Lawrence WD. Reliability of frozen section examination in identifying poor prognostic indications in stage I endometrial adenocarcinoma. Gynecol Oncol 1989; 34:299–304.

44. Manivel C, Wick MR, Sibley RK. Neuroendocrine differentiation in müllerian neoplasms. An immunohistochemical study of a "pure" endometrial small-cell carcinoma and mixed Müllerian tumor containing small-cell carcinoma. Am J Clin Pathol 1986;86: 438–43.

45. Masubuchi K, Nemoto H, Masubuchi S Jr, Fujimoto I, Uchino S. Increasing incidence of endometrial carcinoma in Japan. Gynecol Oncol 1975;3:335–46.

46. Melhem MF, Tobon H. Mucinous adenocarcinoma of the endometrium. Int J Gynecol Pathol 1987;6: 347–55.

47. Montoya F, Martin M, Schneider J, Matia JC, Rodriguez-Escudero FJ. Simultaneous appearance of ovarian and endometrial carcinoma: a therapeutic challenge. Eur J Gynaecol Oncol 1989;10:135–9.

48. Morris WP, Griffin NR, Wells M. Patterns of reactivity with the monoclonal antibodies HMFG1 and HMFG2 in normal endometrium, endometrial hyperplasia and adenocarcinoma. Histopathology 1989;15:179–86.

49. Nogales FF, Gomez-Morales M, Raymundo C, Aguilar D. Benign heterologous tissue components associated with endometrial carcinoma. Int J Gynecol Pathol 1982;1:286–91.

50. Palmer DC, Muir IM, Alexander AI, Cauchi M, Bennett RC, Quinn MA. The prognostic importance of steroid receptors in endometrial carcinoma. Obstet Gynecol 1988;72:388–93.

51. Poropatich C, Nozawa S, Rojas M, Chapman WB, Silverberg SG. MSN-1 antibody in the evaluation of female genital tract adenocarcinomas. Int J Gynecol Pathol 1990;9:73–9.

52. Puts JJ, Moesker O, Aldeweireldt J, Vooijs GP, Ramaekers FC. Application of antibodies to intermediate filament proteins in simple and complex tumors of the female genital tract. Int J Gynecol Pathol 1987;6:257–74.

53. Risberg B, Gröntoft O, Westholm B. Origin of carcinoma in secretory endometrium. Gynecol Oncol 1983;15:32–41.

54. Ross JC, Eifel PJ, Cox RS, Kempson RL, Hendrickson MR. Primary mucinous adenocarcinoma of the endometrium. A clinicopathologic and histochemical study. Am J Surg Pathol 1983;7:715–29.

55. Sasano H, Comerford J, Wilkinson DS, Schwartz A, Garrett CT. Serous papillary adenocarcinoma of the endometrium. Analysis of proto-oncogene amplification, flow cytometry, estrogen and progesterone receptors, and immunohistochemistry. Cancer 1990;65:1545–51.

56. _____ , Fukunaga M, Rojas M, Silverberg SG. Hyperthecosis of the ovary. Clinicopathologic study of 19 cases with immunohistochemical analysis of steroidogenic enzymes. Int J Gynecol Pathol 1989; 8:311–20.

57. Sato Y, Ozaki M, Ueda G, Tanizawa O. Clinical significance of argyrophilia in endometrial carcinomas. Gynecol Oncol 1986;25:53–60.

58. Saurel J, Claverie G. La cytologie endometriale du fonctionnel au tumoral. Gynecologie 1986;37:206–15.

59. Savage J, Subby W, Okagaki T. Adenocarcinoma of the endometrium with trophoblastic differentiation and metastases as choriocarcinoma: a case report. Gynecol Oncol 1987;26:257–62.

60. Schneider ML, Wortmann M, Weigel A. Influence of the histologic and cytologic grade and the clinical and postsurgical stage on the rate of endometrial carcinoma detection by cervical cytology. Acta Cytol 1986;30:616–22.

61. Segreti EM, Novotny DB, Soper JT, Mutch DG, Creasman WT, McCarty KS. Endometrial cancer: histologic correlates of immunohistochemical localization of progesterone receptor and estrogen receptor. Obstet Gynecol 1989;73:780–5.

62. Silva EG, Jenkins R. Serous carcinoma in endometrial polyps. Mod Pathol 1990;3:120–8.

63. Silverberg SG. Significance of squamous elements in carcinoma of the endometrium. A review. Prog Surg Pathol 1982;4:115–36.

64. _____ , Sasano N, Yajima A. Endometrial carcinoma in Miyagi Prefecture, Japan: histopathologic analysis of a cancer registry-based series and comparison with cases in American women. Cancer 1982; 49:1504–10.

65. Simon A, Kopolovic J, Beyth Y. Primary squamous cell carcinoma of the endometrium. Gynecol Oncol 1988; 31:454–61.

66. Sivridis E, Buckley CH, Fox H. The prognostic significance of lymphatic vascular space invasion in endometrial adenocarcinoma. Br J Obstet Gynaecol 1987; 94:991–4.

67. Smith M, McCartney AJ. Occult, high-risk endometrial cancer. Gynecol Oncol 1985;22:154–61.

68. Snowden JA, Harkin PJ, Thornton JG, Wells M. Morphometric assessment of ovarian stromal proliferation. Histopathology 1989;14:369–79.

69. Söderström KO. Lectin binding to human endometrial hyperplasias and adenocarcinoma. Int J Gynecol Pathol 1987;6:356–65.

70. Soothill PW, Alcock CJ, MacKenzie IZ. Discrepancy between curettage and hysterectomy histology in patients with stage I uterine malignancy. Br J Obstet Gynaecol 1989;96:478–81.

71. Stovall TG, Solomon SK, Ling FW. Endometrial sampling prior to hysterectomy [published erratum appears in Obstet Gynecol 1989;74:105]. Obstet Gynecol 1989;73:405–9.

72. Suzuki A, Konishi I, Okamura H, Nakashima N. Adenocarcinoma of the endometrium associated with intrauterine pregnancy. Gynecol Oncol 1984;18: 261–9.

73. Taghian A, Pernot M, Hoffstetter S, Luporosi E, Bey P. Radiation therapy alone for medically inoperable patients with adenocarcinoma of the endometrium. Int J Radiat Oncol Biol Phys 1988;15:1135–40.

74. Thor A, Viglione MJ, Muraro R, Ohuchi N, Schlom J, Gorstein F. Monoclonal antibody B72.3 reactivity with human endometrium. Int J Gynecol Pathol 1987; 6:235–47.

75. Thornton JG, Quirke P, Wells M. Flow cytometry of normal, hyperplastic, and malignant human endometrium. Am J Obstet Gynecol 1989;161:487–92.

76. Tobon H, Watkins GJ. Secretory adenocarcinoma of the endometrium. Int J Gynecol Pathol 1985;4: 328–35.

77. Turner DA, Gershenson DM, Atkinson N, Sneige N, Wharton AT. The prognostic significance of peritoneal cytology for Stage I endometrial cancer. Obstet Gynecol 1989;74:775–80.

78. van der Putten HW, Baak JP, Koenders TJ, Kurver PH, Stolk HG, Stolte LA. Prognostic value of quantitative pathologic features and DNA content in individual patients with stage I endometrial adenocarcinoma. Cancer 1989;63:1378–87.

79. Vergote I, Kjørstad K, Abeler V, Kolstad P. A randomized trial of adjuvant progestagen in early endometrial cancer. Cancer 1989;64:1011–6.

80. Vuopala S. Diagnostic accuracy and clinical applicability of cytological and histological methods for investigating endometrial carcinoma. Acta Obstet Gynecol Scand Suppl 1977;70:1–72.

81. Warhol MJ, Rice RH, Pinkus GS, Robboy SJ. Evaluation of squamous epithelium in adenoacanthoma and adenosquamous carcinoma of the endometrium: immunoperoxidase analysis of involucrin and keratin localization. Int J Gynecol Pathol 1984;3:82–91.

82. Webb GA, Lagios MD. Clear cell carcinoma of the endometrium. Am J Obstet Gynecol 1987;156:1486–91.

83. Yazigi R, Cohen J, Munoz AK, Sandstad J. Magnetic resonance imaging determination of myometrial invasion in endometrial carcinoma. Gynecol Oncol 1989;34:94–7.

84. Zaino RJ, Kurman RJ. Squamous differentiation in carcinoma of the endometrium: a critical appraisal of adenoacanthoma and adenosquamous carcinoma. Semin Diagn Pathol 1988;5:154–71.

85. _____ , Laskaris A, Whitney C, Sharkey FE. Morphometric analysis of endometrial adenocarcinoma: 2. A comparison of architectural differentiation determined morphometrically with subjective grading. Int J Gynecol Pathol 1987;6:20–8.

ENDOMETRIAL STROMAL TUMORS

Although endometrial stromal tumors were first described in 1908 (6), they were not well characterized until the classic study of Norris and Taylor in 1966 (18). The current classification adheres to the nomenclature of Norris and Taylor (although the definitions have undergone alteration) and divides this group of tumors into the following entities:

- stromal nodule—a benign, well-circumscribed tumoral proliferation of uniform cells that resemble the stromal cells of normal proliferative-phase endometrium

- low-grade endometrial stromal sarcoma (endolymphatic stromal myosis)—an infiltrative proliferation of cells cytologically identical to those seen in the stromal nodule, and associated with indolent but aggressive growth characteristics and generally low malignant potential

- high-grade endometrial stromal sarcoma—an infiltrative tumor composed of anaplastic and mitotically active cells bearing at least some morphologic resemblance to endometrial stromal cells.

These tumors are among the rarest primary neoplasms of the uterine corpus. In most reported series from the United States, non-epithelial tumors comprise only about 5 percent of all corporeal malignant tumors, and the endometrial stromal tumors account for 10 percent or less of these. For example, Koss and colleagues (15) state that endometrial stromal sarcomas comprised 0.2 percent of all uterine cancers seen at Memorial Hospital (New York) between 1939 and 1959. In the large series of 177 uterine sarcomas reported from the Mayo Clinic by Aaro and colleagues (1), only 17 (10 percent) were endometrial stromal sarcomas. In our own ongoing review of uterine malignant mesenchymal and mixed tumors collected by the Gynecologic Oncology Group, endometrial stromal tumors have accounted for slightly less than 10 percent of the more than 400 cases reviewed through early 1989. One large study from Finland reported a somewhat higher relative frequency of 23 endometrial stromal sarcomas among 119 uterine sarcomas

and malignant mixed tumors (11). I do not know whether this represents a true geographic difference or just random variation.

Because of the rarity of endometrial stromal sarcomas, very little is known about their epidemiology or pathogenesis. Although early reports (which include tumors referred to as stromatosis, stromal adenomyosis, and stromal endometriosis) suggested that these tumors arise as a stromal form of adenomyosis (4,10, 30), they are currently thought to be true neoplasms. Precursor lesions are essentially unknown, although there are rare cases in which review of prior curettage specimens has revealed an initially unrecognized stromal overgrowth in an apparently benign endometrium. Although no carcinogenic factors are known to antedate or stimulate the development of these tumors in women, one study (28) has demonstrated that normal endometrial stromal cells grown in culture develop morphologic changes resembling those seen in uterine sarcomas after treatment with the carcinogen N-methyl-nitro-N-nitrosoguanidine.

Clinical Features. Although the pathologic features and natural histories of the three types of endometrial stromal tumors are variable, the presenting signs and symptoms recorded in most large series appear to be identical, regardless of tumor type. Most patients present with abnormal uterine bleeding: 35 of 53 patients in the series of Norris and Taylor (18), 22 of 41 patients reported by Fekete and Vellios (8), and 6 of 11 reported by Katz and associates (12). Fekete and Vellios (8) reported that the frequency of vaginal bleeding was essentially identical among the three tumor types; in the large series of benign stromal nodules reported by Tavassoli and Norris (25), 40 of 60 patients presented with abnormal vaginal bleeding. Fekete and Vellios reported pelvic pain and dysmenorrhea with slightly increasing frequency as the tumors increased in malignancy. However, in the series of Tavassoli and Norris, pelvic or abdominal pain was a presenting complaint among 10 of the 60 women in their series who had benign stromal nodules. Asymptomatic patients are also seen among all three groups, although the absence of symptoms varied from a low of 3 of 53 patients reported by Norris and

Taylor (18) to a high of 9 of 41 patients reported by Fekete and Vellios (8).

The age range of these patients also varies in different reported series. However, all authors note a wide age range, with both teenagers and nonagenarians reported. Evans (7) has reported that the median age of patients with low-grade sarcomas (39 years) is notably less than that of patients with high-grade sarcomas (61 years), and this has been the Gynecologic Oncology Group experience as well (Table 4). On the other hand, Fekete and Vellios (8) recorded median ages of 53.5, 42, and 48 years for patients with stromal nodules, low-grade, and high-grade stromal sarcomas, respectively.

Physical examination usually reveals uterine enlargement, and again the frequency of this finding appears to be irrespective of the type of stromal tumor. As would be expected, clinical evidence of disease extension beyond the confines of the uterine corpus is limited to the low-grade and high-grade sarcomas. No radiographic or clinical laboratory data specific to these tumors has been identified.

Very few reports have commented on the possibility of diagnosis of these tumors by exfoliative cytology. Kahanpaa and colleagues (11) mentioned that only 1 of their 23 patients had a positive Papanicolaou smear, but the number of patients who did not have any cytologic examination is not mentioned. Because both the benign stromal nodule and low-grade endometrial stromal sarcoma are composed of essentially normal-appearing endometrial stromal cells, the best possibility of a preoperative cytologic diagnosis is among the high-grade stromal sarcomas (17). Fine-needle aspiration cytology, on the other hand, is potentially useful in confirming the presence of a recurrence or metastasis in a patient with either low-grade or high-grade endometrial stromal sarcoma.

Gross Findings. Regardless of tumor type, these neoplasms are generally described as soft and tan to gray to yellow. They are generally solid but frequently have foci of necrosis, hemorrhage, and cystic degeneration.

Some variability in the gross features is related to the specific tumor type. Stromal nodules

Table 4

COMPARISON OF GYNECOLOGIC ONCOLOGY GROUP CASES OF CLINICAL STAGE I AND II ENDOMETRIAL SARCOMAS *

	Low-Grade Stromal Sarcoma (20 cases)	High-Grade Stromal Sarcoma (21 cases)	Undifferentiated Sarcoma (5 cases) [†]
Mean age (years)	40.9	54.8	60.2
<45 years	85%	33%	20%
Mitoses/10 HPF [‡] (mean)	5.0	45.7	24.2
Abnormal mitoses	0%	85%	80%
Extensive necrosis	20%	66%	100%
Extrauterine extension at laparotomy	50%	29%	20%
Recurrence rate [¶]	10%	50%	60%
Dead of disease [¶]	0%	45%	60%

* From Kaku T, Silverberg SG, Major FJ, et al., unpublished observations.

[†] HPF = high-power fields

[‡] Defined as endometrial sarcoma showing no stromal differentiation.

[¶] Mean follow-up period of 31 months; one high-grade stromal sarcoma case lost to follow-up.

are notable for their discrete rounded contour (8,12,25). They almost always are found within the myometrium but may involve the endometrium as well; rare cases are confined to the endometrium. On gross examination, they are often confused with leiomyomas but tend to be softer and are less likely to show the white color and whorled configuration typical of leiomyomas. I find the term *nodule* to be somewhat misleading because these lesions can measure up to 15 cm in diameter, with median diameters of 4.0 and 5.7 cm in the two largest current series (8,25).

In low-grade endometrial stromal sarcomas, as many as half of the cases may also appear well circumscribed on gross examination. Many of the others are described as demonstrating diffuse myometrial permeation by worm-like masses, whereas others show multiple nodules (pl. III). A polypoid endometrial component is demonstrable in some cases, whereas others appear confined to the myometrium. Extrauterine extension is noted at the gross level in as many as one-third of the cases (7,8,12,25).

High-grade stromal sarcomas may take the form of single polypoid or grossly infiltrative masses, multiple confluent nodules, or tumors that diffusely permeate the myometrium. Endometrial involvement is almost always noted, and gross extension beyond the confines of the uterine corpus is variable. Macroscopic hemorrhage and necrosis are more common than in low-grade tumors.

Microscopic Findings. Because the three tumors in this group are distinguished best by light-microscopic examination of traditional hematoxylin-and-eosin–stained slides, most of the discussion devoted to the microscopic findings emphasizes this aspect.

Stromal Nodule. The stromal nodule is a well-circumscribed tumor with pushing margins between it and the surrounding myometrium or endometrium (fig. 117). The margins, however, are not encapsulated. Tavassoli and Norris noted focal finger-like projections into the adjacent myometrium in 11 of the 60 tumors they studied but noted that none of these projections exceeded 2 to 3 mm (whether in depth or width is not stated) and none invaded blood vessels (25).

The cells within stromal nodules closely resemble the stromal cells of normal proliferative endometrium. They are small and uniform (fig. 118). Cytologic atypia is minimal, and mitotic activity is generally very low; however, more than 10 mitotic figures per 10 high-power fields (HPF) have been reported in 2 of 60 tumors in the series of Tavassoli and Norris (25) and 1 of 12 in the series of Fekete and Vellios (8).

These tumors are characteristically very vascular, and many of the vessels resemble spiral arterioles of the endometrium, with tumor cells arranged in a whorling pattern around them (fig. 119). The vessels are generally thin-walled, evenly spaced, and of uniform size and shape, but occasional dilated or slit-like vessels also may be present. However, lack of vascular uniformity is more common in low-grade endometrial stromal sarcoma (figs. 120, 121).

Variations on the characteristics noted above occur in some tumors. Thick bands of collagen with areas of hyalinization, occasionally in a starburst pattern, may be prominent (figs. 122, 123). Areas of necrosis, cysts, foam cells, calcium deposits, and decidualization also occur but are usually not prominent (fig. 124). Epithelioid differentiation, characterized by a glandular or sex cord-like pattern, was reported in most of the stromal nodules in the series of Fekete and Vellios (8) but in only 5 of the 60 stromal nodules of Tavassoli and Norris (25). Foci of smooth muscle differentiation (fig. 125) were observed in 9 of the 60 cases of Tavassoli and Norris, and the smooth muscle nature of such foci was confirmed at the ultrastructural level by Fekete and Vellios in several of their cases.

Special stains have not been of much use in the diagnosis of these neoplasms, with the possible exception of the silver reticulum stain. With this stain, reticulin fibers surround individual cells, often accentuating the perivascular whorling pattern (fig. 126). Fekete and Vellios have noted that foci of epithelioid differentiation were surrounded rather than permeated by reticulin fibers, as one would expect in true epithelial aggregates. A trichrome stain may be useful in distinguishing endometrial stromal from smooth muscle differentiation, because smooth muscle tumors should contain intracytoplasmic myofibrils.

We are not aware of ultrastructural or immunohistochemical studies of endometrial stromal nodules, although these studies have been reported in cases of low-grade endometrial

Plate III
LOW-GRADE ENDOMETRIAL STROMAL SARCOMA

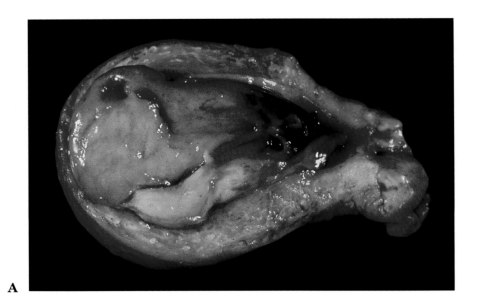

A

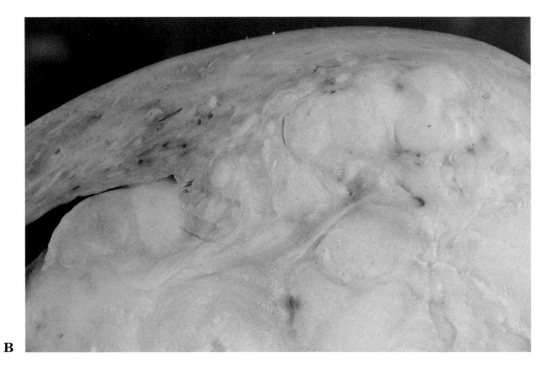

B

This soft, fleshy tumor grows predominantly as a polypoid lesion in the endometrial cavity but also invades the myometrium of the fundus. The bright yellow area was occupied by numerous foam cells, as seen on histologic examination (A) (Courtesy of Dr. Lucien Nochomovitz, Washington, D.C.). This previously fixed specimen shows the typical worm-like plugs of tumor extending through the myometrium in dilated lymphatic spaces (B).

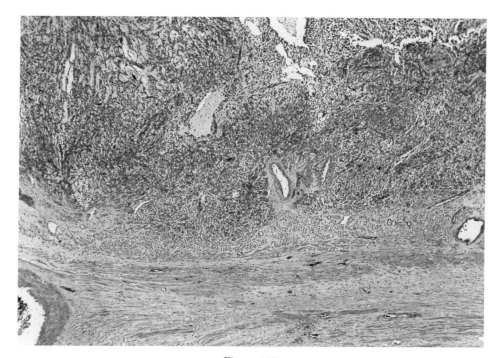

Figure 117
ENDOMETRIAL STROMAL NODULE
Circumscription with pushing margin is demonstrated in this illustration.

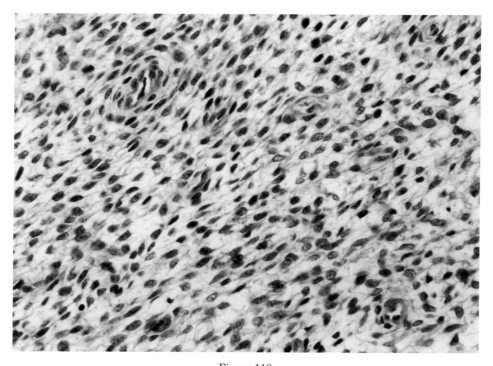

Figure 118
ENDOMETRIAL STROMAL NODULE
In this illustration, small uniform cells closely resemble those of proliferative-phase endometrial stroma.

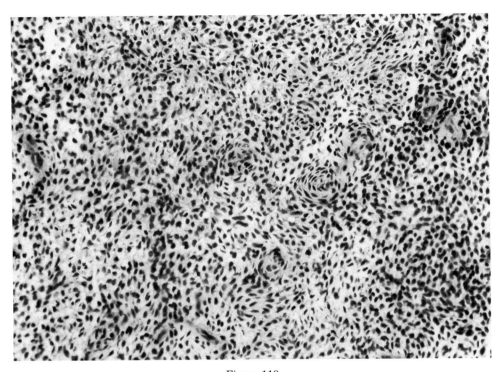

Figure 119
ENDOMETRIAL STROMAL NODULE
This example shows regularly distributed small blood vessels that resemble spiral arterioles.

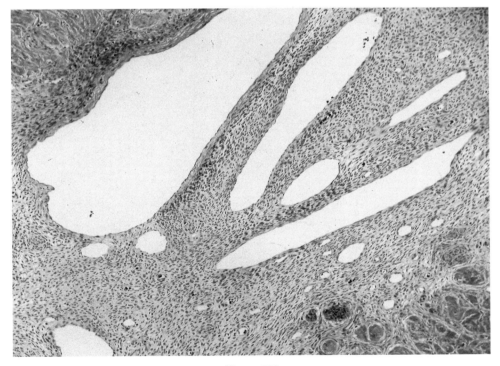

Figure 120
LOW-GRADE ENDOMETRIAL STROMAL SARCOMA
Dilated and slit-like thin-walled vessels are prominent in this example.

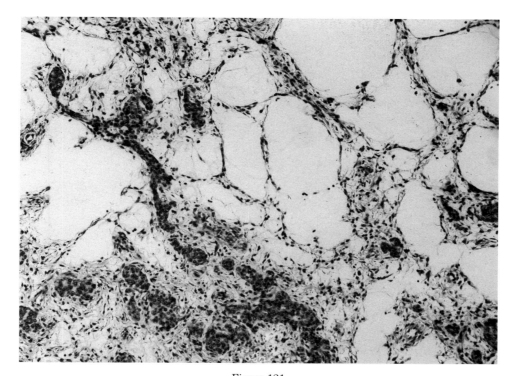

Figure 121
LOW-GRADE ENDOMETRIAL STROMAL SARCOMA
This illustration shows dilated vessels and sex cord-like structures.

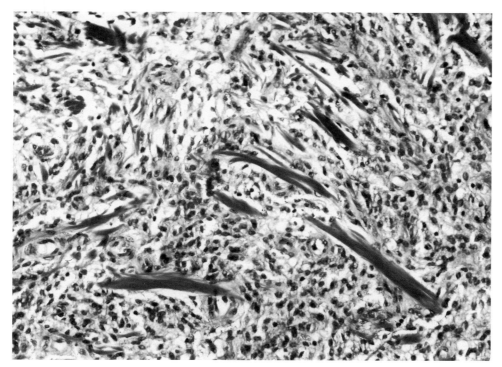

Figure 122
ENDOMETRIAL STROMAL NODULE
Note thick bands of hyalinized collagen in this field.

Figure 123
ENDOMETRIAL STROMAL NODULE
The starburst pattern of hyalinized collagen is featured in this figure.

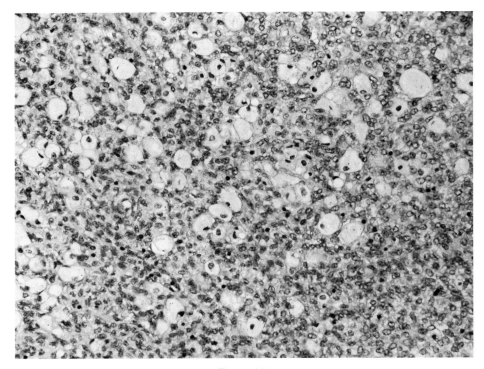

Figure 124
ENDOMETRIAL STROMAL NODULE
There are numerous cells with foamy cytoplasm present in this field.

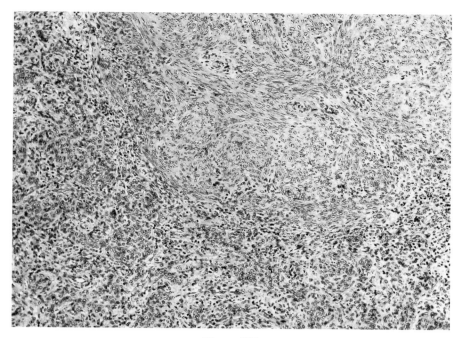

Figure 125
ENDOMETRIAL STROMAL NODULE
Note the large focus (upper) of smooth muscle differentiation. This focus was well within the sharply circumscribed tumor border, distinguishing it from myometrium invaded by tumor.

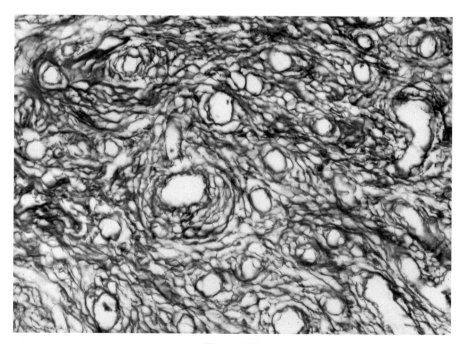

Figure 126
ENDOMETRIAL STROMAL NODULE
Silver reticulum stain demonstrates reticulin fibers wrapping around individual tumor cells and emphasizes the whorling pattern around the blood vessels.

stromal sarcoma, in which the cells are probably the same as in the stromal nodule.

Low-Grade Endometrial Stromal Sarcoma. The cytologic and architectural appearance of low-grade endometrial stromal sarcoma is essentially identical to that of the stromal nodule, with the single exception that the border between tumor and surrounding myometrium is infiltrative (figs. 127, 128). As mentioned previously, a very minor degree of infiltration in an overwhelmingly well-circumscribed neoplasm can be overlooked, because recurrence was never noted in tumors displaying this minor degree of infiltration in the series of Tavassoli and Norris (25). In low-grade endometrial stromal sarcoma, on the other hand, the infiltration is never subtle but is almost always extensive at the microscopic level, and often at the gross level as well. Plugs of tumor are usually identified within lymphatic or venous channels (figs. 127, 129), leading to the frequent designation of this tumor in the older literature as endolymphatic stromal myosis.

Despite the extensive invasion shown by these tumors, they are cytologically no more malignant in appearance than the stromal nodule and are usually equally deficient in mitotic activity. The classic definition of this entity demanded that a tumor displaying more than 10 mitotic figures per 10 HPF be designated high grade, even in the absence of other evidence of cytologic atypia. However, it should be noted that even benign stromal nodules have been recorded as showing as many as 15 mitotic figures per 10 HPF (25). In addition, Evans (7) has noted the typical behavior of low-grade endometrial stromal sarcoma in two cases in which the mitotic rate was 24 and 21 per 10 HPF, respectively. Taina and colleagues (23) also noted that three cases initially placed into their high-grade sarcoma group purely because of increased mitotic activity also ultimately behaved more like low-grade than high-grade tumors, and three cases with 10 to 14 mitotic figures per 10 HPF also behaved like low-grade tumors in our review (Kaku T, Silverberg SG, Major FJ, et al., unpublished observations) of Gynecologic Oncology Group material (Table 4). In the large series of Chang and colleagues (5), 14 percent of cases had more than 10 mitoses per 10 HPF, and these cases also behaved no differently from their stage I cases with lower

mitotic activity. Thus, I favor the concept suggested by Evans (7), that indicates that infiltrating tumors with the typical benign-appearing cytology and endometrial stromal vascular pattern be diagnosed as low grade, regardless of the mitotic rate, and I save the high-grade designation for endometrial stromal neoplasms showing marked cytologic atypia. Atypical mitotic figures, however, were encountered exclusively in high-grade tumors in Gynecologic Oncology Group cases (Table 4).

I emphasize that in most reported series and in my personal experience as well, that low-grade sarcoma is by far the most common of the three tumor types in the endometrial stromal tumor group and indeed is the prototype for most published descriptions of both the appearance and the behavior of endometrial stromal tumors. Because these tumors are the most common, all of the variations on the basic histopathologic characteristics that have been described in the section on Stromal Nodules have actually been noted more frequently in low-grade endometrial stromal sarcomas. Thus, foci of foam cells, decidualization, calcification, cystic degeneration, hemorrhage, necrosis, and particularly epithelioid differentiation (figs. 121, 130, 131) and hyalinization have been described most frequently in this tumor group. However, it cannot be stated definitively that these characteristics are more common in low-grade sarcomas than in stromal nodules. The only good comparison in the literature is that of Fekete and Vellios (8) in which the numbers of cases are, unfortunately, small (12 stromal nodules and 20 low-grade sarcomas). In this series, both epithelioid differentiation and hyalinization were more common in the stromal nodules, whereas necrosis was seen more frequently in low-grade sarcomas (and even more so in high-grade sarcomas), but statistical significance of differences was probably absent.

Immunohistochemical studies of endometrial stromal neoplasms have also focused primarily on low-grade sarcomas (2,16). Both reported studies emphasized that the intermediate filament most frequently expressed by these tumors was vimentin and that epithelial membrane antigen was always absent. Both studies also noted occasional reactivity for both desmin and muscle-specific actin, although Lillemoe and colleagues (16) noted that these

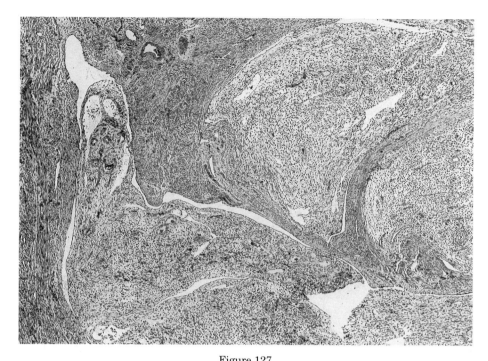

Figure 127
LOW-GRADE ENDOMETRIAL STROMAL SARCOMA
There is extensive myometrial infiltration in this field. Note also slit-like vascular or lymphatic spaces around tumor masses, which represent vascular involvement.

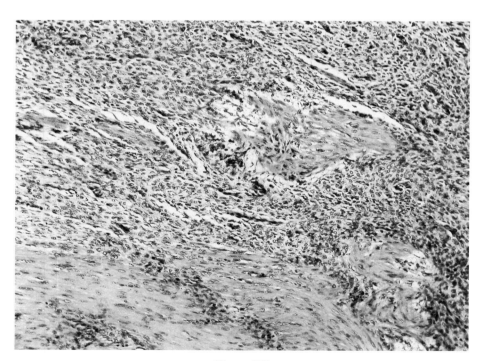

Figure 128
LOW-GRADE ENDOMETRIAL STROMAL SARCOMA
This focus shows the myometrium being infiltrated by uniform small tumor cells.

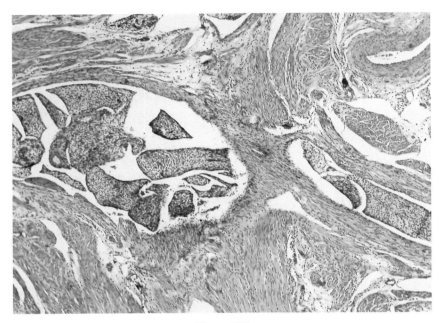

Figure 129
LOW-GRADE ENDOMETRIAL STROMAL SARCOMA
In this illustration, myometrial lymphatics are expanded and infiltrated by tumor.
The lobulated contour of the intravascular tumor is unusual, resembling that seen in
intravenous leiomyomatosis.

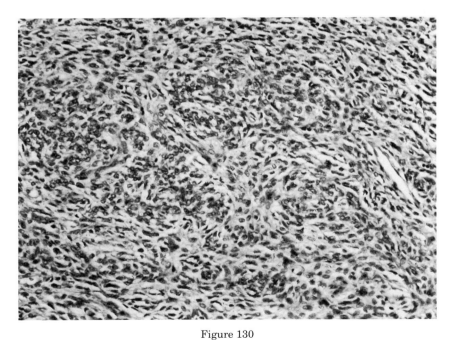

Figure 130
LOW-GRADE ENDOMETRIAL STROMAL SARCOMA
Nests and sex cord-like arrangements blend with intervening stromal cells in this
example.

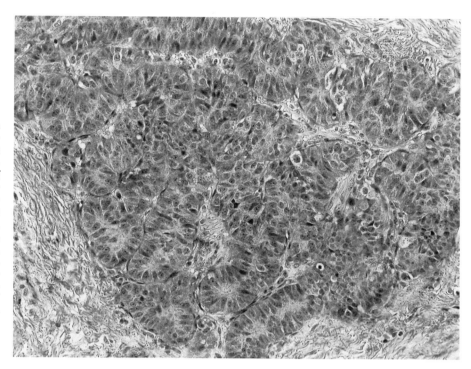

Figure 131
LOW-GRADE ENDO-
METRIAL STROMAL
SARCOMA
This example contains a
focus of glandular differentiation. Note that the glands do
not resemble the normal benign endometrial glands of
adenomyosis, the dilated or
slit-like glands of adenosarcoma, or the carcinomatous
glands of carcinosarcoma.
(Fig. 4 from Chang KL,
Crabtree GS, Lim-Tan SK,
Kempson RL, Hendrickson
MR. Primary uterine endo-
metrial neoplasms. A clinicopathologic study of 117
cases. Am J Surg Pathol
1990;14:415–38.)

filaments were expressed only in foci of epithelioid differentiation. Focal cytokeratin positivity was also reported in a few cases by both
groups of investigators.

Ultrastructurally, low-grade stromal sarcoma has also been the most frequently characterized tumor in the stromal neoplasm group
(3,14). The ultrastructural characteristics of
these neoplasms are generally similar to those
of proliferative-phase endometrial stromal
cells. Mitochondria, Golgi apparatus, micro-
filaments, rough endoplasmic reticulum, and
free ribosomes are present but relatively sparse;
basal lamina and desmosomes are sparse and
poorly formed. Foci with ultrastructural evidence of either epithelial (9) or smooth muscle
(8) differentiation have confirmed the corresponding light-microscopic appearances.

High-Grade Endometrial Stromal Sarcoma.
The microscopic features of high-grade stromal
sarcoma clearly depend on which definition of
this entity one chooses to accept. According to
the classic definition of Norris and Taylor (18),
which has been accepted by most investigators,
a high-grade sarcoma is histologically identical
to a low-grade sarcoma, with the exception that
10 or more mitotic figures per 10 HPF are seen

in the high-grade tumors. Norris and Taylor also
noted that cellular atypia was usually more
pronounced in the high-grade sarcomas but
commented that there was considerable overlap
in degree of atypia among all three groups of
stromal tumors and that there seemed to be no
consistent relationship of atypia to behavior.

On the other hand, I have noted for many
years that, although mitotic activity varies significantly between low-grade and high-grade
tumors, the general appearances of the two
tumor types are so different that it is not necessary to count mitoses to make the distinction.
Evans (7) has made this observation in his
material as well. Furthermore, Evans believes
that there are two fundamentally different
tumor types and uses the terms *endometrial
stromal sarcoma* and *poorly differentiated endometrial sarcoma* to refer to low-grade and high-
grade sarcomas, respectively. Kempson and
Hendrickson (13) also favor this concept and
terminology. This system, however, eliminates
the category of high-grade stromal sarcoma entirely. In the schema presented here (fig. 132)
and in the International Society of Gynecological Pathologists classification, we have retained
the nomenclature of Norris and Taylor with

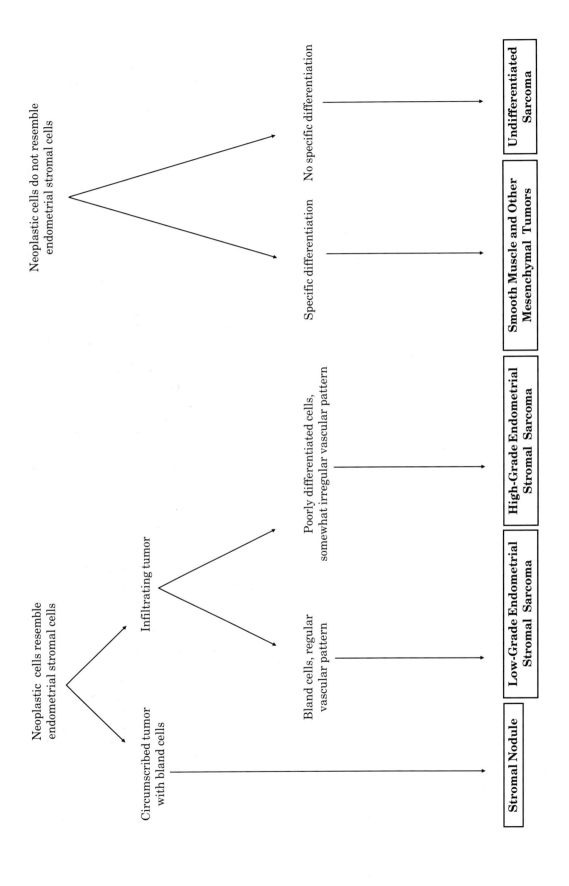

Figure 132

DIAGNOSTIC ALGORITHM FOR UTERINE PURE MESENCHYMAL NEOPLASMS

Mitoses need not be counted to distinguish between low-grade and high-grade tumors, if the criteria outlined above are observed.

respect to low-grade and high-grade endometrial stromal sarcoma, but we use criteria other than mitotic activity to distinguish between them. In addition, we use the term *undifferentiated endometrial sarcoma* to characterize a pure sarcoma arising in the endometrium but showing no evidence of endometrial stromal differentiation (fig. 132).

If one accepts this definition of high-grade stromal sarcoma, the microscopic features are those of an invasive tumor with at least moderate nuclear pleomorphism and hyperchromasia (fig. 133). The cells are rounded or ovoid, and in their distribution and appearance still have some resemblance to endometrial stromal cells. Small vascular channels permeate the tumor but are less regularly distributed than those of a low-grade endometrial stromal sarcoma. Focally, there may be huge cells with bizarre solitary or multiple nuclei, but if the tumor is to be classified as endometrial stromal sarcoma, it should be composed predominantly of cells showing endometrial stromal differentiation. Sarcomas composed predominantly of spindle cells (fig. 134), giant cells (fig. 135), other anaplastic cells, or combinations of these and not differentiating in any specific direction (such as smooth or striated muscle) are diagnosed as undifferentiated sarcoma. Evans (7) has pointed out that these often resemble the sarcomatous component of carcinosarcoma of the endometrium (see Mixed Epithelial-Nonepithelial Tumors), and thus a careful search should be made for an epithelial component before the diagnosis of undifferentiated sarcoma is made.

As in both stromal nodules and low-grade stromal sarcomas, foci of smooth muscle (leiomyosarcomatous) differentiation may be noted in high-grade stromal sarcomas. If these are focal and the tumor appears to arise from the endometrium, retain the designation high-grade endometrial stromal sarcoma. On the other hand, if the tumor is largely myometrial or the leiomyosarcomatous component is dominant, the diagnosis of leiomyosarcoma or mixed sarcoma is more appropriate.

On rare occasions, I have seen foci of heterologous differentiation (specifically rhabdomyosarcoma and chondrosarcoma) in high-grade stromal sarcomas in the absence of a carcinomatous element. This type of tumor should be diagnosed as high-grade endometrial stromal sarcoma with heterologous elements. A careful search should be made in many tissue sections for either a benign or malignant glandular component because heterologous differentiation is far more frequent in adenosarcoma and carcinosarcoma than in pure stromal sarcoma.

I emphasize that, with this definition of high-grade endometrial stromal sarcoma, the typical vascular pattern described for stromal nodules and low-grade sarcomas will be present but not as well developed. Foci of epithelioid or sex cord-like differentiation are usually absent but were present in 2 of 21 cases in our Gynecologic Oncology Group series. Vascular and lymphatic invasion are frequently seen. However, the pattern of worm-like plugs of tumor within vessels and slit-like vascular spaces at the periphery of infiltrating but rounded nests of tumor, which is so typical of low-grade stromal sarcoma, is rarely encountered. Tumor generally invades both on a broad front and in angular pointed proliferations, and necrosis is more frequently seen than in low-grade sarcomas (Table 4) (8).

Differential Diagnosis. The differential diagnosis of the three types of endometrial stromal tumor is largely with each other and with undifferentiated endometrial stromal sarcoma, and the pertinent diagnostic features have been discussed in the previous section. Differential diagnosis is otherwise dependent on the specific type of stromal tumor being considered, as well as the prominence of various associated features. For example, because of their prominent vascular pattern, stromal nodule and low-grade stromal sarcoma may be confused with hemangiopericytoma. In considering this differential diagnosis, remember that, although the endometrial stromal tumors are rare, hemangiopericytoma of the uterus is even rarer, and most cases reported in the literature probably really represent examples of endometrial stromal tumors. Furthermore, neither a silver reticulum stain nor immunostains would help to make this distinction, and thus we would only accept a diagnosis of hemangiopericytoma of the uterus in a case showing clear-cut ultrastructural evidence of pericytic differentiation (21). Large, branching, staghorn-shaped blood vessels seen by routine light microscopy might also suggest hemangiopericytoma. Finally, hormone receptor analysis may be useful in this

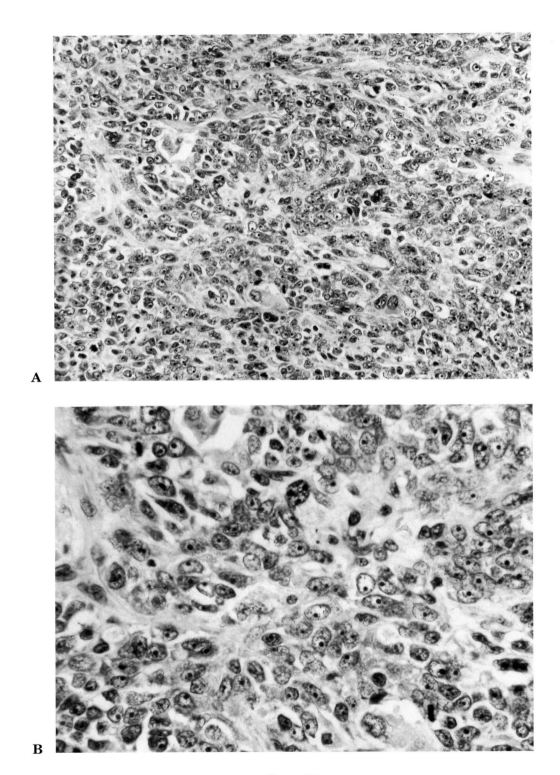

Figure 133
HIGH-GRADE ENDOMETRIAL STROMAL SARCOMA
The round cells resemble endometrial stromal cells but are large and pleomorphic. The regular vascular pattern of the low-grade tumors is absent in this field (A). A higher magnification of this tumor shows anaplastic nuclear features and mitotic figures (B).

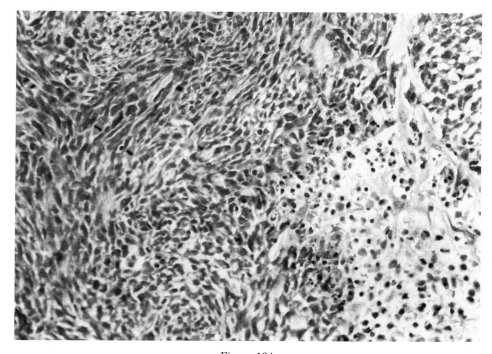

Figure 134
UNDIFFERENTIATED SARCOMA OF THE ENDOMETRIUM
This field consists of poorly differentiated spindled cells. Mitoses are numerous, and necrosis is seen at the lower right.

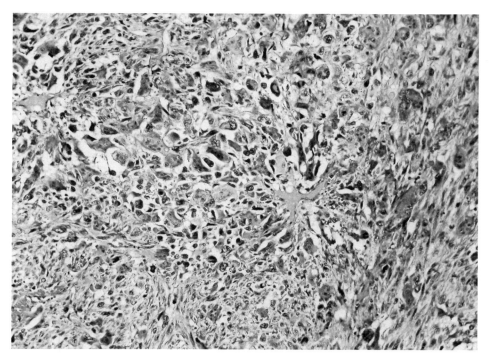

Figure 135
UNDIFFERENTIATED SARCOMA OF THE ENDOMETRIUM
This field is composed of pleomorphic giant and spindle cells.

differential diagnosis because the well-differentiated endometrial stromal tumors are almost always positive and hemangiopericytomas would be expected to be negative. However, receptor negativity is still possible in some low-grade stromal tumors. This represents the only real clinical significance of making the distinction between a low-grade stromal sarcoma and a hemangiopericytoma, since (based on the behavior of extrauterine hemangiopericytomas) both are characterized by favorable short-term survival and frequent late recurrences and metastases.

A more frequent differential diagnostic consideration involving the low-grade stromal tumors is that of a smooth muscle tumor. Indeed, because smooth muscle differentiation has been reported in both stromal nodules and low-grade stromal sarcomas, the real question is how much of such differentiation to accept before designating the lesion as a mixed tumor containing both components (stromomyoma) (24). Again, practical considerations should be taken into account here. If the tumor is well circumscribed, it will behave benignly regardless of whether it is a stromal nodule or a leiomyoma. If, on the other hand, the tumor shows infiltrative borders and vascular invasion, the differential diagnosis lies between intravenous leiomyomatosis, a benign entity, and low-grade endometrial stromal sarcoma, a malignant one. Although endometrial stromal tumors often show smooth muscle differentiation, the converse is very uncommon, so that a tumor of this sort that shows both endometrial stromal and smooth muscle elements should be diagnosed as low-grade endometrial stromal sarcoma.

The question of endometrial stromal differentiation versus smooth muscle differentiation is usually easy to resolve in low-grade tumors if epithelioid or sex cord-like elements are not dominant. Endometrial stromal tumors are characterized by regularly distributed spiral arterioles with cells that are small and round to slightly spindled whorling around them; tumor cell cytoplasm is scanty, nuclei are round to ovoid, and intracellular myofibrils are not demonstrable with trichrome stains or electron microscopy. On the other hand, smooth muscle tumors have irregularly distributed and thick-walled blood vessels; spindled cells with cigar-shaped nuclei arranged in interlacing fascicles;

moderate amounts of cytoplasm with myofibrils demonstrable with trichrome stains; and ultrastructural findings of myofilaments, dense bodies along the filaments and adjacent to the plasma membrane, and pinocytotic vesicles attached to the plasma membrane. Desmin and muscle-specific actin, which should in theory be specific for smooth muscle cells, have been reported in endometrial stromal tumors as well. Therefore, immunohistochemistry is not definitive in distinguishing between these two pathways of differentiation.

The other kind of differentiation that leads to diagnostic difficulties in the low-grade stromal tumors is the epithelioid pattern. If glandular differentiation is present, the differential diagnosis will include carcinosarcoma and adenosarcoma. In the former of these two entities, both glandular and stromal elements are cytologically malignant, so this should not pose a difficult problem. In adenosarcoma, the glandular component frequently forms papillary folds, may comprise cystically dilated or slit-like glands cuffed by an increased density of stromal cells, and invariably demonstrates benign-appearing glandular epithelium that looks different from the surrounding stroma, which is generally poorly differentiated. In low-grade stromal tumors, on the other hand, the glandular formations are generally small and round, and composed of cells with nuclei that are identical to those of the surrounding stromal cells; subtle transitions between the glandular and stromal components can often be identified. Epithelioid (particularly plexiform) leiomyoma must also be considered, and foci of typical smooth muscle differentiation should be carefully searched for to confirm this diagnosis.

If sex cord-like differentiation is a prominent feature in a low-grade stromal tumor, the differential diagnosis consists of the uterine tumor specifically diagnosed as sex cord-like (see Miscellaneous and Secondary Tumors). Although I accept the latter tumor as a separate entity, I believe most of the tumors with sex cord-like elements can be characterized as either endometrial stromal or leiomyomatous, based on the demonstration of more typical appearances of one or the other of these pathways of differentiation somewhere within the tumor. Thus, this differential diagnosis is usually not an issue. In theory, stromal tumors with glandular or sex cord-like differentiation could also be confused with metastatic carcinomas, particularly lobular carcinoma of mammary origin, but in practice the lack of atypia within these endometrial stromal tumors would hardly suggest a metastasis. Additional differential diagnostic possibilities include malignant lymphoma, leukemia, and lymphangiomyomatosis; in all of these, a history of extrauterine disease is usually present before the uterine presentation, and in the first two, an immunostain for leukocyte-common antigen would be positive.

The high-grade endometrial stromal sarcomas present an entirely different set of differential diagnostic possibilities. Because these tumors only rarely contain foci of glandular or sex cord-like differentiation and generally do not show a completely regular vascular pattern, the differential diagnostic possibilities mentioned previously rarely apply. On the other hand, the differential diagnosis is with other poorly differentiated sarcomas and carcinomas. The diagnosis of endometrial stromal sarcoma should not be made unless the tumor demonstrates obvious endometrial stromal differentiation. Soft-tissue sarcomas of other types (e.g., pure rhabdomyosarcoma, osteosarcoma, malignant fibrous histiocytoma, etc.) occur in rare instances in the endometrium and myometrium and should be diagnosed as such (see Smooth Muscle and Other Mesenchymal Tumors). A sarcoma that arises in the endometrium but that lacks endometrial stromal or other specific differentiation is an undifferentiated endometrial sarcoma. In addition, extremely poorly differentiated endometrial carcinomas may present the appearance of malignant spindle cell tumors. Careful search for foci of glandular or squamous differentiation can often be rewarding, as can ultrastructural or immunohistochemical demonstration of epithelial differentiation. Remember, however, that cytokeratin (but not epithelial membrane antigen) positivity may be seen focally in otherwise typical endometrial stromal sarcomas.

Clinical Behavior. The reason for the distinction among the types of endometrial stromal neoplasms is the marked difference in their clinical behavior. Stromal nodules are usually benign. The 60 cases reported by Tavassoli and Norris (25) included the 18 cases previously reported by Norris and Taylor (18). None of these 60 patients experienced a recurrence, including five who had been treated by excision without subsequent hysterectomy. Eighty-five percent of the patients were followed 5 years or more and 63 percent 10 years or more. Six of the patients of Fekete and Vellios (8) were followed from 4 to 10 years, also without recurrence or metastasis, and all six patients reported by Thatcher and Woodruff were alive for 5 years or more without evidence of recurrence (26).

Both low-grade and high-grade endometrial stromal sarcomas behave in a malignant fashion, although the levels of aggressiveness are different. Only a few high-grade stromal sarcomas with follow-up are available for analysis in even the largest reported series, and the diagnostic criteria used vary, but their prognosis appears uniformly grim. Taina and colleagues (23) noted three deaths among five patients but also commented that the three patients with prolonged survival were placed in the high-grade group solely on the basis of high mitotic count and thus perhaps really belonged in the low-grade group. This comment might also be applied to the cases reported by Norris and Taylor (18); however, only four (26.5 percent) of their patients were alive without evidence of tumor at last contact, and the 5-year survival rate was 55 percent. Three of the five patients followed and reported by Fekete and Vellios (8) (who also used the mitotic rate as their main diagnostic criterion) experienced recurrence or metastasis within 2 years. All seven patients reported by Sutton and colleagues died within 27 months (22).

On the other hand, in Evans' series (7), where poorly differentiated endometrial sarcoma was diagnosed by criteria similar to those recommended here for undifferentiated endometrial sarcoma, six of seven patients died within 3 years. The seventh patient had a tumor diagnosed by curettage and treated initially with radium, no tumor remained in the hysterectomy specimen; this patient was alive and well 19 years after treatment. However, this series includes no high-grade stromal sarcoma category, so I assume that some of the cases classified as such by me might have been included among his endometrial stromal sarcomas or poorly differentiated endometrial sarcomas, or both. Among our own Gynecologic Oncology Group cases, 10 of 20 high-grade stromal sarcomas recurred within 2 years, and nine patients had died within the same period of time (Table 4). Results were similar for undifferentiated sarcoma, with three of five patients dead of recurrent tumor. It should be noted that no other series has separated these two tumors in this manner and presented follow-up data for both groups, so these results must still be confirmed.

In low-grade stromal sarcomas, on the other hand, although up to 50 percent of patients may eventually develop recurrences, survival rates at 5 and even 10 years are generally very favorable. In the series of Norris and Taylor (18), the actuarial 5-year and 10-year survival rates were both 100 percent, but 6 of 19 patients were known to be living with recurrent tumor. In the large collaborative study of Piver and colleagues (19), survival rates were identical at 5 and 10 years and were quoted as 88 percent for cases in surgical stage I, 66 percent in stage II, 100 percent in stage III, and 75 percent in stage IV (the staging system used was the same as that used for endometrial carcinoma). Among patients whose tumors were in stage I at the time of primary surgery, initial recurrences were noted as long as 274 months after surgical treatment (median time 34 months), and deaths due to tumor occurred as long as 143 months after initial treatment. Among the 11 cases that Evans reported (7), four patients experienced recurrence, but three were alive between 47 and 89 months after initial treatment, and one died at 65 months. Both Evans (7) and Thatcher and Woodruff (26) included cases with high mitotic rates among their low-grade tumors, and in neither report did the mitotic rate correlate with clinical behavior. In our Gynecologic Oncology Group series (Table 4), 10 of 20 cases had extra-uterine disease at initial presentation, but only two subsequently recurred, and no patient died in an average follow-up period of 31 months. The median time to recurrence in stage I cases in the series of Chang and colleagues (5) was 79 months; 23 percent of the patients died. Initial recurrences of low-grade stromal sarcomas tend to be limited to the pelvis, although a small but significant proportion of patients may first present with distant (usually pulmonary) metastases (8,18,20,26). There is a suggestion in the literature that patients with high-grade sarcomas are more likely to experience recurrence with distant metastases and to develop extrapulmonary

distant metastases (7,18), but the available data do not justify a firm conclusion about this.

Treatment. Treatment of low-grade, high-grade, and undifferentiated endometrial sarcomas is predominantly surgical, the usual procedure performed being total abdominal hysterectomy with bilateral salpingo-oophorectomy. Because of the indolent nature of the low-grade tumors, surgical debulking of extrauterine tumor is also advisable. Fresh tumor tissue should always be submitted for steroid hormone receptor analysis. In cases of benign stromal nodule, hysterectomy has usually been performed, but follow-up has been benign even in cases treated by local excision only (25). However, remember that the differential diagnosis between a stromal nodule and low-grade endometrial stromal sarcoma depends on the microscopic evaluation of the margins of the tumor. Thus, a definitive diagnosis cannot be rendered on a curettage specimen, and the gynecologist usually proceeds on the assumption that he or she may be treating a low-grade stromal sarcoma. When a stromal nodule is initially thought to be a leiomyoma and is removed by myomectomy, additional surgery is probably not required.

An important adjunct to surgical treatment in cases of low-grade stromal sarcoma is therapy with progestational agents. Numerous studies have demonstrated the presence of estrogen and progesterone receptors in most cases of low-grade stromal sarcoma, and in some high-grade stromal sarcomas as well (12,19,22,27). Many of the tumors containing progesterone receptors will respond to therapy with progestins, although it is unclear whether these agents should be used as adjuvant therapy in all cases or only in those with advanced or recurrent disease. A trial of progestin therapy might also be justified in cases of high-grade stromal sarcoma, but the results have generally not been encouraging.

Nonhormonal chemotherapy and radiation therapy have both been utilized for both low-grade and high-grade sarcomas, with variable but generally unimpressive results (11,19,29). Because progestins are generally effective and nontoxic in most cases of low-grade endometrial stromal sarcoma, the use of other modalities is usually reserved for the high-grade and undifferentiated tumors or those low-grade tumors without receptors or with progression despite progestin therapy.

REFERENCES

1. Aaro LA, Symmonds RE, Dockerty MB. Sarcoma of the uterus. A clinical and pathologic study of 177 cases. Am J Obstet Gynecol 1966;94:101–9.
2. Abrams J, Corson JM, Gee B, Farhood A. Immunohistochemistry of endometrial stromal sarcoma (ESS). Hum Pathol 1991;22:224–30.
3. Akhtar M, Kim PY, Young I. Ultrastructure of endometrial stromal sarcoma. Cancer 1975;35:406–12.
4. Casler DB. A unique, diffuse uterine tumor, really an adenomyoma, with stroma, but no glands; menstruation after complete hysterectomy due to uterine mucosa in remaining ovary. Surg Gynecol Obstet 1920;31:150–9.
5. Chang KL, Crabtree GS, Lim-Tan SK, Kempson RL, Hendrickson MR. Primary uterine endometrial stromal neoplasms. A clinicopathologic study of 117 cases. Am J Surg Pathol 1990;14:415–38.
6. Doran AH, Lockyer C. Two cases of uterine fibroids showing peritheliomatous change: long immunity from recurrence after operation. Proc R Soc Med 1908;2:25–39.
7. Evans HL. Endometrial stromal sarcoma and poorly differentiated endometrial sarcoma. Cancer 1982;50:2170–82.
8. Fekete PS, Vellios F. The clinical and histologic spectrum of endometrial stromal neoplasms: a report of 41 cases. Int J Gynecol Pathol 1984;3:198–212.
9. _____, Vellios F, Patterson BD. Uterine tumor resembling an ovarian sex-cord tumor: report of a case of an endometrial stromal tumor with foam cells and ultrastructural evidence of epithelial differentiation. Int J Gynecol Pathol 1985;4:378–87.
10. Hunter WC, Nohlgren JE, Lancefield SM. Stromal endometriosis or endometrial sarcoma—a re-evaluation of old and new cases, with special reference to duration, recurrences and metastases. Am J Obstet Gynecol 1956;72:1072–88
11. Kahanpaa KV, Wahlström T, Gröhn P, Heinonen E, Nieminen U, Widholm O. Sarcomas of the uterus: a clinicopathologic study of 119 patients. Obstet Gynecol 1986;67:417–23.
12. Katz L, Merino MJ, Sakamoto H, Schwartz PE. Endometrial stromal sarcoma: a clinicopathologic study of 11 cases with determination of estrogen and progestin receptor levels in three tumors. Gynecol Oncol 1987;26:87–97.
13. Kempson RL, Hendrickson MR. Pure mesenchymal neoplasms of the uterine corpus: selected problems. Semin Diagn Pathol 1988;5:172–98.
14. Komorowski RA, Garancis JC, Clowry LJ Jr. Fine structure of endometrial stromal sarcoma. Cancer 1970;26:1042–7.
15. Koss LG, Spiro RH, Brunschwig A. Endometrial stromal sarcoma. Surg Gynecol Obstet 1965;121:531–7.
16. Lillemoe I, Perrone T, Norris HJ, Dehner LP. Epithelial-like areas of endometrial stromal sarcomas. Hum Pathol 1991;115:215–9.
17. Massoni EA, Hajdu SI. Cytology of primary and metastatic uterine sarcomas. Acta Cytol 1984;28:93–100.
18. Norris HJ, Taylor HB. Mesenchymal tumors of the uterus. I. A clinical and pathological study of 53 endometrial stromal tumors. Cancer 1966;19:755–66.
19. Piver MS, Rutledge FN, Copeland L, Webster K, Blumenson L, Suh O. Uterine endolymphatic stromal myosis. Obstet Gynecol 1984;64:173–8.
20. Rose PG, Piver MS, Tsukada Y, Lau T. Patterns of metastasis of uterine sarcoma. An autopsy study. Cancer 1989;63:935–8.
21. Silverberg SG, Willson MA, Board J. Hemangiopericytoma of the uterus: an ultrastructural study. Am J Obstet Gynecol 1971;110:397–404.
22. Sutton GP, Stehman FB, Michael H, Young PC, Ehrlich CE. Estrogen and progesterone receptors in uterine sarcomas. Obstet Gynecol 1986;68:709–14.
23. Taina E, Maenpaa J, Erkkola R, Ikkala J, Söderström O, Viitanen A. Endometrial stromal sarcoma. Gynecol Oncol 1989;32:156–62.
24. Tang CK, Toker C, Ances IG. Stromomyoma of the uterus. Cancer 1979;43:308–16.
25. Tavassoli FA, Norris HJ. Mesenchymal tumours of the uterus. VII. A clinicopathological study of 60 endometrial stromal nodules. Histopathology 1981;5:1–10.
26. Thatcher SS, Woodruff JD. Uterine stromatosis: a report of 33 cases. Obstet Gynecol 1982;59:428–34.
27. Tosi P, Sforza V, Santopietro R. Estrogen receptor content, immunohistochemically determined by monoclonal antibodies, in endometrial stromal sarcoma. Obstet Gynecol 1989;73:75–8.
28. Walton LA, Siegfried JM, Nelson KG, Siegal G, Kaufman DG. Endometrial stromal cells in culture: an attempt to understand the genesis of biologic activity of uterine sarcomas. Gynecol Oncol 1986;24:247–57.
29. Wheelock JB, Krebs HB, Schneider V, Goplerud DR. Uterine sarcoma: analysis of prognostic variables in 71 cases. Am J Obstet Gynecol 1985;151:1016–22.
30. Wheelock MC, Strand CM. Endometrial sarcoma—relationship to certain instances of stromal endometriosis. Obstet Gynecol 1953;2:384–90.

❖❖❖

SMOOTH MUSCLE AND OTHER MESENCHYMAL TUMORS

LEIOMYOMA

Definition. Leiomyoma is a benign neoplasm composed of smooth muscle cells with variable amounts of fibrous stroma. This type of tumor is often referred to clinically as a fibroid.

General Features. Leiomyoma is not only the most common neoplasm of the uterus, it is also one of the most common tumors of women because it is estimated to occur in between 20 and 40 percent of women beyond the age of 30 years (11,55). The tumor is rare in women under the age of 18 and is found less frequently after menopause. Its distribution appears to be worldwide.

Leiomyomas may vary in size from incidental microscopic findings to huge tumors that produce clinical signs and symptoms (4). They are usually multiple but may be solitary.

Although the exact stimulus to the development of a uterine leiomyoma is unknown, it is generally accepted that the continued growth of these tumors is related to female sex hormones. Evidence for this hormonal influence includes 1) the rarity of leiomyomas before menarche and their usual regression after menopause; 2) occasional rapid growth and hemorrhagic degeneration of leiomyomas associated with pregnancy and clomiphene and progestin treatment; 3) regression of leiomyomas after treatment with gonadotropin-releasing hormone agonists; 4) increased mitotic activity in leiomyomas during the secretory phase of the menstrual cycle; 5) ultrastructural evidence of increased differentiation (myofilaments, dense bodies) in leiomyoma cells cultured with estrogen and progesterone added to the medium; and 6) the presence of estrogen and progesterone receptors in leiomyoma cells, with variation in their concentration during the menstrual cycle (13,21,22,30,33,47,48,51,55).

Clinical Features. Small leiomyomas are usually asymptomatic. Larger or multiple leiomyomas may be associated with pain, menorrhagia or metrorrhagia, dysmenorrhea, urinary disturbances, or constipation (4). Infertility is occasionally attributed to the presence of leiomyomas. In pregnant women, leiomyomas may be associated with abruptio placentae, intrapartum pain, and premature labor (42).

Uterine leiomyomas are usually diagnosed by manual pelvic examination, but their presence and position may be confirmed by radiologic and ultrasonographic techniques. Submucous leiomyomas (immediately beneath the endometrium) may occasionally be diagnosed by endometrial curettage. A submucous leiomyoma that becomes pedunculated and prolapses through the internal os into the cervix may also be seen in a cervical biopsy or endocervical curettage specimen.

Gross Findings. Most leiomyomas have a similar gross appearance, presenting as solitary or multiple, spherical, well-circumscribed tumors within the myometrium, with a firm, pearly white cut surface showing whorled intersecting fascicles (fig. 136, pl. IV-A). The tumors are generally described as being intramural if they are entirely surrounded by myometrium, submucous if they lie immediately under the endometrium, and subserous if they project onto the serosal surface of the uterus. As mentioned above, submucous tumors may also project as polyps into the endometrial cavity (fig. 136) or, when pedunculated, even into the cervix or vagina. Similarly, subserous tumors may extend into the broad ligament or elsewhere into the pelvic cavity, occasionally being attached to the uterine corpus by only a thin stalk. In some instances, this stalk may become severed, and the tumor may become secondarily adherent to other pelvic organs, giving the false impression that it arose from one of them rather than from the uterus (parasitic leiomyoma). However, primary peritoneal leiomyomas may also occur, so it should not be assumed that such tumors necessarily are of uterine origin.

Numerous variations of the firm, white, whorled type of tumor occur, most of which are considered to represent forms of degeneration (pl. IV-B) (23). These include 1) hemorrhage, manifested by central dark red softening; 2) hyalinization, appearing as smooth white depressed zones; 3) hydropic, myxoid, or mucinous degeneration, identifiable as soft mucoid areas, sometimes with cystic change; 4) true necrosis, with a creamy yellow appearance; and 5) calcification, which is usually seen in elderly women as dense rock-like masses that cannot be cut with a knife. Occasionally, a polypoid submucous

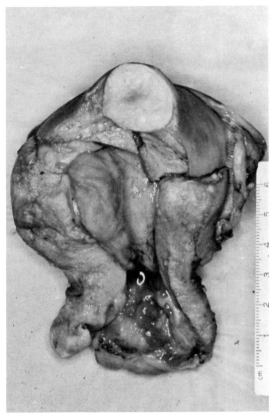

Figure 136
HYSTERECTOMY SPECIMEN CONTAINING
TWO LEIOMYOMAS
In this illustration, the tumor at the apex shows the typical well-demarcated, firm, white, whorled cut surface and is in subserosal location. Projecting into the endometrial cavity is a submucous leiomyoma that is soft and gray but nonetheless proved to be benign.

leiomyoma may undergo torsion and hemorrhagic infarction, with a dark red, unstructured, "beefsteak" gross appearance.

Several of these features, particularly hemorrhage, necrosis, and myxoid and mucinous degeneration, are important because they may also be seen in leiomyosarcoma and other malignant tumors. Any gross change of this sort in a uterine smooth muscle tumor should be examined microscopically in multiple sections.

Microscopic Findings. Typical leiomyoma constitutes almost all uterine smooth muscle tumors and is characterized by an admixture of bland smooth muscle cells, fibroblasts, and collagen (figs. 137–139). The smooth muscle cells are generally arranged in anastomosing whorled fascicles of uniform fusiform cells. The nuclei are elongated and cigar shaped, with relatively blunt ends (fig. 139). The nuclei vary little in size and shape, and mitotic figures are either absent or few and are never atypical. Nuclear chromatin is fine and evenly distributed, and nucleoli are not prominent. Blood vessels are irregularly distributed, usually thick walled, and usually not prominent.

Stains other than hematoxylin and eosin are generally not performed in cases of typical leiomyoma, but a trichrome stain usually demonstrates collagen fibers between smooth muscle cells and myofilaments within them. Reticulin stains demonstrate reticulum fibers around individual smooth muscle cells. Immunohistochemical staining reveals the usual presence of desmin and muscle-specific actin within the tumor cells. Cytokeratins and vimentin may also be present.

Ultrastructural examination reveals the usual markers (fig. 140) of smooth muscle cells: abundant 6- to 8-nm myofilaments arranged longitudinally parallel to the long axis of the cell, dense bodies associated with the filaments and the plasma membrane, pinocytotic vesicles associated with the plasma membrane, and incomplete basal lamina around individual cells. In minute (< 3 mm) leiomyomas, central immature cells characterized by more sporadically located filaments may be identified (27). Fibroblasts, collagen fibers, and blood vessels are seen in the interstitium.

Estrogen and progesterone receptors can be demonstrated within uterine leiomyomas (22, 47). All of the 33 typical leiomyomas studied by flow cytometry in one series were diploid (19).

Numerous variations from the typical appearance may be seen focally within an otherwise typical leiomyoma or occasionally as a diffuse change. One of the most common of these is hyalinization, which occurs initially in the stromal component separating the smooth muscle cells (figs. 141, 142). Eventually, this hyalinization may progress to the point where large portions of a tumor show no residual identifiable smooth muscle cells (fig. 143). The latter picture may sometimes represent a healed infarct.

The vascular component of uterine leiomyomas may be quite variable in its development; occasionally, blood vessel proliferation is so

PLATE IV

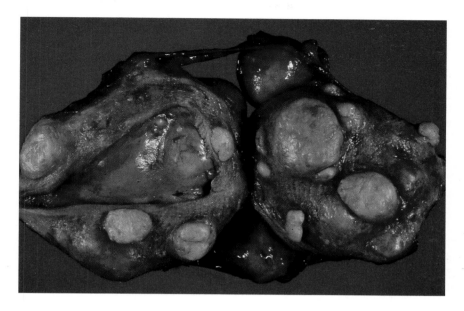

A

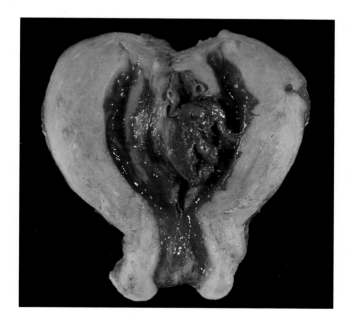

B

A. MULTIPLE LEIOMYOMAS OF THE UTERUS

The firm, white, whorled cut surfaces of the tumors and their tendency to pop up above the surrounding cut surface of the myometrium are well illustrated here.

B. NECROTIC SUBMUCOUS LEIOMYOMA OF THE UTERUS

The soft consistency and brown discoloration of this tumor raised the suspicion of malignancy. Multiple microscopic sections were examined, and the tumor proved to be a necrotic benign leiomyoma. (Courtesy of Dr. Lucien Nochomovitz, Washington, D.C.)

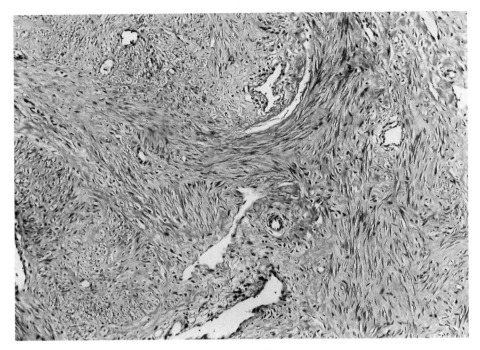

Figure 137
LEIOMYOMA
This typical leiomyoma consists of whorled fascicles of smooth muscle cells separated by a fibrovascular stroma.

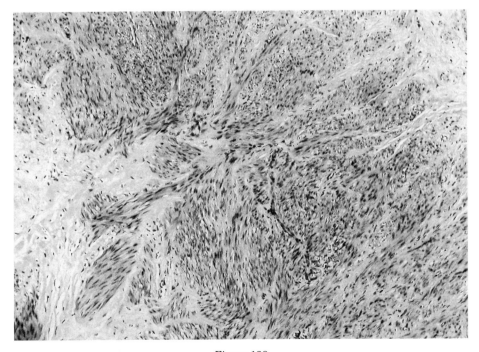

Figure 138
LEIOMYOMA
This tumor also shows intersecting bands of small, uniform smooth muscle cells that are separated by a fibrous stroma with focal hyalinization.

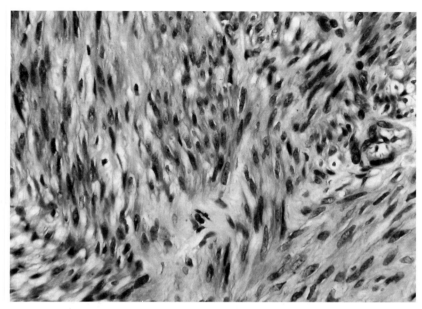

Figure 139
LEIOMYOMA
This high magnification of a leiomyoma shows small spindle cells with uniform nuclei that are spindled, have blunt ends, and are normochromatic, with generally inconspicuous nucleoli.

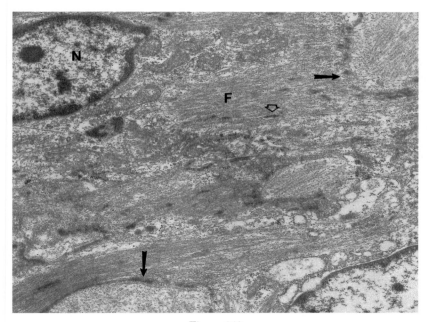

Figure 140
LEIOMYOMA
The typical features in this electron micrograph are neoplastic smooth muscle cells, which include 6- to 8-nm myofilaments (F) arranged parallel to the long axis of the cell, dense bodies associated with the filaments (open arrow) and the plasma membrane (vertical arrow), pinocytotic vesicles (horizontal arrow) associated with the plasma membrane, and incomplete basal lamina (vertical arrow) around individual cells. N, usual cigar-shaped nucleus. X8160. (Courtesy of Dr. Jan M. Orenstein, Washington, D.C.)

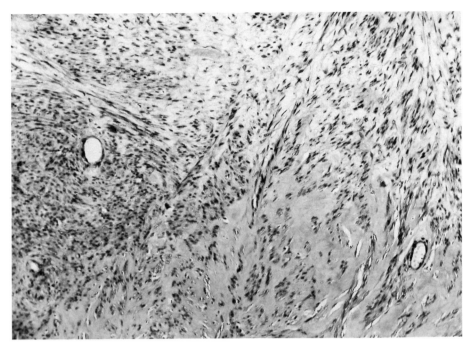

Figure 141
(Figures 141 and 142 are from the same patient)
LEIOMYOMA WITH HYALINIZATION
In this example, smooth muscle cells are entrapped and isolated within extensive fields of hyalinized stroma.

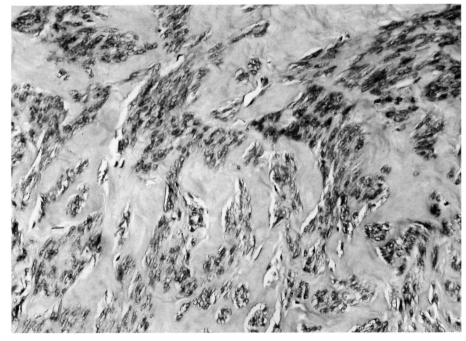

Figure 142
LEIOMYOMA WITH HYALINIZATION
A higher magnification of the same case seen in figure 141 shows the bland appearance of the smooth muscle cells and the extensive hyalinization.

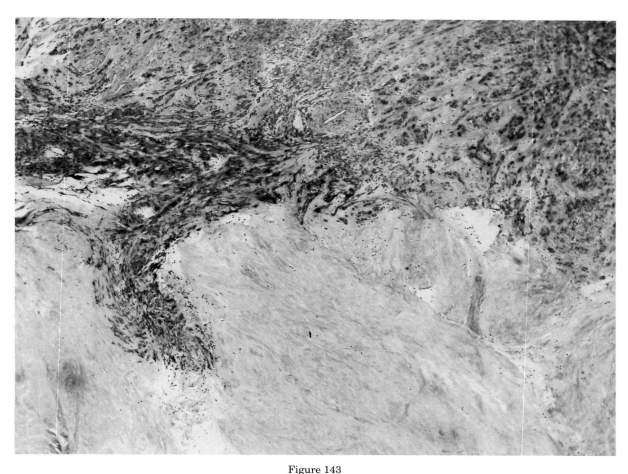

Figure 143
LEIOMYOMA WITH HYALINIZATION
In this case, the sharp demarcation of a large field of hyalinization from a more typical leiomyoma suggests a healed infarct.

prominent that the term *vascular leiomyoma* may be applied (fig. 144). A leiomyoma in which palisading of nuclei is a prominent feature is known as a *neurilemmoma-like leiomyoma* (fig. 145); if necessary, such tumors may be proven to be of smooth muscle rather than schwannian nature by ultrastructural or immunohistochemical study (15).

A tumor with extensive myxoid change may be diagnosed as *myxoid leiomyoma* (figs. 146, 147). Such a tumor may present two diagnostic challenges. First, the myxoid degeneration may be so extensive that it is difficult to identify the smooth muscle nature of the tumor; a trichrome, desmin, or actin stain may be help-

ful in this situation. Even more important is the difficulty in distinguishing myxoid leiomyoma from myxoid leiomyosarcoma (25,35). The latter tumor may have relatively little nuclear atypia and a low mitotic rate, so often the most important distinguishing feature is the markedly infiltrative border of a myxoid leiomyosarcoma compared with the well-circumscribed border of a myxoid leiomyoma.

Some leiomyomas may contain massive lymphoid infiltrates. These uncommon lesions are discussed in more detail in the chapter on Miscellaneous and Secondary Tumors.

The variants of uterine leiomyoma listed in the International Society of Gynecological

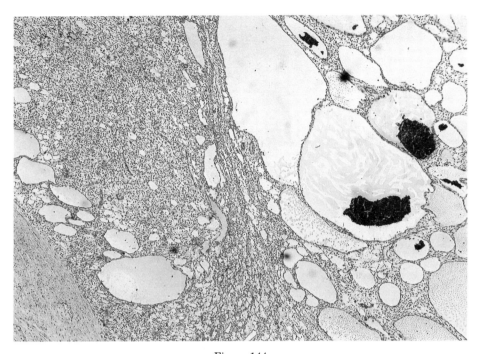

Figure 144
LEIOMYOMA WITH PROMINENT VASCULARITY
Parts of this tumor would be difficult to distinguish from hemangioma.

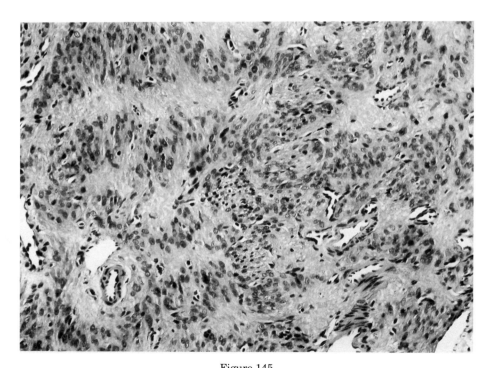

Figure 145
NEURILEMMOMA-LIKE LEIOMYOMA
This leiomyoma contains foci in which tumor cells line up in formations resembling the Verrocay bodies of neurilemmoma.

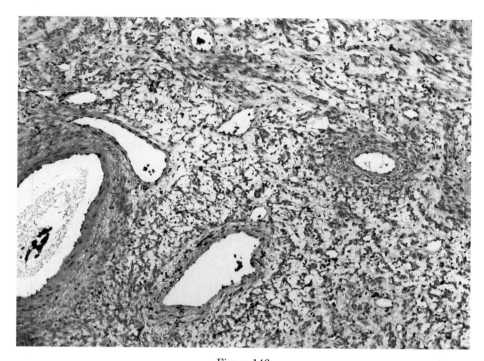

Figure 146
LEIOMYOMA WITH PROMINENT VASCULARITY AND MYXOID CHANGE
Smooth muscle cells are difficult to identify in this field but were numerous elsewhere in the tumor.

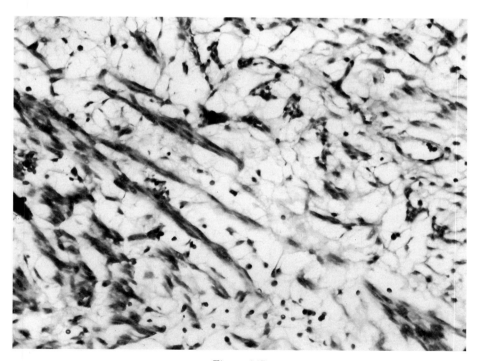

Figure 147
LEIOMYOMA WITH MYXOID DEGENERATION
Only very attenuated fascicles of smooth muscle cells can be identified in this example.

Pathologists classification are cellular, epithelioid, and bizarre leiomyomas and lipoleiomyoma.

Cellular Leiomyoma. This is a benign smooth muscle tumor that is significantly more cellular than the surrounding myometrium. The frequency with which this diagnosis is made by different pathologists is likely to be variable because most leiomyomas are more cellular than surrounding myometrium, and therefore the definition of "significantly" may vary considerably. Our own application of this term results in no more than 5 percent of all uterine leiomyomas being classified as cellular (figs. 148–150).

Cellular leiomyomas do not differ clinically or grossly from other leiomyomas, although they may be more fleshy and less whorled, but they are significant because hypercellularity is one of the characteristics of uterine leiomyosarcoma. Thus, in a cellular smooth muscle tumor, features such as increased mitotic activity, nuclear atypia, and atypical mitoses must be absent before a diagnosis of cellular leiomyoma is made. Some cellular smooth muscle tumors invariably fall into the category of smooth muscle tumor of uncertain malignant potential.

Another potential problem in the differential diagnosis of cellular leiomyoma is its distinction from a stromal nodule or low-grade endometrial stromal sarcoma (23,24). This distinction may be particularly difficult in fields in which most of the nuclei are cut in cross section and appear rounded (fig. 150). If the tumor lacks atypia and mitotic activity and its borders are well demarcated, the alternative diagnosis to cellular leiomyoma would be stromal nodule. Because both of these diagnoses are benign, it can be argued that the distinction may not be clinically significant. If, on the other hand, the margins are poorly defined or inapparent (as in a curettage specimen) or if vascular invasion is present, the distinction becomes extremely important because the differential diagnosis is then between a benign smooth muscle tumor (perhaps intravenous leiomyomatosis) and a low-grade endometrial stromal sarcoma. In this situation, trichrome stains and ultrastructural examination may be useful; immunohistochemistry generally is not because some endometrial stromal tumors may stain for desmin and muscle-specific actin. In some cases, a hysterectomy may be required to determine the correct diagnosis.

A specific type of cellular leiomyoma that may also cause diagnostic difficulty is the *hemorrhagic cellular leiomyoma*(fig. 151), also known as apoplectic leiomyoma (33). This tumor occurs almost exclusively in young women who are taking oral contraceptives or are pregnant and is characterized by discrete foci of hemorrhage and tearing artifact, with increased mitotic activity confined to a narrow zone adjacent to the hemorrhage, and with little or no nuclear atypia. The cellularity, hemorrhage, and mitotic activity may lead to confusion with leiomyosarcoma if the clinical history, the lack of atypia, and the focal distribution of the mitotic activity are not taken into account.

Epithelioid Leiomyoma. This is a benign smooth muscle tumor the cells of which resemble epithelial cells. This category is itself divided into the entities of *leiomyoblastoma* (6,28), *clear cell leiomyoma* (18,28), and *plexiform leiomyoma* (20). These are all rare tumors with no significant clinical differences from typical leiomyomas, except that plexiform leiomyoma is often an incidental microscopic finding. At the gross level, they tend to be softer than the usual leiomyoma and often are yellow rather than white. They are usually solitary and large, with the exception of the plexiform type, which tends to be only a few millimeters in diameter and may be multiple.

By definition, these tumors are all composed of round or polygonal cells, rather than the usual spindled cells seen in typical leiomyomas. It is not infrequent for a single tumor to contain both epithelioid and classic leiomyomatous foci, and the presence of the latter is often the best clue to the smooth muscle origin of these lesions.

In leiomyoblastoma, the tumor cells are round to polygonal, with granular eosinophilic cytoplasm and nuclei that are generally eccentrically situated (figs. 152, 153). Hyalinization is a frequent finding in these tumors and may result in an appearance even more suggestive of an epithelial neoplasm (fig. 154). In clear cell leiomyoma (fig. 155), the cells are also round or polygonal, but the most prominent feature is voluminous clear cytoplasm. The nuclei tend to be smaller and more uniform than those of the leiomyoblastoma type, which are often large

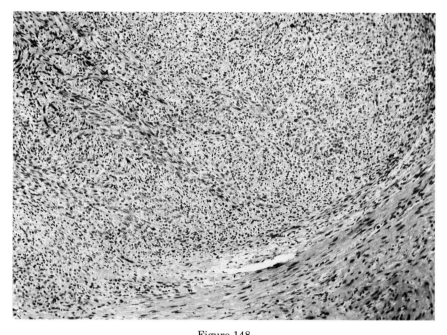

Figure 148
CELLULAR LEIOMYOMA
(Figures 148 and 149 are from the same patient)
This tumor is well demarcated from surrounding myometrium and is considerably
more cellular than the myometrial smooth muscle.

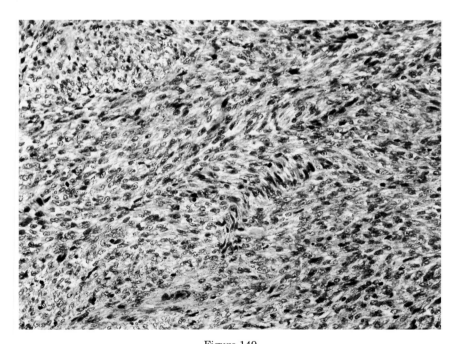

Figure 149
CELLULAR LEIOMYOMA
A higher magnification of the same tumor seen in figure 148 shows the lack of nuclear
atypia and mitotic activity.

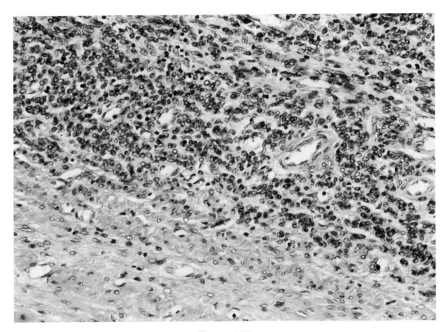

Figure 150
CELLULAR LEIOMYOMA
This tumor is considerably more cellular than the surrounding myometrial smooth muscle, but the cells are mostly cut in cross section, and it is difficult to distinguish the lesion from an endometrial stromal nodule. However, the usual vascular pattern of a stromal nodule is not present, and elsewhere the tumor showed typical smooth muscle differentiation.

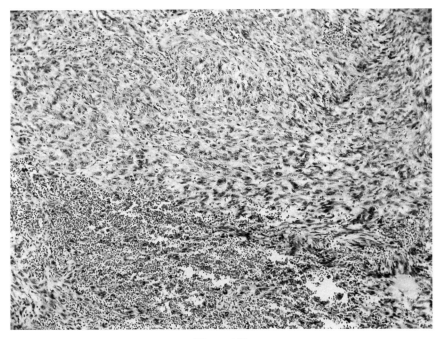

Figure 151
HEMORRHAGIC CELLULAR LEIOMYOMA (APOPLECTIC LEIOMYOMA)
Recent hemorrhage is seen in the lower third of the photograph. (Courtesy of Dr. Henry J. Norris, Washington, D.C.)

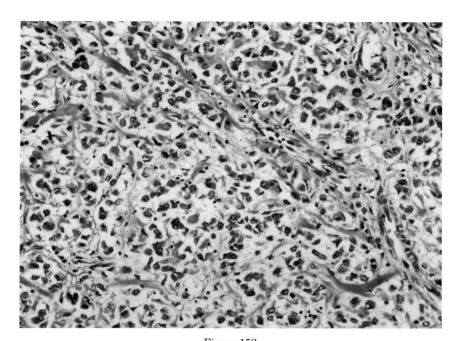

Figure 152
EPITHELIOID LEIOMYOMA (LEIOMYOBLASTOMA TYPE)
The tumor cells in this field are round to polygonal, poorly cohesive, and separated by only small amounts of collagenous stroma.

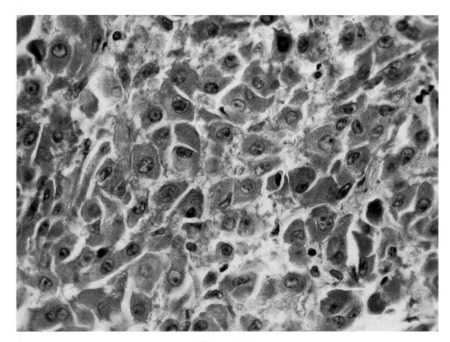

Figure 153
EPITHELIOID LEIOMYOMA (LEIOMYOBLASTOMA TYPE)
Cells that are round to polygonal with voluminous granular eosinophilic cytoplasm and moderately atypical, often eccentric nuclei are visible in this field. (Fig. 2 from Kurman RJ, Norris HJ. Mesenchymal tumors of the uterus. IV. Epithelioid smooth muscle tumors including leiomyoblastoma and clear cell leiomyoma: a clinical and pathologic analysis of 26 cases. Cancer 1976;37:1853–65.)

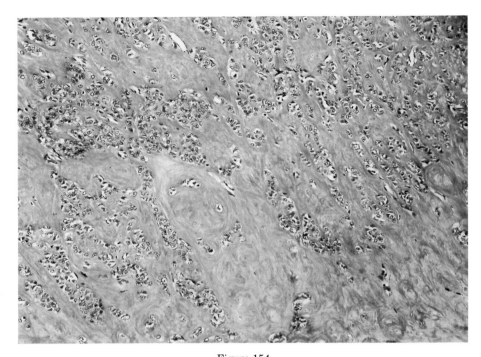

Figure 154
EPITHELIOID LEIOMYOMA (LEIOMYOBLASTOMA TYPE)
This example shows extensive hyalinization. In some areas, only isolated tumor cells are identified.

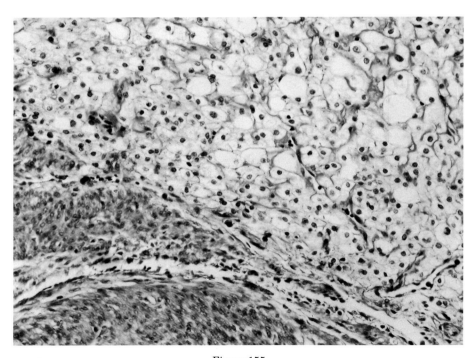

Figure 155
EPITHELIOID LEIOMYOMA (CLEAR CELL TYPE)
The tumor cells in this illustration contain central small nuclei surrounded by voluminous clear cytoplasm. A focus of more typical leiomyoma is seen within the tumor.

and atypical. In plexiform leiomyoma, the tumor cells are arranged in rows and columns separated by fibrous or hyalinized stroma and generally show scanty cytoplasm and indistinct cell borders (figs. 156, 157). These tumors are often incidental microscopic findings in the superficial myometrium near its junction with the endometrium and have been designated *plexiform tumorlets* in this situation (20).

Because of their epithelioid appearance, the differential diagnosis of these tumors includes both epithelial and endometrial stromal neoplasms. Metastatic carcinoma in the myometrium may be particularly difficult to rule out, and ultrastructural or immunohistochemical studies demonstrating smooth muscle differentiation may be necessary. The presence or absence of a known extrauterine primary carcinoma is obviously also pertinent to the differential diagnosis. The clear cell variant may also be difficult to distinguish at the routine microscopic level from clear cell adenocarcinoma of the endometrium and the plexiform type from a stromal nodule or a uterine tumor resembling ovarian sex cord tumor. In these instances, it is extremely helpful if part of the tumor shows typical leiomyomatous differentiation (fig. 155). Differentiation from a primary endometrial carcinoma is also facilitated by knowing that the tumor originates in the myometrium. The diagnosis of uterine tumor resembling ovarian sex cord tumor (see Miscellaneous and Secondary Tumors) should be made only if the entire tumor is composed of sex cord-like structures, and even focal smooth muscle differentiation should lead to the diagnosis of an epithelioid smooth muscle tumor.

One of the greatest problems in the field of epithelioid smooth muscle tumors is predicting their clinical behavior. Plexiform leiomyomas have never been reported to metastasize and thus may safely be considered benign. Most leiomyoblastomas and clear cell leiomyomas have also been clinically benign, but the number of cases reported is still small, follow-up has often been short, and the exact criteria for distinguishing benign from malignant tumors in this group are not yet defined. Thus, it may be safest to regard all tumors in these groups as smooth muscle tumors of uncertain malignant potential, with the exception of small, completely circumscribed and extensively

hyalinized tumors lacking mitotic activity, which are clearly benign, and large ones with numerous mitoses and infiltrating margins, which can be considered malignant (55). Remember, however, that these histologic patterns may be seen in intravenous leiomyomatosis and that this pattern of vascular invasion with otherwise circumscribed borders is still considered benign.

Bizarre Leiomyoma. This tumor is also known as symplastic, pleomorphic, or atypical leiomyoma and is a benign smooth muscle tumor characterized by the presence of pleomorphic tumor giant cells (figs. 158, 159). These tumors usually resemble typical leiomyomas in gross appearance and generally are well circumscribed. The tumors are often hyalinized but may be normocellular or even hypercellular. The symplastic changes are usually focal and may occur in scattered individual cells or groups of cells (fig. 158) within an otherwise typical leiomyoma.

The symplastic giant cells may be mononuclear or multinucleate (fig. 159) and are often characterized by huge, angular nuclei with very dark, generally smudged chromatin. Intranuclear invaginations of cytoplasm are common. Cytoplasm is usually abundant, eosinophilic, and granular. Mitoses are often entirely absent but by definition cannot be numerous, and abnormal mitotic figures are not seen.

The main differential diagnostic problem with bizarre leiomyoma is the distinction from leiomyosarcoma. Hypercellularity, frequent or abnormal mitotic figures, tumor cell necrosis, and myometrial or vascular invasion are all features of leiomyosarcoma. Similar findings may also be encountered in other rarer soft tissue sarcomas, such as malignant fibrous histiocytoma.

Lipoleiomyoma. This tumor resembles the ordinary leiomyoma but contains benign adipocytes. These tumors are rare and occur primarily in postmenopausal women (43). For this reason, it has been suggested by some authors that this tumor represents a degenerative phenomenon in a preexisting leiomyoma; however, in some cases, simultaneous adipose and smooth muscle differentiation appear to take place. Other leiomyomas and adenomyosis often accompany these tumors (43). Microscopic examination shows benign adipocytes intermingled

127

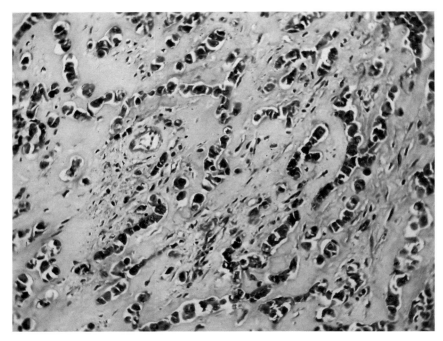

Figure 156
EPITHELIOID LEIOMYOMA (PLEXIFORM TYPE)
This tumor has a hyalinized stroma, with tumor cells growing in slender anastomosing cords. (Fig. 9 from Kurman RJ, Norris HJ. Mesenchymal tumors of the uterus. IV. Epithelioid smooth muscle tumors including leiomyoblastoma and clear cell leiomyoma: a clinical and pathologic analysis of 26 cases. Cancer 1976;37:1853–65.)

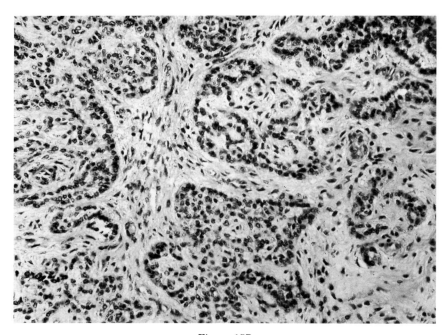

Figure 157
EPITHELIOID LEIOMYOMA (PLEXIFORM TYPE)
This tumor resembles an ovarian sex cord-like tumor. However, between the plexiform structures and elsewhere in the tumor are more typical smooth muscle cells.

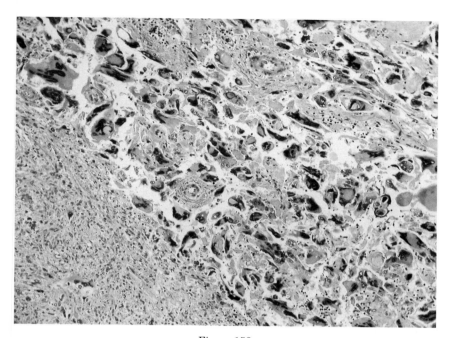

Figure 158
(Figures 158 and 159 are from the same patient)
BIZARRE LEIOMYOMA
Typical leiomyoma is seen at the lower left of this photomicrograph, but most of the
field is occupied by large, bizarre symplastic cells.

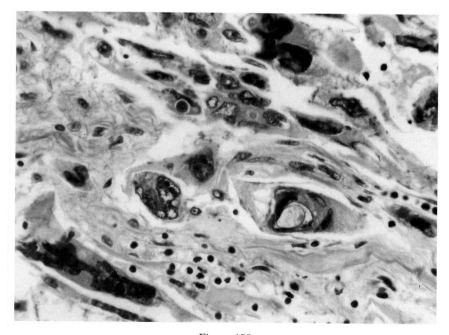

Figure 159
BIZARRE LEIOMYOMA
Higher magnification of the tumor illustrated in figure 158 shows mononuclear and
multinucleate giant cells with bizarre nuclei, some with cytoplasmic invaginations and
others with hyperchromatic smudged chromatin.

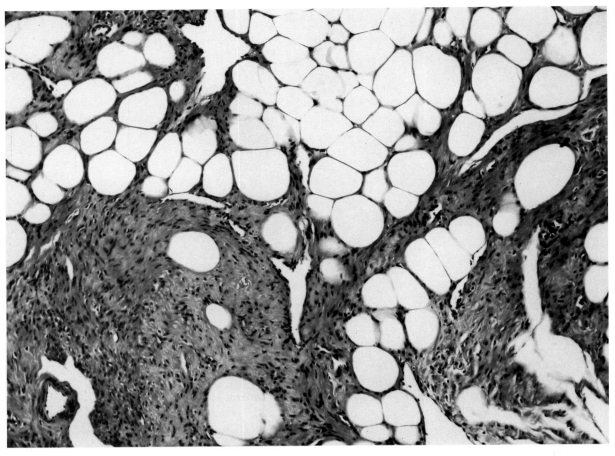

Figure 160
LIPOLEIOMYOMA
This field contains approximately equal amounts of benign adipose tissue and smooth muscle.

with typical leiomyomatous tissue in various proportions (fig. 160). These tumors have a benign evolution.

LEIOMYOSARCOMA

Definition. Leiomyosarcoma is a malignant tumor showing smooth muscle differentiation.

Leiomyosarcomas are rare tumors, representing only about 25 percent of all uterine sarcomas and mixed malignant tumors and slightly over 1 percent of all corporeal malignant tumors (55). They usually arise in postmenopausal women and are not known to be related to the known risk factors for endometrial carcinoma (nulliparity, obesity, diabetes mellitus, hypertension, etc.) or carcinosarcoma

(prior radiation therapy). They may occur in uteri that also bear typical benign leiomyomas, but leiomyosarcomas rarely can be proven to have arisen in or from benign leiomyomas.

The signs and symptoms of leiomyosarcoma are similar to those of leiomyoma, with the exception that the patients are usually older. Rapid increase in the size of a uterine tumor after menopause may arouse suspicion. Evidence of extrauterine extension or distant metastases may be the presenting feature in occasional cases. Although the diagnosis is sometimes made by endometrial curettage or rarely by a cytologic sampling of the lower genital tract, the diagnosis most commonly is established for the first time after hysterectomy.

Gross Findings. Although an occasional leiomyosarcoma may closely resemble a benign leiomyoma macroscopically, the usual gross appearance is quite different (fig. 161). Unlike leiomyomas, which are usually multiple, leiomyosarcomas are more often solitary and usually present as a large, poorly circumscribed mass with a soft, fleshy consistency and a variegated cut surface that is gray-yellow to pink, with foci of hemorrhage and necrosis. Benign leiomyomas may be seen in the same uterus, and their appearance is usually in sharp contrast to that of leiomyosarcomas (fig. 161). In advanced cases, leiomyosarcomas may show gross evidence of extension beyond the uterine corpus. Gross evidence of vascular invasion is much less common than in either intravenous leiomyomatosis or endometrial stromal sarcoma.

Occasional benign leiomyomas may also demonstrate many of the gross features typical of leiomyosarcoma. Indeed, not only is the ratio of leiomyomas to leiomyosarcomas in ordinary practice astronomical (29), but even among uterine tumors with a suspicious gross appearance, more benign leiomyomas than leiomyosarcomas will be seen. Nevertheless, either a suspicious gross appearance or an unusual clinical presentation (e.g., rapid growth of a myometrial tumor in a postmenopausal woman) should prompt the submission of multiple blocks of tissue (at least 1 per 1–2 cm of maximal tumor diameter) for microscopic examination (24,49).

Microscopic Findings. The typical leiomyosarcoma (12,23,55) is a highly cellular tumor composed predominantly of intersecting fascicles of large spindled cells with markedly atypical nuclei, numerous mitotic figures, and frequent atypical mitotic figures (figs. 162–166). The nuclei tend to have blunt or rounded ends, coarsely clumped chromatin, and solitary or multiple prominent nucleoli; multinucleate giant cells are frequently seen (fig. 166). Giant cells resembling osteoclasts, which appear to be derived from macrophages, are occasionally present and may be prominent (31). Small amounts of collagenous stroma are usually seen between tumor cells, and foci of hemorrhage and necrosis may be prominent. The margins of the tumor usually show at least focal infiltration of the surrounding myometrium, and massive invasion of both myometrium and blood vessels may be present.

Rarely, microscopic examination provides a suggestion of the origin of the leiomyosarcoma in a benign leiomyoma (fig. 167).

Most leiomyosarcomas show the combination of hypercellularity, atypia, and numerous mitotic figures (usually over 20 per 10 HPF), but occasional diagnostic problems arise in the case of tumors that are less cellular, less atypical, or less mitotically active (12,23,24,44,45,55). Most authors believe that mitotic activity is the single most reliable indicator of malignancy in these tumors, but opinions vary concerning the exact level of mitotic activity required and the manner in which mitotic counting is to be performed; it has also been shown that mitosis counts are often not reproducible among different observers (45). Thus, if mitoses are to be counted, we strongly recommend that this be done uniformly and point to the caveats quoted by Kempson and Hendrickson (23,24): 1) the specimen must be promptly and well fixed; 2) sections must be thin and well stained; 3) only indisputable mitotic figures should be accepted, with care taken to eliminate lymphocytes, mast cells, naked nuclei, degenerated cells, and precipitated stain; 4) counting should begin in an area of highest mitotic activity and should be performed at a total magnification of X400; 5) four sets of 10 consecutive fields should be counted and the highest count chosen.

Given these caveats, Kempson and Hendrickson recommend that a mitotic count of greater than 10 mitotic figures per 10 HPF for cellular neoplasms, and over 5 mitotic figures per 10 HPF for tumors demonstrating anaplasia, pleomorphism, giant cells, or epithelioid patterns be considered diagnostic of leiomyosarcoma. They note, and we agree, that lower mitotic counts do not necessarily guarantee benignity. Conversely, it should also be noted that cytologically bland tumors with more than 5 mitotic figures per 10 HPF occasionally seen in young women generally have a benign evolution (fig. 168) (34,37). In contrast to leiomyosarcomas, these *mitotically active leiomyomas* are typically small, well circumscribed, and lack significant nuclear pleomorphism and necrosis.

In general, the histochemical, immunohistochemical, and ultrastructural findings discussed for leiomyoma are also noted in leiomyosarcoma. However, the more poorly differentiated the sarcoma, the less likely it is to

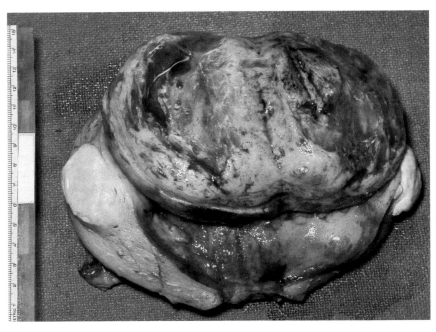

Figure 161
LEIOMYOSARCOMA
The large bisected tumor has a "fish-flesh" appearance with foci of hemorrhage and cystic degeneration. This appearance is in marked contrast to that of the adjacent typical leiomyoma.

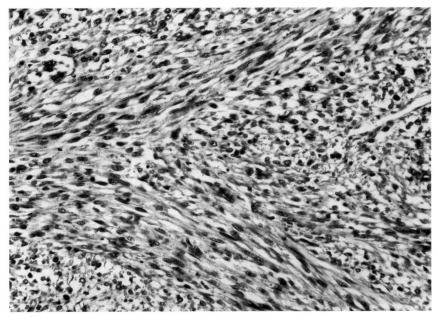

Figure 162
(Figures 162 and 163 are from the same patient)
LEIOMYOSARCOMA
This very cellular tumor displays intersecting fascicles of large atypical cells. Frequent mitotic figures were also seen.

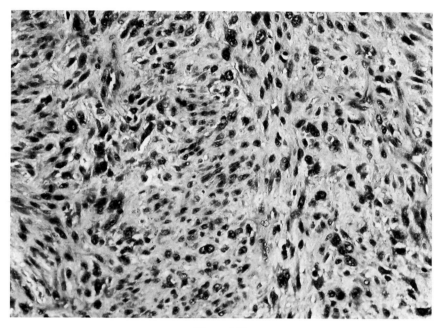

Figure 163
LEIOMYOSARCOMA
This is another field from the same tumor illustrated in figure 162. The tumor cells here are more rounded and are separated by more collagenous stroma but are still large and atypical.

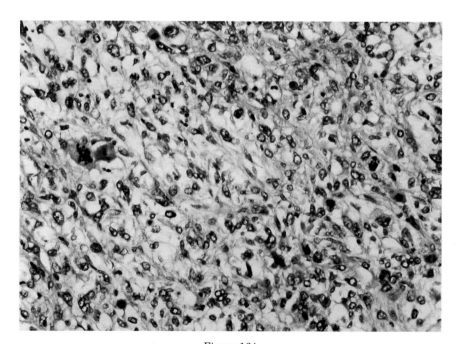

Figure 164
LEIOMYOSARCOMA
This field shows hypercellularity, cytologic atypia, and numerous mitotic figures, including a large atypical mitosis.

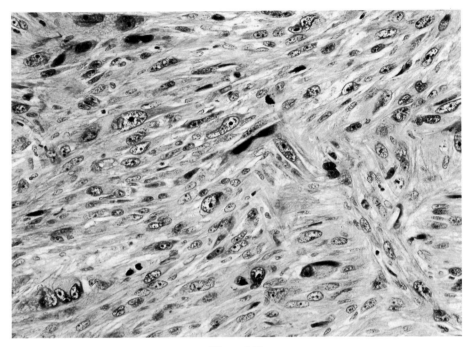

Figure 165
LEIOMYOSARCOMA
Note the nuclear atypia, pleomorphism, anisonucleosis, and prominent nucleoli in this example.

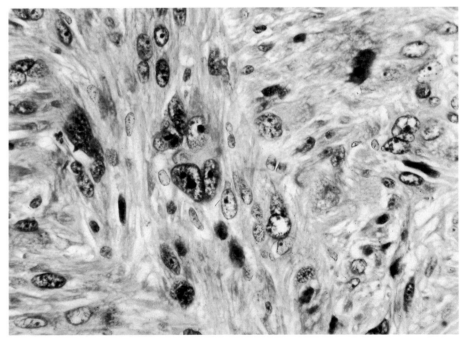

Figure 166
LEIOMYOSARCOMA
This high-power photomicrograph demonstrates the nuclear atypia and scattered multi-nucleate forms typical of this tumor.

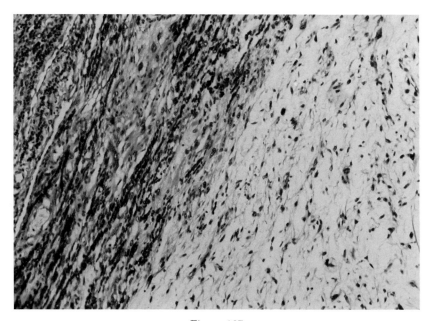

Figure 167
LEIOMYOSARCOMA POSSIBLY ARISING IN A CELLULAR LEIOMYOMA
The myxoid portion of this tumor contained bizarre cells and frequent mitotic figures, whereas the more cellular portion had little atypia and a lower mitotic count. This could be interpreted as variable differentiation within a leiomyosarcoma or as leiomyosarcoma focally involving (and presumably arising from) a leiomyoma.

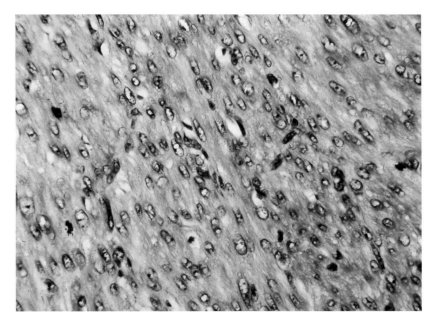

Figure 168
MITOTICALLY ACTIVE BENIGN LEIOMYOMA
This tumor occurred in a 30-year-old woman and resembled an ordinary leiomyoma at gross and low-power microscopic examination. Closer inspection revealed numerous mitotic figures (about 14 per 10 HPF in the most active region), none of which were atypical. The patient is alive and well 6 years after hysterectomy.

demonstrate these typical findings and therefore the less likely they are to be useful in differential diagnosis. Leiomyosarcomas can be either diploid or aneuploid, and therefore are also not very helpful in doubtful cases (19).

Microscopic Types. Although any of the morphologic variations mentioned above in leiomyoma may be encountered in leiomyosarcoma, the two variants specifically included in the International Society of Gynecological Pathologists classification are the epithelioid and myxoid types. These are included as separate variants primarily because they may be particularly difficult to distinguish from benign leiomyomas of similar type. In *epithelioid leiomyosarcoma* (fig. 169) the cells are round or polygonal rather than spindled and usually have voluminous eosinophilic or clear cytoplasm. Because most epithelioid leiomyomas show hypercellularity and nuclear atypia, excess mitotic activity as defined above and in Table 5 may be the only way to distinguish benign from malignant epithelioid smooth muscle neoplasms, particularly if obvious invasion is not demonstrable. However, the natural history of so few of these neoplasms is known (24,28) that it is probably preferable to regard any suspicious epithelioid smooth muscle neoplasm as having uncertain malignant potential.

Myxoid leiomyosarcoma (figs. 170, 171) (25,35) is classified separately because its myxoid appearance may obscure its smooth muscle nature and because its paucity of mitotic figures and typical lack of nuclear pleomorphism may lead to its being misdiagnosed as a benign myxoid leiomyoma. It should be emphasized that this paucity is more apparent than real because the mitotic activity per unit number of cells is probably similar to that of most other leiomyosarcomas; however, because so much of each high-power field is composed of intercellular myxoid substance rather than cells, the mitotic rate per 10 HPF is usually between 0 and 2. In these tumors, it is important to search for non-myxoid areas, which are generally more atypical, more mitotically active, and more obviously of smooth muscle nature. In contrast to myxoid leiomyomas, myxoid leio myosarcomas extensively infiltrate the myometrium and, in some cases, myometrial `vessels. Ultrastructural study has shown typical smooth muscle differentiation (25). Despite their relatively benign appearance, these tumors behave in a highly malignant manner.

Differential Diagnosis. As mentioned earlier, the main differential diagnosis of leiomyosarcoma is with benign leiomyoma, and that of the epithelioid and myxoid variants is with the corresponding benign leiomyoma variants. Despite the controversy concerning the exact criteria that should be applied in these differential diagnoses, particularly with reference to mitotic counts, I emphasize that in the vast majority of both leiomyomas and leiomyosarcomas the diagnosis is immediately apparent. I believe that, even in the most difficult cases, the correct diagnosis can be made by applying some principles of common sense. For example, at least two members of the triad of hypercellularity, cytologic atypia, and increased mitotic activity should be present for a diagnosis of leiomyosarcoma and preferably all three. Tumors with only hypercellularity are best diagnosed as cellular leiomyomas, those with only atypia are bizarre leiomyomas. Those with only increased (but not atypical) mitotic figures are best classified as mitotically active benign leiomyomas when they occur in young women (below the age of 35 years) and as smooth muscle tumors of uncertain malignant potential when they occur in older women. Epithelioid smooth muscle tumors are almost certainly benign if they are of the plexiform type, probably benign if they are of clear cell type, and most suspicious if they are of leiomyoblastoma type. In the last type, mitotic activity, tumor size, and the pushing or invasive nature of the tumor margins are important considerations. In all problematic smooth muscle tumors, the age of the patient and other clinical data are important considerations. I am always hesitant to diagnose leiomyosarcoma in any woman who is under the age of 30 years, pregnant, or taking oral contraceptives or to call unequivocally benign any cellular or atypical smooth muscle tumor in an elderly woman. Exceptions at both extremes of age exist, but they are rare enough that the prudent pathologist should never rely on them when rendering an otherwise tenuous diagnosis.

If mitotic counts are to be used as an important part of the diagnosis, they should be performed diligently, as discussed earlier. The actual count should be specified in the pathology

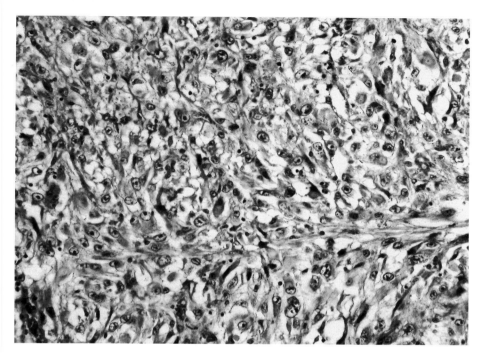

Figure 169
LEIOMYOSARCOMA (EPITHELIOID TYPE)
The tumor cells in this illustration resemble those of epithelioid leiomyoma (cf. fig. 152) but show somewhat more nuclear atypia in this field. Mitotic figures were also present, the tumor infiltrated the myometrium, and metastases were present at the time of laparotomy.

Table 5

SMOOTH MUSCLE TUMORS OF UNCERTAIN MALIGNANT POTENTIAL*

Usual histologic appearance with
- Cytologic atypia and 2 to 5 mitotic figures per 10 HPF [†]
- Hypercellularity, no atypia, and 5 to 10 mitotic figures per 10 HPF
- 10–15 mitotic figures per 10 HPF, without hypercellularity or atypia
- Infiltrating margins and 5 to 9 mitotic figures per 10 HPF
- Any abnormal mitotic figures or necrosis

Epithelioid pattern with 2 to 5 mitotic figures per 10 HPF

Bizarre (symplastic) pattern with 2 to 5 mitotic figures per 10 HPF

Vascular invasion within the tumor and 2 to 5 mitotic figures per 10 HPF

Intravenous leiomyomatosis (vascular invasion outside the tumor) with 2 to 5 mitotic figures per 10 HPF

Parasitic leiomyoma (detached from uterus, attached elsewhere) with 5 to 9 mitotic figures per 10 HPF

* Modified from Kempson and Hendrickson (23).

[†] HPF = high-power fields

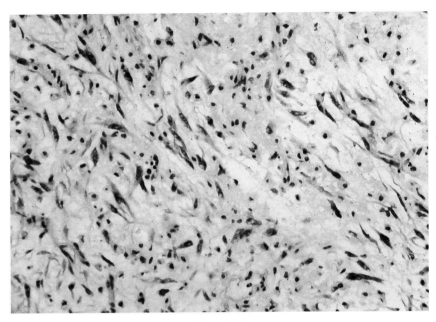

Figure 170
(Figures 170 and 171 are from the same patient)
MYXOID LEIOMYOSARCOMA
This tumor shows the same massive myxoid stroma as the myxoid leiomyoma illustrated in figure 147, but in this case the tumor margins were infiltrative and cytologic atypia more pronounced. However, mitotic figures are difficult to find.

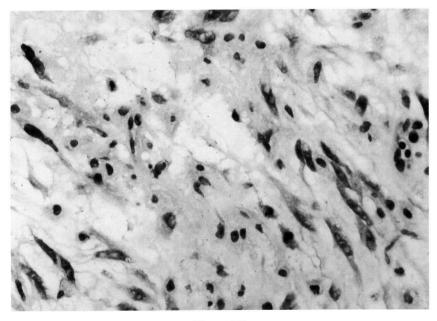

Figure 171
MYXOID LEIOMYOSARCOMA
Note the moderate degree of nuclear atypia and voluminous myxoid stroma in this higher magnification of the tumor illustrated in figure 170. Many of these tumors have little or no atypia but extensively infiltrate the myometrium.

report if it is relied on heavily, and a second observer should probably be used to confirm the count, a good general rule for any difficult diagnosis in surgical pathology. Further comments on mitotic counts appear in the section on Smooth Muscle Tumors of Uncertain Malignant Potential. Unfortunately, ploidy determinations have not been found to be useful in distinguishing atypical leiomyomas from leiomyosarcomas (19,52).

Leiomyosarcoma is also easily confused with intravenous leiomyomatosis, particularly when the latter tumor is of epithelioid, bizarre, cellular, or myxoid type. Further discussion on this differential diagnosis appears in the section on Intravenous Leiomyomatosis.

Finally, a less frequent but occasionally vexing differential diagnostic problem concerns the distinction of leiomyosarcoma from other types of malignant tumors. High-grade endometrial stromal sarcoma, undifferentiated sarcoma, and poorly differentiated or undifferentiated endometrial carcinoma are the most common considerations, but various metastases to the uterus as well as rare primary sarcomas such as malignant fibrous histiocytoma and rhabdomyosarcoma may also occasionally be considered. Location of the tumor entirely within the myometrium is often the best way to rule out an endometrial carcinoma or endometrial stromal sarcoma, but often the tumor is so large that its exact site of origin may not be clear. Growth of the tumor in intersecting fascicles of spindled cells with blunt-ended nuclei and the lack of a uniformly distributed vascular network are useful features of most leiomyosarcomas, as are the usual presence of symplastic and multinucleate giant cells. The presence of any glandular or squamous features indicates either a metaplastic carcinoma or a carcinosarcoma. If the location of the tumor and its routine light-microscopic features are not adequate to confirm the diagnosis, a trichrome stain demonstrating intracytoplasmic myofibrils, immunoreactivity for desmin or smooth muscle actin, or ultrastructural evidence of smooth muscle differentiation may be helpful. However, it should be remembered that the less differentiated the tumor, the less likely it is to show the characteristic features and that desmin and actin may also be present in some carcinomas and stromal sarcomas. Finally, it should be emphasized that

the differential diagnosis can sometimes be facilitated by the submission and examination of additional tissue blocks, which may disclose better differentiated areas of the tumor where the correct diagnosis is more obvious.

Spread and Metastases. Because most large surgical staging and autopsy studies of uterine nonepithelial tumors have included stromal sarcomas and carcinosarcomas as well as leiomyosarcomas, the evolution of these tumors is poorly understood. However, it is generally accepted that leiomyosarcomas frequently have spread beyond the confines of the uterine corpus at the time of initial diagnosis, usually by direct spread into the pelvic cavity. Lymph nodal metastases are uncommon, but distant metastases to the lungs and, less commonly, the bones and liver occur late in the course of the disease (12). As with endometrial carcinoma, spread to the cervix and vagina is frequently seen.

Treatment. The treatment of uterine leiomyosarcoma is predominantly surgical and usually consists of total abdominal hysterectomy with bilateral salpingo-oophorectomy. Radiotherapy and single-agent chemotherapy have generally not significantly influenced the natural history of the disease. Multiple-agent chemotherapy including doxorubicin produces some responses but probably no cures (2).

Prognosis. Because the diagnostic criteria for leiomyosarcoma have varied in different reported series, the survival rates have also varied considerably. Five-year survival rates probably range between 40 and 50 percent for stage I and II tumors, with the staging system used being similar to that for endometrial carcinoma. Features associated with an unfavorable prognosis have varied in different published series but usually include very high mitotic rates, marked anaplasia, vascular invasion, large tumor size, spread beyond the uterus, and elderly or postmenopausal status of the patient.

SMOOTH MUSCLE TUMOR OF UNCERTAIN MALIGNANT POTENTIAL

Definition. The smooth muscle tumor of uncertain malignant potential is a smooth muscle tumor that cannot be diagnosed reliably as benign or malignant on the basis of generally applied criteria.

The degree of experience that a pathologist has with benign and malignant smooth muscle tumors will determine how frequently he or she uses this intermediate diagnostic category. If this diagnosis is made, the reason should be specified (e.g., many mitoses but no atypia, marked atypia and cellularity but few mitoses, etc.).

Table 5 presents the criteria of Kempson and Hendrickson (23) for the diagnosis of uterine smooth tumors of uncertain malignant potential when mitosis counting is deemed necessary. It is questionable whether the 5 to 10 mitotic figures per 10 HPF quoted in some sections is really meant to be different from the 5 to 9 quoted in others. It is also questionable why parasitic leiomyomas should be judged by criteria different from those applied to intrauterine leiomyomas without hypercellularity or atypia and whether necrosis should automatically place a tumor in the uncertain malignant potential category (particularly when it is seen in young women who are pregnant or taking oral contraceptives). Finally, recent studies have indicated that mitotically active (5–10 mitotic figures per 10 HPF) but cytologically bland smooth muscle tumors in young women may be considered benign (34,37). It is understood that, according to the classification in Table 5, tumors with lower mitotic counts than those specified are considered benign and those with higher mitotic counts are classified as leiomyosarcomas.

OTHER SMOOTH MUSCLE TUMORS

These lesions all represent variations in patterns of growth of otherwise morphologically unremarkable leiomyomas. However, on rare occasions, these lesions may demonstrate one of the morphologic variants (cellular, bizarre, epithelioid, myxoid, etc.) described above. These conditions are rare, and their natural history is still in the process of being defined.

Metastasizing Leiomyoma

Definition. The rare metastasizing leiomyoma is a benign-appearing smooth muscle tumor of the uterus that, usually after many years, appears to metastasize to extrauterine tissues.

Because by definition the uterine smooth muscle tumor must appear benign, it is apparent that this diagnosis can be made only in retrospect (after metastasis has occurred), and in such cases it is often found that the uterus and its leiomyomas have been sampled in only a cursory manner. Thus, most of the cases reported in the literature probably are not adequately documented by careful sampling of both the uterus and metastases to rule out the possibility of a low-grade leiomyosarcoma (55). On the other hand, there is also evidence to indicate that some reported examples may represent the multifocal origin of benign smooth muscle tumors rather than metastases from a benign tumor (7). However, the fact that these lesions almost always occur after an operative procedure (hysterectomy or myomectomy) in which manipulation of the uterine tumor has taken place, combined with hormone receptor positivity in the extrauterine lesions in some cases and their almost exclusive occurrence in females, gives credence to the concept of a benign metastatic process. Thus, this entity still appears in the current classification of uterine tumors, but it is open to careful scrutiny in the future.

Metastases. The reported metastases in most cases have been pulmonary, where they also raise the question of primary pulmonary tumors (54). Other sites have included pelvic soft tissues and lymph nodes, mesentery, mediastinum, and extrapelvic soft tissues. These secondary lesions usually occur many years after hysterectomy or myomectomy and are generally compatible with many additional years of life.

Intravenous Leiomyomatosis

Definition. Intravenous leiomyomatosis is a benign uterine smooth muscle proliferation extensively involving myometrial veins.

Although this is by definition a benign lesion, the intravenous tumor may extend outside the uterus within venous channels and may cause significant morbidity and even mortality.

Gross Findings. This condition, like the others in this group of other smooth muscle tumors, is rare and is usually not diagnosed clinically. On gross examination, convoluted worm-like masses of firm to soft tissue are seen within the veins of the uterus, often extending into the broad ligament or other pelvic veins. It is not uncommon for extension into the inferior vena cava or even the right side of the heart to occur.

Microscopic Findings. Tumor may be found exclusively within venous lumina (fig. 172), in lumina with continuity with the surrounding venous wall (fig. 173), or confined to the muscularis of venous walls (fig. 174). In the latter two situations, it is postulated that the tumor originates in venous muscle, whereas in other cases it appears that an ordinary leiomyoma of the myometrium extends secondarily into uterine veins (55). In the former situation, the tumor is predominantly or entirely intravascular.

The cellular composition of the intravascular growth in this condition is varied. In some cases, the intravascular tissue resembles the usual uterine leiomyoma, but in most cases it has a clefted or lobulated contour and is extensively hyalinized, hydropic, or both (figs. 172, 173). Blood vessels may also be prominent and, when accompanied by atrophy of the smooth muscle cells, may be the exclusive component (angiomatoid pattern). In other cases, the intravascular growth pattern may be manifested by tumors showing any of the histologic variations of leiomyoma: bizarre (figs. 175, 176), cellular, epithelioid, myxoid, lipoleiomyoma, etc. (3,8, 10,32). In these instances, the differential diagnosis from leiomyosarcoma with extensive vascular invasion may be extremely difficult. If mitotic activity is absent or minimal and if the tumor is either exclusively intravascular or shows vascular invasion but no other evidence of myometrial invasion (especially if the vascular invasion is apparent on gross inspection), a benign diagnosis is justified.

It should also be noted that vascular invasion within a leiomyoma does not warrant the diagnosis of intravenous leiomyomatosis if such invasion does not extend beyond the confines of the leiomyoma and is a microscopic finding only. This phenomenon, unlike true intravenous leiomyomatosis, which by definition is always seen outside the confines of a leiomyoma, has not been shown to be associated with extension of tumor outside the uterus or other evidence of aggressive behavior (23,55).

Diffuse Leiomyomatosis

Diffuse leiomyomatosis is a rare condition defined by the presence of myriads of small leiomyomas replacing much of the uterine parenchyma. Only about a dozen cases of this very rare entity have been reported (9). The patients are in the usual age range for leiomyoma and undergo hysterectomy with that diagnosis. The uterus is usually massively enlarged and the myometrium is almost completely replaced by innumerable confluent nodules, which microscopically are composed of benign cellular smooth muscle (figs. 177, 178). To make this diagnosis, intravenous growth, atypia, and mitotic activity should be minimal, ruling out intravenous leiomyomatosis, low-grade endometrial stromal sarcoma, and leiomyosarcoma.

MIXED ENDOMETRIAL STROMAL AND SMOOTH MUSCLE TUMORS

Definition. These lesions are tumors that show both endometrial stromal and smooth muscle differentiation by light microscopy.

Mixed endometrial stromal and smooth muscle tumors may be benign (fig. 179), sarcomatous, or of uncertain malignant potential. The diagnosis of a mixed type of tumor should be made on the basis of conventional light microscopy because not all apparent stromal and smooth muscle tumors will be studied ultrastructurally. Additionally, some ultrastructural features of paradoxical differentiation may be present very focally in tumors that are classic pure leiomyomas or stromal tumors by light microscopy. Similarly, because a significant proportion of otherwise typical endometrial stromal tumors can be stained immunohistochemically with antibodies to desmin or smooth muscle actin, immunohistochemical findings alone should not change the diagnosis of an endometrial stromal tumor unless smooth muscle differentiation is also apparent with routine histologic stains (see Endometrial Stromal Tumors for further discussion).

The classification of these mixed tumors as benign, malignant, or of uncertain malignant potential should be made on the basis of the most malignant element present. Usually, both elements are of a comparable degree of histologic

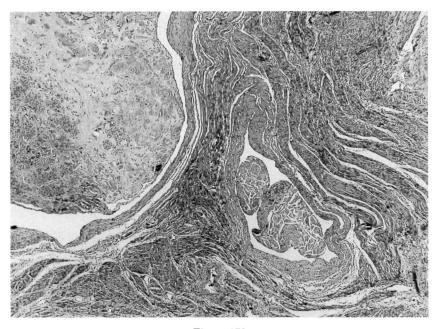

Figure 172
INTRAVENOUS LEIOMYOMATOSIS
In this figure, two myometrial veins are filled with intraluminal leiomyomatous tissue, most of which is hyalinized.

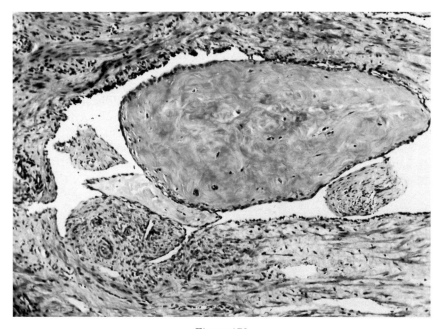

Figure 173
INTRAVENOUS LEIOMYOMATOSIS
The vein illustrated contains a large mass of hyalinized smooth muscle in its lumen. Some of the intravascular tumor consists of more cellular smooth muscle in direct continuity with smooth muscle of the underlying venous wall.

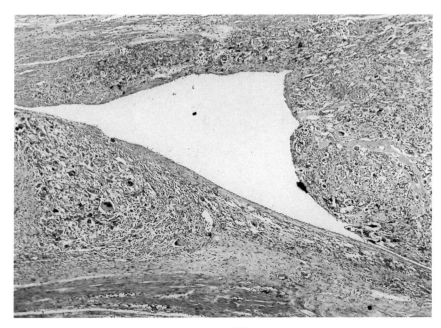

Figure 174
(Figures 174–176 are from the same patient)
INTRAVENOUS LEIOMYOMATOSIS (BIZARRE TYPE)
The vein illustrated shows almost total replacement of its muscular wall by leiomyomatous tissue with numerous bizarre symplastic giant cells. Elsewhere, similar tissue projected into the lumina of veins outside the confines of an otherwise typical bizarre leiomyoma.

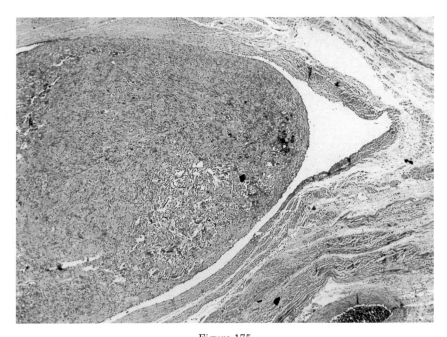

Figure 175
INTRAVENOUS LEIOMYOMATOSIS (BIZARRE TYPE)
This photomicrograph shows a vein lumen filled with a plug of bizarre leiomyomatous tissue.

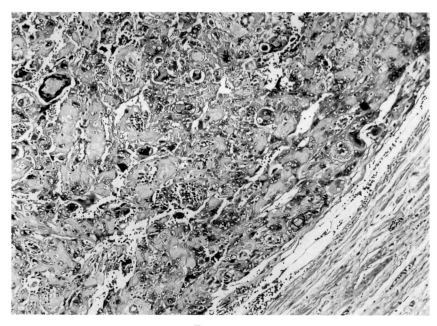

Figure 176
(Figures 174–176 are from the same patient)
INTRAVENOUS LEIOMYOMATOSIS (BIZARRE TYPE)
This high magnification of the lesion illustrated in figures 174 and 175 shows the bizarre nature of the leiomyomatous proliferation (cf. figs. 158 and 159). Mitotic figures were rare, and the patient is alive and well 2 years after hysterectomy.

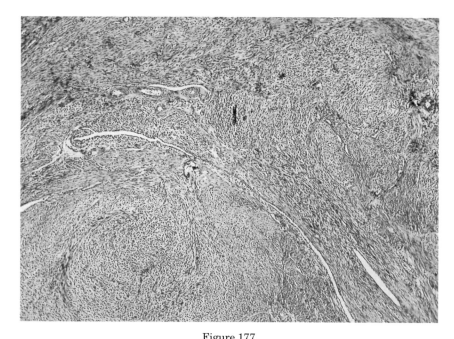

Figure 177
DIFFUSE LEIOMYOMATOSIS
This low-power photomicrograph shows numerous leiomyomatous nodules replacing most of the myometrium.

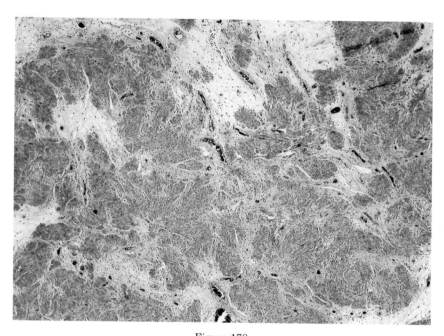

Figure 178
DIFFUSE LEIOMYOMATOSIS
This illustration also shows innumerable minute leiomyomas separated by a somewhat hyalinized stroma. Cellular atypia and mitotic activity were absent.

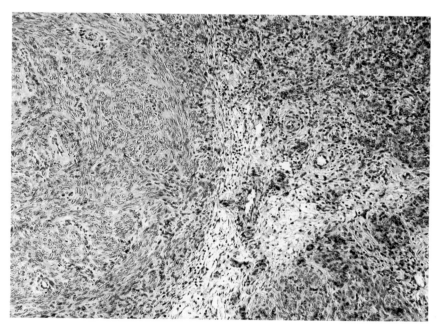

Figure 179
BENIGN UTERINE TUMOR SHOWING MIXED ENDOMETRIAL STROMAL
AND SMOOTH MUSCLE DIFFERENTIATION
The left half of the figure appears to be a typical leiomyoma, whereas the right half resembles a stromal nodule. The entire tumor had pushing margins.

differentiation, but the clinical behavior of the two elements if seen alone might still be different. For example, a histologically benign smooth muscle tumor invading myometrial veins is diagnosed as benign (intravenous leiomyomatosis), whereas an equally bland-appearing endometrial stromal tumor infiltrating veins is diagnosed as low-grade endometrial stromal sarcoma. Thus, if these two elements were encountered in the same tumor the diagnosis would be low-grade sarcoma of mixed endometrial stromal and smooth muscle type.

ADENOMATOID TUMOR

Definition. Adenomatoid tumors are tumors of the uterine serosa and myometrium, originating from serosal mesothelium.

Although the name of this tumor reflects its histologic appearance rather than its originally unknown histogenesis, it is now well accepted that these tumors represent benign mesotheliomas, as demonstrated by numerous immunohistochemical and ultrastructural studies (17,41,50,55). They may rarely be associated with other histologic patterns of mesothelial proliferation.

Gross Findings. Adenomatoid tumors are usually encountered in women of reproductive age, are seen in about 1 percent of hysterectomy specimens if carefully searched for (17,50), and usually resemble small leiomyomas in gross appearance but with a softer consistency and ill-defined margins. They are usually seen in the myometrium near the serosal surface but may extend toward the endometrium if they become large and have even been detected in an endometrial curettage specimen (5).

Microscopic Findings. The adenomatoid tumor usually infiltrates the myometrium, at least focally and often extensively (figs. 180, 181). The most common pattern is the adenoid or tubular configuration, consisting of anastomosing tubules lined by cells that are flattened to cuboidal (figs. 180–183). An angiomatoid configuration is often present, and these tumors were frequently confused with lymphangiomas in the past. Solid and cystic growth patterns are less commonly seen.

Electron-microscopic study reveals long slender microvilli, intracellular lumina, and bundles of intracytoplasmic filaments, all characteristic of mesothelial cells.

Differential Diagnosis. The most common differential diagnosis is with lymphangioma; if there is any doubt, the diagnosis of adenomatoid tumor can be confirmed by a positive immunostain for cytokeratin.

Another common differential diagnosis is with adenocarcinoma, either arising in the endometrium or metastatic to the uterus. The deep-seated location of the tumor usually rules out an endometrial origin, and the generally flattened lining cells with inconspicuous nuclei should rule out any type of malignant tumor (fig. 181). However, in cases with more cuboidal cells and larger nuclei, the distinction from carcinoma may be more difficult (fig. 182, 183). In such cases, it should be noted that adenomatoid tumors generally lack mitotic activity and a desmoplastic stromal reaction; their lumina contain hyaluronic acid but mucicarmine stains are negative, as are immunostains for carcinoembryonic antigen. Other less common differential diagnoses include epithelioid leiomyoma (particularly the plexiform type) and uterine tumor resembling ovarian sex cord tumor. The dilated lumina that are virtually always encountered in adenomatoid tumors rule out either of these possibilities. Again, if in doubt, the histochemical, immunohistochemical, and ultrastructural evidence of mesothelial differentiation should be diagnostic.

OTHER SOFT TISSUE TUMORS (BENIGN AND MALIGNANT)

This group of soft tissue tumors has not been discussed in this chapter, and is divided in the International Society of Gynecological Pathologists classification into homologous and heterologous varieties. This category represents a rare group of generally unrelated tumors, all of which are more common in extrauterine locations.

Some of the benign soft tissue tumors occasionally encountered in the uterine corpus include hemangioma, lymphangioma (fig. 184), and lipoma (36,40). The distinction between lymphangioma and adenomatoid tumor has already been discussed, as have the

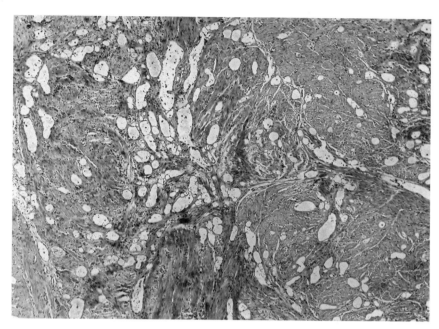

Figure 180
(Figures 180 and 181 are from the same patient)
ADENOMATOID TUMOR
This low-power photomicrograph illustrates the diffusely infiltrating nature of the mesothelial tubules in the myometrium.

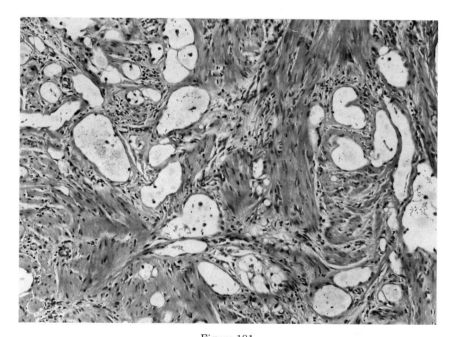

Figure 181
ADENOMATOID TUMOR
A high magnification of the lesion illustrated in figure 180 shows that the infiltrating tubules are variable in size and shape and are lined by a single layer of flattened cells without nuclear atypia.

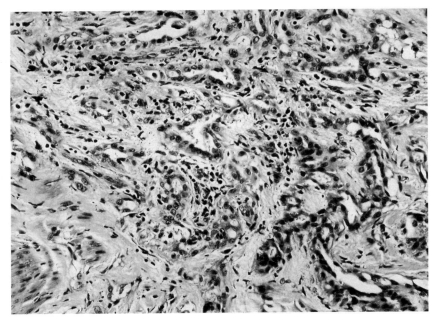

Figure 182
(Figures 182 and 183 are from the same patient)
ADENOMATOID TUMOR
In this lesion, the tubules show complex anastomoses and cuboidal rather than flattened lining cells.

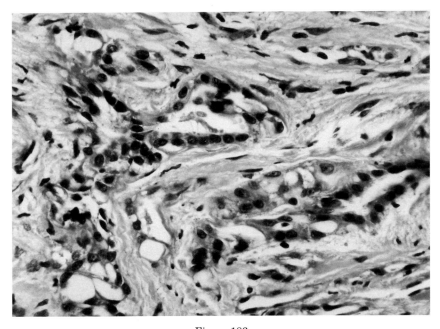

Figure 183
ADENOMATOID TUMOR
A higher magnification of the lesion illustrated in figure 182 shows that the tumor cells are cuboidal and contain unusually large but uniform nuclei, without significant pleomorphism or mitotic activity.

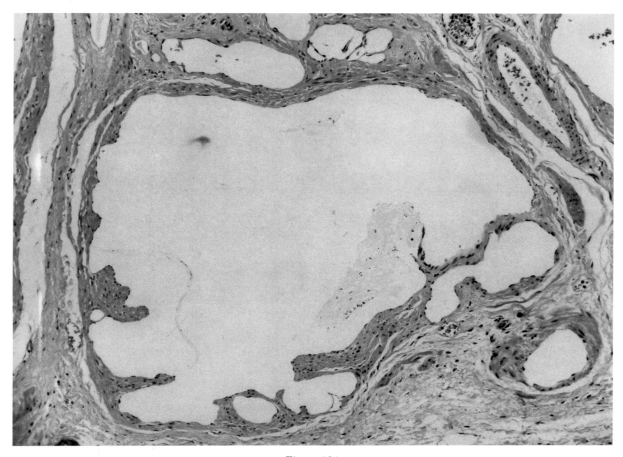

Figure 184
LYMPHANGIOMA OF THE UTERUS
This photomicrograph shows a small portion of a larger tumor that consisted of lymphatic channels, some of which are cystic, infiltrating the myometrium.

facts that vascular leiomyomas are far more common than hemangiomas of the uterus, and lipoleiomyomas are more common than pure lipomas.

Among the malignant soft tissue tumors reported in the uterus are malignant fibrous histiocytoma (14), rhabdomyosarcoma (39), angiosarcoma (53), liposarcoma (1), chondrosarcoma (26), osteosarcoma (38), and alveolar soft part sarcoma (16). The histologic features and differential diagnosis of each of these are similar to those of their extrauterine counterparts, but it should be mentioned that, in the uterine corpus, an overgrowth of an adenosarcoma or carcinosarcoma must always be ruled out. Not enough of these tumors are reported for the

proper characterization of their clinical features, natural history, or treatment.

A final soft tissue tumor that has been reported to occur in the uterus but that has been controversial is hemangiopericytoma. This tumor is so similar histologically to endometrial stromal nodule or low-grade endometrial stromal sarcoma that its existence in the uterus has been denied by some authors (55). It is safe to assume that most uterine tumors that resemble hemangiopericytoma can be proven to be of endometrial stromal type if investigated thoroughly. Both ultrastructural evidence of pericytic differentiation (46) and lack of hormone receptors should be demanded before accepting the diagnosis of hemangiopericytoma.

REFERENCES

1. Bapat K, Brustein S. Uterine sarcoma with liposarcomatous differentiation: report of a case and review of the literature. Int J Gynaecol Obstet 1989;28:71–5.

2. Berchuck A, Rubin SC, Hoskins WJ, Saigo PE, Pierce VK, Lewis JL Jr. Treatment of uterine leiomyosarcoma. Obstet Gynecol 1988;71:845–50.

3. Brescia RJ, Tazelaar HD, Hobbs J, Miller AW. Intravascular lipoleiomyomatosis: a report of two cases. Hum Pathol 1989;20:252–6.

4. Buttram VC Jr, Reiter RC. Uterine leiomyomata: etiology, symptomatology, and management. Fertil Steril 1981;36:433–45.

5. Carlier MT, Dardick I, Lagace AF, Sreeram V. Adenomatoid tumor of the uterus: presentation in endometrial curettings. Int J Gynecol Pathol 1986;5:69–74.

6. Chang V, Aikawa M, Druet R. Uterine leiomyoblastoma: ultrastructural and cytological studies. Cancer 1977;39:1563–9.

7. Cho KR, Woodruff JD, Epstein JI. Leiomyoma of the uterus with multiple extrauterine smooth muscle tumors: a case report suggesting multifocal origin. Hum Pathol 1989;20:80–3.

8. Clement PB. Intravenous leiomyomatosis of the uterus. Pathol Annu 1988;23:153–83.

9. _____ , Young RH. Diffuse leiomyomatosis of the uterus: a report of four cases. Int J Gynecol Pathol 1987;6:322–30.

10. _____ , Young RH, Scully RE. Intravenous leiomyomatosis of the uterus. A clinicopathologic analysis of 16 cases with unusual histologic features. Am J Surg Pathol 1988;12:932–45.

11. Duperroy G. Contribution à l'étude clinique et histopathologique de l'utérus myomateux en rapport avec la pathogénie de l'hémorragie utérine anormale chez la femme. Rev Belge Pathol 1954;23:(Suppl 9):1–166.

12. Evans HL, Chawla SP, Simpson C, Finn KP. Smooth muscle neoplasms of the uterus other than ordinary leiomyoma. A study of 46 cases, with emphasis on diagnostic criteria and prognostic factors. Cancer 1988;62:2239–47.

13. Friedman AJ, Harrison-Atlas D, Barbieri RL, Benacerraf B, Gleason R, Schiff I. A randomized, placebo-controlled, double-blind study evaluating the efficacy of leuprolide acetate depot in the treatment of uterine leiomyomata. Fertil Steril 1989;51:251–6.

14. Fujii S, Kanzaki H, Konishi I, Yamabe H, Okamura H, Mori T. Malignant fibrous histiocytoma of the uterus. Gynecol Oncol 1987;26:319–30.

15. Gisser SD, Young I. Neurilemnoma-like uterine myomas: an ultrastructural reaffirmation of their non-Schwannian nature. Am J Obstet Gynecol 1977;129:389–92.

16. Gray GF Jr, Glick AD, Kurtin PJ, Jones HW III. Alveolar soft part sarcoma of the uterus. Hum Pathol 1986;17:297–300.

17. Honoré LH. Uterine mesothelioma [Letter]. Am J Obstet Gynecol 1979;135:162.

18. Hyde KE, Geisinger KR, Marshall RB, Jones TL. The clear-cell variant of uterine epithelioid leiomyoma. An immunohistologic and ultrastructural study. Arch Pathol Lab Med 1989;113:551–3.

19. Janney C, Weinberg D, Lage J. Ploidy of uterine smooth muscle tumors [Abstract]. Mod Pathol 1990;3:47a.

20. Kaminski PF, Tavassoli FA. Plexiform tumorlet: a clinical and pathologic study of 15 cases with ultrastructural observations. Int J Gynecol Pathol 1984;3:124–34.

21. Kawaguchi K, Fujii S, Konishi I, Nanbu Y, Nonogaki H, Mori T. Mitotic activity in uterine leiomyomas during the menstrual cycle. Am J Obstet Gynecol 1989;160:637–41.

22. _____ , Fujii S, Konishi I, Okamura H, Mori T. Ultrastructural study of cultured smooth muscle cells from uterine leiomyoma and myometrium under the influence of sex steroids. Gynecol Oncol 1985;21:32–41.

23. Kempson RL, Hendrickson MR. Pure mesenchymal neoplasms of the uterine corpus. In: Fox H, ed. Haines and Taylor obstetrical and gynaecological pathology. 3rd ed. Edinburgh: Churchill Livingstone, 1987:411–56.

24. _____ , Hendrickson MR. Pure mesenchymal neoplasms of the uterine corpus: selected problems. Semin Diagn Pathol 1988;5:172–98.

25. King ME, Dickersin GR, Scully RE. Myxoid leiomyosarcoma of the uterus. A report of six cases. Am J Surg Pathol 1982;6:589–98.

26. Kofinas AD, Suarez J, Calame RJ, Chipeco Z. Chondrosarcoma of the uterus. Gynecol Oncol 1984;19:231–7.

27. Konishi I, Fujii S, Ban C, Okuda Y, Okamura H, Tojo S. Ultrastructural study of minute uterine leiomyomas. Int J Gynecol Pathol 1983;2:113–20.

28. Kurman RJ, Norris HJ. Mesenchymal tumors of the uterus. VI. Epithelioid smooth muscle tumors including leiomyoblastoma and clear cell leiomyoma. Cancer 1976;37:1853–65.

29. Leibsohn S, d'Ablaing G, Mishell DR Jr, Schlaerth JB. Leiomyosarcoma in a series of hysterectomies performed for presumed uterine leiomyomas. Am J Obstet Gynecol 1990;162:968–76.

30. Letterie GS, Coddington CC, Winkel CA, Shawker TH, Loriaux DL, Collins RL. Efficacy of a gonadotropin-releasing hormone agonist in the treatment of uterine leiomyomata: long-term follow-up. Fertil Steril 1989;51:951–6.

31. Marshall RJ, Braye SG, Jones DB. Leiomyosarcoma of the uterus with giant cells resembling osteoclasts. Int J Gynecol Pathol 1986;5:260–8.

32. Nogales FF, Navarro N, Martinez de Victoria JM, et al. Uterine intravascular leiomyomatosis: an update and report of seven cases. Int J Gynecol Pathol 1987;6:331–9.

33. Norris HJ, Hilliard GD, Irey NS. Hemorrhagic cellular leiomyomas ("apoplectic leiomyoma") of the uterus associated with pregnancy and oral contraceptives. Int J Gynecol Pathol 1988;7:212–24.

34. O'Connor DM, Norris HJ. Mitotically active leiomyomas of the uterus. Hum Pathol 1990;21:223–7.

35. Peacock G, Archer S. Myxoid leiomyosarcoma of the uterus: case report and review of the literature. Am J Obstet Gynecol 1989;160:1515–9.

36. Pedowitz P, Felmus LB, Grayzel DM. Vascular tumors of the uterus. I. Benign vascular tumors. Am J Obstet Gynecol 1955;69:1291–303.

37. Perrone T, Dehner LP. Prognostically favorable "mitotically active" smooth-muscle tumors of the uterus. A clinicopathologic study of ten cases. Am J Surg Pathol 1988;12:1–8.

38. Piscioli F, Govoni E, Polla E, Pusiol T, Dalri P, Antolini M. Primary osteosarcoma of the uterine corpus. Report of a case and critical review of the literature. Int J Gynaecol Obstet 1985;23:377–85.

39. Podczaski E, Sees J, Kaminski P, et al. Rhabdomyosarcoma of the uterus in a postmenopausal patient. Gynecol Oncol 1990;37:439–42.

40. Pounder DJ. Fatty tumours of the uterus. J Clin Pathol 1982;35:1380–3.

41. Quigley JC, Hart WR. Adenomatoid tumors of the uterus. Am J Clin Pathol 1981;76:627–35.

42. Rice JP, Kay HH, Mahony BS. The clinical significance of uterine leiomyomas in pregnancy. Am J Obstet Gynecol 1989;160:1212–6.

43. Sieinski W. Lipomatous neometaplasia of the uterus. Report of 11 cases with discussion of histogenesis and pathogenesis. Int J Gynecol Pathol 1989;8:357–63.

44. Silverberg SG. Leiomyosarcoma of the uterus. A clinicopathologic study. Obstet Gynecol 1971;38:613–28.

45. _____ . Reproducibility of the mitosis count in the histologic diagnosis of uterine smooth muscle tumors. Hum Pathol 1976;7:451–4

46. _____ , Willson MA, Board JA Hemangiopericytoma of the uterus: an ultrastructural study. Am J Obstet Gynecol 1971;110:397–404.

47. Soules MR, McCarty KS Jr. Leiomyomas: steroid receptor content. Variation within normal menstrual cycles. Am J Obstet Gynecol 1982;143:6–11.

48. Tamaya T, Fujimoto J, Okada H. Comparison of cellular levels of steroid receptors in uterine leiomyoma and myometrium. Acta Obstet Gynecol Scand 1985;64:307–9.

49. Taylor HB, Norris HJ. Mesenchymal tumors of the uterus. IV. Diagnosis and prognosis of leiomyosarcoma. Arch Pathol 1966;82:40–4.

50. Tiltman AJ. Adenomatoid tumours of the uterus. Histopathology 1980;4:437–43.

51. _____ . The effect of progestins on the mitotic activity of uterine fibromyomas. Int J Gynecol Pathol 1985;4:89–96.

52. Tsushima K, Stanhope CR, Gaffey TA, Lieber MM. Uterine leiomyosarcomas and benign smooth muscle tumors: usefulness of nuclear DNA patterns studied by flow cytometry. Mayo Clin Proc 1988;63:248–55.

53. Witkin GB, Askin FB, Geratz JD, Reddick RL. Angiosarcoma of the uterus: a light microscopic, immunohistochemical, and ultrastructural study. Int J Gynecol Pathol 1987;6:176–84.

54. Wolff M, Silva F, Kaye G. Pulmonary metastases (with admixed epithelial elements) from smooth muscle neoplasms. Am J Surg Pathol 1979;3:325–42.

55. Zaloudek C, Norris HJ. Mesenchymal tumors of the uterus. In: Kurman RJ, ed. Blaustein's pathology of the female genital tract. 3rd ed. New York: Springer-Verlag, 1987:373–408.

◇◇◇

MIXED EPITHELIAL-NONEPITHELIAL TUMORS

The mixed epithelial-nonepithelial tumors comprise an extremely interesting but rare group of lesions, the exact clinical and pathologic features of which are still being defined and the epidemiology and histogenesis of which are largely unknown. They are classified as follows:

- Benign
    Adenofibroma
    Adenomyoma
        variant—atypical polypoid
            adenomyoma

- Malignant
    Adenosarcoma
        homologous
        heterologous
    Carcinosarcoma (malignant mixed
        mesodermal tumor; malignant
        mixed müllerian tumor)
        homologous
        heterologous
    Carcinofibroma.

By definition, these are all tumors in which epithelial and nonepithelial elements, at least at the standard light-microscopic level, are intimately admixed. The nomenclature presented provides a prefix (*adeno* or *carcino*), which conveys the benign or malignant appearance of the epithelial component, and a suffix (*fibroma, myoma,* or *sarcoma*), which conveys the benign or malignant appearance of the nonepithelial component. The terms *homologous* and *heterologous*, respectively, define tumors without and with malignant stromal components with types of differentiation not seen in the normal endometrium (rhabdomyosarcoma, chondrosarcoma, osteosarcoma, liposarcoma).

Both the benign and malignant variants share a few common clinical and pathologic features in addition to their mixed nature. All of these tumors present in the uterus as polypoid, usually solitary masses projecting into the endometrial cavity. In general, the malignant tumors in this group are larger than the benign ones, but there is overlap in size, with large benign and small malignant neoplasms encountered often. All of these tumors present clinically with abnormal vaginal bleeding. In general,

although again there is considerable overlap, the tumors with malignant epithelial or stromal elements tend to occur in older, usually postmenopausal women, whereas the totally benign tumors are often encountered in premenopausal women.

ADENOFIBROMA

Adenofibroma was first described in the uterine cervix in 1971 (1) and in the corpus 2 years later (38). These tumors have often been reported subsequently in conjunction with adenosarcomas (13,29,37,40), and terms used for the combination of these two tumors have included *benign* and *low-grade variant of mixed müllerian tumor* (29) and *uterine cystosarcoma phyllodes* (37). The exact frequency of this tumor is difficult to ascertain, but in the large series of Clement and Scully, it comprised only about 5 percent of tumors in the adenofibroma-adenosarcoma group (11).

As mentioned previously, adenofibromas may be encountered at any age, although they are more frequent in postmenopausal women. They most commonly arise from the endometrium, but about 10 percent of the tumors originate in the endocervix (13). They usually present as broad-based polypoid masses that often have a villous surface and a spongy cut surface, with cystic spaces surrounded by firm tissue that is white to tan.

Microscopic Features. The surface of the tumor usually has broad club-shaped papillae (figs. 185, 186), although it may occasionally be relatively flat. The main diagnostic feature is an admixture of epithelial and stromal elements, both of which appear histologically benign (figs. 186, 187). The epithelium is usually of proliferative endometrial type but may be flattened to a single layer of cuboidal cells or show various metaplastic changes. The stroma is composed of cells that resemble either fibroblasts, benign endometrial stromal cells, or both. Smooth muscle may be present focally, but heterologous elements have not been described. Various degrees of stromal cellularity and sclerosis may be present, but stromal atypia is absent, periglandular cuffing by more cellular stroma is not seen, and mitotic activity is absent

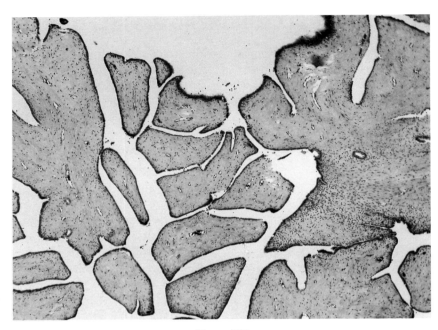

Figure 185
ADENOFIBROMA
(Figures 185 and 186 are from the same patient)
This tumor is composed of broad club-shaped papillae projecting into the endometrial cavity.

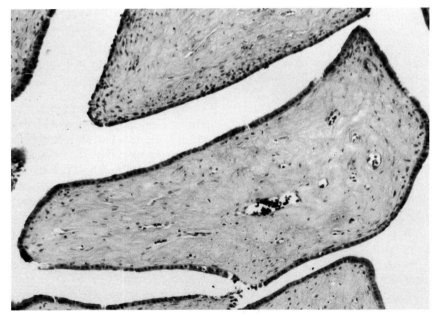

Figure 186
ADENOFIBROMA
A higher magnification of the tumor illustrated in figure 185 clearly demonstrates the histologically benign appearance of both epithelial and stromal components of the tumor.

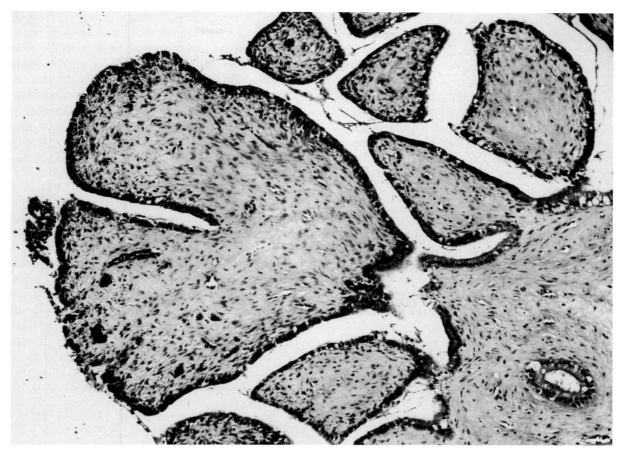

Figure 187
ADENOFIBROMA
The stroma of this tumor is more cellular than that illustrated in figures 185 and 186; however, atypia and a hypercellular "cambium layer" beneath the benign epithelium (as would be seen in adenosarcoma) are both absent.

or minimal, with different observers reporting fewer than 4 (40) or fewer than 2 (11) mitotic figures per 10 HPF.

Although adenofibroma has thus far been reported as a benign lesion, three cases have been reported to invade the myometrium, including one that also invaded large myometrial veins (9,11). Nevertheless, metastasis has not been reported.

Differential Diagnosis. The differential diagnosis of adenofibroma is with either endometrial polyp or adenosarcoma. The papillary architecture of the adenofibroma and the regularity of the relationship between the epithelial and stromal components should distinguish adenofibromas from benign polyps. If the stromal component is atypical and mitotically active, and particularly if it condenses to form more cellular cuffs around glands, the diagnosis of adenosarcoma should be made. In the case of borderline lesions, it is probably safer to diagnose adenosarcomas because these are many times more common than adenofibromas.

ADENOMYOMA

Although about 1 or 2 percent of all endometrial polyps may have some smooth muscle in their stroma, the designation of adenomyoma should be reserved for those polypoid lesions in which the stromal component is largely or exclusively composed of smooth muscle. The term *adenomyoma* is not recommended here to define a solitary myometrial nodule of adenomyosis.

Although atypical polypoid adenomyoma is listed as a variant of adenomyoma, the variant is probably more common than the basic type, although both are certainly rare. The term *atypical polypoid adenomyoma* was first coined in 1981 by Mazur (25), although illustrations of this lesion had appeared in print previously, including in the First Series of the *Atlas of Tumor Pathology* (20). The largest series of these lesions reported to date, which still comprises most of the cases reported, consisted of 27 cases (39).

Clinical Features and Gross Findings. Atypical polypoid adenomyoma typically occurs in premenopausal women (average age 39 years) who are first seen because of abnormal vaginal bleeding. Three atypical polypoid adenomyomas have been seen in patients with Turner's syndrome, at least two of whom had been on long-term estrogen therapy (14).

Similar to the other tumors in this mixed group, the atypical polypoid adenomyoma presents as a polypoid mass, but it is more likely than most of the tumors in this group to be situated in the lower uterine segment or endocervix (39). The average size is about 2 cm in diameter. The tumors may be pedunculated or sessile and are usually well demarcated from the underlying myometrium or cervical wall. However, many tumors are removed totally or almost totally by curettage, so gross descriptions of intact specimens are rare.

Microscopic Findings. The ordinary adenomyoma is characterized by an intimate admixture of benign endometrial glands without architectural complexity and a stroma consisting predominantly or exclusively of equally benign-appearing smooth muscle (fig. 188). In the atypical polypoid adenomyoma, in contrast, the glands invariably exhibit architectural atypia and may show cytologic atypia (usually slight but occasionally marked) as well (figs. 189–191). Squamous or morular metaplasia is found in most of the cases and is often extensive (fig. 191). Although central necrosis may be present in these large metaplastic foci, their cytologic appearance is benign. The stromal component consists of swirling and interlacing fascicles of smooth muscle cells that appear cytologically benign. Mitotic activity in this compartment has been reported as less than 2 mitotic figures per 10 HPF, but I have seen a

case with a mitotic rate of 9 mitotic figures per 10 HPF, which recurred outside the uterus 6 years after hysterectomy. With the exception of this case (which perhaps is better classified as an adenosarcoma), malignant behavior has thus far not been reported, although adenocarcinoma has been noted within and associated with the atypical polypoid adenomyoma (39).

Differential Diagnosis. The most important differential diagnosis of atypical polypoid adenomyoma, particularly in a curettage specimen, is with endometrial carcinoma invading the myometrium. However, it is unusual for myometrial invasion to be demonstrated in a curettage specimen: the glands of atypical polypoid adenomyoma lack cytologic and architectural features of malignancy, and the smooth muscle component exhibits a cellularity and fascicular pattern that would be unusual for myometrium invaded by carcinoma and lacks the usual stromal response to invasive cancer.

Other differential diagnoses of atypical polypoid adenomyoma include the other tumors in the mixed epithelial-nonepithelial group. The benign smooth muscle nature of the stroma and the absence of a papillary component should be sufficient to distinguish atypical polypoid adenomyoma from both adenofibroma and adenosarcoma, and the lack of densely cellular stromal cuffs should distinguish it from adenosarcoma. Both the stroma and the benign (albeit atypical) glandular component should facilitate the distinction from carcinosarcoma.

ADENOSARCOMA

First described in 1974 by Clement and Scully (10), adenosarcoma is characterized as a tumor containing a benign epithelial and a malignant stromal component. Although adenosarcomas are still rare, they are considerably more frequent than adenofibromas and adenomyomas. As with the other tumors in this group, although most of them occur in the uterus, ovarian and other extrauterine primary sites have been reported (8,23).

Gross Findings. As with the other tumors in this group, adenosarcomas are usually polypoid masses arising from the endometrium. Endocervical tumors, multiple tumors, and intramyometrial tumors (presumably arising in adenomyosis) have all been reported (11,13).

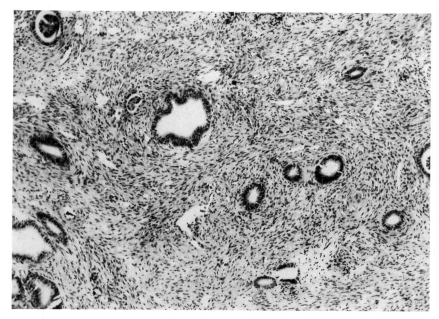

Figure 188
ADENOMYOMA
In this illustration, benign endometrial glands without architectural complexity or cytologic atypia are surrounded by stroma that consists predominantly of smooth muscle. This lesion presented as a polyp projecting into the endometrial cavity.

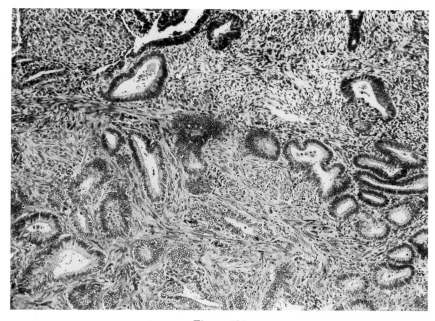

Figure 189
ATYPICAL POLYPOID ADENOMYOMA
Endometrial glands that vary in size and shape are separated by swirling fascicles of cytologically benign, cellular smooth muscle. The upper portion of the illustration consists of surface endometrium that is uninvolved by the lesion. The junction between the adenomyoma and adjacent endometrium is well demarcated (pushing).

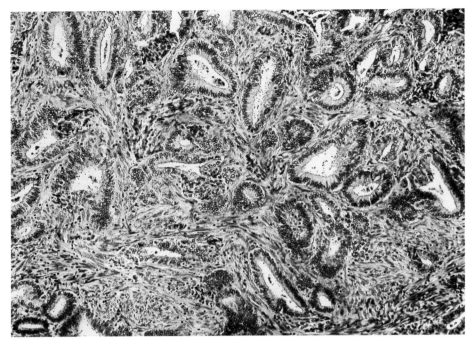

Figure 190
ATYPICAL POLYPOID ADENOMYOMA
This photomicrograph demonstrates the architectural irregularity of the proliferative glands comprising the epithelial component of this lesion. Intervening stroma is made up of interlacing fascicles of smooth muscle.

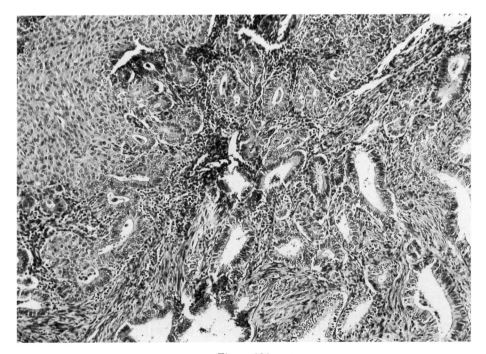

Figure 191
ATYPICAL POLYPOID ADENOMYOMA
Part of the epithelial component of this lesion consists of large benign morules.

The cut surface is usually more fleshy than that of an adenofibroma, and on rare occasions necrosis may be noted on gross inspection; myometrial invasion may also be noted on gross inspection. Otherwise the appearance of this tumor is similar to that of adenofibroma and adenomyoma.

Microscopic Findings. The tumor shows an admixture of a benign epithelial component and a sarcomatous stroma (figs. 192–195). Some of the tumors are encountered within an otherwise banal endometrial polyp (fig. 192). The surface is often papillary, and a leaf-like appearance similar to cystosarcoma phyllodes of the breast may be prominent (fig. 193) (37). Although the stroma is generally cellular throughout the tumor, it tends to coalesce as more densely hypercellular cuffs around the epithelial component (figs. 194, 195), a feature that separates adenosarcoma from most of the other mixed epithelial-nonepithelial tumors.

The epithelial component usually consists of an admixture of small, cystically dilated, and compressed slit-like glands lined by benign proliferative-type endometrium. In some glands, the epithelium may be flattened and cuboidal, and various types of metaplastic and related changes are also encountered (figs. 194, 196). The epithelium may show some cytologic atypia, but by definition invasive carcinoma is absent.

The stromal component appears cytologically malignant and is composed of spindled or round cells that resemble endometrial stromal cells or fibroblasts (figs. 195, 196). Smooth muscle cells and foam cells (fig. 197) may also be present (13,21). The stroma generally shows moderate cellularity but is more cellular in the periglandular cuffs (figs. 194–196). The nuclear atypia of the stromal component is usually mild or moderate, so that most of these cases resemble low-grade sarcomas. However, a high-grade stromal sarcomatous component may also be encountered, particularly in those cases with stromal overgrowth. The mitotic count is greater than 20 mitotic figures per 10 HPF in many cases, but may be as low as 2 or 3 per 10 HPF (11,21). Foci of stromal fibrosis, hyalinization, hemorrhage, and necrosis are common, and in some cases the stromal fibrosis may be extensive, imparting a deceptively benign appearance to parts of the tumor. Heterologous elements, particularly rhabdomyosarcoma

(fig. 198) and less commonly chondrosarcoma (fig. 199), may be encountered and should be noted in the diagnosis. It is not clear whether the presence of these elements has an unfavorable prognostic significance, because the presence of rhabdomyosarcoma was reported as unfavorable in one large series (21) but not in two others (11,40). Approximately 25 percent of all adenosarcomas invade the myometrium, and some of these show vascular or lymphatic space invasion; such invasion is invariably by the sarcomatous component, sometimes accompanied by the glandular component. Distant metastases (11, 21) are always purely sarcomatous.

Occasionally, adenosarcomas contain sex cord-like elements within the stromal component (12). These consist of solid nests, trabeculae, and solid or hollow tubules composed of benign-appearing epithelial-type cells, sometimes with abundant foamy cytoplasm (fig. 197). The clinical and pathologic features of adenosarcomas containing these elements are otherwise similar to those of typical adenosarcomas.

Sarcomatous Overgrowth. Another variant of the usual pattern that has been emphasized recently is sarcomatous overgrowth (7, 21). This is an overgrowth of the adenosarcoma by a pure sarcoma, usually but not necessarily of higher grade and mitotic rate, that accounts for at least 25 percent of the total tumor volume (figs. 200, 201). This phenomenon has been reported in 10 of 125 cases in one series (7) and 17 of 31 in another (21), probably reflecting differences in the sources of the cases. However, in both series, sarcomatous overgrowth was an ominous prognostic sign, with tumor recurrence developing in 44 to 70 percent of cases, compared with 14 to 25 percent of cases without sarcomatous overgrowth. Thus, although sarcomatous overgrowth is not included in the current classification of these tumors, I believe that its presence or absence should always be noted.

Clinical Features. As mentioned previously, myometrial and vascular invasion (figs. 201, 202), as well as distant metastases, are invariably composed predominantly or exclusively of the sarcomatous element. Recurrences are usually initially in the pelvis, but distant metastases may occur, sometimes after many years. Death resulting from tumor progression is generally reported to occur in from 10 to 25 percent of cases, with a much higher figure for

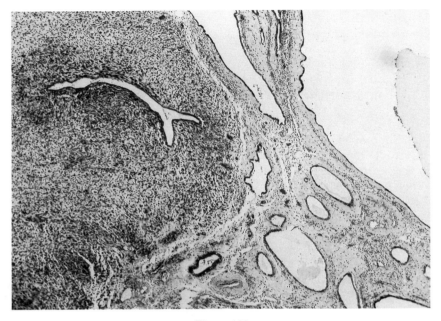

Figure 192
ADENOSARCOMA
This tumor is shown arising in an endometrial polyp. One compressed gland in this
field is cuffed by hypercellular and atypical stroma. The other glands, some of which are
dilated, are separated by the usual stroma of an endometrial polyp.

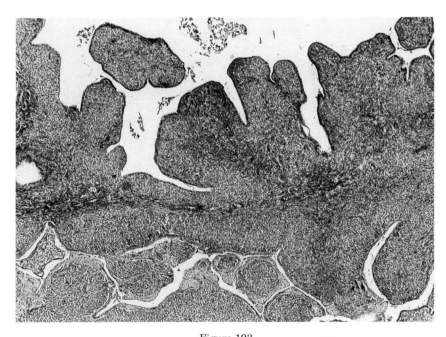

Figure 193
ADENOSARCOMA
The surface of this tumor has a leaf-like appearance similar to that of cystosarcoma
phyllodes of the breast. Note the cellularity of the stroma at low power compared with
the adenofibroma illustrated in figure 185.

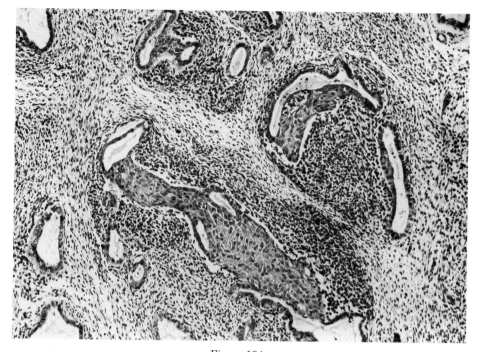

Figure 194
ADENOSARCOMA
The cellular stroma of this tumor forms hypercellular cuffs surrounding the benign-appearing, mostly slit-like glands. Foci of squamous metaplasia are present.

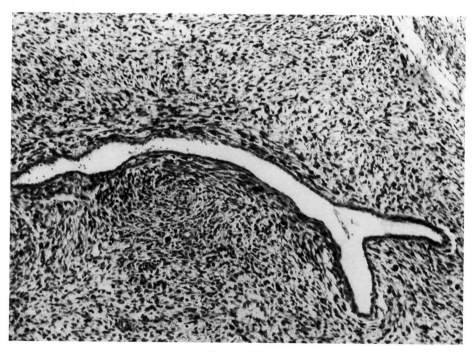

Figure 195
ADENOSARCOMA
Cuffing of stroma around a compressed slit-like gland is evident in this illustration.

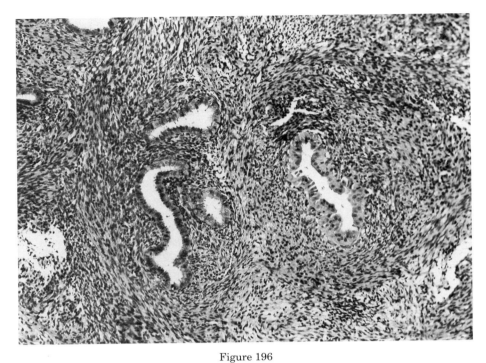

Figure 196
ADENOSARCOMA
Several of the benign-appearing glands in this illustration show eosinophilic cell change. Cuffing by hypercellular stroma is apparent.

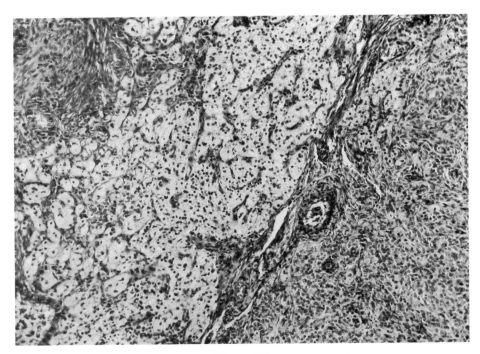

Figure 197
ADENOSARCOMA
This illustration shows foam cells that are forming sex cord-like structures in the stromal component.

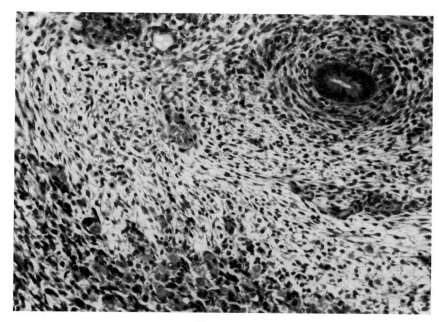

Figure 198
ADENOSARCOMA
A hypercellular cuff of stroma surrounds the single benign gland in this illustration, whereas another hypercellular band of stroma shows rhabdomyosarcomatous differentiation.

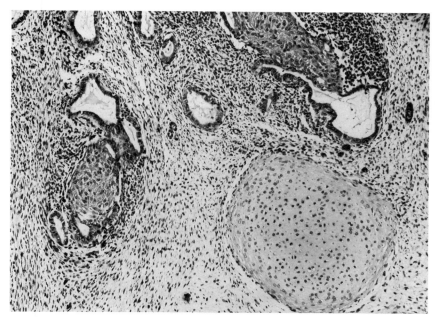

Figure 199
ADENOSARCOMA
A large focus of well-differentiated chondrosarcoma is present in this example. Also note foci of squamous metaplasia and of hypercellular stromal cuffs around the glandular component.

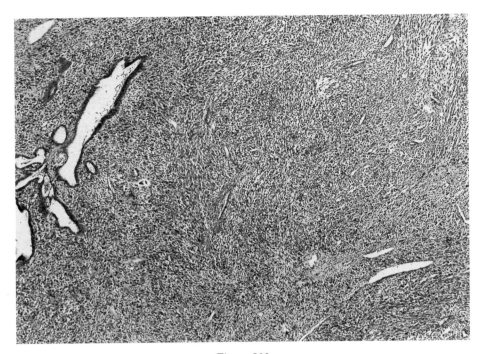

Figure 200
ADENOSARCOMA WITH SARCOMATOUS OVERGROWTH
A pure sarcomatous component extends from the few benign glands illustrated.

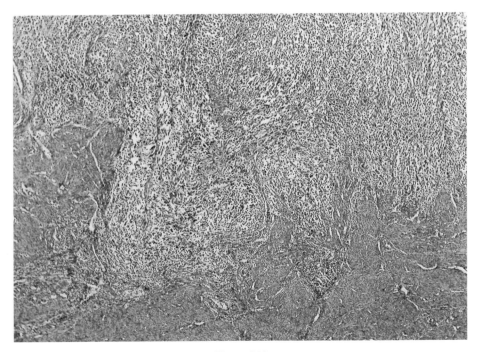

Figure 201
ADENOSARCOMA WITH SARCOMATOUS OVERGROWTH
Pure sarcoma invades the underlying myometrium at the base of this tumor.

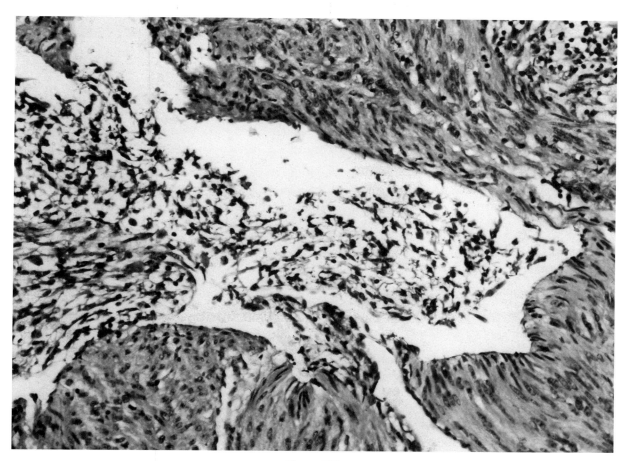

Figure 202
ADENOSARCOMA WITH SARCOMATOUS OVERGROWTH
Venous invasion by the stromal component is noteworthy in this example.

adenosarcomas with sarcomatous overgrowth. Both recurrence and death may occur late (about one-third of initial recurrences 5 years or more after hysterectomy) (11). In one series (21), most of the deaths from adenosarcoma with sarcomatous overgrowth were encountered in cases also containing rhabdomyosarcoma.

Other Findings and Treatment. Ultrastructural findings in adenosarcoma (24) have been relatively nonspecific, and the immunohistochemical, receptor, and flow-cytometric findings have not been characterized in a large series of cases. The treatment is predominantly surgical, and again too few cases have been reported for an evaluation of other modes of therapy.

Differential Diagnosis. The main differential diagnosis of adenosarcoma is with either adenofibroma or carcinosarcoma. Clement and Scully (11) have recommended a diagnosis of adenosarcoma rather than adenofibroma when one or more of the following signs are present: 1) a stromal mitotic count of 2 or more mitotic figures per 10 HPF, 2) marked stromal cellularity, and 3) more than mild degrees of stromal nuclear atypia. Periglandular stromal cuffing also appears to be a useful differential diagnostic feature. The differential diagnosis with carcinosarcoma depends on the presence or absence of carcinoma within the tumor. By definition, an adenosarcoma with even focal carcinoma is diagnosed as carcinosarcoma, but it may be that such lesions are more likely to behave like adenosarcomas. Other differential diagnoses that should generally not pose a significant problem include those with endometrial polyps and adenomyomas.

CARCINOSARCOMA

Definition. Carcinosarcomas are mixed tumors in which both the epithelial and nonepithelial components are histologically malignant. By definition, these should occur in the same tumor, as opposed to a carcinoma and a sarcoma occurring synchronously in different portions of the same uterus. Carcinosarcomas are also known as malignant mixed mesodermal tumors or malignant mixed müllerian tumors and are further subdivided into homologous and heterologous types.

Although carcinosarcomas are rare tumors, comprising only 2 to 3 percent of uterine cancers (35), they are by far the most common of the mixed epithelial-nonepithelial endometrial tumors.

Clinical Features. The epidemiologic background of these tumors is incompletely characterized, but a relationship with prior pelvic radiation has been well known for many years (13). Some of the epidemiologic features associated with endometrial carcinoma (obesity, nulliparity, diabetes mellitus, etc) have also been noted in women with carcinosarcomas, but the associations are not as strong (13,33). Occasional cases have been reported as a complication in functioning ovarian lesions and exogenous estrogen therapy (6,32).

Most carcinosarcomas occur in older postmenopausal patients, but occasional tumors have been reported in young women, and one even has been documented in a 4-year-old girl (2,6). The patients generally present with abnormal vaginal bleeding, but pelvic or abdominal pain is also frequent because many patients have clinical evidence of extensive extrauterine disease at initial presentation. The tumors are generally polypoid, frequently bulky, and often protrude through the external cervical os. Diagnosis is usually made before hysterectomy by endometrial curettage, but often only the carcinomatous or the sarcomatous component is recognized initially. In addition, the initial cytologic diagnosis is more often adenocarcinoma than carcinosarcoma (36).

Gross Findings. Carcinosarcomas are the largest of the mixed tumors and often the largest of any uterine tumors. They are generally soft and friable, broad-based polypoid tumors that fill the endometrial cavity and invade deeply into the myometrium (pl. V). The surface is often smoother than that of an endometrial carcinoma, and the cut surface generally is more fleshy, variegated, hemorrhagic, and necrotic. Bone or cartilage may impart a hard consistency focally. Occasionally, a carcinosarcoma may be removed completely by curettage, with no residual tumor in the hysterectomy specimen. Equally as rarely, it may represent a microscopic finding within an otherwise benign polyp or low-grade adenosarcoma.

Microscopic Findings. Carcinosarcomas are characterized by an admixture of malignant epithelial and nonepithelial elements (13,27, 28,34). The glandular component is usually of endometrioid type but may represent any of the types of endometrial carcinoma described in the chapter on Endometrial Carcinoma (figs. 203–205). Because the stromal component of the tumor is malignant, recognition of the usual stromal changes associated with invasive endometrial carcinoma may be difficult or impossible, and the diagnosis of carcinoma must usually be made on cytologic grounds alone. The cytologic atypia is always greater than that seen in the epithelial component of an adenosarcoma, so this distinction is usually not difficult. However, otherwise typical carcinosarcomas may contain rare glands with a benign appearance (fig. 206).

The sarcomatous component may be either homologous or heterologous. The term *carcinosarcoma* is now used to include both of these types, although the older literature frequently refers to only the homologous tumors as carcinosarcomas and the heterologous ones as mixed mesodermal or mixed müllerian tumors (27, 28). The homologous sarcomatous component is usually high grade and may consist predominantly of spindle cells (figs. 203, 204), round cells (fig. 207), or giant cells (fig. 208). Occasionally, however, the stromal component resembles a low-grade fibrosarcoma or leiomyosarcoma (fig 205).

Carcinosarcoma may arise within an endometrial polyp or adenosarcoma (fig. 206). If a large adenosarcoma contains only a few frankly malignant glands, the diagnosis is carcinosarcoma, but such a tumor may continue to behave more like an adenosarcoma (34).

PLATE V

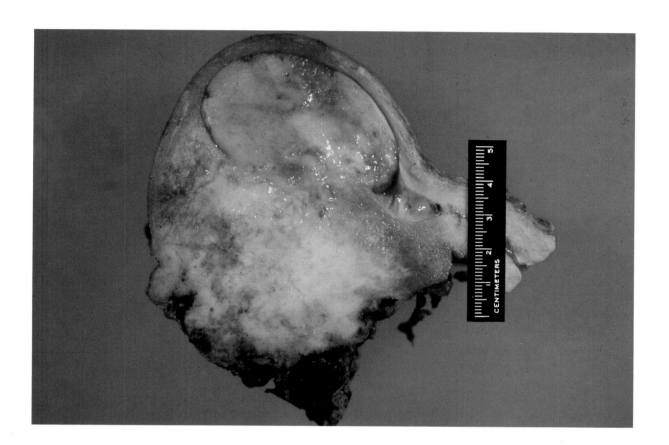

CARCINOSARCOMA OF THE ENDOMETRIUM

As is usually the case, this tumor is massive, filling the endometrial cavity, extending down into the endocervical canal and invading into and through the myometrium. The variegated "fish-flesh" cut surface is characteristic.

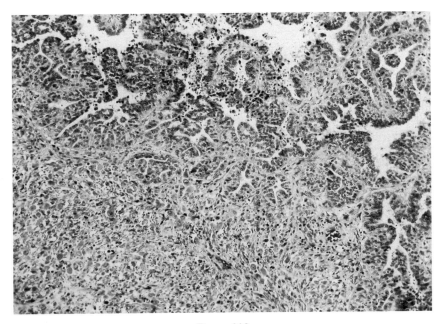

Figure 203
CARCINOSARCOMA
This figure illustrates an intimate admixture of adenocarcinoma and poorly differentiated sarcoma.

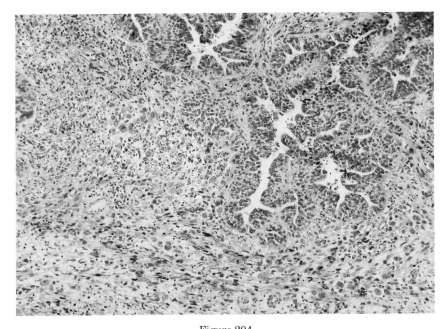

Figure 204
CARCINOSARCOMA
In this field, the sarcomatous component is a high-grade spindle cell tumor. The carcinoma forms glands but is poorly differentiated cytologically, thus it is grade II endometrioid adenocarcinoma.

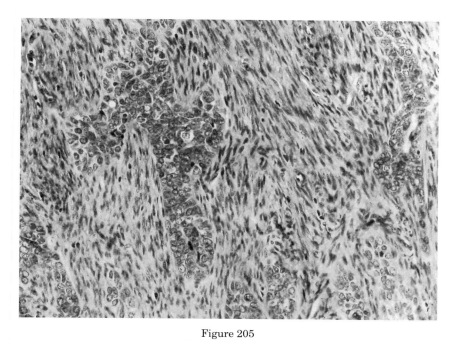

Figure 205
CARCINOSARCOMA
The carcinomatous element of this tumor is poorly differentiated, but the sarcoma is a relatively low-grade spindle cell sarcoma.

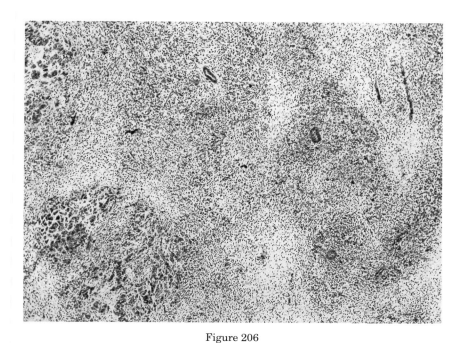

Figure 206
CARCINOSARCOMA
Most of the tumor in this illustration could be mistaken for adenosarcoma with small benign-appearing glands cuffed by hypercellular stroma. However, at the lower left-hand corner, a focus of adenocarcinoma is also present.

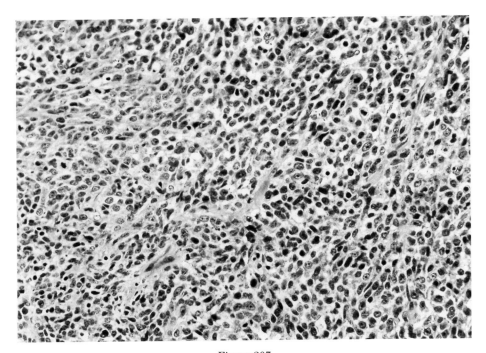

Figure 207
CARCINOSARCOMA
The poorly differentiated sarcomatous component in this field is composed of round cells.

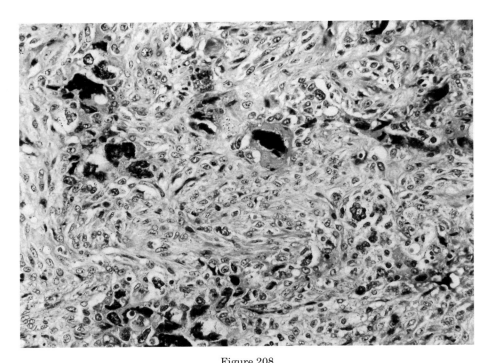

Figure 208
CARCINOSARCOMA
The sarcomatous component illustrated here is anaplastic and contains numerous giant cells.

The heterologous carcinosarcomas contain foci of rhabdomyosarcoma (figs. 209, 210), chondrosarcoma (fig. 211), osteosarcoma (fig. 212), or liposarcoma (fig. 213), in that order of frequency, or often mixtures of these histologic types. In rare instances, other pathways of differentiation, such as neuroectodermal, may be seen (19).

Ultrastructural and Immunohistochemical Findings. Ultrastructural and immunohistochemical studies of uterine carcinosarcomas (3,4,15,18) have generally been directed toward trying to ascertain whether these tumors represent collision tumors (a mixture of two distinct malignant cell populations), combination tumors (in which both cell populations are derived from a common progenitor), or composition tumors (carcinomas with reactive but benign stromal elements). Most ultrastructural studies have emphasized the distinctness of the malignant stromal and epithelial populations, but the largest series of cases examined ultrastructurally has demonstrated permeation of the stromal component by isolated epithelial cells and occasional hybrid forms between the carcinomatous and sarcomatous phenotypes (15). Additionally, some immunohistochemical studies have suggested distinct carcinomatous and sarcomatous populations (3,18), whereas others have noted that epithelial markers such as cytokeratins and epithelial membrane antigen are frequently displayed by the sarcomatous-appearing cells (4,15). It is well known that pure endometrial carcinomas frequently contain vimentin filaments in tumor cells, and this is true of the epithelial component of carcinosarcomas as well (15). In addition, rhabdomyosarcoma cells show immunohistochemical reactivity for myoglobin and foci of chondrosarcomatous differentiation for S-100 protein. These latter markers may be useful in demonstrating foci of heterologous differentiation that are questionable on routine light-microscopic examination.

Differential Diagnosis. The main differential diagnosis of carcinosarcoma is with poorly differentiated endometrial carcinoma. In a typical poorly differentiated endometrial carcinoma with spindle cell metaplasia, the poorly differentiated foci of adenocarcinoma or squamous cell carcinoma gradually blend into a sarcomatoid spindle cell component (fig. 214). In typical carcinosarcoma, on the other hand, the glandular and stromal elements are well defined (figs. 204, 205). I favor making this distinction on the basis of routine light microscopy alone, because our own ultrastructural and immunohistochemical study (15) has shown that over half of otherwise typical carcinosarcomas show evidence of epithelial differentiation in the sarcomatous component. Furthermore, there was no difference in clinical behavior or survival between those tumors that did or did not show such evidence of epithelial differentiation, whereas the small number of metaplastic carcinomas diagnosed by routine light microscopy in our study had a more favorable prognosis.

Other differential diagnostic problems concern the presence or absence of heterologous elements. One common mistake is to confuse stromal cells containing eosinophilic hyaline droplets (figs. 215, 216) with cells showing rhabdomyosarcomatous differentiation. These droplets are common in both homologous and heterologous tumors, do not stain for myoglobin, and look quite different, even in hematoxylin and eosin stains, from the densely and diffusely eosinophilic cells of rhabdomyosarcoma, which sometimes have cross striations, (figs. 209, 210). An additional problem concerning heterologous elements is the distinction of foci of chondrosarcoma from foci of squamous cell carcinoma (fig. 217). Chondrosarcoma cells have a glassier cytoplasm, less prominent cell membranes, and a more lacunar appearance. An immunostain for S-100 protein may be useful in identifying chondrosarcoma. Remember that foci of benign chondroid, osseous, or fatty differentiation may be seen in rare, otherwise typical, endometrial carcinomas (or for that matter in totally benign endometria) and do not justify the diagnosis of heterologous carcinosarcoma. Similarly, pure rhabdomyosarcomas, chondrosarcomas, osteosarcomas, and liposarcomas of the endometrium exist, albeit rarely, and should not be diagnosed as carcinosarcoma in the absence of a malignant epithelial component. Finally, the differential diagnosis with adenosarcoma has already been discussed; a malignant epithelial component should be clearly present before the diagnosis of carcinosarcoma is made.

Treatment. The treatment of carcinosarcoma is predominantly surgical, but adjuvant radiation and chemotherapy are often utilized

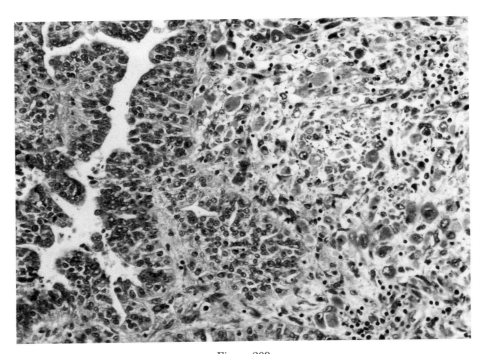

Figure 209
CARCINOSARCOMA
This figure shows rhabdomyosarcomatous differentiation.

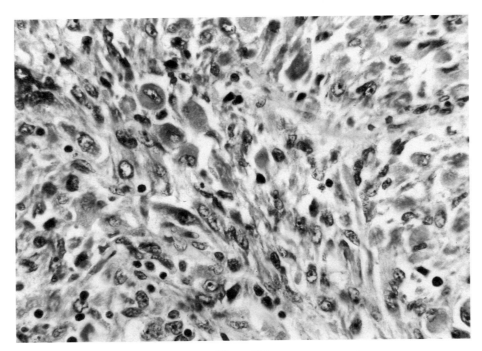

Figure 210
CARCINOSARCOMA
In another case with rhabdomyosarcomatous differentiation, cross striations were not demonstrated, but these large eosinophilic cells were immunoreactive for myoglobin. No carcinoma is present in this field.

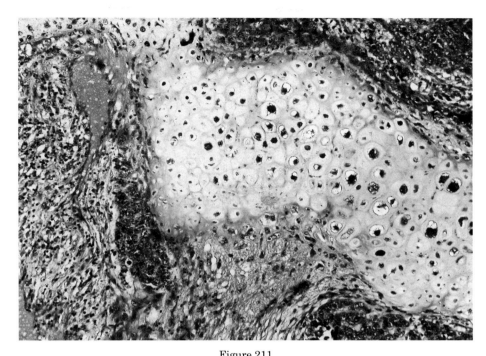

Figure 211
CARCINOSARCOMA
A focus of chondrosarcoma is illustrated. Several foci of poorly differentiated adenocarcinoma border the chondrosarcoma.

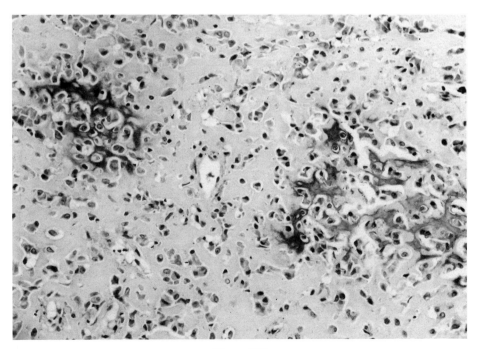

Figure 212
CARCINOSARCOMA
In this field, osteosarcoma is present.

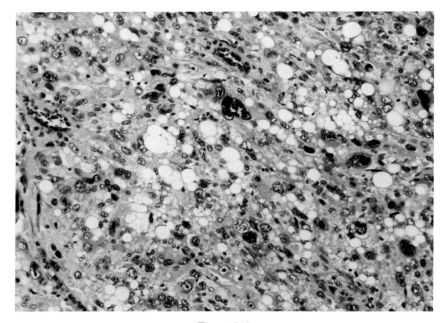

Figure 213
CARCINOSARCOMA
This photomicrograph shows liposarcomatous differentiation.

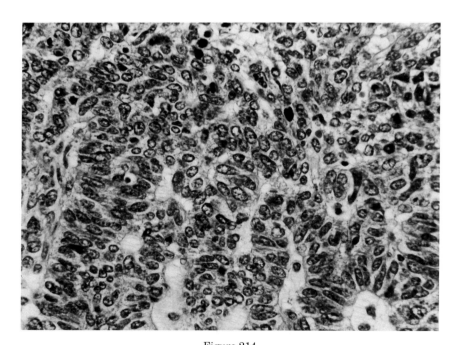

Figure 214
METAPLASTIC CARCINOMA OF THE ENDOMETRIUM
In this illustration, the cells of the adenocarcinoma gradually merge with a malignant stromal component (sarcomatoid carcinoma) rather than showing a sharp transition, as in carcinosarcoma.

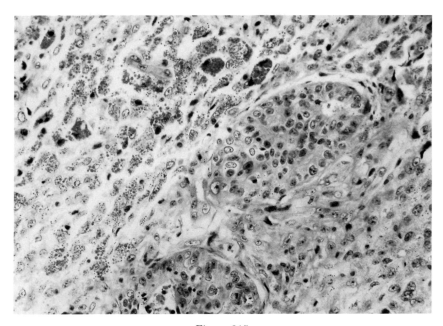

Figure 215
(Figures 215 and 216 are from the same patient)
CARCINOSARCOMA
The stromal cells in this example contain numerous hyaline globules.

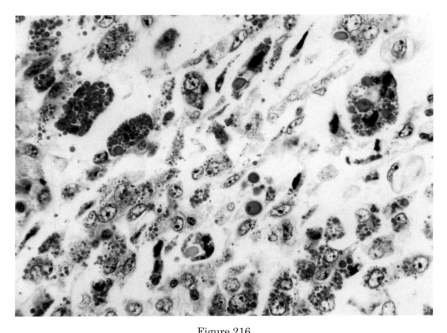

Figure 216
CARCINOSARCOMA
This is a higher magnification of the hyaline globules in stromal cells illustrated in figure 215. Compare this with figure 210, which shows sarcomatous rhabdomyoblasts at similar magnification.

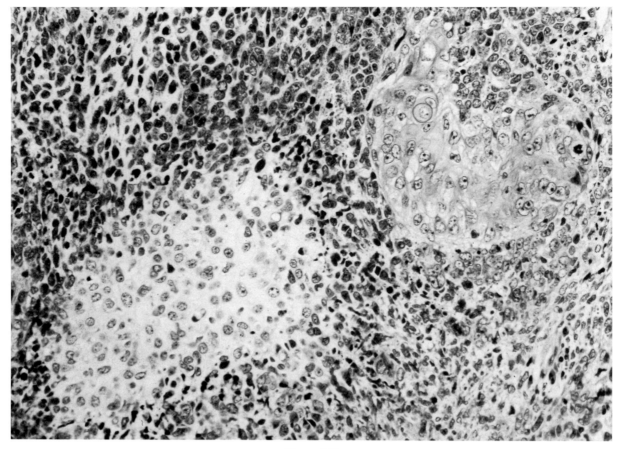

Figure 217
CARCINOSARCOMA
This illustration compares a focus of chondrosarcoma (left) with one of squamous metaplasia (right). The chondrosarcoma cells have a more glassy cytoplasm, less prominent cell membranes, and a more lacunar appearance.

because of the poor prognosis. Combination chemotherapy appears to be useful both as adjuvant treatment and for recurrent disease (30).

Prognosis. It is generally agreed that the prognosis of carcinosarcoma is considerably worse than that of endometrial carcinoma, with 5-year survival rates in recently reported series ranging between 18 and 39 percent (16,26,31). In part, this reflects the fact that many of the cases present with advanced-stage disease (staging is the same as for endometrial carcinoma) in which the prognosis is particularly poor. Although patients with heterologous tumors are said to fare more poorly than patients with homologous tumors in some reports (27,28), most recent studies have shown no significant difference (16,26,31,34). Surgical stage

and depth of myometrial invasion, on the other hand, have usually been important prognostic indicators, as was peritoneal cytology in one recent series (22). Nevertheless, even carcinosarcomas with no demonstrated myometrial invasion have recurred in about 25 percent of the cases in one large series (34).

In a large Gynecologic Oncology Group study (34), the type and grade of the carcinomatous component seemed to reflect the behavior of the tumor more than the appearance of the sarcomatous component did. Indeed, these tumors behaved like poorly differentiated carcinomas in that they metastasized relatively frequently (16 percent) to pelvic or periaortic lymph nodes. If the sarcomatous and carcinomatous components in the primary tumor were separate, it was usually the carcinoma that more closely approximated and invaded the myometrium (fig. 218) and almost invariably the carcinoma that had spread to lymph nodes and other extrauterine sites at the time of initial surgery (fig. 219). However, later metastases may contain both the carcinomatous and the sarcomatous phenotypes (34).

These clinical and pathologic findings, as well as some of the ultrastructural and immunohistochemical findings discussed previously, have suggested that many, most, or even all carcinosarcomas may really be metaplastic carcinomas. Nevertheless, carcinosarcomas diagnosed by the traditional light-microscopic criteria have a considerably poorer prognosis than even high-grade endometrial carcinomas, with recurrences occurring even in 25 percent of the cases lacking myometrial invasion (34).

CARCINOFIBROMA

The last of the mixed tumors is also the rarest, with only a handful of cases reported in the literature (17).

Carcinofibroma is a tumor with a carcinomatous epithelial component and a benign mesenchymal component. The mesenchymal component is classically fibromatous, although it may be questionable whether this component is neoplastic or reactive. A single reported case had a heterologous stromal component that included benign cartilage and adipose tissue (5). Too few carcinofibromas have been reported to be able to predict their clinical behavior.

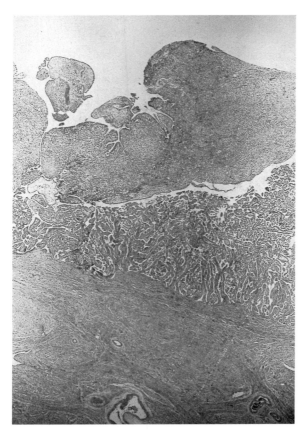

Figure 218
CARCINOSARCOMA
In this example the sarcomatous component is on the surface, underlaid by the carcinomatous component, which is in contact with underlying myometrium.

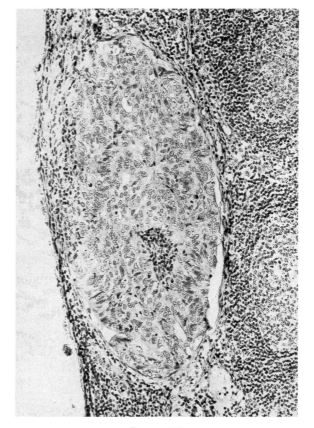

Figure 219
CARCINOSARCOMA
This pelvic lymph node, obtained at the time of hysterectomy and exploratory laparotomy, contains a metastatic lesion consisting of pure carcinoma.

REFERENCES

1. Abell MR. Papillary adenofibroma of the uterine cervix. Am J Obstet Gynecol 1971;110:990–3.
2. Amr SS, Tavassoli FA, Hassan AA, Issa AA, Madanat FF. Mixed mesodermal tumor of the uterus in a 4-year-old girl. Int J Gynecol Pathol 1986;5:371–8.
3. Auerbach HE, LiVolsi VA, Merino MJ. Malignant mixed müllerian tumors of the uterus. An immunohistochemical study. Int J Gynecol Pathol 1988;7:123–30.
4. Bitterman P, Chun B, Kurman RJ. The significance of epithelial differentiation in mixed mesodermal tumors of the uterus. Am J Surg Pathol 1990;14:317–28.
5. Chen KT, Vergon JM. Carcinomesenchymoma of the uterus. Am J Clin Pathol 1981;75:746–8.
6. Chumas JC, Mann WJ, Tseng L. Malignant mixed müllerian tumor of the endometrium in a young woman with polycystic ovaries. Cancer 1983;52:1478–81.
7. Clement PB. Müllerian adenosarcomas of the uterus with sarcomatous overgrowth. A clinicopathological analysis of 10 cases. Am J Surg Pathol 1989;13:28–38.
8. _____, Scully RE. Extrauterine mesodermal (müllerian) adenosarcoma. A clinicopathologic analysis of five cases. Am J Clin Pathol 1978;69:276–83.
9. _____, Scully RE. Müllerian adenofibroma of the uterus with invasion of myometrium and pelvic veins. Int J Gynecol Pathol 1990;9:363–71.
10. _____, Scully RE. Müllerian adenosarcoma of the uterus. A clinicopathologic analysis of ten cases of a distinctive type of müllerian mixed tumor. Cancer 1974;34:1138–49.
11. _____, Scully RE. Müllerian adenosarcoma of the uterus: a clinicopathological analysis of 100 cases with a review of the literature. Hum Pathol 1990;21:363–81.
12. _____, Scully RE. Müllerian adenosarcomas of the uterus with sex cord-like elements. A clinicopathologic analysis of eight cases. Am J Clin Pathol 1989;91:664–72.
13. _____, Scully RE. Uterine tumors with mixed epithelial and mesenchymal elements. Semin Diagn Pathol 1988;5:199–222.
14. _____, Young RH. Atypical polypoid adenomyoma of the uterus associated with Turner's syndrome. A report of three cases, including a review of "estrogen-associated" endometrial neoplasms and neoplasms associated with Turner's syndrome. Int J Gynecol Pathol 1987;6:104–13.
15. de Brito PA, Orenstein JM, Silverberg SG. Carcinosarcoma of the female genital tract: immunohistochemical and ultrastructural analysis of 28 cases. Hum Pathol; in press.
16. Dinh TV, Slavin RE, Bhagavan BS, Hannigan EV, Tiamson EM, Yandell RB. Mixed müllerian tumors of the uterus: a clinicopathologic study. Obstet Gynecol 1989;74:388–92.
17. Engdahl E, Wolfhagen U. Carcinofibroma—a rare variant of mixed müllerian tumor. Acta Obstet Gynecol Scand 1988;67:85–8.
18. Geisinger KR, Dabbs DJ, Marshall RB. Malignant mixed müllerian tumors. An ultrastructural and immunohistochemical analysis with histogenetic considerations. Cancer 1987;59:1781–90.
19. Gersell DJ, Duncan DA, Fulling KH. Malignant mixed müllerian tumor of the uterus with neuroectodermal differentiation. Int J Gynecol Pathol 1989;8:169–78.
20. Hertig AT, Gore H. Tumors of the female sex organs. Pt. 2, Tumors of the vulva, vagina, and uterus. Atlas of tumor pathology, 1st Series, Fascicle 33, Washington, DC: Armed Forces Institute of Pathology, 1960:180–1.
21. Kaku T, Silverberg SG, Major FJ, et al. Adenosarcoma of the uterus. A Gynecologic Oncology Group clinicopathologic study of 31 cases. Int J Gynecol Pathol; in press.
22. Kanbour AI, Buchsbaum HJ, Hall A, Kanbour AI. Peritoneal cytology in malignant mixed müllerian tumors of the uterus. Gynecol Oncol 1989;33:91–5.
23. Kao GF, Norris HJ. Benign and low grade variants of mixed mesodermal tumor (adenosarcoma) of the ovary and adnexal region. Cancer 1978;42:1314–24.
24. Katzenstein AL, Askin FB, Feldman PS. Müllerian adenosarcoma of the uterus: an ultrastructural study of four cases. Cancer 1977;40:2233–42.
25. Mazur MT. Atypical polypoid adenomyomas of the endometrium. Am J Surg Pathol 1981;5:473–82.
26. Nielsen SN, Podratz KC, Scheithauer BW, O'Brien PC. Clinicopathologic analysis of uterine malignant mixed müllerian tumors. Gynecol Oncol 1989;34:372–8.
27. Norris HJ, Roth E, Taylor HB. Mesenchymal tumors of the uterus. II. A clinical and pathologic study of 31 mixed mesodermal tumors. Obstet Gynecol 1966;28:57–63.
28. _____, Taylor HB. Mesenchymal tumors of the uterus. III. A clinical and pathological study of 31 carcinosarcomas. Cancer 1966;19:1459–65.
29. Östör AG, Fortune DW. Benign and low grade variant of mixed müllerian tumour of the uterus. Histopathology 1980;4:369–82.
30. Peters WA III, Rivkin SE, Smith MR, Tesh DE. Cisplatin and adriamycin combination chemotherapy for uterine stromal sarcomas and mixed mesodermal tumors. Gynecol Oncol 1989;34:323–7.
31. Podczaski ES, Woomert CA, Stevens CW Jr, et al. Management of malignant, mixed mesodermal tumors of the uterus. Gynecol Oncol 1989;32:240–4.
32. Press MF, Scully RE. Endometrial "sarcomas" complicating ovarian thecoma, polycystic ovarian disease and estrogen therapy. Gynecol Oncol 1985;21:135–54.
33. Schwartz SM, Thomas DB. A case-control study of risk factors for sarcomas of the uterus. The World Health Organization Collaborative Study of Neoplasia and Steroid Contraceptives. Cancer 1989;64:2487–92.
34. Silverberg SG, Major FJ, Blessing JA, et al. Carcinosarcoma (malignant mixed mesodermal tumor) of the uterus. A Gynecologic Oncology Group pathologic study of 203 cases. Int J Gynecol Pathol 1990;9:1–19.
35. Spanos WJ Jr, Peters LJ, Oswald MJ. Patterns of recurrence in malignant mixed müllerian tumor of the uterus. Cancer 1986;57:155–9.
36. Tenti P, Babilonti L, La Fianza A, et al. Cytology of malignant mixed mesodermal tumour of the uterus: experience of 10 cases. Eur J Gynaecol Oncol 1989;10:125–8.

37. Vellios F. Papillary adenofibroma-adenosarcoma. The uterine cystosarcoma phyllodes. Prog Surg Pathol 1980;1:205–19.

38. _____ , Ng AB, Reagan JW. Papillary adenofibroma of the uterus: a benign mesodermal mixed tumor of müllerian origin. Am J Clin Pathol 1973;60:543–51.

39. Young RH, Treger T, Scully RE. Atypical polypoid adenomyoma of the uterus. A report of 27 cases. Am J Clin Pathol 1986;86:139–45.

40. Zaloudek CJ, Norris HJ. Adenofibroma and adenosarcoma of the uterus: a clinicopathologic study of 35 cases. Cancer 1981;48:354–66.

MISCELLANEOUS AND SECONDARY TUMORS

MISCELLANEOUS TUMORS

The general heading of miscellaneous tumors includes both tumors the histogenesis of which is not known and tumors that do not fit neatly into any of the other groups in the classification. They are all rare in the uterus, although some of them are common in other sites.

Sex Cord-like Tumors

In 1976, under the heading of "uterine tumors resembling ovarian sex-cord tumors," Clement and Scully (6) reported a series of 14 cases of a rather heterogeneous group of uterine neoplasms characterized by pure or predominant histologic patterns that closely resembled those seen more commonly in sex cord tumors of the ovary, specifically granulosa and Sertoli cell tumors. It is believed that previous cases reported as granulosa cell tumor of the uterus represent examples of this entity. Subsequent reports have mostly involved single cases or small series of cases and have emphasized ultrastructural or immunohistochemical findings (7,9,14,18).

The patients have been in the reproductive and postmenopausal age groups and usually presented with abnormal vaginal bleeding. The uterus is usually enlarged and contains myometrial masses ranging from 3 to 10 cm in diameter that are generally solid but occasionally cystic and usually well circumscribed. The cut surfaces are variable in color (although often yellow) and lack the firm consistency and whorled pattern of a leiomyoma. Histologically (figs. 220–223), the tumors are usually well circumscribed but may infiltrate the myometrium, occasionally in lymphatics or veins. The tumor cells generally contain small regular nuclei, but the amount of cytoplasm varies from scant to abundant and is often lipid rich. Characteristically, these cells form cords, tubules, trabeculae, and solid nests and often display a plexiform pattern. True thecal or Leydig cell differentiation has not been observed. Mitotic figures are generally rare but occasionally may be abundant.

It has been noted that the tumor cells co-express cytokeratins and vimentin immunohistochemically and may show epithelial, endometrial stromal, and smooth muscle features ultrastructurally.

The main problem with this group of tumors is that both endometrial stromal tumors and smooth muscle tumors of the uterus may display focal differentiation of this sort. Thus, it is recommended that the less specific diagnosis of sex cord-like tumor be reserved for cases in which extensive sectioning fails to reveal evidence of more classic endometrial stromal or smooth muscle differentiation. If the tumor can be shown to be of endometrial stromal or smooth muscle origin, then the usual rules for predicting behavior apply.

If, on the other hand, only sex cord-like differentiation is demonstrated after extensive sectioning, the behavior of the lesion must be considered unpredictable, and thus it should be regarded as potentially malignant. However, most reported cases have followed a benign clinical course, although a few have recurred or metastasized. Lymphatic or blood vessel invasion in particular has been associated with an unfavorable outcome (7).

Tumors of Germ Cell Type

Rare examples of mature and immature teratomas (1) and yolk sac (endodermal sinus) tumors (13) of the uterus have been reported. These tumors are histologically identical to those seen far more commonly in the gonads and have occurred predominantly in adults. In the case of a malignant germ cell tumor in the uterus, the possibility of a metastasis from a primary ovarian neoplasm must always be ruled out. Also in the differential diagnosis of endodermal sinus tumor is clear cell adenocarcinoma, a far more common lesion in the uterine corpus. Teratoma, of course, should not be diagnosed solely on the basis of heterologous differentiation of tissues of mesodermal origin (bone, cartilage, fat, and striated muscle), because these occur much more commonly in carcinosarcomas and adenosarcomas and, with

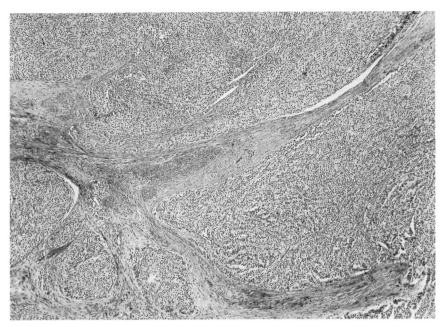

Figure 220
(Figures 220 and 221 are from the same patient)
UTERINE SEX CORD-LIKE TUMOR
This tumor extensively infiltrates the myometrium and is seen as tongues within dilated venous or lymphatic spaces.

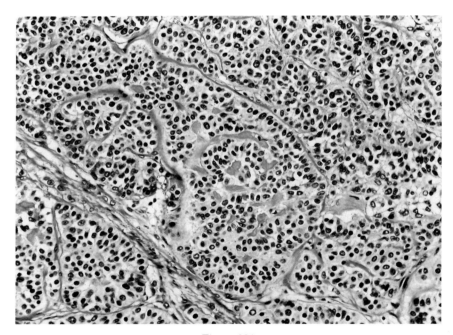

Figure 221
UTERINE SEX CORD-LIKE TUMOR
Higher magnification of the infiltrative tumor illustrated in figure 220 shows a pattern of tubules, trabeculae, and solid nests containing fairly uniform cells with no mitotic figures.

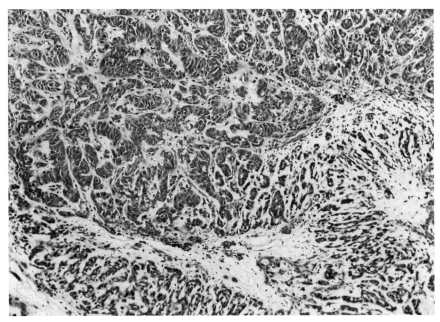

Figure 222
(Figures 222 and 223 are from the same patient)
UTERINE SEX CORD-LIKE TUMOR
This tumor was a sharply defined mass within the myometrium and was composed
entirely of cords and trabeculae.

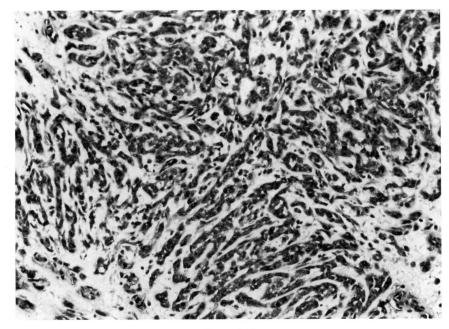

Figure 223
UTERINE SEX CORD-LIKE TUMOR
Higher magnification of the tumor seen in figure 222 shows the sex cord-like pattern
and the uniform small cells lacking atypia or mitotic activity.

the exception of striated muscle, as benign metaplasias in the endometrial stroma. Bone and cartilage may also be of fetal origin, and fat may be present as a result of traumatic perforation of the uterus. Glial tissue can also be seen in the uterus, not only in teratomas but more commonly as benign implants of presumed fetal origin (see Tumor-Like Lesions) and rarely as a primary glioma.

Neuroectodermal Tumors

Rare examples of primitive neuroectodermal tumors with variable neuroblastic, ganglionic, glial, and neuronal differentiation (figs. 224, 225) have been reported in the uterus (12). These tumors have proven to be highly malignant. A case of uterine glioma with a benign clinical course has also been reported (21).

Lymphomas and Leukemias

Although lymphomatous and leukemic infiltrates may be seen in the uterus with some regularity at autopsy, they are only rarely encountered in biopsy or hysterectomy specimens (5, 11). Lymphomas are more common than leukemic infiltrates in this situation, and the latter are almost always granulocytic. A prior history of lymphoma or leukemia can usually be elicited. Lymphomas involving the uterus are almost always of non-Hodgkin's type and are classified and staged by usual lymphoma criteria. Lymphoma presenting as an isolated finding in the uterus has been reported to be associated with an excellent survival rate (11).

The differential diagnosis of these lesions includes other malignant neoplasms, particularly endometrial stromal sarcoma and undifferentiated carcinoma, as well as benign lymphoma-like lesions (10,20). In the first of these situations, the correct diagnosis can usually be made by the application of an immunohistochemical stain for hematopoietic cells (leukocyte-common antigen) or, in the case of granulocytic sarcoma, an esterase stain. However, the distinction of malignant lymphoma from a lymphoma-like lesion may be more complicated. As discussed in the chapter on Tumor-Like

Lesions, a lymphoma-like lesion may massively infiltrate the endometrium, often with considerable nuclear pleomorphism. However, other inflammatory cells are usually admixed, there is seldom a gross mass, and myometrial invasion (figs. 226, 227) is not present. Polyclonality may be demonstrable in these lesions, but this may be difficult or impossible in routinely fixed and embedded specimens. Leiomyomata may also be massively infiltrated by benign lymphoid tissue (fig. 228) (10), with the main differential diagnostic feature here being that the lymphoid infiltrate in such a case is strictly limited to the confines of the leiomyoma, rather than diffusely infiltrating the myometrium. Some cases of chronic endometritis also may develop an inflammatory infiltrate that is massive enough and displays enough nuclear atypia that it may simulate a malignant lymphoma. In such cases, other features of endometritis are usually present, and myometrial involvement is absent.

Other Miscellaneous Tumors

This group comprises a heterogeneous group of tumors that have been or will be reported predominantly as single cases. Examples include Brenner tumor (2), Wilms' tumor (3), and malignant rhabdoid tumor (4).

SECONDARY TUMORS

As with malignant lymphomas and leukemias, other secondary tumors are more commonly seen in the uterus at autopsy than during life (15,16). They may be conveniently divided into two large groups: tumors from genital and tumors from extragenital sites.

Of the genital tumors secondary in the uterine corpus, the most common is represented by direct extension from an invasive or (rarely) in situ carcinoma (usually squamous but occasionally glandular) of the cervix (17). In the case of a cervical squamous carcinoma, the diagnosis is usually apparent, although the rare primary squamous cell carcinoma of the endometrium must be taken into consideration in the differential diagnosis. The distinction between a primary adenocarcinoma of the endocervix and

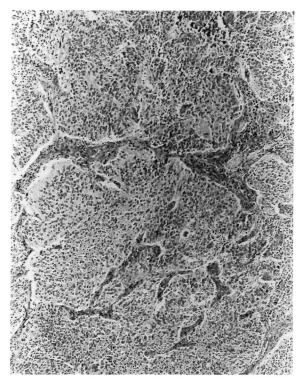

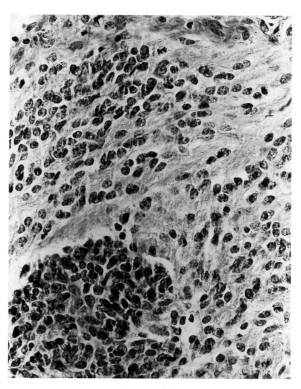

Figure 224
(Figures 224 and 225 are from the same patient)
PRIMITIVE NEUROECTODERMAL TUMOR
This uterine tumor, which was originally interpreted as an endometrial sarcoma, is characterized by prominent branching blood vessels with endothelial cell hyperplasia surrounded by sheets of small round cells.

Figure 225
PRIMITIVE NEUROECTODERMAL TUMOR
Higher magnification of the tumor illustrated in figure 224 shows one compact nest and diffuse infiltration of small neuroblast-like cells in a neurofibrillary background.

Figure 226
(Figures 226 and 227 are from the same patient)
MALIGNANT LYMPHOMA OF THE UTERUS
The infiltrate, which appears focally nodular, extensively infiltrates the myometrium.

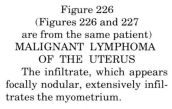

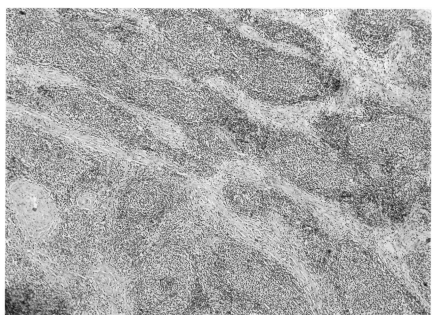

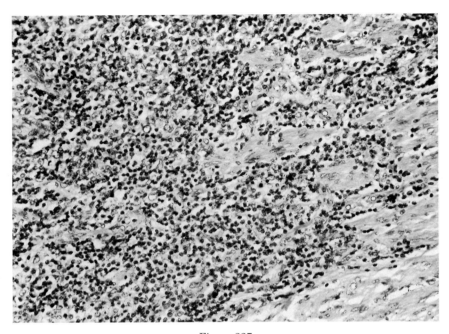

Figure 227
(Figures 227 and 226 are from the same patient)
MALIGNANT LYMPHOMA OF THE UTERUS
Higher magnification of the tumor illustrated in figure 226 shows the lymphoid nature of the tumor cells.

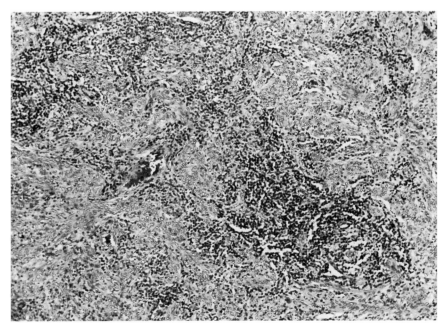

Figure 228
UTERINE LEIOMYOMA WITH LYMPHOID INFILTRATION
SIMULATING LYMPHOMA
The lymphoid infiltrate pictured here was limited to the confines of a well-circumscribed leiomyoma.

primary adenocarcinoma of the endometrium, on the other hand, is one of the more difficult problems in gynecologic pathology and is discussed in more detail in the chapter on Endometrial Carcinoma. Although corporeal extension of a primary cervical carcinoma is said to worsen the prognosis, it has not been accepted as justification for a higher clinical or pathologic stage (17).

A similar diagnostic problem concerns synchronous adenocarcinomas of the endometrium and one or both ovaries (19). It is often difficult to decide whether these lesions represent separate primary tumors or primary endometrial carcinoma metastatic to the ovary, with metastatic spread in the opposite direction being considerably rarer. This problem is discussed in more detail in the chapter on Endometrial Carcinoma. Ovarian cancers frequently metastasize to the uterine serosa, although the question of the primary origin of these serosal tumors from peritoneal mesothelium may also be raised (8). Endosalpingiosis involving the serosa (fig. 229) should not be confused with either primary or secondary carcinoma.

When an extragenital tumor metastasizes to the uterine corpus, there is usually other evidence of dissemination (15,16). However, occasionally a tumor diagnosed by endometrial curettage or hysterectomy may represent the first sign of dissemination from a known or even unknown extragenital primary site. Mammary and gastrointestinal carcinomas are by far the most frequent extragenital sources of metastases to the uterus, although rare examples of metastases of every type have been reported. In the endometrium (figs. 230, 231), metastatic carcinoma may be suspected if one of the following signs is present: 1) a tumor with an unusual gross or histologic pattern for primary endometrial carcinoma, 2) diffuse replacement of endometrial stroma with persistence of intervening benign endometrial glands, 3) lack of accompanying premalignant changes in the residual benign endometrium, and 4) usual lack of tumor necrosis. Metastases that lack cytologic atypia or mitotic activity (such as the lobular carcinoma of mammary origin illustrated in figs. 230 and 231) may be mistaken for

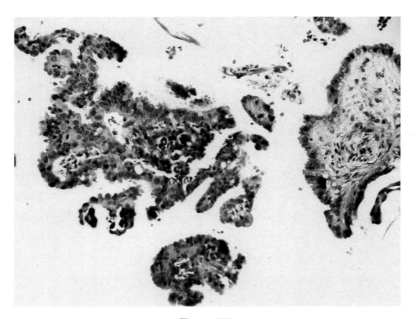

Figure 229
ENDOSALPINGIOSIS INVOLVING UTERINE SEROSA
As is often the case, this lesion is papillary and focally calcified, leading to possible confusion with primary or metastatic adenocarcinoma, particularly of serous type. The lack of cellular stratification (except in areas of tangential sectioning), of more than slight nuclear atypia, and especially of any mitotic activity all contradict the diagnosis of carcinoma. The presence of cilia (not seen in this field) is often a useful criterion of benignity.

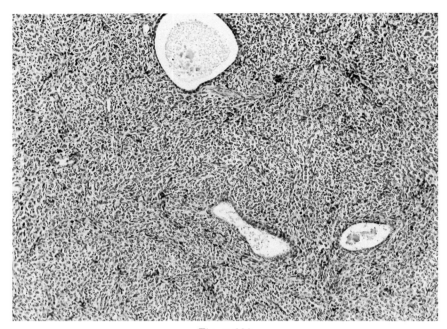

Figure 230
(Figures 230 and 231 are from the same patient)
METASTATIC ADENOCARCINOMA IN ENDOMETRIUM
This infiltrating lobular carcinoma of mammary origin diffusely replaces the endometrial stroma and separates residual benign glands.

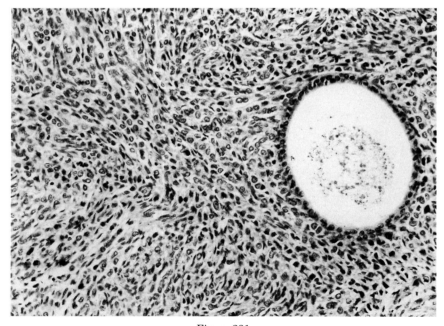

Figure 231
METASTATIC ADENOCARCINOMA IN ENDOMETRIUM
Higher magnification of the lesion illustrated in figure 230 shows small, fairly uniform tumor cells that might be mistaken for endometrial stromal cells. However, the vascular pattern of endometrial stroma is absent, some cells contained intracytoplasmic lumina, and immunohistochemistry revealed the presence of epithelial markers. The patient had a known widely disseminated mammary carcinoma.

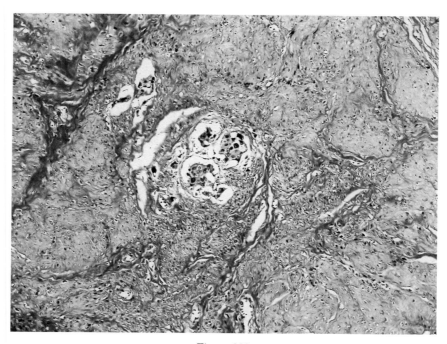

Figure 232
METASTATIC DUCTAL CARCINOMA IN A LEIOMYOMA
This is an example of an infiltrating duct carcinoma of mammary origin in a uterine leiomyoma. (Courtesy of Dr. Toshiaki Manabe, Kurashiki, Japan.)

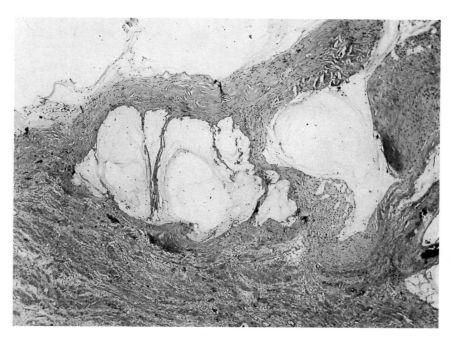

Figure 233
PSEUDOMYXOMA PERITONEI INVOLVING MYOMETRIUM
BY DIRECT EXTENSION
This low-power photomicrograph shows pseudocysts containing mucinous material infiltrating the myometrium near its serosal surface. The patient had pseudomyxoma peritonei derived from a low-grade mucinous adenocarcinoma of the appendix.

endometrial stromal, epithelioid smooth muscle, or sex cord-like tumors if the history of an extrauterine primary cancer is not known and appropriate pathologic and clinical investigations are not performed.

Metastatic tumors can also involve the myometrium, where they usually present as scattered microscopic foci (fig. 232). If the overlying endometrium is benign, the only significant differential diagnoses would be with endometrial carcinoma arising in deep-seated foci of adenomyosis and with adenomatoid tumor (see Smooth Muscle and Other Mesenchymal Tumors). Occasionally, secondary malignant neoplasms can involve the myometrium by direct extension from adjacent organs (fig. 233).

REFERENCES

1. Ansah-Boateng Y, Wells M, Poole DR. Coexistent immature teratoma of the uterus and endometrial adenocarcinoma complicated by gliomatosis peritonei. Gynecol Oncol 1985;21:106–10.
2. Arhelger RB, Bocian JJ. Brenner tumor of the uterus. Cancer 1976;38:1741–3.
3. Bittencourt AL, Britto JF, Fonseca LE Jr. Wilms' tumor of the uterus: the first report in the literature. Cancer 1981;47:2496–9.
4. Cho KR, Rosenshein NB, Epstein JI. Malignant rhabdoid tumor of the uterus. Int J Gynecol Pathol 1989;8:381–7.
5. Chorlton I, Karnei RF Jr, King FM, Norris HJ. Primary malignant reticuloendothelial disease involving the vagina, cervix, and corpus uteri. Obstet Gynecol 1974;44:735–48.
6. Clement PB, Scully RE. Uterine tumors resembling ovarian sex-cord tumors. A clinicopathologic analysis of fourteen cases Am J Clin Pathol 1976;66:512–25.
7. _____ , Scully RE. Uterine tumors with mixed epithelial and mesenchymal elements. Semin Diagn Pathol 1988;5:199–222.
8. Farhi DC, Silverberg SG. Pseudometastases in female genital cancer. Pathol Annu 1982;17(Pt 1):47–76.
9. Fekete PS, Vellios F, Patterson BD. Uterine tumor resembling an ovarian sex-cord tumor: report of a case of an endometrial stromal tumor with foam cells and ultrastructural evidence of epithelial differentiation. Int J Gynecol Pathol 1985;4:378–87.
10. Ferry JA, Harris NL, Scully RE. Uterine leiomyomas with lymphoid infiltration simulating lymphoma. Int J Gynecol Pathol 1989;8:263–70.
11. _____ , Young RH. Malignant lymphoma, pseudolymphoma, and hematopoietic disorders of the female genital tract. Pathol Annu 1991;26:227–63.
12. Hendrickson MR, Scheithauer BW. Primitive neuroectodermal tumor of the endometrium: report of two cases, one with electron microscopic observations. Int J Gynecol Pathol 1986;5:249–59.
13. Joseph MG, Fellows FG, Hearn SA. Primary endodermal sinus tumor of the endometrium. A clinicopathologic, immunocytochemical, and ultrastructural study. Cancer 1990;65:297–302.
14. Kantelip B, Cloup N, Dechelotte P. Uterine tumor resembling ovarian sex cord tumors: report of a case with ultrastructural study. Hum Pathol 1986;17:91–4.
15. Kumar NB, Hart WR. Metastases to the uterine corpus from extragenital cancers. A clinicopathologic study of 63 cases. Cancer 1982;50:2163–9.
16. _____ , Schneider V. Metastases to the uterus from extrapelvic primary tumors. Int J Gynecol Pathol 1983;2:134–40.
17. Perez CA, Camel HM, Askin F, Breaux S. Endometrial extension of carcinoma of the uterine cervix: a prognostic factor that may modify staging. Cancer 1981;48:170–80.
18. Sullinger J, Scully RE. Uterine tumors resembling ovarian sex cord tumors: a clinicopathologic and immunohistochemical study [Abstract]. Mod Pathol 1989;2:93a.
19. Ulbright TM, Roth LM. Metastatic and independent cancers of the endometrium and ovary: a clinicopathologic study of 34 cases. Hum Pathol 1985;16:28–34.
20. Young RH, Harris NL, Scully RE. Lymphoma-like lesions of the lower female genital tract: a report of 16 cases. Int J Gynecol Pathol 1985;4:289–99.
21. _____ , Kleinman GM, Scully RE. Glioma of the uterus. Report of a case with comments on histogenesis. Am J Surg Pathol 1981;5:695–9.

TUMOR-LIKE LESIONS

One of the most important groups of lesions considered in this text is the rather heterogeneous group of endometrial and myometrial changes that are classified together as tumor-like lesions. Although some of these lesions (particularly adenomyosis and chronic endometritis) may be associated with clinical signs and symptoms of their own, the main clinical significance of these lesions as a group is that they may be misinterpreted as neoplastic or preneoplastic conditions. Furthermore, many of these lesions can occur in association with endometrial hyperplasias or carcinomas, although they usually do not seem to alter the behavior of the underlying hyperplastic or neoplastic lesion.

EPITHELIAL METAPLASTIC AND RELATED CHANGES

Definition. This is a group of non-neoplastic lesions, often occurring together or in association with other non-neoplastic or neoplastic lesions in which the normal endometrial epithelium is replaced, usually focally, by another type of non-neoplastic epithelium. The types of epithelial metaplastic and related changes recognized in the new International Society of Gynecological Pathologists classification are

- squamous metaplasia and morules
- mucinous metaplasia (including intestinal)
- ciliary change
- hobnail change
- clear cell change
- eosinophilic cell change (including oncocytic)
- surface syncytial change
- papillary proliferation
- Arias-Stella change.

Although the epithelial metaplastic and related changes are balanced in the International Society of Gynecological Pathologists classification by nonepithelial metaplastic and related changes, the former are both far more frequently encountered and far more likely to be confused with a malignant or premalignant process. Although scattered examples of these epithelial lesions had been published, often as case reports, since the 1950s, much of the current interest in them dates from two publications by Hendrickson and Kempson that appeared in 1980 (23,24). With the exception of Arias-Stella change (which also represents an exception to many of the other general statements about this group of lesions), these lesions were all initially defined as metaplasias. However, because the term *metaplasia* refers to the replacement of a normal epithelium in one site (in this instance, the endometrium) with a mature different type of epithelium inappropriate to that site but appropriate to a different one, the term metaplasia has been replaced by the less restrictive term *change* for most of these entities. With the exception of Arias-Stella change, most of the epithelial metaplastic and related changes occur predominantly in nonsecretory endometria. The latter include atrophic, inactive, normal proliferative, hyperplastic, and carcinomatous endometria, and it must be emphasized that the distinction among these basic patterns is of far greater clinical significance than the correct identification of the specific metaplasia or related change.

General Features. Because the various epithelial metaplastic and related changes often occur in association with one another, it has been assumed that their inciting causes may be similar; exogenous and endogenous hyperestrinism have been implicated as important associated factors (23,24). However, note that the older literature has mentioned such diverse associations for squamous metaplasia as intrauterine administration of chemicals, presence of an intrauterine contraceptive device, vitamin A deficiency, chronic inversion, chronic endometritis, and pyometra (4). We have encountered hobnail and clear cell changes in gestational endometria and hobnail change as a reparative phenomenon after curettage or radiation therapy.

The exact frequency with which these changes occur in benign endometria is unknown, but they appear to be fairly common in the United States, and several Japanese and Korean pathologists have stated to me that

191

these changes are rarely seen in those countries. Anderson and colleagues (1) noted the changes in 15 of 47 endometrial carcinomas.

There are no known clinical features or gross findings specifically associated with the epithelial metaplasias and related changes. If these lesions occur in a hyperplastic or carcinomatous endometrium, the clinical features and gross findings will be those of the hyperplasia or carcinoma.

Squamous Metaplasia and Morules

Microscopic Findings. Both squamous metaplasia and morules are composed of cytologically bland cells with eosinophilic cytoplasm, which can usually be demonstrated to be continuous with an endometrial gland lining. They are seen commonly in endometrial carcinomas, usually of low grade and stage (see Endometrial Carcinoma). They less commonly accompany hyperplastic or normal endometrium, but in such cases, they have frequently led to an inappropriate diagnosis of carcinoma. Crum and colleagues (11) recognized this situation and recommended the use of the term *adenoacanthosis*; they and other authors have emphasized that the diagnosis of adenocarcinoma with squamous differentiation can be made only when the glandular component is indisputably malignant. However, Kurman and Norris (25) have stated that extensive (>2.1 mm) solid squamous proliferations alone justify the diagnosis of carcinoma, a view with which I do not agree.

Morules were first characterized by Dutra (14) and differ from more mature squamous metaplasia in that they lack foci of keratinization, abundant eosinophilic cytoplasm, or intercellular bridges (figs. 234–236). When the individual cellular aggregates reach a certain size, central necrosis is common (fig. 234), but atypia and mitotic activity are still absent (fig. 236).

Differential Diagnosis. Because the constituent cells of morules are often rather spindled (fig. 236), diagnostic confusion may arise with intraendometrial proliferations of stroma or smooth muscle. In a difficult case, positive immunostains for epithelial markers and negative reticulin staining within the morules facilitate the diagnosis. The differential diagnosis

with a solid carcinoma of the endometrium is made by the absence of nuclear atypia, and granulomatous inflammation is ruled out by the absence of admixed inflammatory cells.

In the case of fully developed squamous metaplasia (fig. 237), the constituent cells are by definition obviously epithelial and show clear-cut evidence of squamous differentiation (as defined previously). Squamous carcinoma, whether primary in the endometrium or invading the endometrium by extension from the cervix, is ruled out by the absence of cytologic atypia and stromal invasion. In the rare instance of cervical in situ squamous carcinoma extending to the endometrium, only the former criterion would be useful. As mentioned previously, adenocarcinoma with squamous metaplasia or morules is diagnosed by the usual criteria for malignancy of the glandular component.

Mucinous Metaplasia

Although Hendrickson and Kempson (23,24) refer to mucinous metaplasia as a common endometrial change, we have found it to be one of the rarer forms of endometrial epithelial metaplastic and related changes. This entity was reported as early as 1954 by Solomon and Polishuk (34), who noted its association with myxometra. Demopoulous and Greco (13) have shown that the endometrial epithelial cells in mucinous metaplasia are usually identical to endocervical epithelial cells both ultrastructurally and histochemically; however, in rare instances, intestinal metaplasia may occur as well.

Microscopic Findings. Histologically, this lesion is characterized by glands that are lined focally or completely by mucin-containing cells and are separated by benign endometrial stroma. As with the other metaplastic and related changes, the nuclei are bland and mitotic activity is absent or minimal (figs. 238, 239).

Differential Diagnosis. The microscopic findings form the basis of the most important differential diagnosis, which is with mucinous adenocarcinoma, whether primary in the endometrium, invasive from the endocervix, or metastatic from an extrauterine site. In each of these instances, both nuclear atypia and

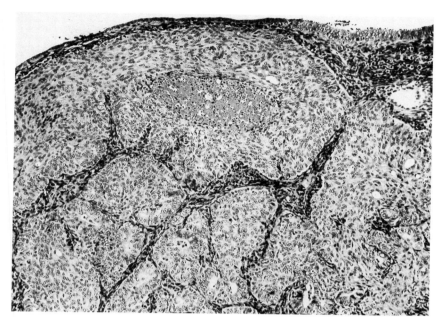

Figure 234
(Figures 234–236 are from the same patient)
ENDOMETRIAL MORULES
Only rare residual endometrial glands (bottom center) are identifiable in this field.
The morules are separated by endometrial stroma, and the largest one (at top center)
has a necrotic center.

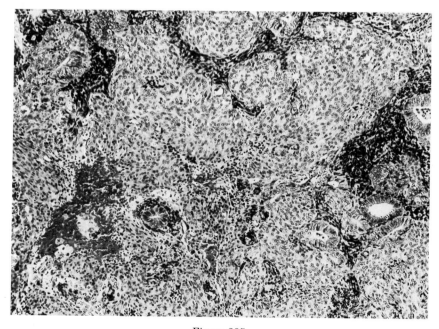

Figure 235
ENDOMETRIAL MORULES
This photomicrograph also shows a few benign glands intermingled with the massive
morular proliferation.

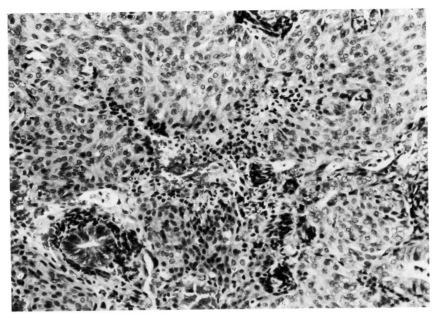

Figure 236
(Figures 234–236 are from the same patient)
ENDOMETRIAL MORULES
Higher magnification of the lesion seen in figures 234 and 235 shows the bland, uniform, ovoid nuclei, without mitotic activity, characteristic of endometrial morules.

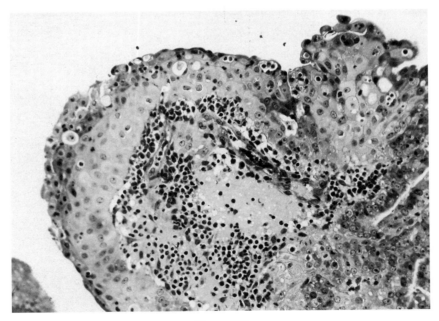

Figure 237
SQUAMOUS METAPLASIA OF THE ENDOMETRIUM
Benign squamous metaplasia appears on the surface of the endometrium in this curettage specimen, with some acute and chronic inflammatory cells in the underlying stroma.

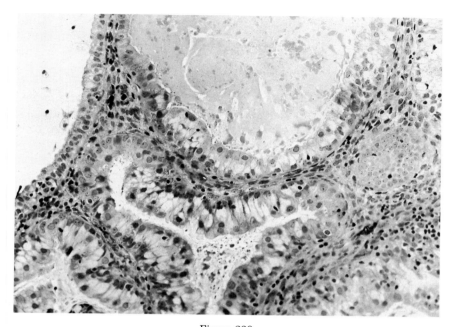

Figure 238
MUCINOUS METAPLASIA OF THE ENDOMETRIUM
In this illustration, endometrial glands show intracytoplasmic and intraluminal mucin, bland nuclei, and separation by endometrial stroma.

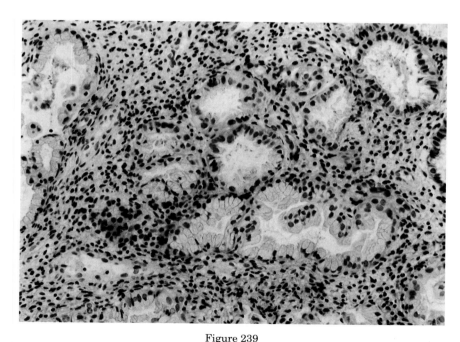

Figure 239
MUCINOUS METAPLASIA OF THE ENDOMETRIUM
Small glands resembling benign endocervical glands are separated by endometrial stroma. Without this stroma, it might be postulated that a fragment of endocervix had been included in this endometrial curettage specimen.

evidence of stromal invasion should be present. In addition, the presence of normal endometrial stroma between mucinous glands rules out the possibility of normal endocervical glands admixed with an endometrial curettage specimen.

Ciliary Change

Microscopic Findings. Although this change is frequently referred to as tubal metaplasia (18), it does not necessarily include the full spectrum of cell types seen in normal adult fallopian tubal epithelium. Because a few ciliated cells are commonly seen in normal endometrium (17), the diagnosis of ciliary change should be made only when one or more endometrial glands are lined predominantly by such cells (fig. 240). Remember that ciliated cells lining endometrial glands but contacting the luminal surface may appear as large round cells with voluminous eosinophilic or clear cytoplasm but without obvious cilia.

Differential Diagnosis. Because ciliated cells are so frequently characterized by eosinophilic cytoplasm, the main differential diagnosis is with atypical hyperplasia of the endometrium, which often features eosinophilic cytoplasm as well. However, in atypical hyperplasia, there is irregular stratification of cells with loss of polarity, as well as considerable nuclear atypia, which are not features of ciliary change. Both conditions can occur in endometria that show the architectural features of simple or complex hyperplasia (fig. 241), and indeed, ciliated cells may be seen within an atypical hyperplasia of the endometrium, although they usually are not prominent. Similarly, scattered ciliated cells may be seen in a well-differentiated endometrioid adenocarcinoma of the endometrium or as a prominent feature in the ciliated cell variant of endometrioid adenocarcinoma (see Endometrial Carcinoma). In either of these situations, the distinction from benign ciliary change is made predominantly by the demonstration of stromal invasion.

Hobnail Change

Microscopic Findings. Hobnail change (fig. 242) is characterized by the presence of pear-shaped cells with a rounded apical bleb containing a large nucleus that is bland to moderately atypical. This change may be seen as a reparative phenomenon after traumata such as curettage or radiation therapy and occurs more diffusely in some gestational endometria.

Differential Diagnosis. Because hobnail cells are also a prominent feature of clear cell adenocarcinoma, this represents the most important differential diagnosis (15). In clear cell adenocarcinoma, there is almost always marked nuclear atypia, as well as the presence of clear cells and evidence of stromal invasion. Arias-Stella change also enters into the differential diagnosis, and in fact hobnail change occurring in the endometrium of a pregnant patient may represent a variant of Arias-Stella change without the stratification and hypersecretion that are also characteristic of the fully developed form.

Clear Cell Change

Clear cell change is also an uncommon and generally focal epithelial change that may be seen in the context of pregnancy but also may occur in otherwise unremarkable proliferative or secretory endometria. The affected glands are characterized by the presence of cells with voluminous clear cytoplasm containing secretions composed predominantly or exclusively of glycogen. The involved glands also contain small bland nuclei and are separated by unremarkable endometrial stroma (figs. 243, 244), in contradistinction to clear cell adenocarcinoma (either primary in the endometrium or metastatic from another site such as the kidney), which represents the most significant differential diagnosis.

Eosinophilic Cell Change

Microscopic Findings. As expected, glands showing eosinophilic cell change are characterized by the presence of bland cells with prominent eosinophilic cytoplasm (figs. 245, 246). These cells may show the typical features of oncocytes (5) at both the light- (fig. 246) and electron-microscopic levels. As with oncocytes in other organs, considerable nuclear atypia

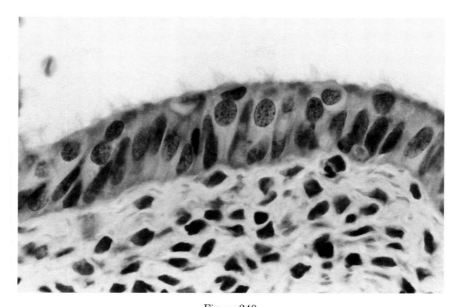

Figure 240
CILIARY CHANGE OF THE ENDOMETRIUM
This gland is lined largely by ciliated cells. The stratification and nuclear atypia that would be expected in atypical hyperplasia are absent from this field.

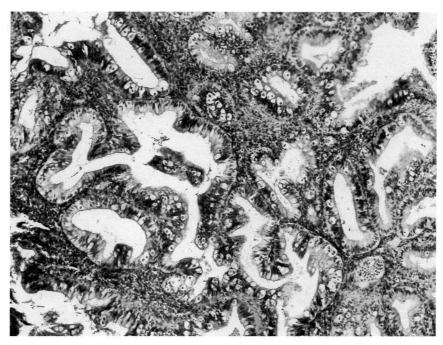

Figure 241
CILIARY CHANGE OCCURRING IN COMPLEX HYPERPLASIA
In this illustration, many of the ciliated cells have not discharged their cilia into gland lumina. This benign change should not be mistaken for ciliated cell endometrioid adenocarcinoma (see Endometrial Carcinoma) or atypical hyperplasia (see Endometrial Polyps and Hyperplasias).

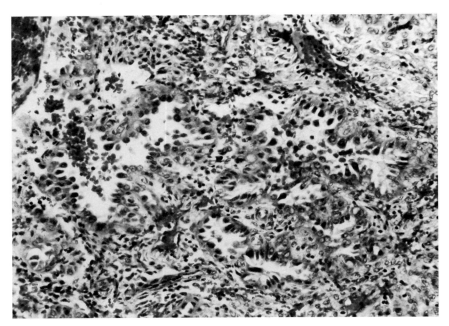

Figure 242
HOBNAIL CHANGE
In this endometrial specimen from a pregnant patient, small glands are lined by a single layer of cells with apical blebs containing uniform small nuclei.

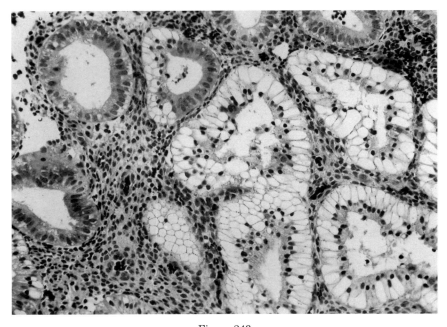

Figure 243
CLEAR CELL CHANGE OF THE ENDOMETRIUM
In this illustration, a small focus of glands in this otherwise proliferative endometrium is lined partially or completely by cells with voluminous clear cytoplasm and small apically situated nuclei. The glands are separated by unremarkable endometrial stroma. The patient was not pregnant.

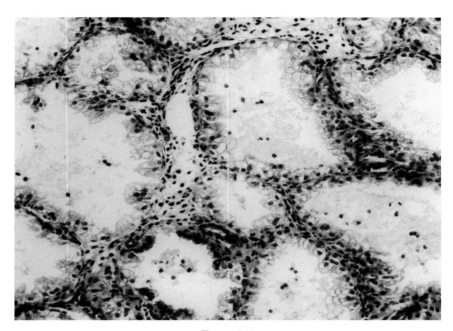

Figure 244
CLEAR CELL CHANGE OF THE ENDOMETRIUM
In this specimen from a pregnant patient, the endometrial glands are focally or diffusely lined by clear cells and contain a few small papillary projections. Stratification and nuclear atypia are absent, and the glands are separated by endometrial stroma. The lack of stratification and nuclear atypia contradict the diagnosis of Arias-Stella change, whereas bland nuclei and intact endometrial stroma rule out clear cell carcinoma.

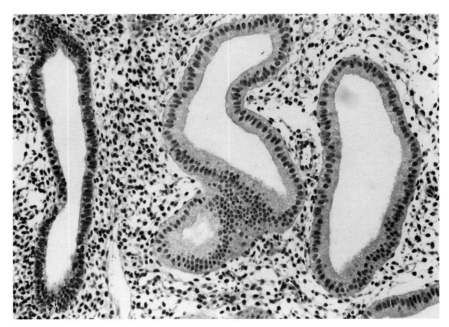

Figure 245
EOSINOPHILIC CELL CHANGE OF THE ENDOMETRIUM
The two glands on the right-hand side in this illustration are lined by cells with cytoplasm that was brightly eosinophilic. The granular appearance of oncocytes was not evident in these cells.

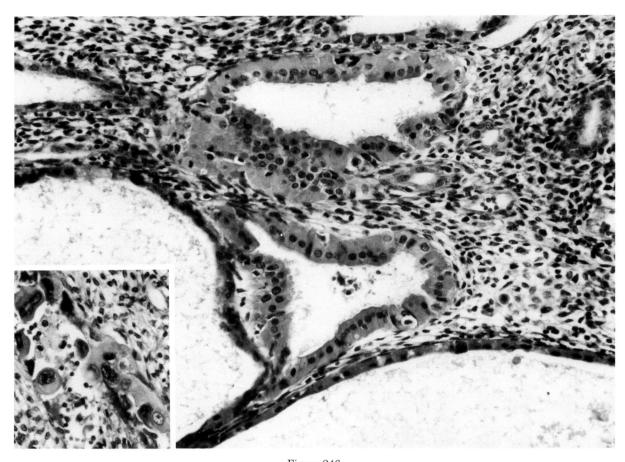

Figure 246
EOSINOPHILIC CELL CHANGE OF THE ENDOMETRIUM (ONCOCYTIC TYPE)
In this photomicrograph, the glands are lined by cells with oncocytic-type granular cytoplasm that was eosinophilic. In the inset, some oncocytes show bizarre nuclei.

may be present (fig. 246), but I am unaware of any reports of oncocytic carcinomas of the endometrium.

Differential Diagnosis. The main differential diagnoses are with other conditions in which eosinophilic cytoplasm is prominent, particularly atypical hyperplasia and ciliary change. The absence of cilia obviously contradicts the latter diagnosis, and the absence of stratification and dyspolarity contradicts the former.

Surface Syncytial Change

Microscopic Findings. This lesion ranks with squamous metaplasia and morules, ciliary change, and Arias-Stella change as one of the more commonly encountered lesions in this section; it also ranks with the first two of those three as one of the lesions most commonly misdiagnosed as atypical hyperplasia or adenocarcinoma. However, its microscopic appearance is characteristic and easily recognized, so that once correctly diagnosed for the first time, it is usually appropriately diagnosed thereafter.

As the name of this lesion suggests, it tends to occur at or near the endometrial surface and is characterized by eosinophilic cells that appear to form a syncytium (figs. 247–252). The lesion resembles microglandular hyperplasia of the endocervix because small glandular lumina or pseudolumina may be formed, and these are often infiltrated by neutrophils (figs. 247–250). The nuclei are generally bland but may be

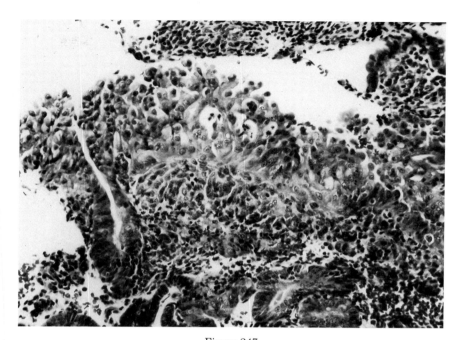

Figure 247
SURFACE SYNCYTIAL CHANGE OF THE ENDOMETRIUM
This photomicrograph from a curettage specimen shows the typical features of this lesion, with stratification of the surface epithelium due to proliferation of small cells with uniform bland nuclei. A few microcystic spaces are formed, and neutrophils are seen within these spaces. The underlying endometrium is proliferative.

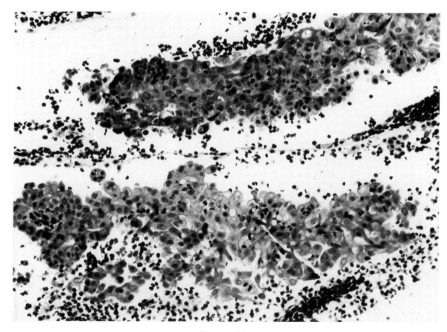

Figure 248
SURFACE SYNCYTIAL CHANGE OF THE ENDOMETRIUM
In this curettage specimen, the surface epithelium showing the same changes as in figure 247 has largely separated from the underlying endometrial stroma. Isolated fragments of this sort could be erroneously interpreted as adenocarcinoma. Note the uniform bland nuclei and focal neutrophilic infiltration.

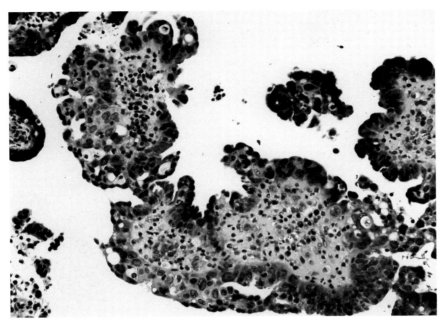

Figure 249
SURFACE SYNCYTIAL CHANGE OF THE ENDOMETRIUM
Another curettage specimen demonstrates a somewhat less florid reaction. As in figure 248, because of the trauma of curettage, it is difficult to identify this change as limited to the surface epithelium.

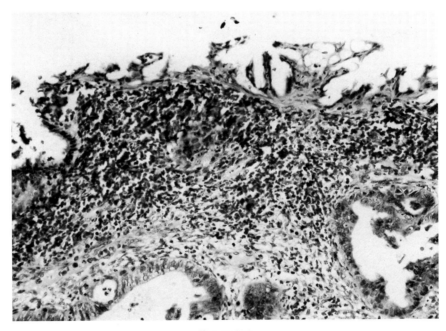

Figure 250
SURFACE SYNCYTIAL CHANGE OF THE ENDOMETRIUM
In this specimen, a papillary arrangement of the surface endometrium is seen, but microcystic spaces with included neutrophils are still present. Underlying endometritis is also present.

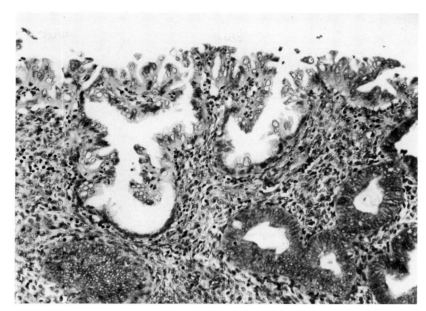

Figure 251
SURFACE SYNCYTIAL CHANGE OF THE ENDOMETRIUM
In this example, the surface change, which is micropapillary as in figure 250, involves the immediately subjacent endometrial glands. More deeply situated glands are of normal proliferative type.

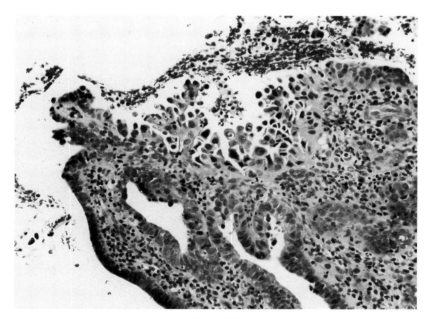

Figure 252
SURFACE SYNCYTIAL CHANGE OF THE ENDOMETRIUM
This photomicrograph shows surface syncytial and micropapillary changes similar to those seen in figures 250 and 251 but with prominent nuclear atypia. The remainder of this microscopic field appears unremarkable, but elsewhere in the curettage specimen there was a moderately differentiated endometrioid adenocarcinoma. Although carcinoma cannot be diagnosed in this field, the unusual degree of atypia is worth noting in a diagnostic comment if no other evidence of a malignant or premalignant process is found in the specimen submitted.

degenerated and pyknotic. Prominent papillarity due to cellular stratification and budding may be present, but the papillae lack stromal cores (figs. 250–252). Squamous metaplasia is also often found at the base of the syncytial proliferation or elsewhere in the same endometrium.

Differential Diagnosis. In a hysterectomy specimen, this lesion usually does not present a significant diagnostic problem. However, in a curettage specimen, where it may be difficult to demonstrate that the lesion is limited to the surface epithelium and immediately subjacent glands, the differential diagnosis with atypical hyperplasia or adenocarcinoma may be difficult. For this reason, it is recommended that the definitive diagnosis of surface syncytial change be made only when the nuclei are completely bland. I have noted that similar changes with cytologically atypical nuclei are often associated with underlying carcinoma more deeply situated in the endometrium (fig. 252).

Papillary Proliferation

Because surface syncytial change frequently has a papillary component, the distinction between these two lesions may be difficult to make, but we recommend the diagnosis of papillary proliferation when the papillary component is extensive and contains fibrovascular stromal cores (figs. 253, 254). This also tends to be a lesion limited to the endometrial surface and immediately subjacent glands. The distinction from papillary serous adenocarcinoma, which also is characterized by the presence of fibrovascular stromal cores, is facilitated by the small, uniform, bland nuclei of the benign papillary proliferation. Serous carcinomas of the endometrium are high-grade cancers with marked atypia, necrosis, stratification, cellular exfoliation, and prominent mitotic activity.

Arias-Stella Change

General Features. In contradistinction to the other epithelial changes already discussed, the changes characterized by Arias-Stella (2,3),

which have come to bear his name, occur almost exclusively in gestational endometria. The change may be encountered in both normal and abnormal (including ectopic) pregnancy and in association with other trophoblastic diseases. It can be demonstrated in curettage material in approximately 80 percent of cases of either spontaneous or induced abortion (32). Although Arias-Stella change is typically associated with an elevated level of chorionic gonadotropin; however, occasionally the lesion is unassociated with any condition known to produce this hormonal picture. Although it is most frequently seen in the endometrium, it is also encountered in foci of endometriosis, adenomyosis, vaginal adenosis, endocervical epithelium, tubal epithelium, ovarian germinal inclusions and cysts, and in other primary and secondary müllerian epithelia.

Microscopic Findings. Arias-Stella change is typically focal and is characterized by glands showing cellular stratification, hypersecretion, and cytomegaly, with enlargement of both nucleus and cytoplasm (fig. 255). Scattered nuclei are large and hyperchromatic, but most of these are dense and smudged, unlike malignant nuclei (figs. 255, 256). The constituent cells have been demonstrated to be polyploid (36). A relatively hyposecretory pattern (fig. 256) is said to be more frequently associated with abnormal than normal pregnancies (3).

Differential Diagnosis. The differential diagnosis of Arias-Stella change is with hobnail and clear cell endometrial changes and with clear cell adenocarcinoma. The two former changes may actually represent variants of Arias-Stella change because they are frequently encountered in gestational endometria. In clear cell adenocarcinoma, the history of pregnancy or trophoblastic disease is usually lacking, other gestational changes (fig. 256) are absent in adjacent endometrium, solid and papillary foci of tumor are usually present in addition to tubuloglandular patterns, and architectural evidence of stromal invasion is present. An increasingly common additional differential diagnosis in recent years is cytomegalovirus infection of the endometrium. This lesion is generally even more focal than Arias-Stella change, being limited to individual cells within endometrial glands, and the typical nuclear and cytoplasmic inclusions are present.

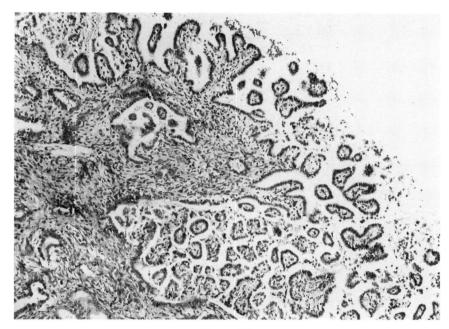

Figure 253
(Figures 253 and 254 are from the same patient)
PAPILLARY PROLIFERATION OF THE ENDOMETRIUM
Numerous papillary processes with fibrovascular connective tissue cores involve the surface of this endometrial specimen. Cytologic atypia is lacking at higher magnification.

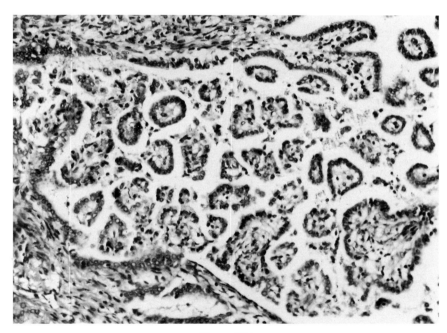

Figure 254
PAPILLARY PROLIFERATION OF THE ENDOMETRIUM
In this higher magnification of the lesion seen in figure 253, the papillary processes are lined by a single layer of small, uniform epithelial cells with bland nuclei and no mitotic activity. A papillary serous adenocarcinoma would show much more atypia, stratification, necrosis, and mitotic activity. This patient underwent hysterectomy, and the specimen showed no carcinoma.

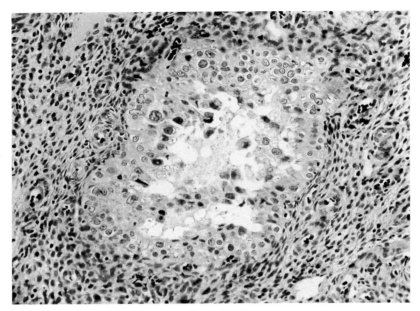

Figure 255
ARIAS-STELLA CHANGE OF THE ENDOMETRIUM
This gland, present in an induced abortion specimen, shows stratification, hypersecretion, cytomegaly, and focal nuclear enlargement and atypia. Many of the atypical nuclei are square and have densely smudged chromatin. Other gestational changes were seen elsewhere in the specimen.

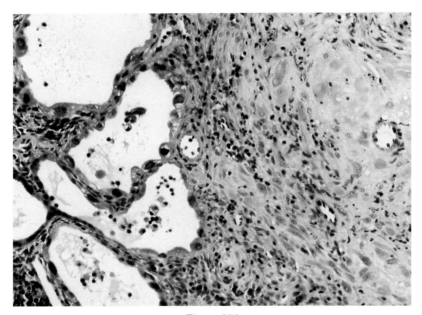

Figure 256
ARIAS-STELLA CHANGE OF THE ENDOMETRIUM
(HYPOSECRETORY TYPE)
This specimen was obtained from a spontaneous abortion. It shows inflamed decidua adjacent to several dilated endometrial glands lined by a single layer of cells. Some of these cells are in hobnail configuration, with smudged hyperchromatic nuclei similar to those seen in figure 255 but without stratification or excessive secretory activity. This less secretory pattern of Arias-Stella change occurs more frequently in abnormal gestations.

NONEPITHELIAL METAPLASTIC AND RELATED CHANGES

Definition. This is a group of changes in which endometrial stroma is focally replaced by non-neoplastic mesenchymal or other tissues that are not encountered in normal cycling endometrium. They are characterized as

- smooth muscle metaplasia
- osseous metaplasia
- cartilaginous metaplasia
- fatty change
- glial tissue
- foam cell change.

These conditions are considerably rarer than the epithelial metaplastic and related changes and do not have the same tendency to occur in association with one another that is seen with the epithelial changes. They are also considerably less likely to be confused with malignant tumors, but, as with the epithelial changes, their major clinical significance lies in their possible misinterpretation as malignant.

Smooth Muscle Metaplasia

Smooth muscle metaplasia is seen occasionally as small foci of typical benign smooth muscle within the endometrium. They have sometimes been referred to as *intraendometrial leiomyomas*. The pathogenesis of this lesion is related to the well-known ability of endometrial stroma to differentiate into smooth muscle (6). Smooth muscle metaplasia is unlikely to be misdiagnosed as malignant but may be confused with morular metaplasia, as mentioned previously.

Osseous and Cartilaginous Metaplasias

In rare instances, foci of osseous (19) and cartilaginous (30) metaplasia are encountered in the endometrium, usually in the postabortal state. In this situation, the tissues may be of fetal origin (fig. 257). In other cases, true metaplasia can be inferred when the tissues arise directly from endometrial stromal cells. This true metaplasia is seen most frequently within the stroma of an endometrial carcinoma or sarcoma (figs. 258, 259). If the osseous or cartilaginous foci are histologically benign, they should not lead to the erroneous diagnosis of carcinosarcoma with a malignant heterologous component (malignant mixed mesodermal tumor) (26).

Fatty Change

Fatty change is seen often as small foci of mature adipose cells within the endometrial stroma. Mature fat is also occasionally encountered within the myometrium. In a curettage specimen, the adipocytes should be completely surrounded by normal endometrium or myometrium, or perforation of the uterus must be suspected. Lipoma and lipoleiomyoma of the uterus are also involved in the differential diagnosis (28).

Glial Tissue

Glial tissue in the uterus represents the most controversial of the nonepithelial metaplastic and related changes because only mesodermal-derived tissues would be expected to be within the metaplastic capabilities of the endometrial stroma. Thus, most cases reported have been presumed to be derived from a previous abortion (22,29). Glial tissue is more frequently found in a cervical polyp than in the endometrium itself. The main differential diagnosis is with a glioma (in which increased cellularity and atypia would be expected) or a teratoma (in which tissues from other germ cell layers should be found). If the residual products of an abortion also include cartilage, bone, and squamous epithelium, the latter differential diagnosis may be difficult.

Foam Cell Change

Lipid-laden foam cells (fig. 260) are found within the endometrial stroma in a variety of conditions, but they are by far most commonly seen in endometrial carcinoma (12). Indeed, the presence of foam cells in a benign endometrial biopsy performed as an office procedure might suggest that formal curettage should be undertaken to rule out the possibility of an underlying

Figure 257
BONY SPICULES IN THE ENDOMETRIUM
These fragments of bone, which were evident on gross examination, occurred in a 17-year-old girl with endometritis and a tubo-ovarian abscess but no known history of pregnancy. The mature bone (at the top of the photomicrograph) is separated from the endometrium (at the bottom) by blood. The bone may be of either fetal or metaplastic origin.

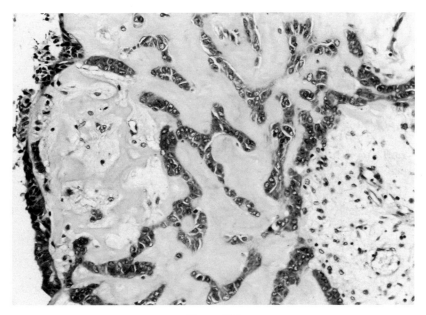

Figure 258
(Figures 258 and 259 are from the same patient)
OSSEOUS METAPLASIA OF THE ENDOMETRIUM
Numerous foci of benign-appearing osseous and cartilaginous metaplasia occurred in this hyperplastic endometrium from a 30-year-old infertile woman. Nuclear atypia is absent, and the osseous tissue appears to arise from endometrial stroma.

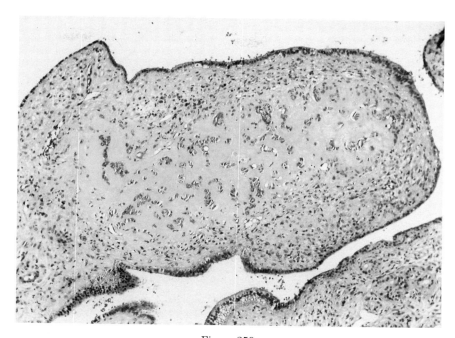

Figure 259
CARTILAGINOUS METAPLASIA OF THE ENDOMETRIUM
This photomicrograph shows a focus of benign cartilaginous tissue arising from endometrial stroma. There is no associated neoplasm, although the patient subsequently developed a focal, well-differentiated endometrioid adenocarcinoma that retained foci of osseous and cartilaginous metaplasia in its stroma.

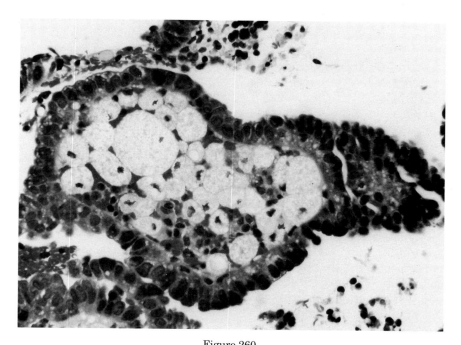

Figure 260
FOAM CELL CHANGE OF THE ENDOMETRIAL STROMA
These stromal foam cells are present within an endometrial carcinoma, although the diagnosis of carcinoma cannot be made in this particular field. Foam cell change is also seen (but less commonly) in benign endometria.

carcinoma. Foam cells are present within 10 to 15 percent of endometrial carcinoma specimens and appear to be unrelated to other clinical or pathologic features of the patients or tumors (12).

Differential Diagnosis. Within an endometrial carcinoma, and also more rarely within hyperplasias and polyps, the foam cells represent converted non-neoplastic endometrial stromal cells. Remember that neoplastic stromal cells in stromal nodules and low-grade endometrial stromal sarcomas may also undergo foam cell change. In these cases, the diagnosis is made by applying the usual diagnostic criteria for these tumors (see Endometrial Stromal Tumors).

Another differential diagnosis is with histiocytic or xanthomatous endometritis (8). In these rare lesions, multinucleated giant cells, plasma cells, lymphocytes, and neutrophils are generally admixed with the foam cells, and evidence of recent or old hemorrhage is usually found. In malakoplakia, Michaelis-Gutmann bodies are also identified (fig. 261).

ADENOMYOSIS

Definition. Adenomyosis is a non-neoplastic condition in which endometrial glands and stroma are found within the myometrium.

Adenomyosis rarely raises a microscopic differential diagnostic problem with any neoplasm but is included among the tumor-like lesions because it often presents clinically with an enlarged uterus, thus entering into the differential diagnosis at the clinical and gross pathologic levels. Adenomyosis was also frequently called *endometriosis interna* in the older literature to distinguish it from *endometriosis externa*, which is characterized by the presence of extrauterine localizations of benign endometrial glands and stroma. The latter condition, however, may involve the uterine serosa and subserosal myometrium, so it should be remembered that not every case of deeply situated endometrium in the uterine corpus represents adenomyosis.

Because the junction between endometrium and myometrium in normal uteri is often irregular, the exact criteria for the histopathologic diagnosis of adenomyosis are controversial, with the diagnosis being made by some pathologists when any penetration of the myometrium by tongues of endometrium is found, whereas others demand either the presence of hypertrophied myometrium around the foci of endometrium or a specific depth of penetration or both. We have recommended the dividing line of one medium-power (X100) microscopic field below the endometrial-myometrial junction as the distinction between physiologic penetration of endometrium into the myometrium and the "disease" of adenomyosis (21).

Clinical Features and Gross Pathology. Both the clinical features and gross pathologic findings of adenomyosis obviously depend on the microscopic diagnostic criteria chosen. If the diagnosis is made as recommended above, adenomyosis occurs in 10 to 20 percent of hysterectomy specimens in the United States and is frequently a symptomatic disease. If the diagnosis is made with less extensive involvement of the myometrium, the prevalence rate will be higher and the condition will more frequently be asymptomatic. The condition occurs primarily in women in their reproductive years, and the most common symptoms are abnormal menstrual bleeding, dysmenorrhea, uterine enlargement, and occasionally infertility. The patients frequently have other lesions in addition to adenomyosis, most commonly leiomyomata and endometriosis; in such cases, the exact cause of the symptoms may be unclear. For this reason and because many patients with adenomyosis are asymptomatic, the diagnosis is usually not made clinically before hysterectomy (27).

The uterus is usually moderately enlarged but may be either of normal size or massively enlarged. The myometrium is generally thickened and often has a trabeculated cut surface, and in some cases the lesions may be visible at the gross level as small, soft, pink or gray-white zones within the myometrium. Small cysts are occasionally seen. If the lesion is large and solitary, it may be designated an *adenomyoma*. I prefer this term, however, for the polypoid lesion discussed in the chapter on Mixed Epitheilial-Nonepithelial Tumors.

Microscopic Findings. The endometrium may form small or large islands within the myometrium that are frequently surrounded by foci of myometrial hypertrophy (fig. 262). The endometrium is generally inactive or proliferative and may consist largely of basalis. In some

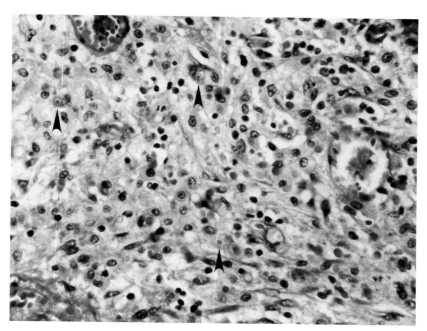

Figure 261
MALAKOPLAKIA
The inflammatory infiltrate is composed of histiocytes and smaller numbers of lymphocytes and plasma cells. The histiocytes contain granular eosinophilic cytoplasm that often contains Michaelis-Gutmann bodies (arrows), which are round, concentrically laminated bodies that stain blue-gray with hematoxylin and eosin and positively for calcium and iron.

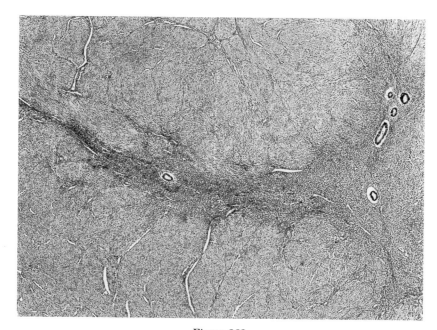

Figure 262
ADENOMYOSIS OF THE UTERUS
In this illustration, benign endometrial glands and stroma surrounded by hypertrophic smooth muscle lie deep in the myometrium. The endometrial glands and stroma appear to be of basalis type.

cases, however, functional changes may be seen, and a stromal decidual reaction may be encountered if the patient is pregnant. The usual lack of secretory activity correlates with the observation by Tamaya and associates that estrogen receptors are always present in foci of adenomyosis, but progesterone receptor levels are low or absent (35). It also correlates with the general lack of hemorrhage or hemosiderin pigment within the foci of adenomyosis, although these are generally seen in endometriosis.

Differential Diagnosis. The most common differential diagnosis of adenomyosis is with a normal uterus. If glands are difficult to find, the possibility of a low-grade endometrial stromal sarcoma may be raised (see Endometrial Stromal Tumors). However, the spiral arteriole-like vessels of that lesion are usually absent in adenomyosis, and lymphatic or venous invasion, if present at all, is much less prominent than in endometrial stromal sarcoma. Perhaps the most effective diagnostic tool is serial sectioning to reveal the presence of benign endometrial glands and surrounding myometrial hypertrophy in adenomyosis or of endometrial involvement in endometrial stromal sarcoma.

Hyperplasias, carcinomas, and other tumors and tumor-like lesions arising in the endometrium may penetrate into tongues of adenomyosis deep in the myometrium. In this case, it is important to exclude the diagnosis of a malignant tumor with true myometrial invasion. This differential diagnosis, which is clinically the most important involving adenomyosis, has been discussed in detail in the chapter on Endometrial Carcinoma.

EPITHELIAL CYSTS OF MYOMETRIUM

Endometrial glands in foci of adenomyosis or serosal mesothelial invaginations may undergo cystic dilatation within the myometrium, and leiomyomata and metastatic adenocarcinomas may undergo cystic degeneration. Specifically indicated in this category, however, are intramyometrial cysts lined by histologically benign epithelium without associated endometrial stroma. Such cysts are usually congenital and may be of either mesonephric or paramesonephric (müllerian) type (31); they are extremely rare.

CHRONIC ENDOMETRITIS

Chronic endometritis is a chronic inflammation of the endometrium. This common lesion, which is reported to occur in approximately 10 percent of endometrial tissue specimens (7), is included among the tumor-like lesions because it may be confused histologically with either an endometrial carcinoma or a lymphoma. However, in the usual case, neither of these problems arise, and the diagnosis is first suspected at low magnification by the finding of an endometrium that is difficult to date, coupled with the presence of a focally or diffusely spindled and possibly edematous stroma. Higher magnification (fig. 263) reveals an inflammatory cell infiltrate that must include at least occasional plasma cells, because lymphocytes are a normal component of the endometrium. An acute inflammatory infiltrate may also be present, and specific agents may induce a histiocytic or granulomatous response.

Differential Diagnosis. Although the clinical and pathologic features of chronic endometritis are interesting on their own accord, the main significance of this lesion for this discussion is the observation that the endometrial glandular epithelium may respond to the inflammatory stimulus in a manner that can suggest the diagnosis of endometrial hyperplasia or even carcinoma to the unwary pathologist, particularly in a biopsy or curettage specimen. This proliferation generally results in marked architectural abnormalities of endometrial glands with minimal cytologic atypia (figs. 264, 265) but may occasionally cause irregular cellular stratification and nuclear atypia as well, particularly when the inflammatory cells extensively infiltrate the glandular epithelium (fig. 266). It is important to recognize that the stroma, although heavily inflamed and often spindled, usually does not show the desmoplastic fibrosis or necrosis that is seen with endometrial carcinoma, and the glands are not confluent or cribriform (see Endometrial Polyps and Hyperplasias and Endometrial Carcinoma). Marked chronic inflammation with plasma cells and the presence of granulomatous inflammation (which may be associated with the most marked examples of reactive endometrial proliferation) are not usually features of endometrial carcinoma.

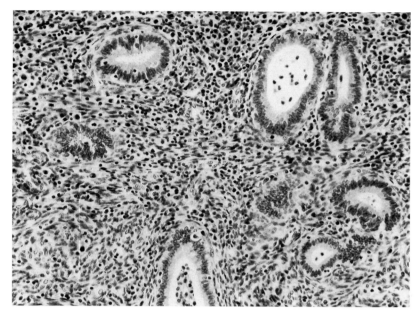

Figure 263
CHRONIC ENDOMETRITIS

This photomicrograph shows irregularly distributed endometrial glands separated by a spindled stroma containing numerous lymphocytes and plasma cells. Some inflammatory cells have also penetrated through basement membranes into endometrial glandular epithelium. This patient was in the second half of her cycle when this biopsy was obtained, but no secretory activity is seen.

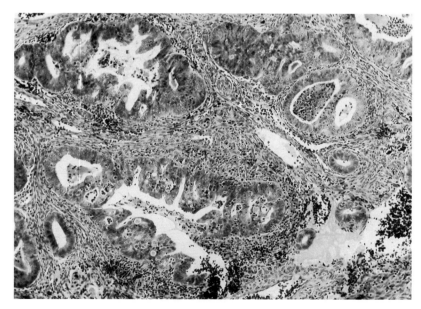

Figure 264
(Figures 264 and 265 are from the same patient)
CHRONIC ENDOMETRITIS WITH REACTIVE ENDOMETRIAL
GLANDULAR PROLIFERATION

In this inflamed endometrium, endometrial glands are enlarged and show papillary and cribriform architectural changes, as well as infiltration by inflammatory cells. However, cytologic atypia is absent (see fig. 265).

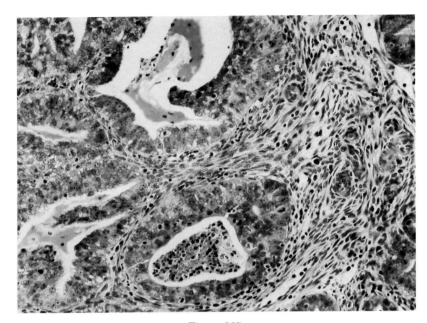

Figure 265
(Figures 265 and 264 are from the same patient)
CHRONIC ENDOMETRITIS WITH REACTIVE ENDOMETRIAL GLANDULAR PROLIFERATION
Higher magnification of the same specimen seen in figure 264 more clearly shows the spindled stroma, the inflammatory infiltrate, and the architectural atypia and cellular stratification of endometrial glands. Nucleoli are prominent within the glandular cells, but significant nuclear atypia is absent.

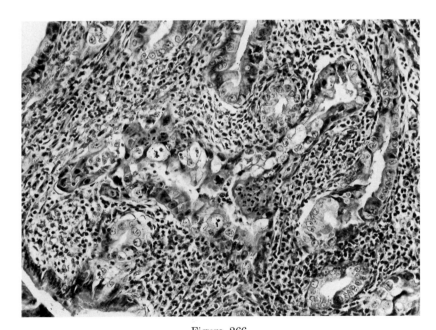

Figure 266
CHRONIC ENDOMETRITIS WITH GLANDULAR ARCHITECTURAL AND CYTOLOGIC ATYPIA
This example shows a marked inflammatory infiltrate. Endometrial glands are irregularly distributed and angular in configuration. Marked nuclear atypia is also present, particularly in the branched gland at the center, which is infiltrated by inflammatory cells. This combination of architectural and cytologic atypia could represent adenocarcinoma, but the stromal appearance does not resemble that usually encountered in endometrial carcinoma.

214

LYMPHOMA-LIKE LESIONS

Lymphoma-like lesions are non-neoplastic proliferations of lymphoid tissue within the endometrium that resemble malignant lymphoma. They probably represent an unusual form of chronic endometritis, but it is for the most part unknown whether they are infectious or autoimmune in etiology. In this condition, the endometrium is massively infiltrated by lymphoid tissue, usually containing numerous large mitotically active lymphoid cells, including immunoblasts (figs. 267, 268). In contradistinction to a true malignant lymphoma, other inflammatory cells (histiocytes, plasma cells) are usually admixed, there is seldom a gross mass, and myometrial invasion is not present. Also, by definition, there is no history of a malignant lymphoma elsewhere. However, these conditions may be difficult to meet in a small biopsy or curettage specimen submitted without an adequate clinical history. In such cases, the demonstration of polyclonality in the atypical cells may occasionally be useful, but this may be difficult or impossible in formalin-fixed paraffin-embedded material (37).

Another situation in which a massive benign lymphoid infiltrate may be encountered within the uterus is in rare cases of leiomyomata (16). In this situation, the main diagnostic feature is that the lymphoid infiltrate is strictly limited to the confines of leiomyomata, whereas a malignant lymphoma would be expected to diffusely infiltrate the myometrium.

INFLAMMATORY PSEUDOTUMOR

Inflammatory pseudotumor is defined as a non-neoplastic myometrial mass characterized by spindled cells of myofibroblastic type, plasma cells, and other inflammatory cells. This lesion has recently been reported in the uterus by Gilks and colleagues (20). The cases presented clinically as solitary leiomyoma-like masses and raised the diagnostic possibility of low-grade sarcoma. The inflammatory cell infiltrate throughout the lesion and the general lack of marked nuclear atypia in the spindled cells (figs. 269, 270) indicated the correct diagnosis, and follow-up has been benign.

OTHER TUMOR-LIKE LESIONS

There are other tumor-like lesions, some already recognized in the uterine corpus and others merely potential in this site, that might be included in this category. Clement (9) has reported a case of postoperative spindle-cell nodule of the endometrium, and we have seen a similar case in a repeat curettage specimen. More common are epithelial and stromal atypia after radiation therapy; in particular, florid hobnail cell change of surface and glandular epithelium may be encountered in this situation (33). Xanthogranulomatous endometritis and malakoplakia (fig. 261) can also be included in this category but are more appropriately considered under the heading of chronic endometritis. Although not reported in the corpus, stromal endometriosis of the cervix may simulate a metastatic low-grade endometrial stromal sarcoma (10). Other tumor-like lesions will no doubt continue to be described and characterized in the future.

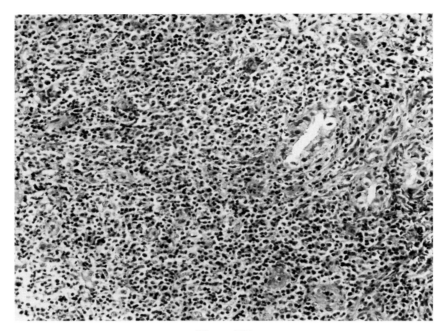

Figure 267
(Figures 267 and 268 are from the same patient)
LYMPHOMA-LIKE LESION OF THE ENDOMETRIUM
This photomicrograph shows a sheet-like lymphoid infiltrate replacing the endometrial stroma. A few residual glands are seen at the left.

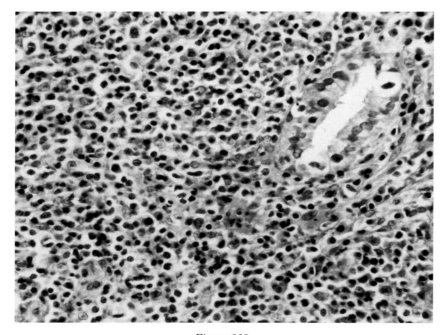

Figure 268
LYMPHOMA-LIKE LESION OF THE ENDOMETRIUM
In this higher magnification of figure 267, the polymorphous nature of the lymphoid infiltrate is apparent, as is its tendency to infiltrate into endometrial glands. This patient had no history of malignant lymphoma, no uterine mass, the myometrium was not involved, and she was alive and well 2 years later without further therapy.

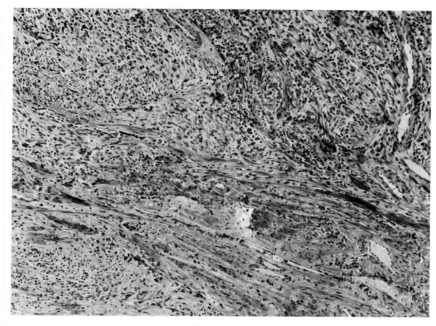

Figure 269
(Figures 269 and 270 are from the same patient)
INFLAMMATORY PSEUDOTUMOR OF THE UTERUS
This low magnification of a myometrial mass shows infiltration of spindled and inflammatory cells through thin strands of residual myometrial smooth muscle. (Courtesy of Dr. Philip Clement, Vancouver, B.C., Canada.)

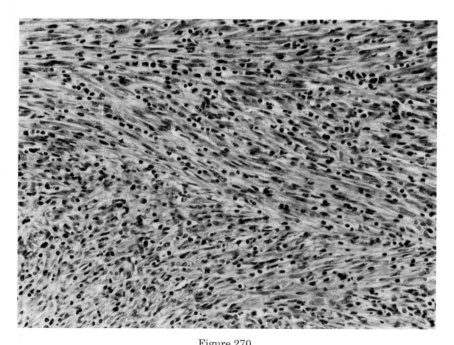

Figure 270
INFLAMMATORY PSEUDOTUMOR OF THE UTERUS
Higher magnification of the lesion illustrated in figure 269 shows spindled myofibroblastic cells with only slight nuclear atypia, separated by a mixed inflammatory infiltrate. (Courtesy of Dr. Philip Clement, Vancouver, B.C., Canada.)

REFERENCES

1. Andersen WA, Taylor PT Jr, Fechner RE, Pinkerton JA. Endometrial metaplasia associated with endometrial adenocarcinoma. Am J Obstet Gynecol 1987;157:597–604.

2. Arias-Stella J. Atypical endometrial changes associated with the presence of chorionic tissue. Arch Pathol 1954;58:112–28.

3. _____. Atypical endometrial changes produced by chorionic tissue. Hum Pathol 1972;3:450–3.

4. Baggish MS, Woodruff JD. The occurrence of squamous epithelium in the endometrium. Obstet Gynecol Surv 1967;22:69–115.

5. Bergeron C, Ferenczy A. Oncocytic metaplasia in endometrial hyperplasia and carcinoma [Letter]. Int J Gynecol Pathol 1988;7:93–5.

6. Bird CC, Willis RA. The production of smooth muscle by the endometrial stroma of the adult human uterus. J Pathol Bacteriol 1965;90:75–81.

7. Buckley CH. Endometrial inflammation. In: Fox H, ed. Haines and Taylor obstetrical and gynaecological pathology. 3rd ed. Edinburgh: Churchill Livingstone, 1987:340–53.

8. _____, Fox H. Histiocytic endometritis. Histopathology 1980;4:105–10.

9. Clement PB. Postoperative spindle-cell nodule of the endometrium. Arch Pathol Lab Med 1988;112:566–8.

10. _____, Young RH, Scully RE. Stromal endometriosis of the uterine cervix. Am J Surg Pathol 1990;14:449–55.

11. Crum CP, Richart RM, Fenoglio CM. Adenoacanthosis of the endometrium: a clinicopathologic study in premenopausal women. Am J Surg Pathol 1981;5:15–20.

12. Dawgne MP, Silverberg SG. Foam cells in endometrial carcinoma. Gynecol Oncol 1982;13:67–75.

13. Demopoulos RI, Greco MA. Mucinous metaplasia of the endometrium: ultrastructural and histochemical characteristics. Int J Gynecol Pathol 1983;1:383–90.

14. Dutra FR. Intraglandular morules of the endometrium. Am J Clin Pathol 1959;31:60–5.

15. Fechner RE. Endometrium with pattern of mesonephroma. Obstet Gynecol 1968;31:485–90.

16 Ferry JA, Harris NL, Scully RE. Uterine leiomyomas with lymphoid infiltration simulating lymphoma. A report of seven cases. Int J Gynecol Pathol 1989;8:263–70.

17. Fleming S, Tweeddale DN, Roddick JW Jr. Ciliated endometrial cells. Am J Obstet Gynecol 1968;102:186–91.

18 Fruin AH, Tighe JR. Tubal metaplasia of the endometrium. J Obstet Gynaecol Br Commonw 1967;74:93–7.

19. Ganem KJ, Parsons L, Friedell GH. Endometrial ossification. Am J Obstet Gynecol 1962;83:1592–4.

20. Gilks CB, Taylor GP, Clement PB. Inflammatory pseudotumor of the uterus. Int J Gynecol Pathol 1987;6:275–86.

21. Gompel C, Silverberg SG. The corpus uteri. In: Pathology in gynecology and obstetrics. 3rd ed. Philadelphia: JB Lippincott, 1985:208–9.

22. Grönroos M, Meurman L, Kahra K. Proliferating glia and other heterotopic tissues in the uterus: fetal homografts? Obstet Gynecol 1983;61:261–6.

23. Hendrickson MR, Kempson RL. Endometrial epithelial metaplasias: proliferations frequently misdiagnosed as adenocarcinoma. Report of 89 cases and proposed classification. Am J Surg Pathol 1980;4:525–42.

24. _____, Kempson RL. Non-neoplastic metaplasias. Epithelial and mesenchymal musical chairs. In: Hendrickson MR and Kempson RL, eds. Surgical pathology of the uterine corpus. Philadelphia: WB Saunders, 1980:158–214. (Bennington JL, ed. Major problems in pathology; Vol 12.)

25. Kurman RJ, Norris HJ. Evaluation of criteria for distinguishing atypical endometrial hyperplasia from well-differentiated carcinoma. Cancer 1982;49:2547–59.

26. Nogales FF, Gomez-Morales M, Raymundo C, Aguilar D. Benign heterologous tissue components associated with endometrial carcinoma. Int J Gynecol Pathol 1982;1:286–91.

27. Owolabi TO, Strickler RC. Adenomyosis: a neglected diagnosis. Obstet Gynecol 1977;50:424–7.

28. Pounder DJ. Fatty tumours of the uterus. J Clin Pathol 1982;35:1380–3.

29. Roca AN, Guajardo M, Estrada WJ. Glial polyp of the cervix and endometrium. Report of a case and review of the literature. Am J Clin Pathol 1980;73:718–20.

30. Roth E, Taylor HB. Heterotopic cartilage in uterus. Obstet Gynecol 1966;27:838–44.

31. Sherrick JC, Vega JG. Congenital intramural cysts of the uterus. Obstet Gynecol 1962;19:486–93.

32. Silverberg SG. Arias-Stella phenomenon in spontaneous and therapeutic abortion. Am J Obstet Gynecol 1972;112:777–80.

33. _____, DeGiorgi LS. Histopathologic analysis of preoperative radiation therapy in endometrial carcinoma. Am J Obstet Gynecol 1974;119:698–704.

34. Solomon C, Polishuk W. Myxometra resulting from mucous metaplasia of the endometrium. Am J Obstet Gynecol 1954;68:1600–3.

35. Tamaya T, Motoyama T, Ohno Y, Ide N, Tsurusaki T, Okada H. Steroid receptor levels and histology of endometriosis and adenomyosis. Fertil Steril 1979;31:396–400.

36. Wagner D, Richart RM. Polyploidy in the human endometrium with the Arias-Stella reaction. Arch Pathol 1968;85:475–80.

37. Young RH, Harris NL, Scully RE. Lymphoma-like lesions of the lower female genital tract: a report of 16 cases. Int J Gynecol Pathol 1985;4:289–99.

✧✧✧

GESTATIONAL TROPHOBLASTIC DISEASE

TROPHOBLASTIC DEVELOPMENT

Definition. Trophoblast is the ectodermal covering of the blastocyst that erodes the uterine mucosa and through which the embryo receives nourishment from the mother.

General Features. The succinct definition belies the complex morphologic and functional properties of this extraordinary tissue. During a relatively brief life span, trophoblast undergoes profound changes as it evolves from the covering of the blastocyst, first identifiable at the 16-cell stage (16), to the highly specialized tissue that makes up the functional unit of the term placenta. During this period, trophoblast matures from a primitive invasive tissue to a highly complex absorptive one involved in the transfer of oxygen and nutrients. Additionally, trophoblast is a potent source of steroid and protein hormones and prevents rejection of the fetal allograft. The various metabolic, endocrinologic, and immunologic properties of trophoblast are briefly discussed, whereas those aspects of the morphology and biology that are relevant to the understanding of the pathology of gestational trophoblastic disease are described in greater detail.

After attachment of the blastocyst to the endometrium, trophoblast invades the endometrium, myometrium, and maternal vasculature to initiate the development of the maternal fetal circulation. As a result, trophoblast enters the systemic circulation, where it disseminates widely and can be identified in the peripheral venous blood throughout gestation (7). It is this property of invasion, together with the highly proliferative and primitive appearance of immature trophoblast, that is responsible for the difficulty that may be encountered in distinguishing normal trophoblast from malignant trophoblastic tumors.

During pregnancy, the trophoblast secretes large amounts of estrogen and progesterone. By term, 300 mg/day of estrogen and 250 mg/day of progesterone are synthesized by the trophoblast, compared to 100 mg/day of estrogen of ovarian origin in the nonpregnant woman. The precise function of these steroid hormones is not known, although progesterone is thought to reduce myometrial contractility (14). In addition to steroid hormones, trophoblast produces a wide variety of protein hormones, notably, human chorionic gonadotropin (hCG) and placental lactogen (hPL). The function of many of the protein hormones is not clear, but hCG, by maintaining the integrity of the corpus luteum early in the first trimester, ensures that progesterone is present at sufficient levels to preserve the secretory endometrium, which is necessary for successful development of the conceptus. In addition, hCG may have an immunosuppressive effect.

It is widely acknowledged that because trophoblast is the only component of the placenta that is in direct contact with maternal tissues, it must play a role in facilitating immunologic tolerance of the fetal allograft. The major histocompatibility system in humans is the leukocyte antigen (HLA) system, which is divided into two groups. Class I antigens are present in most tissues, whereas class II antigens are expressed on B lymphocytes, macrophages, activated T cells, and some hematopoietic precursor cells. Studies have shown that neither class I nor class II antigens are expressed by villous trophoblast (11). In contrast, the intermediate trophoblastic cells that infiltrate the implantation site express class I antigens but do not express class II antigens (6,34). Furthermore, the particular class I antigens expressed by intermediate trophoblast are those that are shared by all individuals. Intermediate trophoblast does not express polymorphic class I HLA specificities that confer antigenic differences among individuals, in this case, the mother and fetus (34). Recently, it has been demonstrated that interleukin 6 (IL-6), a cytokine that is normally present in immunocompetent cells, is localized in syncytiotrophoblast, thus providing further evidence that trophoblast has immunologic functions (17).

Microscopic Findings. Trophoblast is classified according to its anatomic location and the morphology of its constituent cellular populations. After the development of chorionic villi on day 13 (fig. 271), trophoblast can be anatomically categorized into villous and extravillous forms. Before that time, trophoblast is called *previllous trophoblast* (figs. 272–274). The classification of trophoblast according to its constituent cellular populations has been revised in recent years. Since the turn of the century, two types of trophoblast, cytotrophoblast and syncytiotrophoblast, have been clearly defined and recognized. Subsequent light-microscopic (42), histochemical (8,23,40,41), electron-microscopic (38,39,43), and immunocytochemical studies (6,21) have confirmed the presence of an intermediate form of trophoblast with characteristic morphologic and biochemical features. This third type of cell has light-microcopic and ultrastructural features (38,39,43) intermediate between cytotrophoblast and syncytiotrophoblast and has therefore been designated *intermediate trophoblast* (21). In the older literature the intermediate trophoblastic cells that infiltrate the placental site have been called *X cells* (36) or *interstitial trophoblast* and when they are multinucleate, *syncytial wandering cells, syncytial giant cells* (23), and *placental site giant cells* (19). Because most of the trophoblastic cellular population at the implantation site are intermediate trophoblastic cells, the term *extravillous trophoblast* has also been used to refer to these cells. Because intermediate trophoblastic cells are also on the surface of chorionic villi, extravillous trophoblast is not synonymous with intermediate trophoblast.

The morphologic features of the three types of trophoblastic cells are listed in Table 6. The cytotrophoblastic cell is a small, undifferentiated, mononucleate stem cell with a high nuclear/cytoplasmic ratio (figs. 275, 276), a single nucleus, cytoplasm that is clear to granular, and well-defined cell borders. Cytotrophoblast has proliferative activity consistent with its germinative role but lacks functional activity, that is, hormone synthesis. The syncytiotrophoblastic cell is multinucleate, with abundant amphophilic or eosinophilic cytoplasm (figs. 275, 276). In the first 2 weeks of gestation, vacuoles, some of which form lacunae, develop in the cytoplasm of syncytiotrophoblast. These cells overlie the villi and often have a brush border. Mitotic activity is absent.

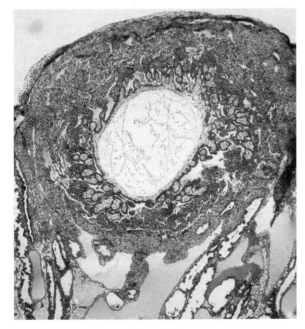

Figure 271
(Figures 271 and 275 are from the same patient)
CONCEPTUS (DAY 16)
Primitive villi are evident in this field, and the trophoblastic shell is composed of all three types of trophoblast. (Fig. 7.2 from Kurman RJ. The pathology of trophoblast. In: Kraus FT, Damjanov I, Kaufman N, eds. The pathology of reproductive failure. Baltimore: Williams and Wilkins. 1991:195–227 [Kaufman N, ed. Monographs in pathology; Vol 33]).

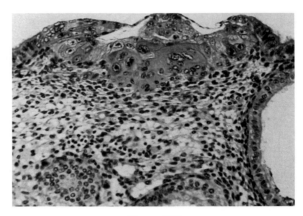

Figure 272
CONCEPTUS (DAY 7.5)
This illustration shows the thick trophoblastic plate that has formed from the blastocyst wall and its junction with the endometrium. The double-layered embryonic mass lies within the blastocyst cavity above the trophoblastic plate. At this point, the trophoblast is undifferentiated, and therefore the various subpopulations of trophoblastic cells cannot be discerned. (Fig. 14 from Fascicle 33, First Series.)

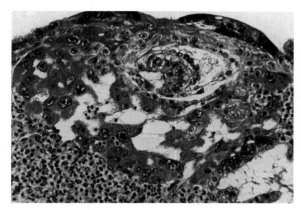

Figure 273
CONCEPTUS (DAY 9)
Further differentiation of the trophoblast is evident at the implantation pole in this illustration. Cytotrophoblast is in close proximity to the embryonic mass, whereas coalescing vacuoles are developing within the primitive syncytiotrophoblast, peripheral to the cytotrophoblast. (Fig. 15 from Fascicle 33, First Series.)

Figure 274
CONCEPTUS (DAY 11)
Further differentiation of the trophoblast can be seen in this illustration. Cytotrophoblast can now be more clearly distinguished from syncytiotrophoblast. Note that the trophoblastic shell completely envelops the developing embryo. (Fig. 16 from Fascicle 33, First Series.)

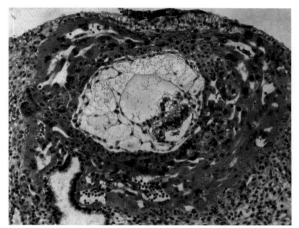

Table 6

MORPHOLOGIC FEATURES OF TROPHOBLASTIC CELLS *

	Cytotrophoblast	Intermediate Trophoblast	Syncytiotrophoblast
Nucleus	Single	One to several	Multiple
Mitotic activity	High	Low	Absent
Shape	Round	Variable; polyhedral to spindle	Irregular, highly variable
Cytoplasm	Scant; clear to granular, well-defined cell borders	Abundant; amphophilic; occasional vacuoles	Abundant; dense; multiple vacuoles; lacunae; red cell lakes

* Modification of Table 4 from Mazur MT, Kurman RJ. Gestational trophoblastic disease. In: Sternberg SS, ed. Diagnostic surgical pathology. Vol. 2. New York: Raven Press, 1989:1495.

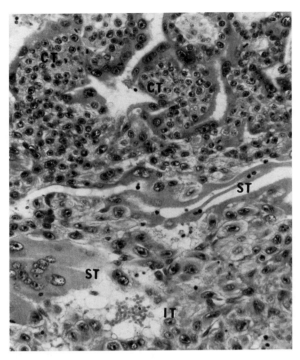

Figure 275
(Figures 275 and 271 are from the same patient)
TROPHOBLASTIC CELL TYPES
High magnification of a day-16 conceptus illustrating the three types of trophoblast. Intermediate trophoblastic cells (IT) are present in the lower right of the field, cytotrophoblastic cells (CT) are in the upper part of the field proliferating from the surface of two chorionic villi, and syncytiotrophoblast (ST) ensheaths the cytotrophoblast in this location. Syncytiotrophoblast is also present in the center, right, and left of the field. (Fig. 2 from Kurman RJ, Main CS, Chen HC. Intermediate trophoblast: a distinctive form of trophoblast with specific morphological, biochemical and functional features. Placenta 1984;5:349–70.)

The intermediate trophoblastic cell is larger and more polyhedral than the cytotrophoblastic cell, with a larger, slightly more hyperchromatic nucleus (figs. 275, 276). The intermediate trophoblastic cells differentiating from the underlying cytotrophoblast have vacuolated cytoplasm. As they infiltrate through the decidua and myometrium, they become less vacuolated and acquire amphophilic cytoplasm. Typical intermediate trophoblastic cells are mononucleate, but some fuse to form binucleate and trinucleate cells, and multinucleate cells, which form syncytiotrophoblastic giant cells (figs. 277, 278). Cell membranes are usually less distinct in intermediate trophoblast. Compared with syncytiotrophoblast, the intermediate tro-

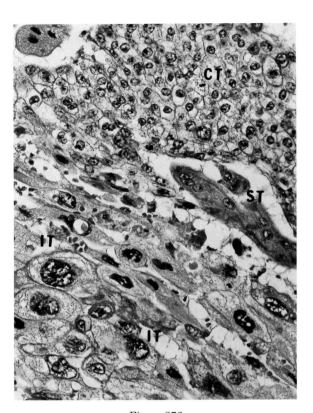

Figure 276
TROPHOBLASTIC CELL TYPES
This illustration shows cytotrophoblast (CT), syncytiotrophoblast (ST), and intermediate trophoblast (IT) proliferating from the surface of a chorionic villus (not shown) of a complete hydatidiform mole. Note that the intermediate trophoblast shows marked cytologic atypia compared with that of the normal conceptus shown in figure 275.

phoblastic cells have slightly larger nuclei, are largely mononucleate, and have distinctly less eosinophilic cytoplasm.

MORPHOLOGIC ASPECTS OF TROPHOBLASTIC DIFFERENTIATION AT THE IMPLANTATION SITE

Trophoblast appears to undergo two different pathways of differentiation that can be correlated with its anatomic distribution. Shortly after implantation, before the formation of chorionic villi, sheets of intermediate trophoblastic cells emanating from cytotrophoblast invade the surrounding endometrium in a centrifugal fashion to form what is known as the trophoblastic shell (figs. 274, 279). Some of the

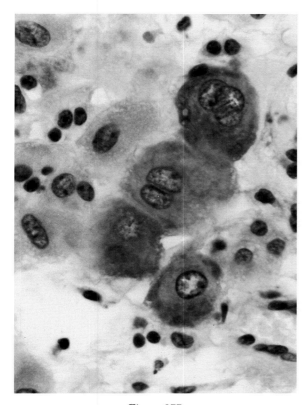

Figure 277
TROPHOBLASTIC CELL TYPES

Mononucleate, binucleate, and trinucleate intermediate trophoblastic cells at the implantation site are shown. When multinucleate, these cells are referred to as syncytiotrophoblastic giant cells. The dark gray cytoplasmic staining represents the localization of human placental lactogen (hPL). Immunoperoxidase hPL with hematoxylin counterstain. (Fig. 9 from Kurman RJ, Main CS, Chen HC. Intermediate trophoblast: a distinctive form of trophoblast with specific morphological, biochemical and functional features. Placenta 1984;5:349–70.)

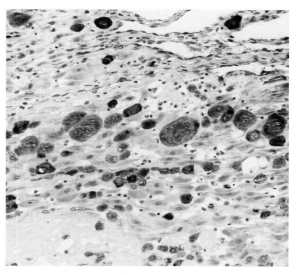

Figure 278
PLACENTAL SITE GIANT CELLS

In this field, multinucleate intermediate trophoblastic cells form syncytiotrophoblastic giant cells at the implantation site, so-called "placental site giant cells". The dark gray cytoplasmic staining represents localization of hPL. Immunoperoxidase hPL with hematoxylin counterstain. (Fig. 10 from Kurman RJ, Main CS, Chen HC. Intermediate trophoblast: a distinctive form of trophoblast with specific morphological, biochemical and functional features. Placenta 1984;5:349–70.)

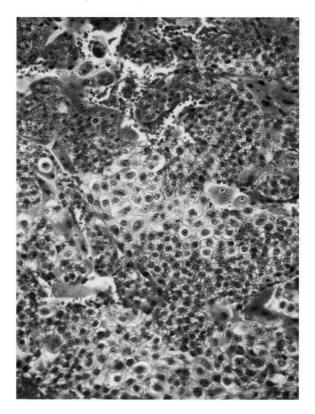

Figure 279
TROPHOBLASTIC CELL TYPES

This is a high magnification of the trophoblastic population that makes up the trophoblastic shell in an early conceptus. The combination of cytotrophoblast capped by syncytiotrophoblast and adjacent intermediate trophoblast resembles choriocarcinoma. (Fig. 7.1 from Kurman RJ. The pathology of trophoblast. In: Kraus FT, Damjanov I, Kaufman N (eds), The pathology of reproductive failure. Baltimore: Williams and Wilkins. 1991;195–227 [Kaufman N, ed. Monographs in pathology; Vol 33].)

intermediate trophoblastic cells fuse to form syncytiotrophoblast (20). (This pattern of differentiation of previllous trophoblast may be recapitulated by choriocarcinoma [see fig. 284].) After the formation of chorionic villi, cytotrophoblastic cells on the villous surface fuse to form syncytiotrophoblast. This is the pattern of differentiation of villous trophoblast (fig. 280). In addition, along one margin of what are to become anchoring villi, cytotrophoblast differentiates into intermediate trophoblast to form solid columns (figs. 280, 281). Intermediate trophoblastic cells infiltrate the decidua and underlying myometrium via these trophoblastic columns to form extravillous trophoblast. Unlike the abrupt transition between cytotrophoblast and syncytiotrophoblast on the villous surface, there is a continuous spectrum of differentiation from cytotrophoblast through intermediate trophoblast to syncytiotrophoblast in these columns (fig. 280). Most of the intermediate trophoblastic cells do not differentiate further.

Immunohistochemical identification of intermediate trophoblastic cells by the localization of hPL and cytokeratin has demonstrated that there is a massive infiltration of the endometrium and myometrium at the implantation site by these cells (figs. 282, 283). Intermediate trophoblastic cells account for most of the trophoblastic cellular population at this location. The intermediate trophoblastic cells infiltrate between decidual cells (figs. 284, 285), surround but do not destroy endometrial glands, and infiltrate the myometrium, separating individual smooth muscle fibers without causing apparent

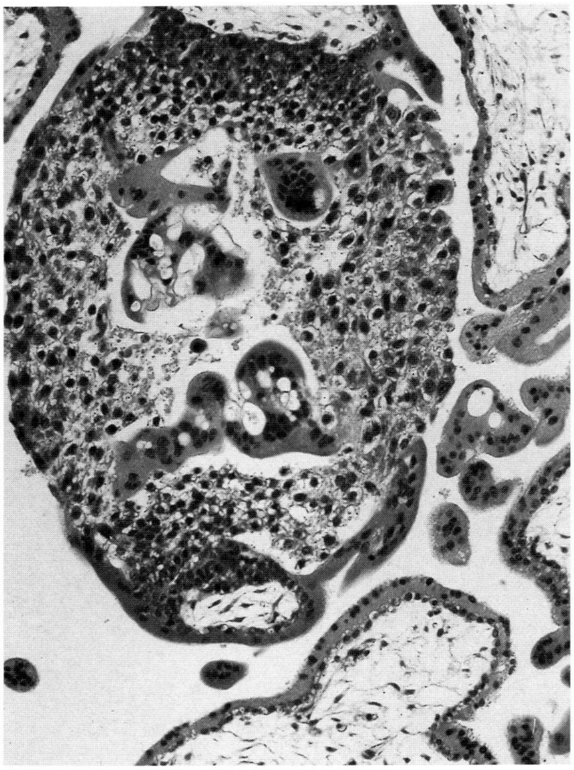

Figure 280
TROPHOBLASTIC CELL TYPES
Primitive chorionic villi are covered by cytotrophoblast and syncytiotrophoblast. In the center of the field, trophoblast extends from the tip of one chorionic villus to form a trophoblastic column. Within the column there is a continuous spectrum of differentiation from cytotrophoblast to intermediate trophoblast to syncytiotrophoblastic giant cells.

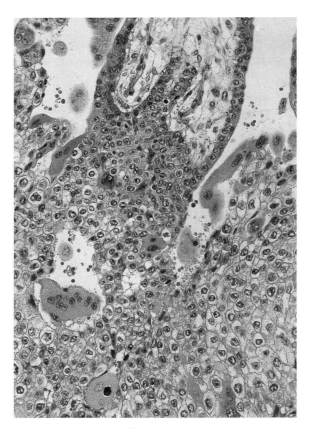

Figure 281
TROPHOBLASTIC COLUMN
Note the continuous spectrum of differentiation from cytotrophoblast through intermediate trophoblast to syncytiotrophoblast in this field.

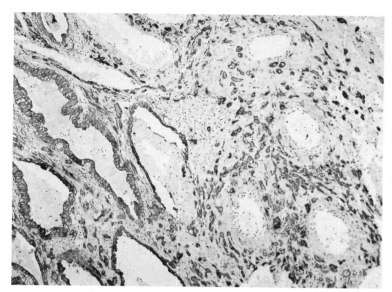

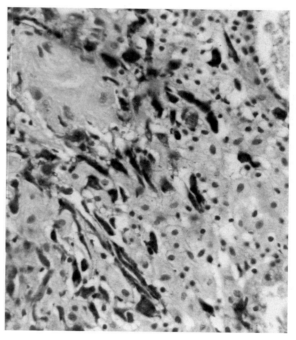

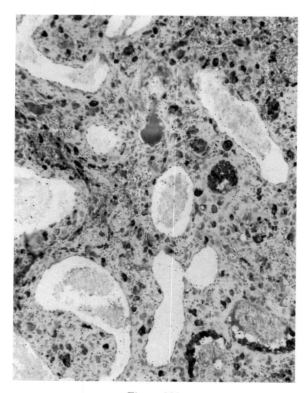

Figure 282
INTERMEDIATE TROPHOBLASTIC
CELLS AT THE IMPLANTATION SITE
Intermediate trophoblastic cells containing immunoreactive cytokeratin surround endometrial glands (left of field) and spiral arteries (right of field). Immunoperoxidase-cytokeratin, AE1/AE3 with hematoxylin counterstain.

Figure 283
INTERMEDIATE TROPHOBLASTIC CELLS
AT THE IMPLANTATION SITE
IN A FIRST-TRIMESTER ABORTUS
The intermediate trophoblastic cells contain intra-cytoplasmic hPL and surround spiral arteries at the implantation site. Most of the cells in this field are immunoreactive for hPL. Immunoperoxidase-hPL with hematoxylin counterstain.

Figure 284
INTERMEDIATE TROPHOBLASTIC CELLS
Spindle-shaped intermediate trophoblastic cells, some with elongated cytoplasmic processes, are intermingled with decidual cells at the implantation site in this example. hPL is localized within intermediate trophoblast only. Immunoperoxidase-hPL with hematoxylin counterstain. (Fig. 7a from Kurman RJ, Main CS, Chen HC. Intermediate trophoblast: a distinctive form of of trophoblast with specific morphological, biochemical and functional features. Placenta 1984;5:349–70.)

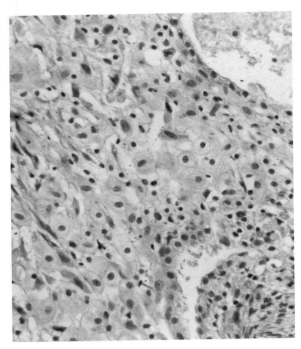

Figure 285
(Figures 285, 287, and 288 are from the same patient)
INTERMEDIATE TROPHOBLASTIC CELLS
Human chorionic gonadotropin (hCG) is not localized in intermediate trophoblastic cells at the implantation site, as shown in this illustration. Immunoperoxidase-hCG with hematoxylin counterstain. (Fig. 7b from Kurman RJ, Main CS, Chen HC. Intermediate trophoblast: a distinctive form of trophoblast with specific morphological, biochemical and functional features. Placenta 1984;5:349–70.)

destruction. A unique form of vascular invasion also characterizes the trophoblastic infiltration of the implantation site. These features of intermediate trophoblastic invasion are recapitulated by the placental site trophoblastic tumor.

The local milieu appears to dictate the differentiation of intermediate trophoblastic cells in extravillous locations. Evidence for this is based on in vitro studies that have shown that cytotrophoblast requires a culture surface coated with an extracellular matrix protein including collagen types I, IV, V, fibronectin, or laminin to differentiate into syncytiotrophoblast; this differentiation does not occur when cytotrophoblast is cultured in serum-free medium (13,18). Similarly, the tendency for intermediate trophoblast to simulate the histologic appearance of adjacent tissues in vivo may be due to local factors exerting an inductive influence on the pheno-

typic expression of trophoblast. For example, in decidua, intermediate trophoblastic cells tend to be polygonal, between the myometrial smooth muscle cells they are often spindle shaped, and when they replace the endothelium of the spiral arteries, they become flattened. This mimicry of the morphologic appearance of cells in adjacent tissue by intermediate trophoblast accounted for the difficulty that early embryologists had in determining whether they were of trophoblastic, decidual, or smooth muscle origin (3,15,25, 28,31). The distinction between decidua and intermediate trophoblast in the placental bed can be diagnostically important.

Immunohistochemical Findings. A panel of antibodies can be used to specifically localize various trophoblastic populations in tissue sections. The discussion that follows describes the localization of various proteins in different trophoblastic populations throughout pregnancy.

The cytotrophoblastic cell fails to react with antibodies against α- and β-hCG, hPL, epithelial membrane antigen, and placental alkaline phosphatase (PlAP); however, as do the other two types of trophoblast, it contains immunoreactive keratin (fig. 286) (4,44). In contrast, the syncytiotrophoblastic cell is a terminally differentiated cell responsible for the synthesis of a wide variety of steroid and protein hormones. Among the latter, hCG and hPL have been the most extensively studied immunohistochemically. The distribution of these two hormones as demonstrated immunohistochemically varies markedly throughout pregnancy (Table 7). β-hCG is identifiable in all syncytiotrophoblastic cells from at least 9 or 10 days gestation (fig. 287) to approximately 8 to 10 weeks, after which it diminishes; by 40 weeks, it is present only focally. Compared with hCG, hPL shows a more focal distribution in syncytiotrophoblast at 9 or 10 days (fig. 288) but increases steadily thereafter. From late in the second trimester until term, hPL is present in all syncytiotrophoblastic cells (4,21). This shift in the synthesis of β-hCG to hPL by syncytiotrophoblast during the course of gestation is thought to reflect trophoblastic maturation.

In addition to β-hCG and hPL, syncytiotrophoblast is focally reactive for epithelial membrane antigen in the second and third trimester (44). The distribution of PlAP is focal in the first trimester, becoming diffuse in the second and third trimesters (4). α–hCG is present diffusely

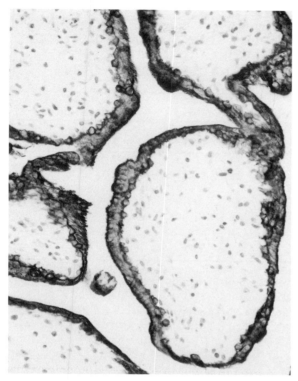

Figure 286
INTERMEDIATE TROPHOBLASTIC CELLS
Immunoreactive cytokeratin is present within the cytotrophoblast and syncytiotrophoblast overlying chorionic villi in the first trimester abortus illustrated here. Immunoperoxidase-cytokeratin, AE1/AE3 and hematoxylin counterstain.

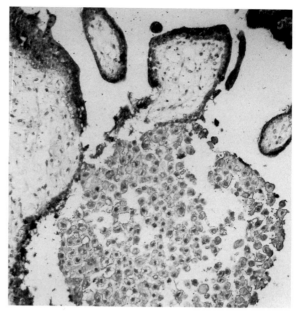

Figure 287
(Figures 287, 285, and 288 are from the same patient)
INTERMEDIATE TROPHOBLASTIC CELLS
This illustration shows localization of hCG, identified by black deposit within the cytoplasm of syncytiotrophoblastic cells in an abortus of 4 weeks gestational age. (Note absence of hCG in cytotrophoblastic and intermediate trophoblastic cells). Immunoperoxidase-hCG with hematoxylin counterstain. (Fig. 3b from Kurman RJ, Main CS, Chen HC. Intermediate trophoblast: a distinctive form of trophoblast with specific morphological, biochemical and functional features. Placenta 1984;5:349–70.)

in the first trimester, decreasing to moderate amounts in the second and third trimesters; there is a greater amount of α-hCG than β-hCG in the last trimester (44).

Although intermediate trophoblastic cells in villous trophoblast contain hPL (fig. 288), the distribution of hPL is more diffuse in these cells at extravillous sites (fig. 283). As in villous trophoblast, the process of fusion of intermediate trophoblastic cells leads to the formation of syncytiotrophoblast and is accompanied by the synthesis of β-hCG. However, with increasing gestational age, there is a gradual increase in the synthesis of hPL and a decrease in hCG in all hormonally active cells. Some syncytiotrophoblastic cells contain both hCG and hPL. In extravillous locations, intermediate trophoblastic cells are also positive for cytokeratin and epithelial membrane antigen but show

only a focal distribution of PlAP and hCG (1,29,35,44).

The immunohistochemical localization of the various trophoblastic proteins, such as hCG and hPL, and cytokeratin can assist in the differential diagnosis of trophoblastic lesions and in the detection of trophoblast in endometrial curettage specimens. For example, in curettage specimens without chorionic villi or fetal tissue from a patient suspected of having an ectopic pregnancy, the identification of trophoblast confirms an intrauterine gestation. The probability of an ectopic pregnancy in this situation is remote. The recognition of intermediate trophoblast in these situations is facilitated by the immunohistochemical localization of hPL and keratin (1,29); intermediate trophoblastic cells are immunoreactive for both, whereas decidua is not.

Table 7

LOCALIZATION OF CHORIONIC GONADOTROPIN β-SUBUNIT AND PLACENTAL LACTOGEN IN DIFFERENT TYPES OF TROPHOBLASTIC CELLS IN THE PLACENTA AND THE PLACENTAL SITE THROUGHOUT GESTATION *

Trophoblastic Cell Type	First Trimester		Second Trimester		Third Trimester	
	hCG [†]	hPL [†]	hCG	hPL	hCG	hPL
Cytotrophoblast	−	−	−	−	−	−
Intermediate trophoblast	+ [‡]	++ [‡]	+/−	+++ [‡]	−	+/++
Syncytiotrophoblast	++++ [‡]	+	+	+++	+	++++

* Modification of Table 24.2 from Mazur MT, Kurman RJ. Gestational trophoblastic disease. In: Kurman RJ, ed. Blaustein's pathology of the female genital tract. 3rd ed. New York: Springer-Verlag, 1987:846.

[†] hCG = human chorionic gonadotropin; hPL = human placental lactogen.

[‡] All symbols denote semiquantitative scoring of the proportion of cells showing a positive reaction: + = 1–24 percent, ++ = 25–49 percent, +++ = 50–74 percent, ++++ = 75–100 percent.

Ultrastructural Findings. Electron micrographs of the various types of trophoblastic cells are included in the sections on Choriocarcinoma and the Placental Site Trophoblastic Tumor because the ultrastructural features of normal trophoblast are similar to those in the trophoblastic neoplasms.

The cytotrophoblastic cell has a nucleus that is round to oval, with a smooth contour and a prominent nucleolus (see fig. 333). The cytoplasm is electron lucent, containing numerous free ribosomes and aggregates of particulate glycogen. In addition, there are mitochondria, scattered strands of rough endoplasmic reticulum, and Golgi complexes. Other organelles are sparse. A few small electron-dense lysosomes, vesicles, and lipid droplets may be present, but cytoplasmic filaments are not. The cells are joined by widely separated, well-formed desmosomes.

In contrast to the simplicity of the cytotrophoblastic cell, the syncytiotrophoblastic cell has a complex cytoplasm and cell membrane structure (see fig. 333) (9,10). Its nucleus has irregular outlines and coarsely clumped chromatin. The cytoplasm is electron dense due to the presence of multiple organelles. There is abundant, often dilated, rough endoplasmic reticulum, resulting in the appearance of multiple tiny vacuoles within the cytoplasm. In addition, there are abundant free cytoplasmic ribosomes, many prominent lipid droplets, vesicles, and lysosomes. Thick bundles of tonofilaments are scattered throughout the cytoplasm, and the surface is covered by many long microvilli. Syncytiotrophoblastic cells are frequently joined by desmosomes.

The intermediate trophoblastic cell displays features shared by both the cytotrophoblastic and the syncytiotrophoblastic cell, confirming its transitional nature (see figs. 334, 351). The intermediate trophoblastic cell usually has one but occasionally more than one nucleus. The cytoplasm is more complex and dense than that of the cytotrophoblastic cell, but it is less well developed than that of the syncytiotrophoblastic cell. It contains numerous organelles, including moderate numbers of mitochondria, dilated rough endoplasmic reticulum, scattered single strands of rough endoplasmic reticulum, and free ribosomes. Some cells contain vesicles of smooth endoplasmic reticulum, Golgi complexes, and pools of glycogen. A characteristic feature is the presence of large bundles of perinuclear intermediate filaments, which are absent in cytotrophoblastic and syncytiotrophoblastic cells. The free surfaces of

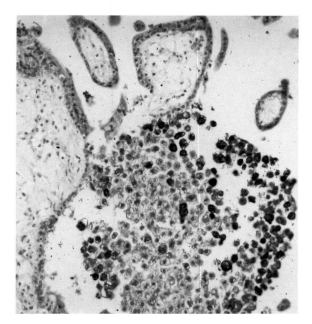

Figure 288
(Figures 288, 285, and 287 are from the same patient)
INTERMEDIATE TROPHOBLASTIC CELLS
This illustration shows localization of hPL, identified by black deposit, within the cytoplasm of intermediate trophoblastic cells sprouting from a chorionic villus. (Note absence of hPL in cytotrophoblast and syncytiotrophoblast. (Fig. 3a from Kurman RJ, Main CS, Chen HC. Intermediate trophoblast: a distinctive form of trophoblast with specific morphological, biochemical and functional features. Placenta 1984;5:349–70.)

the intermediate trophoblastic cell are covered by numerous microvilli, which are more blunt than those of syncytiotrophoblast. When intermediate trophoblastic cells are closely apposed, they are joined by well-formed desmosomes.

FUNCTIONAL ASPECTS OF TROPHOBLASTIC DIFFERENTIATION AT THE IMPLANTATION SITE

One of the most important functions of trophoblast is to establish and maintain implantation of the blastocyst. This process involves invasion of the adjacent endometrium and maternal vasculature to establish the maternal-fetal circulation. During the first week of implantation, before the development of villi, the syncytiotrophoblast invades the endo-

metrium and capillaries (fig. 289). At this time, isolated lacunae appear within the cytoplasm of the syncytiotrophoblast and subsequently coalesce. The invasion of capillaries by the syncytiotrophoblast permits blood to flow into the simultaneously developing lacunae, resulting in the formation of the intervillous space (15). Thus, the invasive properties of the previllous trophoblast reside in syncytiotrophoblast. As discussed in the chapter on Classification and Pathology of Gestational Trophoblastic Disease, choriocarcinoma recapitulates this pattern of vascular invasion. After the development of the chorionic villi, syncytiotrophoblast is mostly confined to villous trophoblast, where it has an absorptive and secretory function. At this point, the invasive properties of trophoblast are assumed by intermediate trophoblast. Intermediate trophoblastic cells engulf and invade the spiral arteries (figs. 282, 290) (5). During the process of invasion, the spiral artery remains intact, but the smooth muscle is replaced by intermediate trophoblast. The trophoblast in the wall of the vessel subsequently undergoes dissolution and is replaced by a fibrinoid matrix, resulting in an inability of the distal segments of the spiral arteries to constrict. This physiologic process accounts in part for the low-pressure system characteristic of the uteroplacental circulation. Syncytiotrophoblastic cells are never found within the walls of the spiral arteries, confirming that the invasive properties of trophoblast after the formation of villi reside in intermediate trophoblast (21). These observations based on morphologic studies have been made not only in the human but also in the hamster, rhesus monkey, and baboon (30,32,33).

The mechanisms that are responsible for the initiation, regulation, and termination of trophoblastic invasion are only now beginning to be elucidated. It is apparent that intermediate trophoblast must elaborate some type of proteolytic enzyme(s) that facilitates the invasive process. Recently, it has been demonstrated that cultured human trophoblast secretes a urokinase-type plasminogen activator (PA). Because PAs are activators of procollagenases (26), these enzymes may play a role in the degradation of the extracellular matrix (2,37). Further evidence supporting the role of PAs in facilitating trophoblastic invasion has been the isolation of two different plasminogen activator

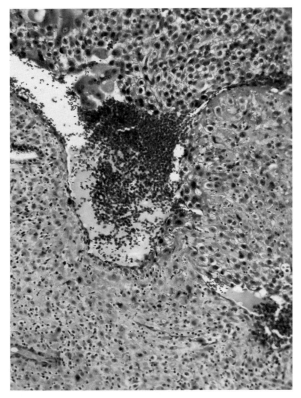

Figure 289
VASCULAR INVASION
This illustration shows vascular invasion by syncytiotrophoblast (overlying intermediate trophoblast) in a 12-day conceptus. This pattern of vascular invasion by previllous trophoblast is recapitulated by choriocarcinoma. (Fig. 7.9 from Kurman RJ. The pathology of trophoblast. In: Kraus FT, Damjanov I, Kaufman N, eds. The pathology of reproductive failure. Chapt 7. Baltimore: Williams and Wilkins 1991:195–227 [Kaufman N, ed. Monographs in pathology; Vol 33].)

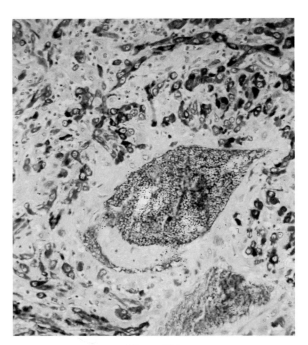

Figure 290
VASCULAR INVASION
This illustration shows invasion of a spiral artery by hPL-positive intermediate trophoblastic cells in a first-trimester abortus. The spiral artery remains intact despite invasion. Immunoperoxidase-hPL with hematoxylin counterstain. (Fig. 6A from Kurman RJ, Young RH, Norris HJ, Main CS, Lawrence WD, Scully RE. Immunocytochemical localization of placental lactogen and chorionic gonadotropin in the normal placenta and trophoblastic tumors, with emphasis on intermediate trophoblast and the placental site trophoblastic tumor. Int J Gynecol Pathol 1984;3:101–21.

inhibitors (PAI 1 and PAI 2) from placental extracts and their subsequent differential immunohistochemical localization within syncytiotrophoblast and intermediate trophoblast (12). Plasminogen activator inhibitors bind PAs and thereby inhibit their proteolytic activity. PAI 1 and PAI 2 have not been identified in cytotrophoblast, consistent with its undifferentiated nature as the germinative trophoblastic element. Recent immunohistochemical studies localizing both PAs (Kliman HJ, personal communication) and PAIs (12) within trophoblast suggest that the synthesis and down regulation of these proteolytic enzymes are autoregulated.

The synthesis of PAs is shared by both trophoblast and endothelium (24). Although it is not readily apparent that these cells have similar functions, immunohistochemical studies of the placenta and implantation site indicate that trophoblast is located at sites where it presumably acts as an endothelial cell. For example, the syncytiotrophoblast that lines the intervillous space can be regarded as a modified type of endothelial cell. Thromboplastin, which converts prothrombin to thrombin in the formation of fibrin, has been demonstrated in trophoblast (27), and as previously indicated, PA, a key component in the dissolution of fibrin, has also been found in this tissue (37). Because both PAI 1 and PAI 2 have been demonstrated on the cell surface of villous syncytiotrophoblast, it is conceivable that they regulate fibrin formation, which in turn plays a role in the maintenance of free blood flow in the intervillous space.

REFERENCES

1. Angel E, Davis JR, Nagle RB. Immunohistochemical demonstration of placental hormones in the diagnosis of uterine versus ectopic pregnancy. Am J Clin Pathol 1985;84:705–9.

2. Blasi F, Vassalli JD, Dano K. Urokinase-type plasminogen activator: proenzyme, receptor, and inhibitors. J Cell Biol 1987;104:801–4.

3. Boyd JD, Hamilton WJ. The giant cells of the pregnant human uterus. J Obstet Gynaecol Br Emp 1960;67:208–18.

4. Brescia RJ, Kurman RJ, Main CS, Surti U, Szulman AE. Immunocytochemical localization of chorionic gonadotropin, placental lactogen, and placental alkaline phosphatase in the diagnosis of complete and partial hydatidiform moles. Int J Gynecol Pathol 1987;6:213–29.

5. Brosens I, Robertson WB, Dixon HG. The physiological response of the vessels of the placental bed to normal pregnancy. J Pathol Bacteriol 1967;93:569–79.

6. Bulmer JN, Johnson PM. Antigenic expression by trophoblast populations in the human placenta and their possible immunobiological relevance. Placenta 1985;6:127–40.

7. Covone AE, Mutton D, Johnson PM, Adinolfi M. Trophoblast cells in peripheral blood from pregnant women. Lancet 1984;2:841–3.

8. Dallenbach-Hellweg G, Nette G. Morphological and histochemical observations on trophoblast and decidua of the basal plate of the human placenta at term. Am J Anat 1964;115:309.

9. Dearden L, Ockleford CD, Gupta M. Structure of human trophoblast. Correlation with function. In: Loke YW, Whyte A, eds. Biology of trophoblast. New York: Elsevier, 1983:70–110.

10. Elston CW. Development and structure of trophoblastic neoplasms. In: Loke YW, White A, eds. Biology of trophoblast. New York: Elsevier, 1983:188–232.

11. Faulk WP, Temple A. Distribution of beta2 microglobulin and HLA in chorionic villi of human placentae. Nature 1976;262:799–802.

12. Feinberg RF, Kao LC, Haimonwitz JE, et al. Plasminogen activator inhibitor types 1 and 2 in human trophoblasts. PAI-1 is an immunocytochemical marker of invading trophoblasts. Lab Invest 1989;61:20–6.

13. Feinman MA, Kliman HJ, Caltabiano S, Strauss JF III. 8-Bromo-3'5'-adenosine monophosphate stimulates the endocrine activity of human cytotrophoblasts in culture. J Clin Endocrinol Metab 1986;63:1211–7.

14. Fox F. Pathology of the placenta. London: WB Saunders, 1978;38–40 [Bennington JL, ed. Major problems in pathology; Vol 7].

15. Hertig AT. Human trophoblast. Springfield, IL: Charles C. Thomas, 1968:63.

16. Heuser CH, Streeter GL. Early stages in the development of pig embryos, from the period of initial cleavage to the time of appearance of limb buds. Contrib Embryol 1929;20:1–29.

17. Kamada T, Matsusaki N, Sawai K, et al. Production of interleukin-6 by normal human trophoblast. Placenta 1990;11:205–13.

18. Kao LC, Caltabiano S, Wu S, Strauss JF III, Kliman HJ. The human villous cytotrophoblast: interactions with extracellular matrix proteins, endocrine function, and cytoplasmic differentiation in the absence of syncytium formation. Dev Biol 1988;130:693–702.

19. Khudr G, Soma H, Benrischke K. Trophoblastic origin of the X cell and the placental site giant cell. Am J Obstet Gynecol 1973;115:530–3.

20. Kliman HJ, Nestler JE, Sermasi E, Sanger JM, Strauss JF III. Purification, characterization, and in vitro differentiation of cytotrophoblasts from human term placentae. Endocrinology 1986;118:1567–82.

21. Kurman RJ, Main CS, Chen HC. Intermediate trophoblast: a distinctive form of trophoblast with specific morphological, biochemical and functional features. Placenta 1984;5:349–70.

22. Laquer WA. A morphological study on chorionepithelial proliferations. J Obstet Gynaecol Br Emp 1945;52:468.

23. Latta JS, Beber CR. The differentiation of a special form of trophoblast in the human placenta. Am J Obstet Gynecol 1957;74:105.

24. Loskutoff DJ, Ny T, Sawdey M, Lawrence D. Fibrinolytic system of cultured endothelial cells: regulation of plasminogen activator inhibitor. J Cell Biochem 1986;32:273–80.

25. Meyer R. Zur Kenntnis der benignen chorioepithelialen Zellinvasion in die Wand des Uterus und der Tuben. Z Geburtsh Gynäk 1906;58:98–134.

26. Mignatti P, Robbins E, Rifkin DB. Tumor invasion through the human amniotic membrane: requirement for a proteinase cascade. Cell 1986;47:487–98.

27. Nilsen PA. The mechanism of hypofibrinogenaemia in premature separation of the normally implanted placenta. Acta Obstet Gynecol Scand 1963;42 (Suppl. 12):1–96.

28. Ober WB. Historical perspectives on trophoblast and its tumors. Ann NY Acad Sci 1959;80:3–20.

29. O'Connor DM, Kurman RJ. Intermediate trophoblast in uterine curettings in the diagnosis of ectopic pregnancy. Obstet Gynecol 1988;72:665–70.

30. Orsini MW. The trophoblastic giant cells and endovascular cells associated with pregnancy in the hamster, *Cricetus auratus*. Am J Anat 1954;94:273–331.

31. Park WW. Disorders arising from the human trophoblast. In: DH Collins, ed. Modern trends in pathology. London: Butterworth, 1959:180.

32. Pijnenborg R, Robertson WB, Brosens I, Dixon G. Review article: trophoblast invasion and the establishment of haemochorial placentation in man and laboratory animals. Placenta 1981;2:71–91.

33. Ramsey EM, Houston ML, Harris JW. Interactions of the trophoblast and maternal tissues in three closely related primate species. Am J Obstet Gynecol 1976;124:647–52.

34. Redmond CW, McMichael AJ, Stirrat GN, et al. Class I major histocompatibility complex antigens on human extravillous trophoblast. Immunology 1984;52:457–68.

35. Sasagawa M, Watanabe S, Ohmomo Y, Honma S, Kanazawa K, Takeuchi S. Reactivity of two monoclonal antibodies (Troma 1 and CAM 5.2) on human tissue sections: analysis of their usefulness as a histological trophoblast marker in normal pregnancy and trophoblastic disease. Int J Gynecol Pathol 1986;5:345–56.

36. Scipiades E, Burg E. Uber die Morphologie der manschilchen Placenta mit besonderer Rücksicht auf unsere eigenen Studien. Arch Gynäk 1930; 141:577–619.

37. Strickland S, Reich E, Sherman MI. Plasminogen activator in early embryogenesis: enzyme production by trophoblast and parietal endoderm. Cell 1976;9:231–40.

38. Terzakis JA. The ultrastructure of the normal human first trimester placenta. J Ultrastruct Res 1963;9:268–84.

39. Tighe JR, Garrod PR, Curran RC. The trophoblast of the human chorionic villus. J Pathol Bacteriol 1967;93:559–67.

40. Wislocki GB. The histology and cytochemistry of the basal plate and septae placentae of the normal human placenta delivered at full term [Abstract]. Anat Rec 1951;109:359a.

41. Wislocki GB. Succinic dehydrogenase, esterases and protein-linked sulfhydryl groups in human placenta. Anat Rec 1953;115:380.

42. Wislocki GB, Bennett HS. The histology and cytology of the human and monkey placenta, with special reference to the trophoblast. Am J Anat 1943;73:335–449.

43. Wynn RM. Cytotrophoblastic specializations: an ultrastructural study of the human placenta. Am J Obstet Gynecol 1972;114:339–55.

44. Yeh IT, O'Connor DM, Kurman RJ. Intermediate trophoblast: further immunocytochemical characterization. Mod Pathol 1990;3:282–7.

CLASSIFICATION AND PATHOLOGY OF GESTATIONAL TROPHOBLASTIC DISEASE

Gestational trophoblastic disease encompasses a heterogeneous group of lesions characterized by an abnormal proliferation of trophoblast. Because the management of gestational trophoblastic disease is largely medical and is often conducted in the absence of a histologic diagnosis (see General Aspects of Clinical Management and Staging), all trophoblastic lesions are frequently combined under the rubric of gestational trophoblastic disease without applying specific pathologic terms. Recent light-microscopic studies, complemented by immunocytochemical and cytogenetic techniques, have demonstrated profound differences in the pathogenesis, morphology, and clinical behavior of various forms of the disease. These studies also suggest that each of the specific forms of gestational trophoblastic disease is related to discrete pathologic aberrations occurring at different stages of gametogenesis and placentation. Hydatidiform moles (complete, partial, and invasive) represent abnormally formed placentas with specific genetic abnormalities that are related to villous trophoblast, whereas choriocarcinoma and the placental site trophoblastic tumor are true neoplasms and are related to previllous and extravillous trophoblast, respectively. The histologic classification of gestational trophoblastic disease used in this presentation was developed by the International Society of Gynecological Pathologists under the auspices of the World Health Organization (Table 8).

HYDATIDIFORM MOLE

Definition. A hydatidiform mole represents a noninvasive abnormal placenta characterized by grossly evident hydropic swelling of chorionic villi accompanied by trophoblastic proliferation.

Recent morphologic and cytogenetic studies (9,38–40,46) have shown that hydatidiform mole is composed of two distinct entities, the *complete* and the *partial* mole. Although the histogenesis and morphology of these two lesions differ, many of their clinical features and their management are similar. Accordingly, the pathologic features of complete and partial mole are discussed separately, but the general aspects, clinical behavior, and treatment of these lesions are discussed in the same section to compare and contrast them.

General Features. Most epidemiologic studies concerning molar gestation have not separated the complete mole from the partial mole because the latter entity has been described only recently. Also, because various studies have failed to clearly define the population at risk and the type of gestational event, the denominator used in the calculation of the incidence varies markedly. Preferably, the denominator should be the number of pregnancies, although some studies use the number of deliveries or live births in determining incidence rates. In many countries, even the latter data are not available. Nonetheless, there does appear to be a marked variation in the incidence of molar pregnancies in different parts of the world (4,6,7,19). Molar pregnancy occurs more frequently in parts of Asia, Latin America, and the Middle East than it does in North America and Europe (Table 9).

Several studies have shown that the risk of hydatidiform mole is increased for women over the age of 45 years and for women under the age of 20 years (4,6). In contrast, in one of the few studies of partial moles, it was shown that maternal age and

Table 8

WORLD HEALTH ORGANIZATION HISTOPATHOLOGIC CLASSIFICATION OF GESTATIONAL TROPHOBLASTIC DISEASE*

Hydatidiform mole
    Complete
    Partial
Invasive hydatidiform mole
Choriocarcinoma
Placental site trophoblastic tumor
Trophoblastic lesions, miscellaneous
    Exaggerated placental site
    Placental site nodule or plaque
Unclassified trophoblastic lesions

*In press

Table 9

COMPARISON OF INCIDENCE OF CHORIOCARCINOMA AND HYDATIDIFORM MOLE *

| Country | Incidence Estimate (per 100,000) | | Choriocarcinoma as Percentage of Hydatidiform Mole |
	Hydatidiform Mole	Choriocarcinoma	
United States	66.1	2.2	3.3
Japan	214.6	12.1	5.6
Sweden	64.8	3.9	6.0
Israel	75.0	5.1	6.8
Singapore (Malay)	113.8	8.9	7.8
Malaysia	136.5	12.5	9.2
Singapore (Chinese)	123.4	12.1	9.8
Paraguay	22.9	2.3	10.0
Greenland	117.6	35.0	29.9

* Table 2-3 from Buckley J. Epidemiology of gestational trophoblastic diseases. In: Szulman A, Buchsbaum H. eds. Gestational trophoblastic disease. New York: Springer-Verlag, 1987:8–26 (Buchsbaum HJ, ed. Clinical perspectives in obstetrics and gynecology; Vol 7).

race do not appear to affect the incidence (27). Although other factors, including smoking, occupation, a history of infertility, consanguinity, blood groups of parents, age at menarche, patterns of menstruation, and use of different types of contraceptives have been analyzed to determine their association with the development of hydatidiform moles, none of these factors appear to be significant (29).

Cytogenetic studies have shown that chromosomal abnormalities play a key role in the development of both complete and partial moles (43,46). Most complete hydatidiform moles are diploid with a 46,XX karyotype (40,43), but rare examples are triploid or tetraploid; all the chromosome complements are paternally derived (49). In the diploid complete mole, both X chromosomes result from duplication of a haploid sperm pronucleus in an empty ovum that has lost its maternal chromosomal haploid set (fig. 291) (22,49,50). Duplication of a 23,Y sperm results in a nonviable 46,YY cell. Approximately 3 to 13 percent of complete moles have a 46,XY chromosome complement, presumably as a result of dispermy, in which an empty ovum is fertilized by two sperm pronuclei, one with an X and the other with a Y chromosome (31,36). The embryo or fetus is absent in the complete mole; cases in which a fetus is present represent twin gestations, one of which is molar.

Karyotypes of the partial mole most frequently show triploidy (69 chromosomes) (43), with two paternal sets and a maternal chromosome complement (fig. 292) (1). Rarely, a partial mole with an identifiable fetus has a 46,XX karyotype (47). Rare examples of tetraploidy with three sets of chromosomes of paternal origin have also been reported (25,37). When triploidy is present in a partial mole, the chromosomal complement is XXY in 70 percent of the cases, XXX in 27 percent, and XYY in 3 percent (43). These abnormal conceptuses result from the fertilization of an egg with a haploid set of chromosomes by either two sperms, each with a set of haploid chromosomes, or by a single sperm with a diploid 46,XY complement (20). A conceptus with a diploid 46,XX maternal genome and a haploid paternal set of chromosomes evolves into an abnormal triploid fetus that is usually a nonmolar pregnancy called a digynic conceptus; it accounts for 15 to 20 percent of cases of triploidy (19). Thus, most well-documented partial moles are triploid, but not all triploid conceptuses are associated with partial moles. Although many partial moles have a triploid karyotype and evidence of an embryo or fetus, there is no consensus that all partial moles have these features. Similarly, not all molar pregnancies with evidence of fetal development are partial moles, because fetal development may occur

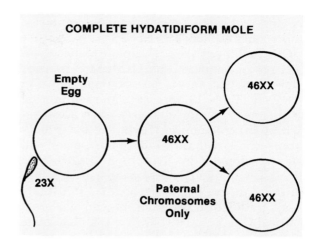

Figure 291
CHROMOSOMAL ORIGIN OF A COMPLETE
HYDATIDIFORM MOLE
In this scheme, a single sperm fertilizes an empty egg.
Reduplication of its 23,X set gives a completely homozygous
diploid genome of 46,XX. A similar process follows fertilization of an empty egg by two sperms with two independent
sets of 23,X or 23,Y chromosomes. Note that both karyotypes
46,XX and 46,XY can ensue. (Modification of fig. 1 from
Szulman AE. Syndromes of hydatidiform moles. Partial vs.
complete. J Reprod Med 1984;29:788–91.)

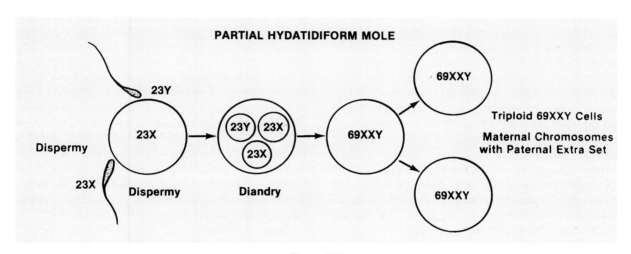

Figure 292
CHROMOSOMAL ORIGIN OF A TRIPLOID PARTIAL HYDATIDIFORM MOLE
In this scheme, a normal egg with a 23,X haploid set is fertilized by two sperms that carry either sex chromosome, to give
a total of 69 chromosomes with a sex configuration of XXY, XXX, or XYY. A similar result can be obtained by fertilization of
a sperm carrying the unreduced paternal genome 46,XY (resulting sex complement, XXY only). (Modification of fig. 2 from
Szulman AE. Syndromes of hydatidiform moles. Partial vs. complete. J Reprod Med 1984;29:788–91.)

in rare instances as a twin gestation in association with a complete mole (19).

Although it is not known why these chromosomal aberrations lead to the formation of a
molar pregnancy, recent experimental studies
suggest that there may be a relationship between the molar phenotype and the ratio of
paternal to maternal haploid sets of chromosomes. The hypothesis has been advanced that
the formation of a mole is associated with an
excess of paternal compared with maternal haploid contributions (35,37). The higher the ratio

of paternal to maternal chromosomes, the
greater the molar change. Complete moles show
a 2:0 ratio of paternal to maternal chromosomes, whereas partial moles show a 2:1 ratio.
This hypothesis is supported by experimental evidence in mice in which enucleated eggs
are implanted with different combinations of a
male or female pronucleus. In a conceptus with
two maternal sets of chromosomes, the embryo
develops to a limited extent, but the trophoblast is stunted. In contrast, in a conceptus with
two paternal sets of chromosomes, there is much

greater trophoblastic development, and the embryo dies earlier (34).

Clinical Features. Complete moles typically present between the 11th and 25th week of pregnancy at an average gestational age of 16 weeks (Table 10) (8,18,28). Marked uterine enlargement is common and is often accompanied by severe vomiting (hyperemesis gravidarum) and pregnancy-induced hypertension and occasionally by hyperthyroidism (8,17). Pregnancy-induced hypertension may be a clinical clue to the diagnosis because it usually occurs in the third trimester in nonmolar pregnancies. Often, patients with a complete mole spontaneously abort, presenting with vaginal bleeding or passage of molar vesicles. Ovarian enlargement due to multiple theca-lutein cysts (hyperreactio luteinalis) and pulmonary embolization occurs in some patients with a complete mole. The hCG level is markedly elevated, and pelvic ultrasonography often discloses a classic "snowstorm" appearance. Although most molar pregnancies are detected before uterine evacuation, the clinical presentation varies, and sometimes the diagnosis is made only after curettage (39,49).

Partial moles account for 25 to 43 percent of all molar pregnancies and occur between the ninth and thirty-fourth week of pregnancy at an average gestational age of about 19 weeks (Table 10) (3,9,39). Usually the patient presents with abnormal uterine bleeding and is clinically thought to have a spontaneous or missed abortion (3,9,39). This presentation differs from that of complete moles, which are usually diagnosed

before curettage. In cases of partial mole, the uterus is typically normal in size or small for the gestational age, and serum hCG levels generally do not show the marked elevation seen in association with the complete mole (33).

COMPLETE HYDATIDIFORM MOLE (COMPLETE MOLE)

Definition. The complete hydatidiform mole is characterized by gross hydropic swelling of most of the chorionic villi. It typically has a diploid karyotype. This term formerly described most lesions designated hydatidiform mole.

Gross Findings. The complete mole is typically voluminous, consisting of 300 to 500 cm^3 or more of bloody tissue, although prior spontaneous passage of a portion of the tissue may decrease this volume substantially. The most characteristic feature of the complete mole is the presence of grape-like transparent vesicles 1 to 2 cm in diameter (fig. 293). Molar specimens evacuated by suction curettage may lack vesicles because this procedure may lead to their collapse. Careful inspection is therefore necessary to identify a mole at the gross level in these cases. When the complete mole is encountered in a hysterectomy specimen, the uterus is enlarged, and molar vesicles protrude when it is opened (fig. 294).

Microscopic Findings. The most prominent feature of the complete mole is generalized hydropic villous change (fig. 295). Although most villi are edematous, some are relatively

Table 10

CLINICAL FEATURES OF COMPLETE AND PARTIAL MOLES *

Feature	Complete	Partial
Clinical presentation	Spontaneous abortion	Missed or spontaneous abortion
Gestational age	16–18 weeks	18–20 weeks
Uterine size	Often large for dates	Often small for dates
Serum hCG [†]	++++	+
Behavior	10–30% develop persistent GTD [†]	4–11% develop persistent GTD

* Modification of Table 24.3 from Mazur MT, Kurman RJ. Gestational trophoblastic disease. In: Kurman RJ, ed. Blaustein's pathology of the female genital tract. 3rd ed. New York: Springer-Verlag, 1987:853.

[†] hCG, human chorionic gonadotropin; GTD, gestational trophoblastic disease.

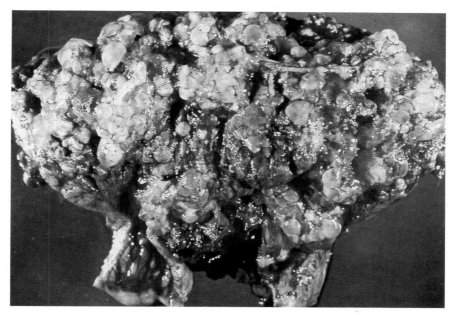

Figure 293
COMPLETE HYDATIDIFORM MOLE
This is the gross appearance of a complete mole, demonstrating the marked generalized villous swelling characteristic of molar gestation. (Fig. 24.21 from Mazur MT, Kurman RJ. Gestational trophoblastic disease. In: Kurman RJ, ed. Blaustein's pathology of the female genital tract. 3rd ed. New York: Springer-Verlag, 1987:835–75.)

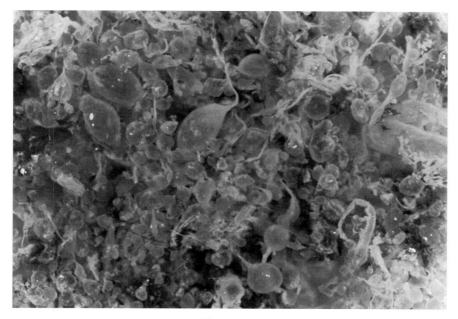

Figure 294
COMPLETE HYDATIDIFORM MOLE
This complete hydatidiform mole contains hydropic villi ranging from a few millimeters to over 1 cm. (Courtesy of Dr. Michael T. Mazur, Syracuse, NY.)

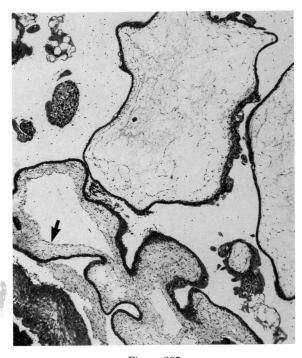

Figure 295
COMPLETE HYDATIDIFORM MOLE
Low magnification of a complete mole demonstrates generalized villous swelling and a cistern (arrow) characterized by a central, acellular, fluid-filled space devoid of mesenchymal cells. Note presence of a small nonhydropic chorionic villus in lower right.

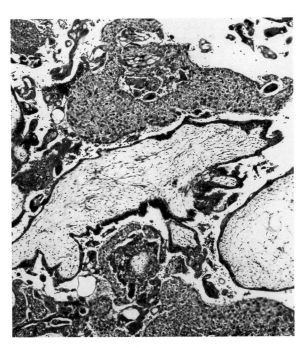

Figure 296
COMPLETE HYDATIDIFORM MOLE
Low magnification of a complete mole demonstrates hydropic villi with marked circumferential hyperplasia of trophoblast.

small. Many have cisterns characterized by a central, acellular, fluid-filled space devoid of mesenchymal cells (fig. 295). A small rim of mesenchyme separates the cistern from the surrounding trophoblast. Often the border of the mesenchyme with the acellular cistern is abrupt and well defined. Necrosis and patchy calcification of villous stroma may be seen.

All complete moles display some degree of trophoblastic proliferation, which is circumferential but haphazard along the villous surface (fig. 296). The degree of proliferation in an individual mole may show wide variation. It may be marked, affecting most villi (fig. 297) or only minimal and focal (figs. 298, 299). The proliferating trophoblast, composed of syncytiotrophoblast, cytotrophoblast, and intermediate trophoblast shows a random, centrifugal growth from the villous surface (figs. 300–302). The trophoblast of a mole, in addition to being hyperplastic, often shows considerable cytologic atypia with

nuclear enlargement, irregularity of the nuclear outline, and hyperchromasia. Mitotic figures, including abnormal forms, may be evident.

In addition to the marked villous swelling and trophoblastic hyperplasia, the complete mole is typically characterized by an absence of development of the embryo/fetus. Neither fetal parts nor amnion are found, and the villous stroma often lacks blood vessels that would normally form if embryogenesis had occurred. In rare instances, small degenerating vascular spaces may be found in a complete mole, and their presence does not exclude the diagnosis.

Because all moles, regardless of their histologic characteristics, should be followed and managed in the same manner, histologic grading is unnecessary.

PARTIAL HYDATIDIFORM MOLE (PARTIAL MOLE)

Definition. The partial hydatidiform mole has two populations of chorionic villi, one of

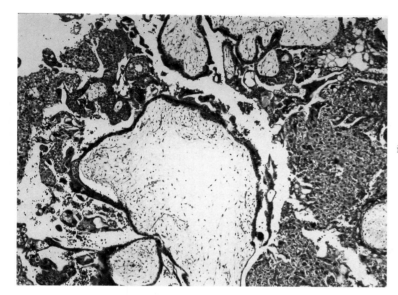

Figure 297
COMPLETE HYDATIDIFORM MOLE
Massive trophoblastic hyperplasia involving several villi is visible.

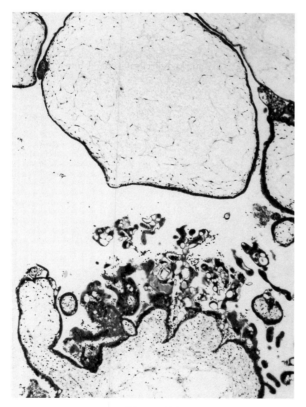

Figure 298
COMPLETE HYDATIDIFORM MOLE
A complete mole shows a variable degree of trophoblastic hyperplasia. Minimal trophoblastic hyperplasia and relatively bland appearing trophoblast on the villi in the upper part of the field contrast with greater hyperplasia on the villus in the lower part of the field.

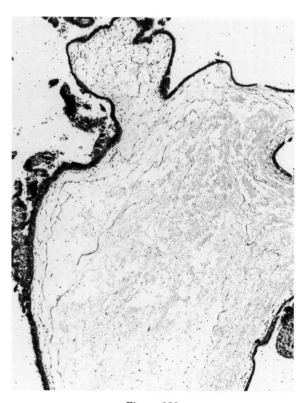

Figure 299
COMPLETE HYDATIDIFORM MOLE
A complete mole shows focal minimal trophoblastic hyperplasia on the surface of a chorionic villus.

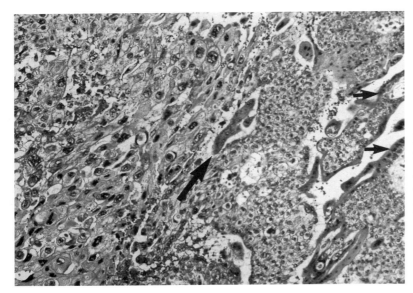

Figure 300
COMPLETE HYDATIDIFORM MOLE
This high-power photomicrograph shows proliferating trophoblast from two chorionic villi (small arrows) in a complete mole. Immediately adjacent to the villi are cytotrophoblastic cells. Intermediate trophoblastic cells occupy the left half of the field, and two syncytiotrophoblastic cells are present between the cytotrophoblast and intermediate trophoblast (large arrow).

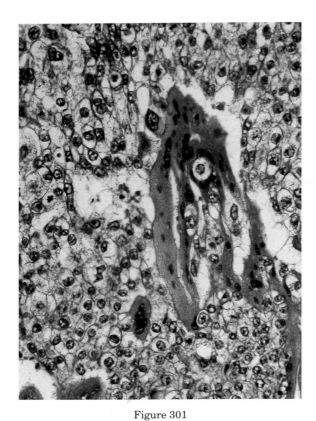

Figure 301
COMPLETE HYDATIDIFORM MOLE
High magnification of a complete mole shows syncytiotrophoblast in the center of the field surrounded by cytotrophoblast.

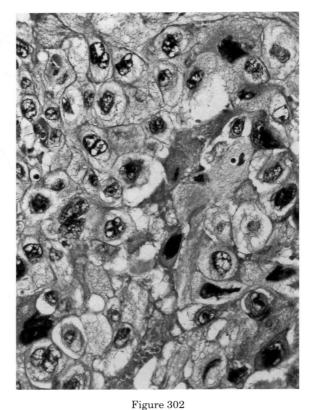

Figure 302
COMPLETE HYDATIDIFORM MOLE
High magnification of a complete mole shows intermediate trophoblastic cells with vacuolated cytoplasm, clearly defined cell membranes, and marked nuclear pleomorphism.

normal size and the other grossly hydropic. It usually has a triploid karyotype. This lesion was formerly termed *transitional mole*.

Gross Findings. Generally, the amount of tissue in a partial mole is less than that found in a complete mole; the total volume is often no greater than 200 cm³. The gross specimen contains large hydropic villi similar to those seen in the complete mole mixed with nonmolar placental tissue, an important distinguishing characteristic (figs. 303, 304). A fetus is nearly always present with a partial mole, although it may require careful examination to detect because early fetal death is the rule (8–9 weeks menstrual age). In some cases, the fetus may show gross developmental abnormalities (44).

Microscopic Findings. The partial mole is characterized by a mixture of large edematous villi and normal-sized villi (fig. 305). In comparison with the complete mole, the degree of hydropic swelling in the partial mole tends to be less pronounced. At least some of the hydropic villi contain a central acellular cistern (fig. 306). The chorionic villi often have a scalloped outline, compared to the typically round, distended appearance of the villi in the complete mole (figs. 307, 308). These irregular outlines produce infoldings of the trophoblast into the villous stroma that, when prominent and sectioned tangentially, appear to be inclusions (figs. 307, 308). Although for practical purposes scalloping and trophoblastic inclusions are very

Figure 303
PARTIAL HYDATIDIFORM MOLE
This illustration shows a partial mole with hydropic villi mixed with smaller villi. (Fig. 24.25 from Mazur MT, Kurman RJ. Gestational trophoblastic disease. In: Kurman RJ, ed. Blaustein's pathology of the female genital tract. 3rd ed. New York: Springer-Verlag, 1987:835–75.)

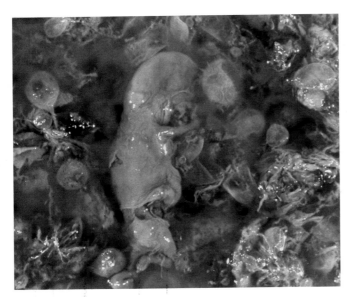

Figure 304
PARTIAL HYDATIDIFORM MOLE
This partial mole contains a macerated fetus and villi with visible hydropic change. (Fig. 24.26 from Mazur MT, Kurman RJ. Gestational trophoblastic disease. In: Kurman RJ, ed. Blaustein's pathology of the female genital tract. 3rd ed. New York: Springer-Verlag, 1987:835–75.)

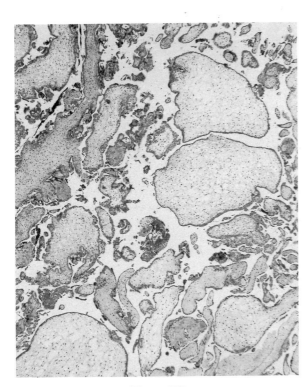

Figure 305
PARTIAL HYDATIDIFORM MOLE
A partial mole with a mixture of large edematous villi and normal-sized villi is illustrated.

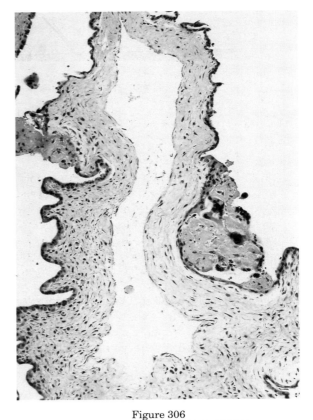

Figure 306
PARTIAL HYDATIDIFORM MOLE
This is a high magnification of an enlarged villus in a partial mole with a central acellular cistern. Note the irregular scalloped outline of the villus and minimal trophoblastic proliferation.

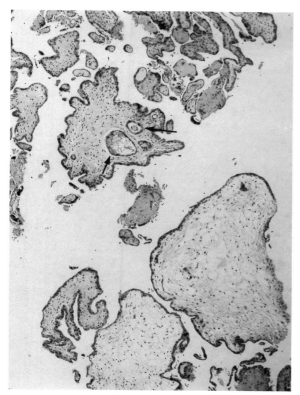

Figure 307
PARTIAL HYDATIDIFORM MOLE
Two populations of chorionic villi can be seen in this partial mole. The hydropic villi have scalloped contours and trophoblastic inclusions (arrows).

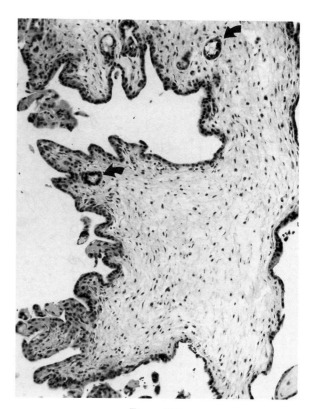

Figure 308
PARTIAL HYDATIDIFORM MOLE
Note the markedly scalloped outline and small trophoblastic inclusions (arrows) in this chorionic villus.

useful diagnostic features of the partial mole, both of these features are occasionally observed in other disorders as well. In addition, the villous stroma of the partial mole frequently undergoes fibrosis, in contrast to that of the complete mole. The villous capillaries of the partial mole frequently contain fetal (nucleated) erythrocytes.

The trophoblast covering the villi is typically only focally and mildly hyperplastic. As in the complete mole, the trophoblastic overgrowth is circumferential rather than polar. The cellular population is composed of cytotrophoblast and syncytiotrophoblast; the latter typically forms focal aggregates on the villous surface. Intermediate trophoblast is rarely encountered. A comparison of the pathologic features of the complete and partial mole is shown in Table 11.

Immunohistochemical Findings. The immunohistochemical localization of hCG, hPL, and PlAP in complete and partial moles is confined mostly to the syncytiotrophoblast and varies according to gestational age, as shown in Table 12. Intermediate trophoblast in complete moles frequently contains hPL but only rarely contains hCG. Cytotrophoblast is uniformly negative for all of these proteins (5,23). As a group, complete moles have widespread diffuse staining for hCG, moderately diffuse staining for hPL, and focal staining for PlAP (figs. 309–311). In contrast, partial moles show focal to moderate staining for hCG and widespread diffuse staining for hPL and PlAP (fig. 312).

Cytogenetics. As noted previously, cytogenetic studies typically reveal that the complete mole is diploid, whereas the partial mole is triploid; however, exceptions to this rule occur. On the basis of the differences in ploidy, flow cytometry performed on fresh tissue or

Table 11

PATHOLOGIC FEATURES OF COMPLETE AND PARTIAL MOLES *

Feature	Complete Mole	Partial Mole
Karyotype	46,XX, 46,XY	Triploid
Embryo/fetus	Absent	Present
Villous outline	Round	Scalloped
Hydropic swelling	Marked	Less pronounced
	Cisterns present	Cisterns less prominent
	All villi involved	Focal villous involvement
	No villous fibrosis	Villous fibrosis
Trophoblastic proliferation	Circumferential	Focal
	Variable, may be marked	Minimal
Trophoblastic atypia	Often present	Absent
Immunocytochemistry		
hCG [†]	++++ [‡]	+ [‡]
PlAP [†]	+	++++

* Modification of Table 24.4 from Mazur MT, Kurman RJ. Gestational trophoblastic disease. In: Kurman RJ, ed. Blaustein's pathology of the female genital tract. 3rd ed. New York: Springer-Verlag, 1987:855.

[†] hCG = human chorionic gonadotropin; PlAP = placental alkaline phosphatase.

[‡] Symbols denote semiquantitative scoring of the proportion of cells showing a positive reaction; + = 1–24 percent; ++++ = 75–100 percent.

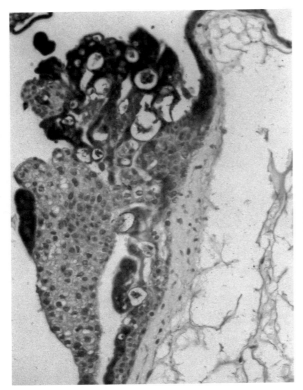

Figure 309
COMPLETE HYDATIDIFORM MOLE
This portion of a hydropic villus from a complete mole shows localization of hCG (intracytoplasmic black deposit) limited to the syncytiotrophoblast. Immunoperoxidase-hCG with hematoxylin counterstain. (Fig. 12 from Kurman RJ, Young RH, Norris HJ, Main CS, Lawrence WD, Scully RE. Immunocytochemical localization of placental lactogen and chorionic gonadotropin in normal placenta and trophoblastic tumors, with emphasis on intermediate trophoblast and the placental site trophoblastic tumor. Int J Gynecol Pathol 1984;3:101–21.)

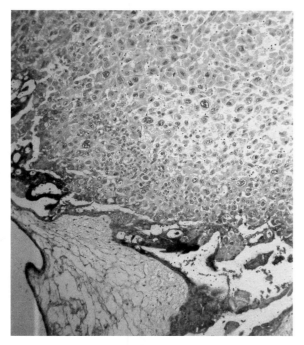

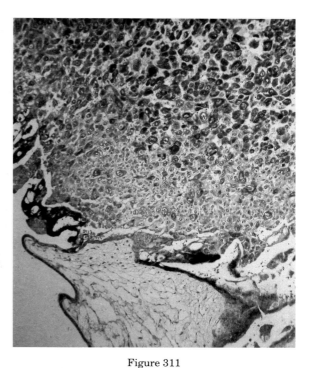

Figure 310
(Figures 310 and 311 are from the same patient)
COMPLETE HYDATIDIFORM MOLE
Localization of hCG in syncytiotrophoblast only is illustrated. Note that most of the proliferating trophoblastic cells are intermediate trophoblast, devoid of hCG. Immunoperoxidase-hCG with hematoxylin counterstain.

Figure 311
COMPLETE HYDATIDIFORM MOLE
The same section as in figure 310 shows localization of hPL in both syncytiotrophoblastic and intermediate trophoblastic cells. Immunoperoxidase-hPL with hematoxylin counterstain.

Figure 312
PARTIAL HYDATIDIFORM MOLE
This partial mole stains diffusely for PlAP in the right panel and focally for hCG in the left panel (arrows). (Fig. 24.30 from Mazur MT, Kurman RJ. Gestational trophoblastic disease. In: Kurman RJ, ed. Blaustein's pathology of the female genital tract. 3rd ed. New York: Springer-Verlag, 1987:835–75.)

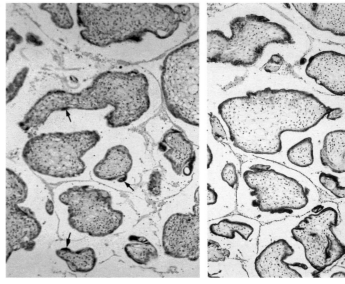

Table 12

COMPARISON OF THE IMMUNOCYTOCHEMICAL DISTRIBUTION OF HUMAN CHORIONIC GONADOTROPIN, HUMAN PLACENTAL LACTOGEN, AND PLACENTAL ALKALINE PHOSPHATASE IN NORMAL PLACENTAS, COMPLETE HYDATIDIFORM MOLES, PARTIAL HYDATIDIFORM MOLES, AND ABORTUSES WITH HYDROPIC SWELLING ACCORDING TO GESTATIONAL AGE *

Diagnosis	No. Cases	Staining Scores [†]		
		hCG [‡]	hPL [‡]	PlAP [‡]
Normal placenta	34			
6–10 weeks	14	3.2	2.2	0.2
11–15 weeks	8	0.8	2.9	1.5
16–24 weeks	12	0.8	3.8	2.6
Complete hydatidiform mole	22			
6–10 weeks	4	3.8	1.8	0.4
11–15 weeks	10	3.9	2.5	0.7
16–20 weeks	8	3.9	2.9	1.1
Partial hydatidiform mole	21			
6–10 weeks	2	3.5	4.0	1.8
11–15 weeks	8	2.3	3.6	1.6
16–33 weeks	11	1.1	3.9	3.8
Abortus with hydropic swelling	13			
6–10 weeks	4	2.3	2.5	1.0
11–15 weeks	8	2.0	3.6	0.2
16–18 weeks	1	2.0	3.0	0

* Modification of Table 4 from Brescia RJ, Kurman RJ, Main CS, Surti U, Szulman AE. Immunocytochemical localization of chorionic gonadotropin, placental lactogen, and placental alkaline phosphatase in the diagnosis of complete and partial moles. Int J Gynecol Pathol 1987;6:213–29.

† A semiquantitative scoring system based on the localization of peroxidase-antiperoxidase reaction product in syncytiotrophoblast. Occasional positive cells = 0.5; 1–24 percent positive cells = 1+; 25–49 percent positive cells = 3+; 75–100 percent positive cells = 4+. Staining scores represent mean values of all cases analyzed.

‡ hCG = human chorionic gonadotropin; hPL = human placental lactogen; PlAP = placental alkaline phosphatase.

formalin-fixed paraffin tissue can be used to distinguish complete from partial moles. An advantage of fixed tissue is that molar tissue can be easily distinguished from decidual tissue that could contaminate the specimen and lead to an erroneous diploid peak (15,25).

Differential Diagnosis. The most common problem in differential diagnosis is the distinction of a complete or partial hydatidiform mole from early nonmolar pregnancy, especially a mole with hydropic change. Comparison of complete and partial moles, a nonmolar abortus, and one showing hydropic change is shown in figures 313–318.

The nonmolar abortus can have several morphologic features that may mimic changes found in molar pregnancy. These include marked proliferation of trophoblast, which typically occurs early in gestation; the presence of immature villi with loose, edematous stroma; and the presence of hydropic villi associated with the so-called "blighted ovum", in which there is no development of an embryo. The edema of the nonmolar abortus including the blighted ovum is usually only a microscopic finding and is focally distributed among the villi. In contrast to complete or partial moles, macroscopic villous swelling is never present in the hydropic abortus. Microscopically, the swollen villi of the common abortus are typically surrounded by attenuated trophoblast (fig. 317). When trophoblastic proliferation occurs in an abortus, it is polar, characterized by column-like growth emanating from only one pole of the villus (fig. 318). In contrast, the trophoblastic proliferation on a chorionic villus of a mole is haphazard and circumferential. Trophoblastic atypia is not a feature of a hydropic abortus; when present, it suggests a hydatidiform mole. Most important, in the nonmolar gestations, central cistern formation is not a significant component, although in a nonmolar gestation, a hydropic villus with a cistern may occasionally be encountered.

The distinction of a nonmolar abortus from a partial mole in which hydropic change is not generalized is difficult. Other features of the partial mole, such as irregular scalloped borders (figs. 306, 307), can be helpful in making the distinction. In the partial mole, there are two distinct populations of hydropic and normal-sized villi (figs. 305, 314), whereas in the abortus with hydropic change, the hydropic villi are scattered haphazardly in a more focal distribution. Furthermore, immunohistochemical staining for PlAP is only focal in abortions with hydropic change, whereas it is more diffuse in partial moles (5). Finally, flow-cytometric analysis of nuclear DNA can be used to identify polyploidy in fresh or fixed tissue and thereby facilitate the diagnosis (24).

Usually it is not difficult to distinguish a complete mole from a partial mole, but sometimes this distinction may be difficult. Clinical and pathologic features helpful in the differential diagnosis are shown in Tables 10 and 11. Although the distinction of a complete from a partial mole is important from a prognostic standpoint, the clinical management is similar. Therefore, the most important distinction is between an abortus with hydropic change from any type of mole.

Clinical Behavior and Treatment. The hydatidiform mole, either partial or complete, is not a true neoplasm. However, its trophoblast may undergo malignant transformation. The mole, although evacuated, may persist and remain confined to the uterine cavity, penetrate the myometrium, embolize to the vagina or lungs, or transform to a choriocarcinoma. Most of the studies that have examined the long-term follow-up of hydatidiform mole were completed before the partial mole was recognized as a distinctive variant, so comprehensive comparison of the clinicopathologic features of the two forms of mole is not always feasible. Nonetheless, available data indicate that 10 to 30 percent of evacuated complete moles are followed by persistent gestational trophoblastic disease that requires therapy, as evidenced by a plateau or rise in hCG titers or the presence of metastases (2,8,26). Currently, there are no morphologic or genetic markers that can be used to predict the behavior of a complete mole. Some studies have suggested that complete moles with a Y chromosome are more likely to undergo malignant transformation (10,48), but other studies have not confirmed this (35). Choriocarcinoma is the most serious form of persistent gestational trophoblastic disease and occurs in about 2 to 3 percent of complete moles (2,26).

Partial mole is associated with less risk of persistent gestational trophoblastic disease, and the percentage of patients requiring therapy

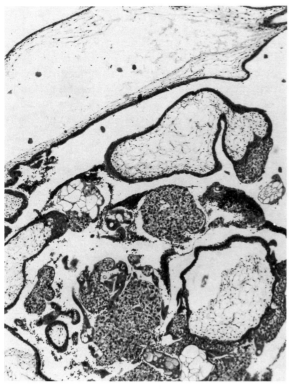

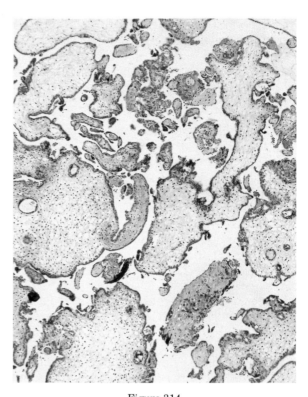

Figure 313
COMPLETE HYDATIDIFORM MOLE
Generalized villous swelling with circumferential hyperplasia of trophoblast is evident. Note the cistern in the villus in the upper part of the field.

Figure 314
PARTIAL HYDATIDIFORM MOLE
Two populations of chorionic villi, one with hydropic swelling and one of normal size, are visible. Note trophoblastic inclusions, minimal trophoblastic hyperplasia, and scalloping of villous outlines.

Figure 315
NONMOLAR ABORTUS
Immature villi have a loose edematous stroma, but hydropic change is not evident.

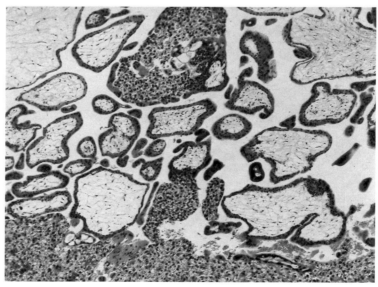

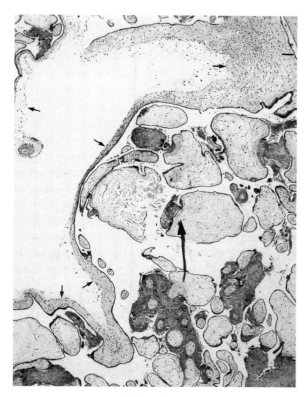

Figure 316
(Figures 316 and 317 are from the same patient)
BLIGHTED OVUM
This is an example of a blighted ovum with a collapsed gestational sac (small arrows), which should not be confused with a cistern. Small villi, some with hydropic change (large arrow), radiate out in a circumferential fashion from the gestational sac.

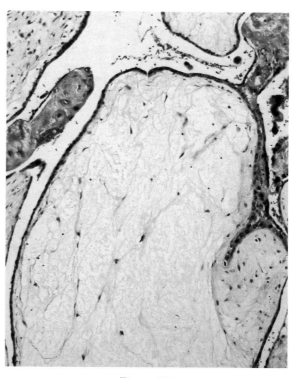

Figure 317
BLIGHTED OVUM
High magnification of a hydropic villus from the blighted ovum illustrated in figure 316 is shown. The trophoblast surrounding the chorionic villus is attenuated, with no trophoblastic proliferation.

Figure 318
NONMOLAR ABORTUS
A nonmolar first-trimester abortus with trophoblastic proliferation is illustrated. Note that the trophoblastic proliferation is polar, characterized by column-like growth emanating from only one pole of the villus.

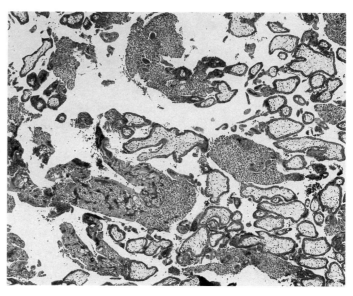

after evacuation of a partial mole has ranged from 4 to 11 percent (3,30,32,39,42,51). In one large study, the risk of persistent gestational trophoblastic disease based on the need for chemotherapy after a partial mole was 1 in 200 compared to 1 in 12 for a complete mole (1). Choriocarcinoma is an extremely rare occurrence after a partial mole; I am aware of only one well-documented case (Lage JM, personal communication). The sequelae of a partial mole have been persistent intrauterine disease or, in rare instances, an invasive mole (16,41).

Because of the risk of persistent gestational trophoblastic disease, close monitoring of serum β-hCG levels, until they fall and remain in the normal range, is necessary after the diagnosis of any form of hydatidiform mole (32,42,43). A chest radiograph after diagnosis is also useful for detecting early metastases, as well as serving as a baseline should pulmonary disease ensue.

INVASIVE HYDATIDIFORM MOLE (INVASIVE MOLE)

Definition. An invasive hydatidiform mole is one in which hydropic chorionic villi are within the myometrium or its vascular spaces or at distant sites, notably the vagina or lung. This lesion was formerly termed *chorioadenoma destruens*, *penetrating mole*, *malignant mole*, and *mola destruens*.

General Features. Invasive hydatidiform mole is a sequela to hydatidiform mole, complete or partial (11,26,28,45). The frequency of invasive mole is difficult to determine because most cases are diagnosed solely on clinical grounds without pathologic confirmation (28). Overall, invasive mole is a clinically significant sequela in about 15 percent of cases of hydatidiform mole. The pathologic diagnosis of invasive mole is made by establishing the presence of molar villi growing into the myometrium and broad ligament. The diagnosis of an invasive mole cannot be made on examination of curettage specimens except when curetted fragments of myometrium contain invasive molar villi. In extrauterine sites the lesion almost always involves the vagina, vulva, or lungs.

Gross Findings. On gross inspection, an invasive mole in the uterus appears as an irregular hemorrhagic lesion that invades the myometrium (fig. 319). It may grow through the myometrium, perforating the serosa and extending into the broad ligament with involvement of the adnexa.

Microscopic Findings. The villi are enlarged but often not as enlarged as the villi of a typical complete mole (fig. 320). The amount of trophoblast around the molar villi varies greatly; it may be abundant and obscure the presence of the molar villus. In such cases, careful scrutiny for villi is necessary to avoid misclassification of the lesion as choriocarcinoma. Similarly, trophoblastic lesions at distant sites after evacuation of a hydatidiform mole may also show an invasive mole with a marked proliferation of trophoblast, underscoring the need for thorough sectioning to ensure the correct diagnosis.

Extrauterine molar disease is typically characterized by the presence of molar villi within blood vessels without invasion of adjacent tissue. Because the trophoblast does not invade the adjacent tissue in extrauterine sites, this process is called *deportation* rather than *metastasis*. Occasionally, in these circumstances, the extrauterine lesion contains trophoblast without villi, and there is a central hemorrhagic zone accompanied by trophoblastic cells and fibrosis at the periphery. The trophoblastic cells are predominantly of the intermediate type, and the lesion closely simulates an exaggerated placental site. In the absence of a dimorphic population of trophoblast, the lesion does not fulfill the criteria for choriocarcinoma.

Immunohistochemistry. Invasive moles display a pattern of staining similar to that of complete moles because most invasive moles are derived from complete moles.

Differential Diagnosis. Invasive moles must be distinguished from noninvasive hydatidiform moles, choriocarcinoma, and placenta increta or percreta (13). Invasive moles should be diagnosed only when molar villi are identified in the myometrium and its vessels or at distant sites. Marked trophoblastic proliferation associated with an intracavitary hydatidiform mole in the absence of villi in the myometrium does not fulfill the criteria for an invasive mole. Invasive moles are distinguished from choriocarcinoma by the presence of chorionic villi. In placenta increta or percreta, the chorionic villi lack hydropic change.

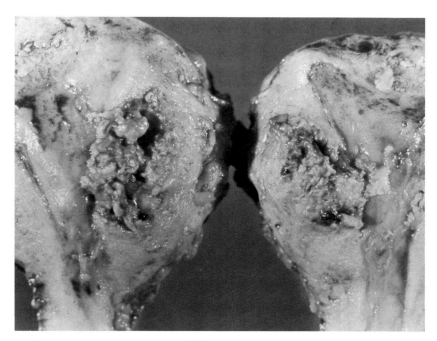

Figure 319
INVASIVE HYDATIDIFORM MOLE
The invasive mole infiltrates deeply into the myometrium, forming a ragged irregular mass. (Fig. 24.32 from Mazur MT, Kurman RJ. Gestational trophoblastic disease. In: Kurman RJ, ed. Blaustein's pathology of the female genital tract. 3rd ed. New York: Springer-Verlag, 1987:835–75.)

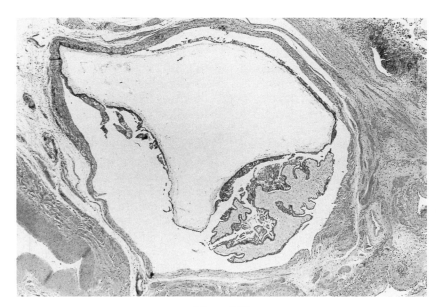

Figure 320
INVASIVE HYDATIDIFORM MOLE
Invasive mole deep within the myometrium. A hydropic villus and nonhydropic villi with minimal trophoblastic proliferation are shown. (Courtesy of Dr. Michael T. Mazur, Syracuse, NY.)

Clinical Behavior and Treatment. In the past, invasive hydatidiform moles sometimes resulted in life-threatening hemorrhage due to transmural invasion of the uterus and parametrial tissues, a complication that almost never occurs with chemotherapy (12,14). The pathologic diagnosis of invasive mole is rarely made because most patients with gestational trophoblastic disease are managed medically. Elevated or rising serum hCG titers that persist after evacuation of a mole may signify either an invasive mole or choriocarcinoma. Because tissue is usually not available to make the distinction, elevated serum hCG titers are usually attributed to persistent gestational trophoblastic disease without more specific classification. The risk of progression of invasive mole to choriocarcinoma appears to be no greater than that of progression from a noninvasive hydatidiform mole. Invasive moles may regress spontaneously. Before the chemotherapy era, it was observed that spontaneous regression of pulmonary lesions often occurred after hysterectomy (21). Nonetheless, if hCG titers persist or rise, the patient is usually treated with chemotherapy in the absence of a histologic diagnosis, and the lesion usually responds.

CHORIOCARCINOMA

Definition. Choriocarcinoma is a malignant neoplasm composed of trophoblast arranged in a dimorphic pattern and lacking chorionic villi. It has also been termed *chorionepithelioma*.

General Features. The reported prevalence of choriocarcinoma varies widely throughout the world, being greatest in Asia, Africa, and Latin America and substantially lower in North America, Europe, and Australia (Table 9) (4,6). However, studies of geographic prevalence suffer from methodological problems. Often, the total population at risk is not identified, and the rate of occurrence for all conceptions is difficult to determine. Furthermore, the clinical classification of gestational trophoblastic disease without identification of the specific pathologic lesion has obscured the prevalence rate of choriocarcinoma in many studies.

Women who are sexually active are at risk for development of these tumors, but the frequency is substantially higher in older women. Women over the age of 40 years are at increased risk for choriocarcinoma (4), although the absolute number of cases of choriocarcinoma in women over 40 years of age is smaller because of their lower fertility.

Choriocarcinoma may be associated with any form of gestation. More abnormal types of pregnancy are more likely to be associated with choriocarcinoma. Thus, the frequency is 1:160,000 for normal gestations, 1:15,386 for spontaneous abortions, 1:5,333 for ectopic pregnancies, and 1:40 for molar pregnancies (74). One half the cases of choriocarcinoma are preceded by hydatidiform mole, with 25 percent after an abortion, 22.5 percent after a normal pregnancy, and 2.5 percent after an ectopic pregnancy (73). Finally, there have been a few well-documented examples of choriocarcinoma arising from the trophoblast overlying the villi in an otherwise normal placenta (56,64).

An association has been reported between ABO blood groups and the occurrence of choriocarcinoma. Blood group A is more frequent and group O less common in patients with choriocarcinoma (53). On the other hand, some studies have found no association or even a decrease in the frequency of group A among patients with malignant gestational trophoblastic disease (82,91). In contrast to ABO blood group interactions, there has been no consistent pattern in human leukocyte antigen distribution of women with choriocarcinoma and their consorts (82,100).

The elucidation of the chromosomal abnormalities in cases of hydatidiform mole has had little impact on the understanding of the etiology of choriocarcinoma. The few choriocarcinomas that have been karyotyped to date have had aneuploid or polyploid chromosome complements (96,99). In one study, 74 percent of cases of choriocarcinoma contained Y-chromatin (60). The significance of this observation is not clear, but it indicates that there is a difference between the genomes of most hydatidiform moles and choriocarcinoma.

Clinical Features. Generally, choriocarcinoma follows an identifiable gestational event such as a hydatidiform mole, an abortion, or a term gestation by a few months. Choriocarcinoma not associated with hydatidiform mole is often not suspected clinically (71,86). It has been estimated that approximately

5 percent of choriocarcinomas arise in the fallopian tube as a result of an ectopic gestation (87). The signs and symptoms of choriocarcinoma are protean, whether they occur in association with a molar or nonmolar pregnancy (71,86,89). Abnormal uterine bleeding is one of the most frequent presentations (89), but uterine lesions restricted to the myometrium may be asymptomatic. Not all patients have a demonstrable lesion in the uterus after intrauterine gestation, and many examples of metastatic choriocarcinoma with no detectable uterine tumor have been described (75,81). The neoplasm has probably undergone regression in the uterus after metastasizing to distant sites (75,89). In such cases, symptoms related to metastasis may be the first manifestation of choriocarcinoma (56). The lungs are the most frequent site for blood-borne metastasis (78,81,86), and the patient may present with hemoptysis (95). Symptoms related to hemorrhagic events in the central nervous system, liver, and gastrointestinal or urinary tracts may also occur (62,68,86). Occasionally, thyroxicosis may be associated with choriocarcinoma because of the thyrotropic activity of hCG (83). Choriocarcinoma may have an unusually long latent period (69,77,89), occurring 10 or more years after hysterectomy or tubal ligation; rare examples of choriocarcinoma in postmenopausal women have been reported (63).

Gross Findings. The typical gross appearance of choriocarcinoma is that of a circumscribed hemorrhagic mass, due to its rapid proliferation combined with blood vessel invasion (fig. 321). The tumors vary from pinpoint-sized lesions to large destructive masses (fig. 322). The central portion of the lesion is typically hemorrhagic and necrotic, with only a thin rim of viable tumor at the periphery.

Microscopic Findings. The classic histologic pattern of choriocarcinoma is dimorphic or biphasic, indicating an alternating arrangement of cytotrophoblast and syncytiotrophoblast or intermediate trophoblast and syncytiotrophoblast (figs. 323–326).

Cytotrophoblast is composed of primitive cells that show mitotic activity. Typically, they are mononucleate cells of small to moderate size that contain a small amount of pale cytoplasm that is granular to clear (figs. 327, 328); cell borders are prominent. The syncytiotrophoblastic cells, in contrast, are highly developed multinucleate cells that are terminally differentiated and show no mitotic activity. The cytoplasm is dense and stains deeply eosinophilic to basophilic (figs. 301, 327) and often contains multiple vacuoles and lacunae formed by complex infoldings of the cell surface (figs. 324, 326). Erythrocytes may be seen in the lacunae. Sometimes a distinct brush border is identified along the membrane surfaces of syncytiotrophoblast. The intermediate trophoblastic cells, as their name implies, have features between those of cytotrophoblast and syncytiotrophoblast. They are typically large and polyhedral, with one nucleus and abundant cytoplasm (figs. 302, 328). Binucleate, trinucleate, and multinucleate cells may also be encountered. The cytoplasm is densely eosinophilic to amphophilic and lacks the vacuoles seen in syncytiotrophoblast. Cell membranes are less distinct than in cytotrophoblast, except when trophoblast infiltrates as individual cells or cords and clusters of cells. All of the cell types found in choriocarcinoma may show cytologic variation. There may be marked differences in the degree of cytologic atypia from one case to the other. Nuclear pleomorphism and hyperchromasia is often marked, and nucleoli may be prominent.

An unusual variant of choriocarcinoma composed predominantly of mononucleate cells growing in a nesting pattern with an intrinsic fibrovascular network has been reported (fig. 329) (80). The latter feature is not usually found in choriocarcinoma. Syncytiotrophoblastic cells are a relatively minor component. The mononucleate cells, which have irregular nuclei, amphophilic cytoplasm, and indistinct cell borders, most closely resemble intermediate trophoblastic cells. However, on electron microscopy, these intermediate trophoblastic cells are different from those in the placental site tumor and in the normal implantation site (see Ultrastructural Findings in this section). This variant of choriocarcinoma has been reported after chemotherapy (80) but may also arise de novo (Mazur MT, personal communication).

Because of the extensive necrosis associated with the rapid proliferation of choriocarcinoma, trophoblastic tissue may be scant, and extensive sectioning may be necessary to find the diagnostic biphasic pattern. Vascular invasion is often prominent in choriocarcinoma (fig. 330).

Chorionic villi are not a component of chorio-carcinoma except for the rare cases that arise in an otherwise normal placenta. In these cases, choriocarcinoma clearly arises from the villous covering of normal-appearing chorionic villi (fig. 331) (64,88). Choriocarcinoma arising from the villi of a nonmolar abortus has also been observed but is rare (Kurman RJ, personal observation). Chorionic villi in association with trophoblastic proliferations under any other circumstance rule out the diagnosis of choriocarcinoma.

Immunohistochemical Findings. As in normal placentation and molar disease, syn-cytiotrophoblast and intermediate tropho-blast in choriocarcinoma are hormonally active. Immunohistochemical studies with antibodies

to hCG or hPL can therefore be extremely help-ful in identifying these cells and defining the characteristic biphasic pattern in evaluating cases of suspected choriocarcinoma (23). In typ-ical choriocarcinoma, the syncytiotrophoblastic cells stain intensely for β-hCG and to a variable but lesser extent for hPL (fig. 332). Intermediate trophoblastic cells also stain to some extent for hCG and hPL (see fig. 337). All forms of tropho-blastic cells in choriocarcinoma, including cyto-trophoblast, are reactive to antibodies for cyto-keratin that recognize species of low as well as high molecular weight.

Ultrastructural Findings. Typically, a spectrum of cell types ranging from primitive to highly complex cells with specialized cytoplas-mic organelles is observed (65). Cytotrophoblastic

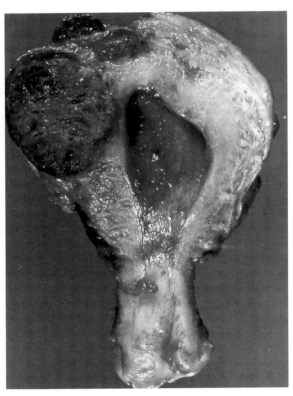

Figure 321
CHORIOCARCINOMA
Choriocarcinoma forms a circumscribed mass within the myometrium and does not involve the endometrium. (Fig. 24.35 from Mazur MT, Kurman RJ. Gestational tropho-blastic disease. In: Kurman RJ, ed. Blaustein's pathology of the female genital tract. 3rd ed. New York: Springer-Verlag, 1987:835–75.)

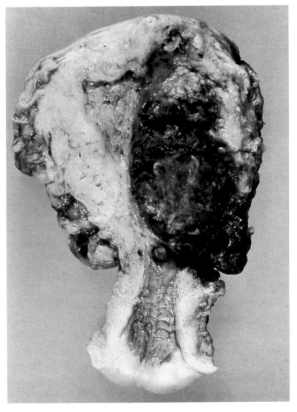

Figure 322
CHORIOCARCINOMA
Choriocarcinoma within the uterus forms a large hem-orrhagic destructive mass that involves both the endome-trium and myometrium. (Fig. 24.34 from Mazur MT, Kurman RJ. Gestational trophoblastic disease. In: Kurman RJ, ed. Blaustein's pathology of the female genital tract. 3rd ed. New York: Springer-Verlag, 1987:835–75.)

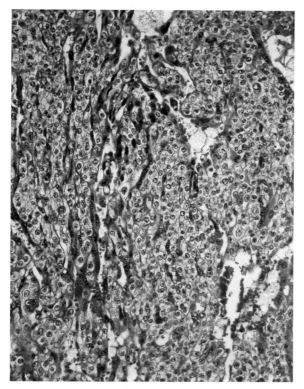

Figure 323
CHORIOCARCINOMA
A dimorphic pattern of cytotrophoblast and syncytio-
trophoblast lining vascular channels is illustrated.

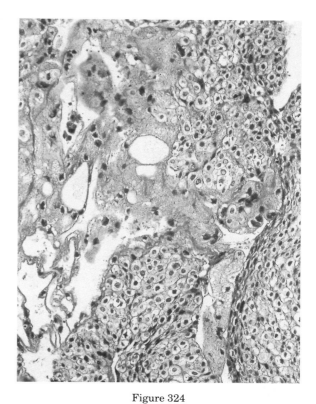

Figure 324
CHORIOCARCINOMA
In this illustration, choriocarcinoma is characterized by
a population of cytotrophoblast directly apposed to syncytiotrophoblast with prominent cytoplasmic vacuolization.

Figure 325
CHORIOCARCINOMA
Cytotrophoblast occupies the lower portion of the field, syncytiotrophoblast is visible just below the center and in the upper
left, and intermediate trophoblast occupies the upper half of the
field.

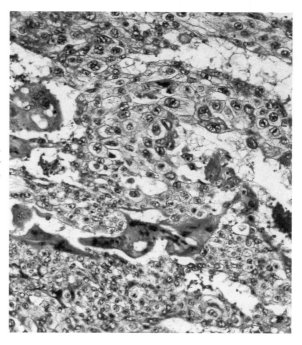

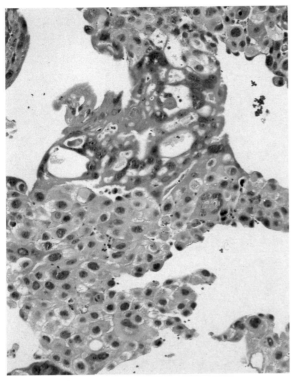

Figure 326
(Figures 326 and 327 are from the same patient)
CHORIOCARCINOMA
Intermediate trophoblastic cells are in direct apposition to syncytiotrophoblastic cells with marked cytoplasmic vacuolization.

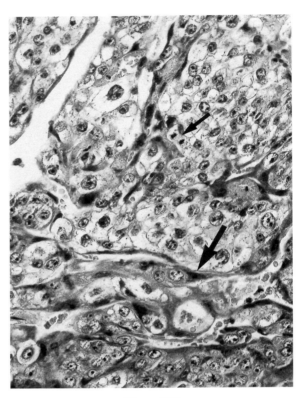

Figure 327
CHORIOCARCINOMA
Higher magnification of the tumor illustrated in figure 326 shows the relatively uniform population of cytotrophoblast overlying syncytiotrophoblast (large arrow). Cytotrophoblast is composed of mononucleate cells that are small to moderate in size, with granular or clear cytoplasm. Mitotic figures (small arrow) are usually evident.

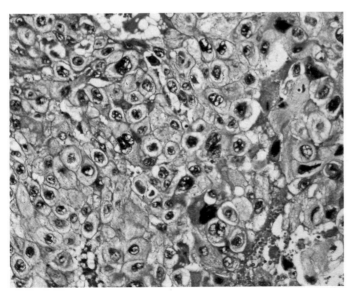

Figure 328
CHORIOCARCINOMA
Cytotrophoblast in the left-hand portion of the field is characterized by small mononucleate cells with prominent cell borders. In the right-hand portion of the field, intermediate trophoblastic cells are larger, with more pleomorphic nuclei and somewhat less distinct cell membranes.

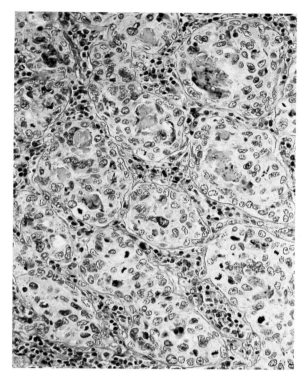

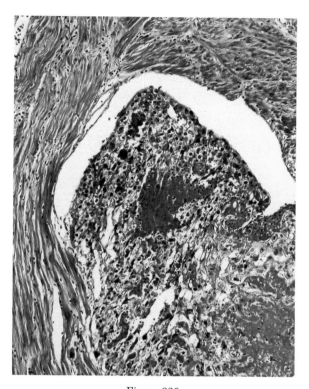

Figure 329
CHORIOCARCINOMA
An unusual variant of choriocarcinoma occurring after chemotherapy is shown. Most of the trophoblastic cells are mononucleate, suggesting that they are a form of intermediate trophoblast. The tumor cells are arranged in rounded nests surrounded by a chronic inflammatory infiltrate. (Courtesy of Dr. Michael T. Mazur, Syracuse, NY.)

Figure 330
CHORIOCARCINOMA
As shown in this illustration, vascular involvement by choriocarcinoma is characterized by a mass of trophoblastic cells expanding and growing out from a vascular lumen.

Figure 331
CHORIOCARCINOMA
Choriocarcinoma arising in a placenta with malignant trophoblast arising from the surface of normal villi is illustrated. (Fig. 24.40 from Mazur MT, Kurman RJ. Gestational trophoblastic disease. In: Kurman RJ, ed. Blaustein's pathology of the female genital tract. 3rd ed. New York: Springer-Verlag, 1987:835–75.)

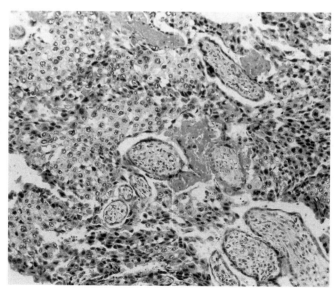

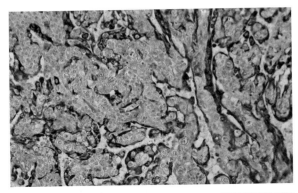

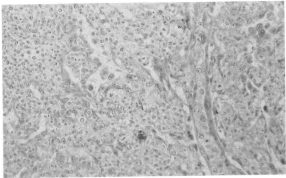

Figure 332
CHORIOCARCINOMA
In the upper panel of this illustration, immunoreactive hCG is localized in syncytiotrophoblast. Immunoperoxidase-hCG with hematoxylin counterstain. In the lower panel, hPL is absent from the field. Immunoperoxidase-hPL with hematoxylin counterstain.

cells contain a single large variably shaped nucleus with cytoplasm that has a paucity of organelles (fig. 333). The organelles include perinuclear mitochondria and a small amount of smooth and rough endoplasmic reticulum. Cytotrophoblastic cells are connected by desmosomes with tonofilaments. Syncytiotrophoblastic cells have irregular nuclei with condensed heterochromatin. The cytoplasm contains mitochondria, dilated smooth and rough endoplasmic reticulum, free ribosomes, vesicles, glycogen, and tonofilaments. There are multiple uniform thin microvilli on the plasma membrane (fig. 333).

Intermediate trophoblastic cells are mononucleate, with more complicated cytoplasmic structures than cytotrophoblast but less complex cytoplasm than syncytiotrophoblast. The cytoplasm contains dilated rough endoplasmic reticulum and occasional bundles of tonofilaments (65). In the unusual postchemotherapy variant of choriocarcinoma, the predominant cellular population is composed of intermediate trophoblastic cells that lack the perinuclear intermediate filaments that characterize this cell in the placental site trophoblastic tumor (fig. 334) (80).

Differential Diagnosis. Most choriocarcinomas have the typical biphasic pattern, but variations may exist. Portions of a tumor can show a predominance of cytotrophoblastic, intermediate trophoblastic, or syncytiotrophoblastic cells. When cytotrophoblastic or intermediate trophoblastic cells predominate, choriocarcinoma may simulate a poorly differentiated carcinoma (figs. 335–337). Occasionally, syncytiotrophoblastic cells are spindle shaped, causing confusion with a sarcoma (figs. 338, 339). Usually, additional sampling reveals the more typical biphasic arrangement of cytotrophoblastic and syncytiotrophoblastic cells or intermediate and syncytiotrophoblastic cells. The syncytiotrophoblast is the most distinctive cell in choriocarcinoma, so it is the most important diagnostic cell. At times, these cells may be difficult to identify, even with extensive sectioning. In such cases, the predominant cell is somewhat larger than cytotrophoblast, has one or several nuclei, and has indistinct cell membranes, features suggesting intermediate trophoblast (fig. 336). Immunohistochemical detection of hCG can assist in these cases because diffuse localization of hCG rarely, if ever, occurs in tumors other than choriocarcinoma (figs. 337, 339).

Choriocarcinoma is considered in the differential diagnosis of normal trophoblast from early gestations and in the proliferation of trophoblast associated with hydatidiform mole (66). When trophoblastic proliferations are encountered in uterine curettage specimens and no chorionic villi are found, the differential diagnosis includes choriocarcinoma or an abortus in which there are no villi, presumably because these were passed before the curettage. In a normal abortion without villi, there is usually only a small amount of trophoblastic tissue, whereas in choriocarcinoma the trophoblast is more abundant and arranged in the characteristic biphasic pattern. Tumor necrosis and cytologic atypia are additional characteristic features of choriocarcinoma. Often, trophoblast

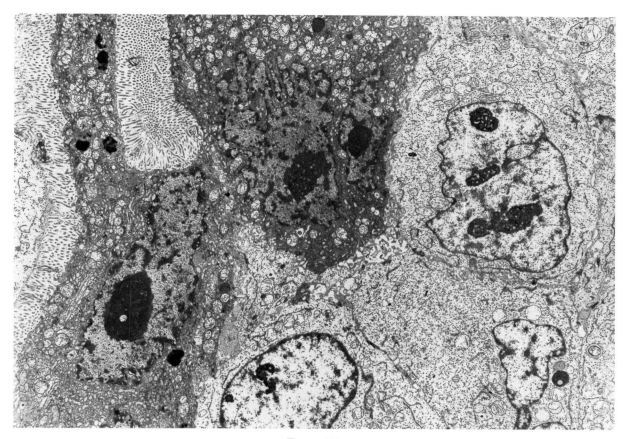

Figure 333
CHORIOCARCINOMA
Cytotrophoblastic cells shown on the right side of the field have a central nucleus and simple cytoplasm. Desmosomes join cells. The multinucleate syncytiotrophoblastic cell shown on the left side of the field has dense, complex cytoplasm containing dilated rough endoplasmic reticulum. Numerous slender microvilli project from surface. X3880. (Fig. 3 from Duncan DA, Mazur MT. Trophoblastic tumors: ultrastructural comparison of choriocarcinoma and placental site trophoblastic tumor. Hum Pathol 1989;20:370–81.)

without villi in curettage specimens may be suspicious for choriocarcinoma but difficult to categorize with certainty. A careful obstetric history in such cases may be extremely helpful. Atypical trophoblast without villi is more likely to represent choriocarcinoma if the preceding pregnancy was nonmolar, whereas similar-appearing trophoblast after evacuation of a mole may only represent a persistent intrauterine mole. In questionable cases, careful monitoring of serum β-hCG levels and chest radiographs may help establish the diagnosis.

At sites of metastasis, the differential diagnosis includes deported invasive mole, carcinomas with areas of choriocarcinomatous differen-

tiation, and poorly differentiated carcinomas with tumor giant cells. Choriocarcinoma is distinguished from invasive mole by the absence of chorionic villi. As previously noted, however, trophoblastic tissue in extrauterine sites after a molar pregnancy may in rare instances lack villi. In these cases, the trophoblast is composed almost entirely of intermediate trophoblast. The absence of a dimorphic population of cytotrophoblast or intermediate trophoblast in close approximation with syncytiotrophoblast distinguishes this lesion from choriocarcinoma.

In nongestational tumors with choriocarcinomatous differentiation or with areas that mimic choriocarcinoma, the differential

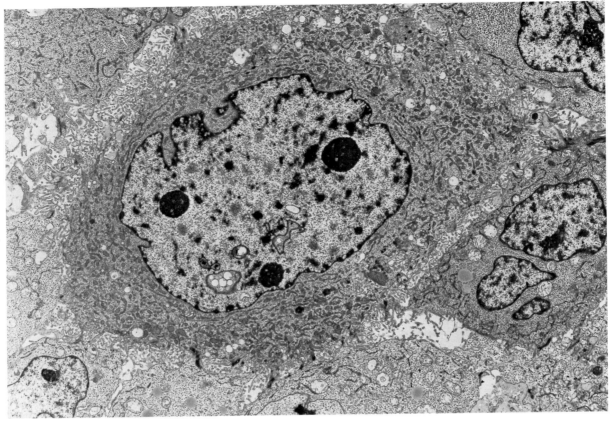

Figure 334
CHORIOCARCINOMA
This illustration shows an intermediate trophoblastic cell with numerous microvilli on the surface and many cytoplasmic organelles including dilated rough endoplasmic reticulum. X3750. (Courtesy of Dr. Michael T. Mazur, Syracuse, NY.)

diagnosis may be difficult, especially in young women in whom gestational trophoblastic disease is suspected. Choriocarcinoma occurs as a form of differentiation in some primary visceral neoplasms such as carcinomas of the gastrointestinal tract, urinary bladder, breast, liver, lung, and uterus (72,76,85,90,92,94). In such cases, the sections usually reveal areas of carcinoma typical of the primary site. When the differential diagnosis includes carcinoma with giant cell change suggestive of syncytiotrophoblast, immunohistochemistry may be useful in establishing the correct diagnosis. In choriocarcinoma, the syncytiotrophoblast and the intermediate trophoblast stain with hCG and hPL, whereas the giant cells in nontrophoblastic proliferations do not, although on rare occasions, trophoblastic-type

giant cells immunoreactive for hCG have been reported (58). It should be emphasized that tumors without the morphologic features of choriocarcinoma may be associated with the production of various trophoblastic proteins such as hCG or hPL (74).

Pure nongestational choriocarcinoma arising in the ovary is extremely rare (98) and is usually a component of a malignant germ-cell tumor. Accordingly, other germ-cell tumor elements, such as dysgerminoma, teratoma, or yolk sac tumor, are present. α-Fetoprotein is typically produced by yolk sac tumor and less commonly by teratoma, so immunostaining tissue and serum α-fetoprotein levels can be useful in diagnosing these mixed germ-cell tumors. The differential diagnosis of the placental site trophoblastic tumor with choriocarcinoma is

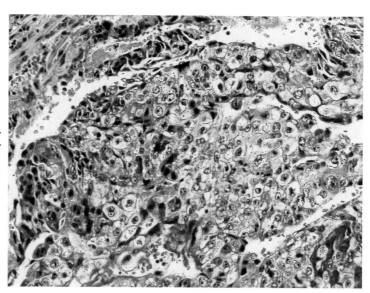

Figure 335
CHORIOCARCINOMA
Choriocarcinoma composed mostly of cytotrophoblastic cells is illustrated. Because of the paucity of syncytiotrophoblast, this tumor may be confused with a poorly differentiated carcinoma.

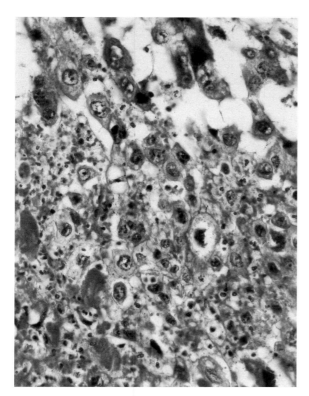

Figure 336
(Figures 336 and 337 are from the same patient)
CHORIOCARCINOMA
Intermediate trophoblastic cells are illustrated in this field. When this cellular population predominates, the neoplasm may be confused with a poorly differentiated carcinoma or placental site trophoblastic tumor.

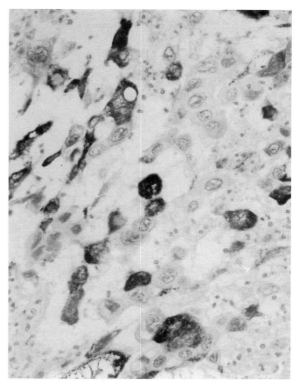

Figure 337
CHORIOCARCINOMA
Localization of hCG in intermediate trophoblastic cells from the choriocarcinoma illustrated in figure 336 is useful in distinguishing this tumor from a poorly differentiated carcinoma.

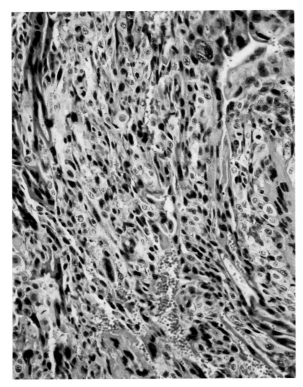

Figure 338
(Figures 338 and 339 are from the same patient)
CHORIOCARCINOMA
In this choriocarcinoma, the syncytiotrophoblastic cells show a prominent spindle-cell pattern that can be confused with a sarcoma.

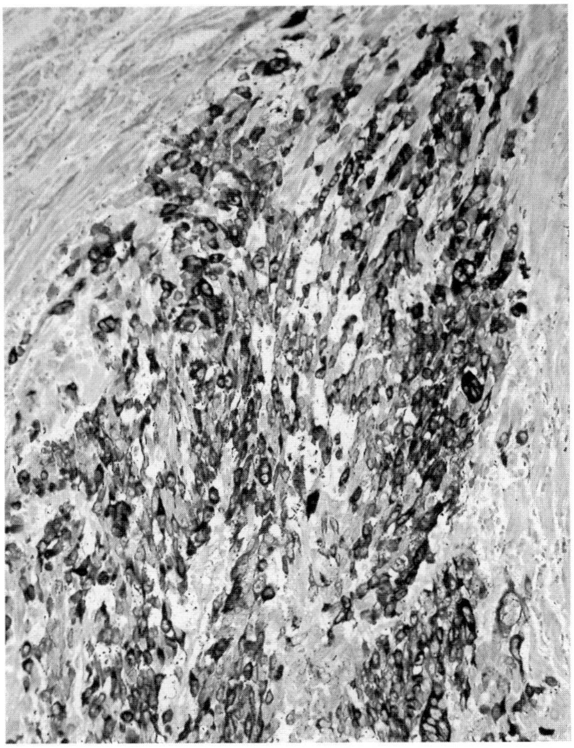

Figure 339
CHORIOCARCINOMA
Immunolocalization of hCG in the spindle-shaped cells of the tumor illustrated in figure 338 confirms the diagnosis of choriocarcinoma.

considered in the discussion of the placental site trophoblastic tumor.

Clinical Behavior and Treatment. More than 90 percent of patients with extrauterine spread of gestational choriocarcinoma will have lung metastases (75,78,81,86,89). The frequency of involvement of other sites varies, depending on whether the rates are based on autopsy studies and whether the patients have received chemotherapy. Brain and liver metastases occur in 20 to 60 percent of the patients. The kidney and gastrointestinal tract are the other common sites, but almost any organ, including the skin, may be involved (67,81,86). Lymph nodes contain tumor on occasion, often as tertiary metastases from other organs (81, 86). Vaginal involvement has been reported in 16 to 32 percent of patients (81,84,86,89). There have been a few isolated reports of metastatic choriocarcinoma occurring during pregnancy (97)

and in the mother and child of a term pregnancy (57,59). Usually the infant is free of disease (52).

Before modern cytotoxic chemotherapy, treatment was hysterectomy, which had a survival rate of only 41 percent when no metastases were present and 19 percent when metastases were present (56). Chemotherapy has dramatically improved the prognosis. The survival rate is 81 percent for all patients but only 71 percent for those with metastatic disease (79). In contrast, the overall survival rate for all cases of persistent and metastatic gestational trophoblastic disease is now over 90 percent (79).

Death from choriocarcinoma is usually due to hemorrhagic events at metastatic sites, pulmonary insufficiency caused by a large tumor burden, or the effects of irradiation and cytotoxic chemotherapy (72,81). Several prognostic factors help predict the response to treatment (53,54,71,93) (see General Aspects of Clinical

Management and Staging). Some investigators have suggested that gestational trophoblastic disease with minimal differentiation toward syncytiotrophoblast has a worse prognosis (61). Further study is needed to determine whether such histologic patterns have clinical significance. As noted, chemotherapy may alter the histologic appearance in isolated cases (80,81), but the influence of these histologic changes on the clinical outcome has not been established.

PLACENTAL SITE TROPHOBLASTIC TUMOR

Definition. The placental site trophoblastic tumor forms a variably cellular mass, occupying the endometrium and myometrium, that resembles the non-neoplastic trophoblastic infiltration of the implantation site. This tumor was formerly called *syncytioma*, *atypical choriocarcinoma*, *chorioepitheliosis*, and *trophoblastic pseudotumor*.

General Features. The placental site trophoblastic tumor is the rarest form of gestational trophoblastic disease. The epidemiologic and risk factors for the placental site trophoblastic tumor are not well known because the entity has only recently been recognized as a distinct form of trophoblastic disease (108). So far, there are only approximately 80 reported and unreported cases of placental site trophoblastic tumor (112). As expected, this is a disorder of the reproductive years, although several patients have been over 50 years of age when the tumor was diagnosed (101,110). Most patients have been parous, and several have had a prior hydatidiform mole (101,104,108). Both term pregnancies and spontaneous abortions have preceded the diagnosis of placental site trophoblastic tumor. Usually the relationship to the previous gestations is uncertain because the tumors are diagnosed some time after the last known pregnancy.

The pathogenesis of the placental site trophoblastic tumor is not precisely known. Comparison of placental site trophoblastic tumor with choriocarcinoma suggests that the placental site trophoblastic tumor represents a neoplastic transformation of extravillous intermediate

trophoblast at a later stage of trophoblastic maturation. A number of lines of evidence support this view: 1) the morphology of the placental site trophoblastic tumor with its characteristic pattern of vascular and myometrial invasion recapitulates the normal infiltration of intermediate trophoblast at the implantation site (23,107); 2) the immunohistochemical distribution of hPL and hCG in the placental site trophoblastic tumor closely simulates that in the intermediate trophoblastic cells of the implantation site (107); 3) the preponderance of hPL relative to hCG in the placental site trophoblastic tumor compared with choriocarcinoma is thought to reflect trophoblastic maturation because the synthesis of hPL follows that of hCG in normal gestation (23); 4) the behavior of placental site trophoblastic tumor, which is usually benign and associated with low serum levels of hCG, compared with choriocarcinoma, which is invariably malignant and associated with high serum levels of hCG, indicates that placental site trophoblastic tumor is not as primitive a neoplasm as choriocarcinoma (112).

Clinical Features. Patients with placental site trophoblastic tumor may present either with amenorrhea or with abnormal bleeding (101,103,108). The uterus is often enlarged, so the patient may be thought to be pregnant. The results of pregnancy tests vary but are almost always positive when a sensitive immunologic assay is used. When progressive uterine enlargement ceases, a diagnosis of missed abortion is made. Because of the deep myometrial penetration, perforation may occur during curettage (108). One case of placental site trophoblastic tumor has been associated with virilization (109). A few cases of placental site trophoblastic tumor have been associated with an apparently unique form of renal disease in which the nephrotic syndrome is a major component (113).

Gross Findings. The gross appearance of placental site trophoblastic tumor is highly variable. The lesions range from microscopic to diffuse tumors that enlarge and distort the fundus. Usually the tumors are well defined; however, some are poorly demarcated (fig. 340). Tumor may project into the uterine cavity or may be confined to the myometrium. The neoplasm is soft and tan and may have areas of hemorrhage or necrosis. Many cases have been associated with invasion through the entire

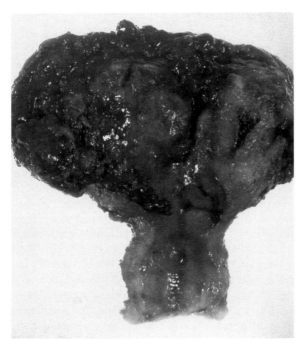

Figure 340
PLACENTAL SITE TROPHOBLASTIC TUMOR
This placental site trophoblastic tumor involves most of the fundus and invades into the serosa. (Fig. 24.42 from Mazur MT, Kurman RJ. Gestational trophoblastic disease. In: Kurman RJ, ed. Blaustein's pathology of the female genital tract. 3rd ed. New York: Springer-Verlag, 1987:835–75.)

thickness of the myometrium, extending to the serosa.

Microscopic Findings. The placental site trophoblastic tumor is composed predominantly of intermediate trophoblast; cytotrophoblast and syncytiotrophoblast are relatively minor constituents. The typical growth pattern is that of infiltration of the myometrium by large polygonal intermediate trophoblastic cells that insinuate themselves between the smooth muscle fibers at the interface between the tumor and the myometrium (figs. 341, 342). Although some tumors appear to cause little tissue destruction, others are associated with extensive necrosis. The cells may be present singly or in large nests or masses. Usually the cells are polyhedral (figs. 341, 343) but may be spindle shaped in areas (fig. 344). Extensive deposition of fibrinoid material is characteristic (fig. 345). The placental site trophoblastic tumor also characteristically invades the walls of blood vessels from the

periphery to the lumen, eventually replacing the entire wall (fig. 346). Fibrinoid material is also deposited in the vessel wall. A central lumen containing erythrocytes typically identifies the structure as a vessel. Placental site trophoblastic tumor also contains syncytiotrophoblastic cells that may have vacuolated cytoplasm (fig. 345). In most cases, the syncytiotrophoblast is a relatively minor component, but occasionally it is prominent. The placental site trophoblastic tumor usually is not associated with the presence of chorionic villi. Decidua may be present in the uninvolved endometrium.

Certain microscopic features may be useful in predicting prognosis. The malignant cases of placental site trophoblastic tumor are often composed of larger masses and sheets of cells that tend to have clear instead of amphophilic cytoplasm (fig. 347). Necrosis is more extensive in the malignant tumors, and the mitotic rate is higher. In the benign placental site trophoblastic tumors, the mean mitotic rate has been 2 mitotic figures per 10 HPF, with the highest reported rate being 5 mitotic figures per 10 HPF (fig. 348). In contrast, malignant lesions usually have more than 5 mitotic figures per 10 HPF. In one fatal case, however, the mean mitotic rate was only 2 mitotic figures per 10 HPF (104,105). Abnormal mitotic figures may be found in either benign or malignant tumors. The malignant cases tend to stain more diffusely for hCG than hPL, more closely resembling the distribution of these hormones in choriocarcinoma.

Immunohistochemical Findings. Typically, most of the intermediate trophoblastic cells of the placental site trophoblastic tumor contain hPL, whereas only a few contain hCG (fig. 349). All of the morphologic variants of intermediate trophoblastic cells stain positively (Table 13). Multinucleate giant cells corresponding to syncytiotrophoblastic giant cells are occasionally positive for hPL and are almost always positive for hCG. Cells that contain one hormone usually do not contain the other, but occasionally both hormones appear to be present in the same cell. Cells that are negative for hCG and hPL cannot be distinguished morphologically from those that are positive. In approximately 15 percent of placental site trophoblastic tumors, hCG either predominates or is equal in amount to hPL. The immunohistochemical features of these tumors resemble

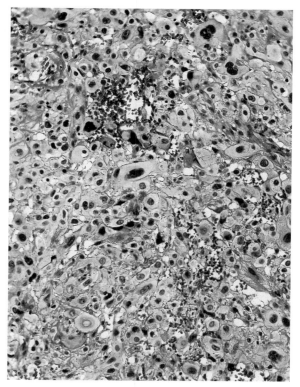

Figure 341
PLACENTAL SITE TROPHOBLASTIC TUMOR
The tumor is characterized by sheets of predominantly mononucleate pleomorphic cells with abundant cytoplasm and sharp cell borders. (Fig. 4 from Kurman RJ, Scully RE, Norris HJ. Trophoblastic pseudotumor of the uterus. An exaggerated form of "syncytial endometritis" simulating a malignant tumor. Cancer 1976;38:1214–26.)

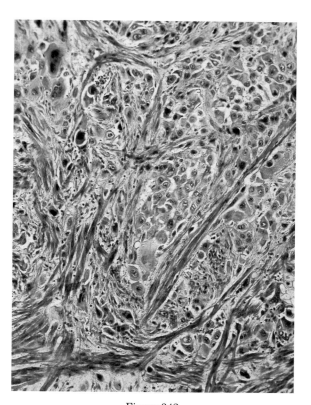

Figure 342
PLACENTAL SITE TROPHOBLASTIC TUMOR
This tumor is composed of masses of intermediate trophoblastic cells invading the myometrium and disrupting its architecture. (Fig. 2 from Kurman RJ, Scully RE, Norris HJ. Trophoblastic pseudotumor of the uterus. An exaggerated form of "syncytial endometritis" simulating a malignant tumor. Cancer 1976;38:1214–26.)

Figure 343
PLACENTAL SITE
TROPHOBLASTIC TUMOR
High magnification of a placental site trophoblastic tumor composed of a relatively uniform population of rounded-to-polygonal cells infiltrating and separating individual muscle fibers is illustrated.

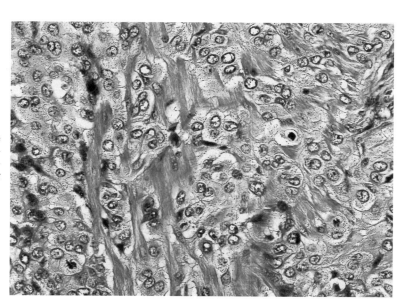

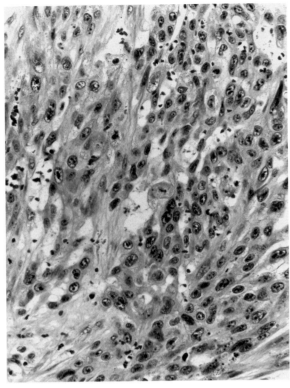

Figure 344
PLACENTAL SITE TROPHOBLASTIC TUMOR
This tumor has a spindle-cell pattern that is particularly evident in the lower right of the field. Tumor cells have nuclei with prominent granular, clumped chromatin. This tumor behaved in a malignant fashion.

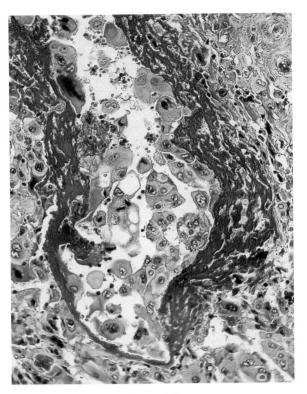

Figure 345
PLACENTAL SITE TROPHOBLASTIC TUMOR
In this tumor, a blood vessel wall is replaced by fibrinoid. Trophoblast containing vacuoles is present within the lumen. (Fig. 10 from Kurman RJ, Scully RE, Norris HJ. Trophoblastic pseudotumor of the uterus. An exaggerated form of "syncytial endometritis" simulating a malignant tumor. Cancer 1976;38:1214–26.)

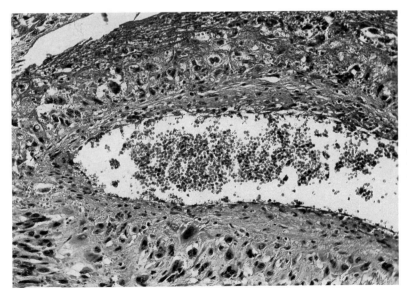

Figure 346
PLACENTAL SITE
TROPHOBLASTIC TUMOR
The wall of a large blood vessel in this tumor is infiltrated by intermediate trophoblastic cells. Note that the overall structure of the vessel is maintained with an intact lumen despite massive trophoblastic invasion.

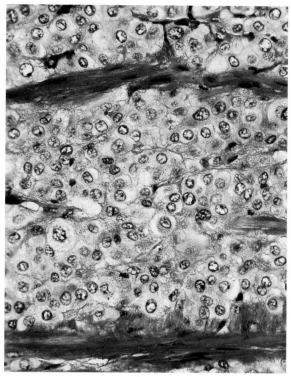

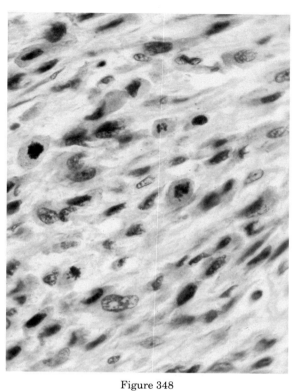

Figure 347
PLACENTAL SITE TROPHOBLASTIC TUMOR
This tumor is composed of a relatively uniform monomorphic population of intermediate trophoblast in which many of the cells have clear cytoplasm. (Fig. 24.43 from Mazur MT, Kurman RJ. Gestational trophoblastic disease. In: Kurman RJ, ed. Blaustein's pathology of the female genital tract. 3rd ed. New York: Springer-Verlag, 1987:835–75.)

Figure 348
PLACENTAL SITE TROPHOBLASTIC TUMOR
The spindle-shaped intermediate trophoblastic cells simulate a sarcoma. There are four mitotic figures in this field. (Fig. 5 from Kurman RJ, Scully RE, Norris HJ. Trophoblastic pseudotumor of the uterus. An exaggerated form of "syncytial endometritis" simulating a malignant tumor. Cancer 1976;38:1214–26.)

Figure 349
PLACENTAL SITE TROPHOBLASTIC TUMOR
Most of the intermediate trophoblastic cells in the upper panel of this illustration contain immunoreactive hPL. Immunoperoxidase-hPL with hematoxylin counterstain. In the lower panel, all of the intermediate trophoblastic cells are devoid of hCG. Immunoperoxidase-hCG with hematoxylin counterstain.

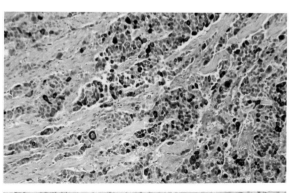

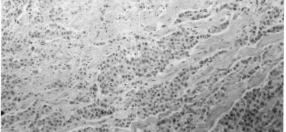

Table 13

LOCALIZATION OF CHORIONIC GONADOTROPIN β-SUBUNIT AND PLACENTAL LACTOGEN IN DIFFERENT TYPES OF TROPHOBLASTIC CELLS IN PLACENTAL SITE TROPHOBLASTIC TUMOR, AND CHORIOCARCINOMA *

	hCG [†]	hPL [†]
Placental site trophoblastic tumor		
Intermediate trophoblast	– /+ [‡]	+++/++++ [‡]
Syncytiotrophoblastic giant cells [†]	++/+++ [‡]	– /+
Choriocarcinoma		
Cytotrophoblast	– /+	–
Intermediate trophoblast	– /+	– /++
Syncytiotrophoblast	+++/++++	– /++

* Modification of Table 2 from Kurman RJ, Young RH, Norris HJ, Main CS, Lawrence WD, Scully RE. Immunocytochemical localization of placental lactogen and chorionic gonadotropin in the normal placenta and trophoblastic tumors, with emphasis on intermediate trophoblast and the placental site trophoblastic tumor. Int J Gynecol Pathol 1984;3:101–21.

[†] hCG = human chorionic gonadotropin; hPL = human placental lactogen.

[‡] All symbols denote semiquantitative scoring of the proportion of cells showing a positive reaction; + = 1–24 percent; ++ = 25–49 percent; +++ = 50–74 percent; ++++ = 75–100 percent.

those of choriocarcinoma more closely than the usual placental site trophoblastic tumor (23). Immunoreactive cytokeratin is detected in all of the various trophoblastic cells in placental site trophoblastic tumors when broadly reactive keratin antibodies are used (fig. 350).

Ultrastructural Findings. Consistent with the light-microscopic appearance, the predominant cellular population of the placental site trophoblastic tumor is the intermediate trophoblastic cell. Cytotrophoblastic cells are usually not identified. The intermediate trophoblastic cells are mononucleate, with complex cytoplasm containing free ribosomes, partially dilated rough endoplasmic reticulum, and glycogen. Cell junctions are present, and there are scattered blunt microvilli. A distinctive feature of this cell is the presence of bundles of intermediate filaments in a perinuclear location (fig. 351). The syncytiotrophoblastic cell in the placental site tumor is similar to its analogue in choriocarcinoma, except it has fewer microvilli on the free cell surface (65).

Differential Diagnosis. The placental site trophoblastic tumor must be differentiated from choriocarcinoma, an exaggerated implantation site, placental site nodule, and a variety of other malignant tumors. Usually the distinction of placental site trophoblastic tumor from chorio-

carcinoma is not difficult. The clinical and pathologic features that assist in this distinction are listed in Tables 14 and 15. A number of histologic features distinguish choriocarcinoma from placental site trophoblastic tumor. The placental site trophoblastic tumor is composed predominantly of intermediate trophoblastic cells. Syncytiotrophoblast may be present, but these cells are widely scattered in placental site trophoblastic tumor, in contrast to their alternating biphasic arrangement in choriocarcinoma.

Besides the differing proportions of the various trophoblastic populations in placental site trophoblastic tumors compared with choriocarcinoma, these tumors have different patterns of invasion. Choriocarcinoma tends to have an expansile margin at the interface with the adjacent myometrium and invades and fills vessel lumina (fig. 330). In contrast, the placental site trophoblastic tumor has a more irregular margin, invading the adjacent myometrium by infiltrating between individual muscle fibers and groups of muscle fibers (figs. 342, 343). This tumor also exhibits a characteristic pattern of vascular invasion in which mononucleate intermediate trophoblastic cells surround, migrate through, and replace the vessel walls (fig. 352). Subsequently, the intermediate trophoblastic cells are replaced by a fibrinoid matrix. Invaded

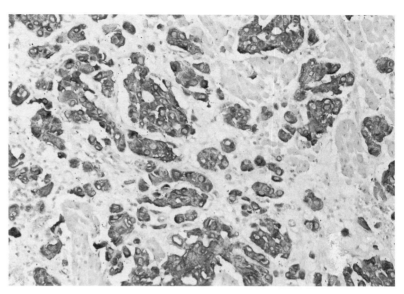

Figure 350
PLACENTAL SITE
TROPHOBLASTIC TUMOR
The cells in this field contain immuno-reactive cytokeratin. Unstained cells represent myometrial cells infiltrated by the tumor. Immunoperoxidase-cytokeratin AE1/AE3 with hematoxylin counterstain.

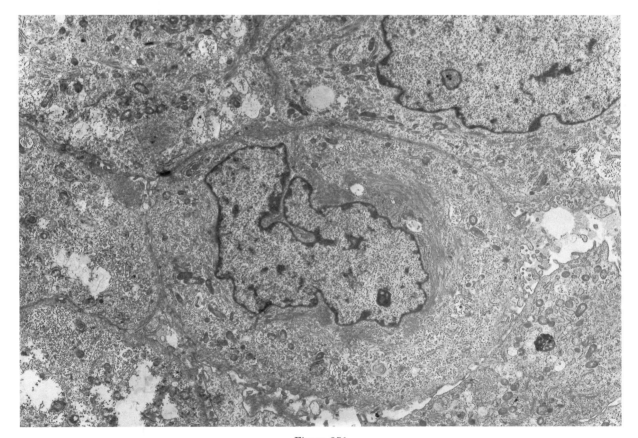

Figure 351
PLACENTAL SITE TROPHOBLASTIC TUMOR
This large intermediate trophoblastic cell contains paranuclear filaments and irregular blunt microvilli. X5820. (Fig. 9 from Duncan DA, Mazur MT. Trophoblastic tumors: ultrastructural comparison of choriocarcinoma and a placental site trophoblastic tumor. Hum Pathol 1989;20:370.)

Table 14

CLINICAL FEATURES OF PLACENTAL SITE TROPHOBLASTIC TUMOR AND CHORIOCARCINOMA *

Feature	PSTT [†]	Choriocarcinoma
Clinical presentation	Missed abortion	Persistent GTD [†] after hydatidiform mole
Serum hCG [†]	Low	High
Behavior	Self-limited	Highly aggressive
	Persistent or highly aggressive	
Response to chemotherapy	Poor	Good
Treatment	Surgery (hysterectomy)	Chemotherapy

* Table 24.5 from Mazur MT, Kurman RJ. Gestational trophoblastic disease. In: Kurman RJ, ed. Blaustein's pathology of the female genital tract. 3rd ed. New York: Springer-Verlag, 1987:863.

[†] PSTT = placental site trophoblastic tumor; GTD = gestational trophoblastic disease; hCG = human chorionic gonadotropin.

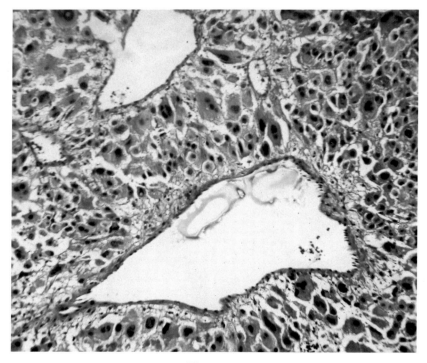

Figure 352
PLACENTAL SITE TROPHOBLASTIC TUMOR
Vascular invasion in a placental site trophoblastic tumor is characterized by intermediate trophoblastic cells engulfing vessels.

Table 15

PATHOLOGIC FEATURES OF PLACENTAL SITE TROPHOBLASTIC TUMOR AND CHORIOCARCINOMA *

Feature	PSTT [†]	Choriocarcinoma
Cellular population	Monomorphic	Dimorphic
	Intermediate trophoblast	Mainly cytotrophoblast and syncytiotrophoblast
Margin	Infiltrating	Circumscribed
Hemorrhage	Focal and haphazard	Massive and central
Vascular invasion	From periphery to lumen	From lumen to periphery
Fibrinoid change	Present	Absent
Immunocytochemistry		
hCG [†]	+ [‡]	++++ [‡]
hPL [†]	++++	+

* Modfication of Table 24.6 from Mazur MT, Kurman RJ. Gestational trophoblastic disease. In: Kurman RJ, ed. Blaustein's pathology of the female genital tract. 3rd ed. New York: Springer-Verlag, 1987:865.

[†] PSTT = placental site trophoblastic tumor; hCG = human chorionic gonadotropin; hPL = human placental lactogen.

[‡] All symbols denote semiquantitative scoring of the proportion of cells showing a positive reaction; + = 1–24 percent; ++++ = 75–100 percent.

vessels often remain intact within the substance of the tumor (fig. 352). The presence of fibrinoid within and outside of blood vessel walls is a characteristic feature of the placental site trophoblastic tumor (fig. 345). Fibrinoid is not found in association with choriocarcinoma. The placental site trophoblastic tumor also has a different immunohistochemical staining pattern than choriocarcinoma. Because the tumor is composed primarily of intermediate trophoblast, staining for hPL is diffuse throughout the neoplasm. In contrast, hCG immunostaining is usually focal because syncytiotrophoblastic cells are less prominent. In addition, the serum β-hCG levels tend to be much lower in placental site trophoblastic tumors than in choriocarcinoma.

Occasionally, a placental site trophoblastic tumor may contain a choriocarcinoma component. These neoplasms should be designated *placental site trophoblastic tumor with foci of choriocarcinoma* or *mixed placental site trophoblastic tumor and choriocarcinoma*, depending on the extent of involvement by the two components (figs. 353–355). The behavior of these mixed tumors compared with the pure types is not known. Occasionally, a poorly differentiated placental site trophoblastic tumor is not readily distinguishable from a choriocarcinoma that lacks the typical pattern of cytotrophoblast and intermediate trophoblast. In these cases, the relative proportion of hCG to hPL may assist in the diagnosis because there is typically a much greater distribution of hPL to hCG in placental site trophoblastic tumors.

The normal implantation site is composed of intermediate trophoblastic cells much like those seen in placental site trophoblastic tumor. Consequently, curettage or hysterectomy specimens that include an implantation site without accompanying villi and villous trophoblast can mimic the placental site trophoblastic tumor. This resemblance can be particularly problematic when there is a florid proliferation of intermediate trophoblast, the so-called "exaggerated placental site", which is composed of large nests of intermediate cells infiltrating the decidua and the superficial myometrium. An exaggerated placental site is only a microscopic phenomenon in contrast to the placental site trophoblastic tumor, which usually forms a large mass. Furthermore, because the exaggerated placental site is essentially a physiologic

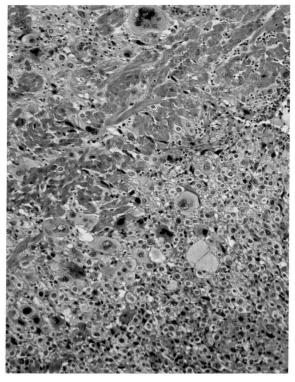

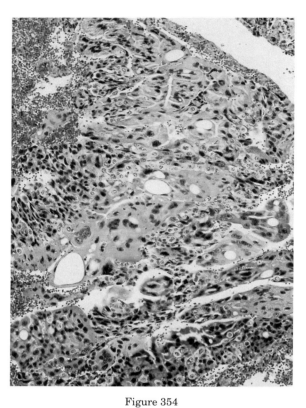

Figure 353
(Figures 353–355 are from the same patient)
MIXED PLACENTAL SITE TROPHOBLASTIC
TUMOR AND CHORIOCARCINOMA
In the lower part of the field, the predominant cellular
population is cytotrophoblast intermixed with intermediate
trophoblastic cells. The latter infiltrate the myometrium; a
single syncytiotrophoblastic giant cell is present in the
center at the upper part of the field.

Figure 354
MIXED PLACENTAL SITE TROPHOBLASTIC
TUMOR AND CHORIOCARCINOMA
The choriocarcinomatous component of the mixed tumor
is shown. Syncytiotrophoblastic cells predominate in this
field.

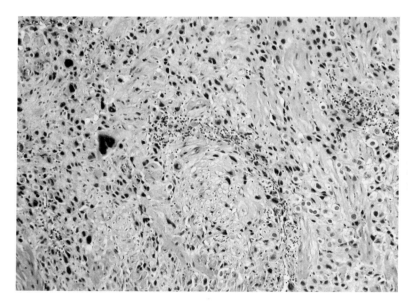

Figure 355
MIXED PLACENTAL SITE
TROPHOBLASTIC TUMOR
AND CHORIOCARCINOMA
The placental site trophoblastic tumor
component is characterized by intermediate
trophoblastic cells infiltrating through the
myometrium.

process, it does not distort the normal architecture of the endometrium and myometrium. At times it may be difficult or impossible to determine whether a process in curettage specimens represents an exaggerated implantation site or a placental site trophoblastic tumor. In such cases, close clinical follow-up with monitoring of serum hCG levels is prudent. In normal gestation, the hCG levels return to normal and menstruation resumes, whereas in the placental site trophoblastic tumor, low but elevated serum hCG levels persist after the curettage. Accordingly, careful clinical follow-up with monitoring of serum hCG levels is a safe procedure in questionable cases. Plateauing or rising hCG titers are ominous and require careful clinical evaluation.

The placental site trophoblastic tumor can be confused with a wide variety of nontrophoblastic cancers. The differential diagnosis between an epithelioid leiomyosarcoma and placental site trophoblastic tumor can be especially difficult because placental site trophoblastic tumors often have a highly infiltrative pattern within the myometrium, appearing to originate from smooth muscle cells. Helpful clues in the differential diagnosis include the distinctive pattern of vascular invasion and the deposition of fibrinoid material in the placental site trophoblastic tumor that are not found in leiomyosarcoma or most other malignant tumors. In addition, the placental site trophoblastic tumor shows a diffuse distribution for hPL and cytokeratin, whereas sarcomas do not. On rare occasions, placental site trophoblastic tumors may be difficult to distinguish from a clear cell carcinoma with minimal or no glandular differentiation or from a markedly hyalinized squamous cell carcinoma of the cervix (fig. 356). Immunostaining for hPL and hCG can be particularly helpful in distinguishing placental site trophoblastic tumors from these other tumors. Although other tumors may, on occasion, stain focally for hCG or hPL, the combination of the histologic features, the more diffuse and intense immunostaining for hPL, and the definite but more focal staining for hCG in placental site trophoblastic tumors should resolve difficult cases.

Clinical Behavior and Treatment. The placental site trophoblastic tumor tends to have an indolent behavior. In most cases, it remains con-

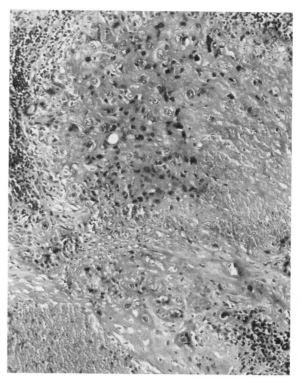

Figure 356
SQUAMOUS CELL CARCINOMA
This hyalinized squamous cell carcinoma of the cervix resembles a placental site trophoblastic tumor. Hyalinization and necrosis are evident. (Courtesy of Dr. Robert H. Young, Boston, MA.)

fined to the uterus. Most placental site trophoblastic tumors are benign, but approximately 10 to 15 percent behave in a highly malignant fashion (101–103,106,108,110–112). In the few overtly malignant cases, lungs, liver, abdominal cavity, and brain have been involved by metastases; the metastases retain the same histologic pattern as that of the uterine primary tumor. Metastases usually develop rapidly after the initial diagnosis, but one reported tumor recurred 5 years after hysterectomy (104). Although serum hCG levels are very useful in monitoring disease, the serum level of hCG is typically low despite a large tumor burden (103) because the predominant cellular population of the tumor is intermediate trophoblast, which secretes only small amounts of hCG. The malignant cases have not responded to the multiagent chemotherapy used to treat choriocarcinoma. Currently, the criteria to distinguish benign from malignant placental site trophoblastic tumors have not been completely established. The microscopic criteria that have been proposed as prognostic indicators have been described previously (see Microscopic Findings in this section).

EXAGGERATED PLACENTAL SITE

Definition. The exaggerated placental site is an exuberant infiltrative proliferation of intermediate trophoblast at the placental site. This lesion was formerly called *syncytial endometritis* or *benign chorionic invasion*.

Clinical and Pathologic Findings. An exaggerated placental site may occur in association with normal pregnancy, an abortion, and frequently, a hydatidiform mole (115). The lesion is characterized by extensive trophoblastic invasion of the endometrium (figs. 357, 358) and underlying myometrium (fig. 359). In addition to mononucleate intermediate trophoblastic cells, there are large numbers of syncytiotrophoblastic giant cells. Despite the extensive infiltration by intermediate trophoblastic cells, the overall architecture is not disturbed. For example, endometrial glands may be completely surrounded by trophoblast but are not destroyed. On examination of curettage specimens, distinction from a placental site trophoblastic tumor may be particularly difficult. If the process is microscopic, lacking in mitotic activity, separated by masses of hyalin, and admixed with fragments of decidua and chorionic villi, it is probably an exaggerated placental site. Invasion of spiral arteries by intermediate trophoblast normally occurs at the placental site and should not be considered evidence for a neoplasm. In contrast, a lesion with features of an exaggerated placental site but composed of confluent masses of trophoblast or containing more than a rare mitotic figure should be classified as a placental site trophoblastic tumor. Villi are usually not identified in placental site trophoblastic tumors.

PLACENTAL SITE NODULE AND PLAQUE

Definition. Discrete nodules or plaques of intermediate trophoblastic cells surrounded by hyalinized material characterize the placental site nodule or plaque.

Clinical and Pathologic Findings. These lesions are found in the endometrium or superficial myometrium and are usually detected in an endometrial curettage performed for abnormal bleeding. These lesions may also be incidental findings. Patients range in age from 27 to 45 years. Some women have had hydatidiform moles, and a few patients have had tubal ligations, sometimes as long as 4 years before the diagnosis (114,116).

The lesions are usually not evident on gross examination. When they are, they appear as a yellow excrescence in the endometrium or as a tan or hemorrhagic nodule in the myometrium. Microscopic examination reveals single or multiple well-circumscribed round, oval, or plaquelike lesions that are extensively hyalinized (figs. 360, 361). The cells in the lesion have abundant amphophilic, eosinophilic, or occasionally vacuolated cytoplasm with round, slightly irregular nuclei that have a degenerative appearance (fig. 362). Mitotic figures are rare or absent. The cells are typically diffusely positive for keratin when broadly reactive antibodies are used (fig. 363). They are usually focally positive for hPL and rarely positive for hCG.

The microscopic and immunohistochemical findings indicate that these cells are intermediate trophoblast. Based on their clinical and pathologic features, the lesions appear to represent an involuted placental site that has not been completely resorbed. The nodules often appear to have central collapsed vascular lumina that are probably the remains of spiral arteries that were invaded by intermediate trophoblast and then became hyalinized (fig. 363). They may remain in the uterus for several years after an obvious gestational event or perhaps an unrecognized pregnancy.

Differential Diagnosis. These lesions may be confused with a placental site trophoblastic tumor. The placental site nodule is distinguished from a placental site trophoblastic tumor by its small size, circumscription, extensive hyalinization, and low levels of mitotic activity. The clinical setting also differs. The placental site nodule is discovered in the curettage specimens taken from a patient who is not considered pregnant at the time of diagnosis, whereas the placental site trophoblastic tumor is typically diagnosed in curettage specimens taken from a patient who

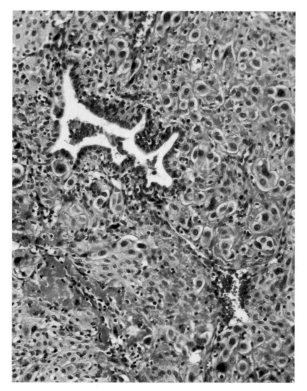

Figure 357
EXAGGERATED PLACENTAL SITE
Note the extensive replacement of the endometrial stroma by intermediate trophoblastic cells. The infiltrative process replaces the endometrial stroma but does not destroy endometrial glands.

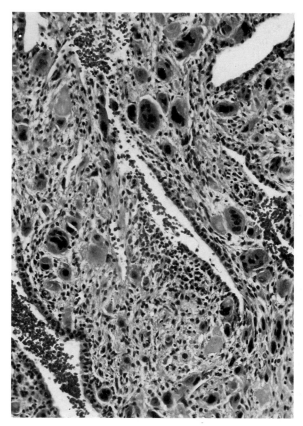

Figure 358
EXAGGERATED PLACENTAL SITE
The predominant trophoblastic population in this illustration is intermediate trophoblast; however, large numbers of syncytiotrophoblastic giant cells are also present.

Figure 359
EXAGGERATED PLACENTAL SITE
The underlying myometrium is invaded by trophoblastic cells, most of which are syncytiotrophoblastic giant cells.

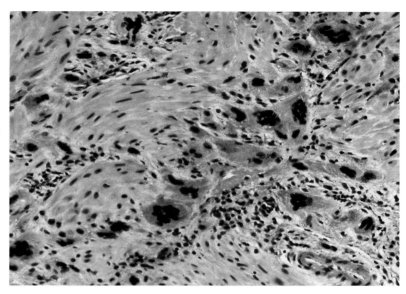

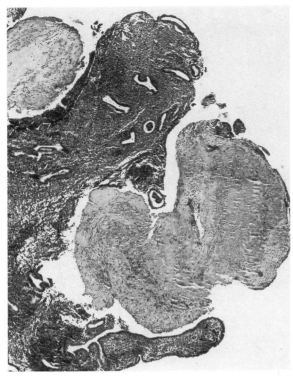

Figure 360
PLACENTAL SITE NODULE
Under low magnification, this placental site nodule appears as a well-circumscribed hyalinized masses admixed with normal endometrium.

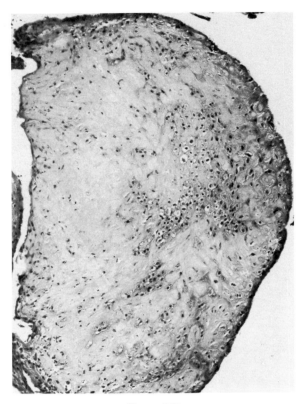

Figure 361
PLACENTAL SITE NODULE
A well-circumscribed rounded hyalinized lesion with vacuolated intermediate trophoblastic cells in its center is illustrated.

is clinically thought to have a missed abortion. Occasionally, a placental site trophoblastic tumor may, in areas, have a nodular appearance. If this represents the only material in the curettage specimen, the tumor may closely simulate a placental site nodule. The diagnosis of a placental site trophoblastic tumor should be suspected if there are more than just a few discrete nodules and if there are fragments of tissue that are more cellular, contain larger more atypical nuclei, and lack hyalin. In these cases, close follow-up with serial serum hCG titers should be undertaken. If the levels remain even slightly elevated, a repeat curettage is indicated.

The placental site nodule may be confused with the rare hyalinized squamous cell carcinoma of the cervix (fig. 356). In contrast to the placental site nodule, this carcinoma is larger, has a greater degree of cytologic atypia and mitotic activity, and is hPL negative. Also, careful search usually discloses typical keratinized squamous cells.

Clinical Behavior and Treatment. So far, all patients who have been reported have had no evidence of recurrent disease, and the lesion is regarded as benign. After the diagnosis in curettage specimens, no further treatment is necessary.

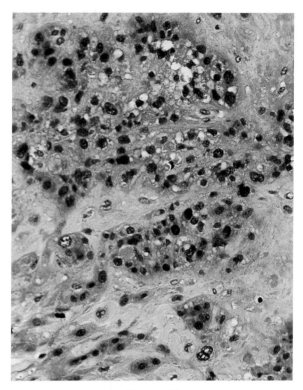

Figure 362
PLACENTAL SITE NODULE
At high magnification, this placental site nodule shows intermediate trophoblastic cells with slightly vacuolated cytoplasm and round, irregular nuclei that have a degenerative appearance.

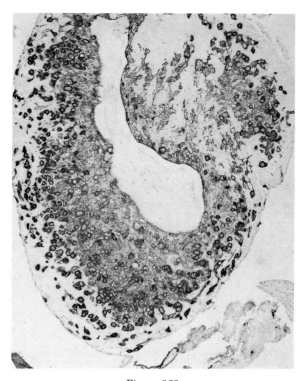

Figure 363
PLACENTAL SITE NODULE
All of the intermediate trophoblastic cells in this placental site nodule are immunoreactive for cytokeratin. Note the central space, probably representing the remains of a vascular lumen. Immunoperoxidase-cytokeratin AE1/AE3 with hematoxylin counterstain.

UNCLASSIFIED TROPHOBLASTIC LESIONS

Occasionally, trophoblastic lesions do not conform with the histologic criteria described for specific lesions. This category includes lesions with gross features of a mole but lacking abnormal trophoblastic activity and lesions displaying abnormal trophoblastic proliferation in association with nonmolar villi or without a villous component. The latter lesions lack the typical appearance of choriocarcinoma or placental site trophoblastic tumor. They should be described accurately and not classified specifically until their significance has been determined.

At times, curettage specimens obtained from a patient in whom a previous diagnosis of gestational trophoblastic disease has been made or after a normal pregnancy or abortion may contain small and scant fragments of trophoblast showing no clear-cut delineation into cytotrophoblast and syncytiotrophoblast (fig. 364) or a specimen consisting mainly of intermediate trophoblast admixed with blood clot (fig. 365) (66). In these instances, a diagnosis of atypical trophoblast consistent with persistent trophoblastic disease or atypical trophoblast suspicious but not diagnostic of choriocarcinoma or placental site trophoblastic tumor, as the case may be, may be appropriate. Careful clinical follow-up with serum hCG assays usually resolves the problem.

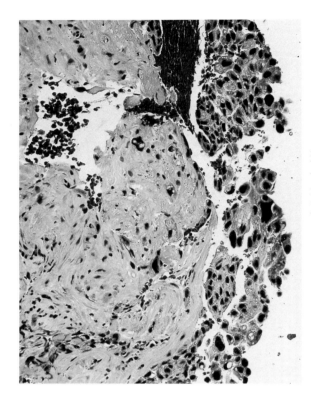

Figure 364
UNCLASSIFIED TROPHOBLASTIC LESION
A fragment of myometrium with overlying trophoblast shows no clear-cut delineation into cytotrophoblast or syncytiotrophoblast. The trophoblast probably represents intermediate trophoblast. When found in a curettage specimen from a patient with a previous diagnosis of gestational trophoblastic disease, a diagnosis of atypical trophoblast consistent with persistent trophoblastic disease is appropriate.

Figure 365
UNCLASSIFIED TROPHOBLASTIC LESION
Intermediate trophoblast is admixed with blood clot in a curettage specimen obtained from a patient with a prior diagnosis of a complete hydatidiform mole. In this instance, the diagnosis of atypical trophoblast consistent with persistent trophoblastic disease is appropriate.

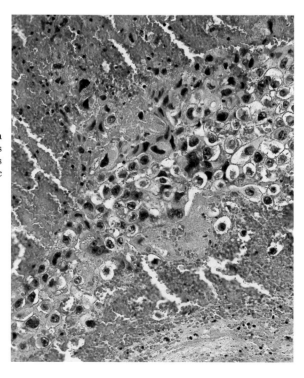

REFERENCES

Hydatidiform Mole (complete, partial, and invasive)

1. Bagshawe KD, Lawler SD, Paradinas FJ, Dent J, Brown P, Boxer GM. Gestational trophoblastic tumours following initial diagnosis of partial hydatidiform mole. Lancet 1990;335:1074–6.
2. Bagshawe KD, Wilson H, Dublon P, Smith A, Baldwin M, Kardana A. Follow-up after hydatidiform mole: studies using radioimmunoassay for urinary human chorionic gonadotrophin (HCG). J Obstet Gynaecol Br Commonw 1973;80:461–8.
3. Berkowitz RS, Goldstein DP, Bernstein MR. Natural history of partial molar pregnancy. Obstet Gynecol 1985;66:677–81.
4. Bracken MB, Brinton LA, Hayashi K. Epidemiology of hydatidiform mole and choriocarcinoma. Epidemiol Rev 1984;6:52–75.
5. Brescia RJ, Kurman RJ, Main C, Surti U, Szulman AE. Immunocytochemical localization of chorionic gonadotropin, placental lactogen, and placental alkaline phosphatase in the diagnosis of complete and partial hydatidiform moles. Int J Gynecol Pathol 1987;6:213–29.
6. Buckley J. Epidemiology of gestational trophoblastic diseases. In: Szulman AE, Buchsbaum HJ, eds. Gestational trophoblastic disease. New York: Springer-Verlag, 1987:8–26 (Buchsbaum HJ, ed. Clinical perspectives in obstetrics and gynecology; Vol 7).
7. Craighill MC, Cramer DW. Epidemiology of complete molar pregnancy. J Reprod Med 1984;29:784–7.
8. Curry SL, Hammond CB, Tyrey L, Creasman WT, Parker RT. Hydatidiform mole: diagnosis, management, and long-term followup of 347 patients. Obstet Gynecol 1975;45:1–8.
9. Czernobilsky B, Barash A, Lancet M. Partial moles: a clinicopathologic study of 25 cases. Obstet Gynecol 1982;59:75–7.
10. Davis JR, Surwit EA, Garay JP, Fortier KJ. Sex assignment in gestational trophoblastic neoplasia. Am J Obstet Gynecol 1984;148:722–5.
11. Dehner LP. Gestational and nongestational trophoblastic neoplasia: a historic and pathobiologic surgery. Am J Surg Pathol 1980;4:43–58.
12. Elston CW. Development and structure of trophoblastic neoplasms. In: Loke YW, Whyte A, eds. Biology of trophoblast. New York: Elsevier, 1983:188–232.
13. Elston W. The histopathology of trophoblastic tumours. J Clin Pathol Suppl (R Coll Pathol) 1976;10:111–31.
14. Elston CW. Trophoblastic tumors of the placenta. In: Fox H, ed. Pathology of the placenta. Philadelphia: WB Saunders, 1978:368–425 (Bennington, JL, ed. Major problems in pathology; Vol 7).
15. Fisher RA, Lawler SD, Ormerod MG, Imrie PR, Povey S. Flow cytometry used to distinguish between complete and partial hydatidiform moles. Placenta 1987;8:249–56.
16. Gaber LW, Redline RW, Mostoufi-Zadeh M, Driscoll SG. Invasive partial mole. Am J Clin Pathol 1986;85:722–4.
17. Goldstein DP, Berkowitz RS. Gestational trophoblastic neoplasms. Clinical principles of diagnosis and management. Philadelphia: WB Saunders, 1982 (Friedman EA, ed. Major problems in obsetrics and gynecology; Vol 14).
18. Hertig AT, Sheldon WH. Hydatidiform mole—pathologico-clinical correlation of 200 cases. Am J Obstet Gynecol 1947;53:1–36.
19. Jacobs PA, Hunt PA, Matsuura JS, Wilson CC, Szulman AE. Complete and partial hydatidiform mole in Hawaii: cytogenetics, morphology and epidemiology. Br J Obstet Gynaecol 1982;89:258–66.
20. Jacobs PA, Szulman AE, Funkhouser J, Matsuura JS, Wilson CC. Human triploidy: relationship between parental origin of the additional haploid complement and development of partial hydatidiform mole. Ann Hum Genet 1982;46:223–31.
21. Jacobson TJ, Enzer N. Hydatidiform mole with benign metastasis to lung. Histologic evidence of regressing lesions in the lung. Am J Obstet Gynecol 1959;78:868–75.
22. Kajii T, Ohama K. Androgenetic origin of hydatidiform mole. Nature 1977;268:633–4.
23. Kurman RJ, Young RH, Norris HJ, Main CS, Lawrence WD, Scully RE. Immunocytochemical localization of placental lactogen and chorionic gonadotropin in the normal placenta and trophoblastic tumors, with emphasis on intermediate trophoblast and the placental site trophoblastic tumor. Int J Gynecol Pathol 1984;3:101–21.
24. Lage JM, Driscoll SG, Yavner DL, Olivier AP, Mark SD, Weinberg DS. Hydatidiform moles. Am J Clin Pathol 1988;89: 596–600.
25. Lage JM, Weinberg DS, Yavner DL, Bieber FR. The biology of tetraploid hydatidiform moles: histopathology, cytogenetics, and flow cytometry. Hum Pathol 1989;20:419–25.
26. Lurain JR, Brewer JI, Torok EE, Halpern B. Natural history of hydatidiform mole after primary evacuation. Am J Obstet Gynecol 1983;145:591–5.
27. Matsuura J, Chiu D, Jacobs PA, Szulman AE. Complete hydatidiform mole in Hawaii: an epidemiologic study. Genet Epidemiol 1984;1:271–84.
28. Mazur MT, Kurman RJ. Gestational trophoblastic disease. In: Kurman RJ, ed. Blaustein's pathology of the female genital tract. 3rd ed. New York: Springer-Verlag, 1987:835–75.
29. Messerli ML, Lilienfeld AM, Parmley T, Woodruff JD, Rosenshein NB. Risk factors for gestational trophoblastic neoplasia. Am J Obstet Gynecol 1985;153: 294–300.
30. Mostoufi-Zadeh M, Berkowitz RS, Driscoll SG. Persistence of partial mole. Am J Clin Pathol 1987;87:377–80.
31. Ohama K, Kajii T, Okamoto E, et al. Dispermic origin of XY hydatidiform moles. Nature 1981;292:551–2.
32. Rice LW, Berkowitz RS, Lage JM, Goldstein DP, Bernstein MR. Persistent gestational trophoblastic tumor after partial hydatidiform mole. Gynecol Oncol 1990;36:358–62.
33. Smith EB, Szulman AE, Hinsaw W, Tyrey L, Surti U, Hammond CB. Human chorionic gonadotropin levels in complete and partial hydatidiform moles and in nonmolar abortuses. Am J Obstet Gynecol 1984; 149:129–32.
34. Surani MA, Barton SC, Norris ML. Development of reconstituted mouse eggs suggests imprinting of the genome during gametogenesis. Nature 1984;308:548–50.

35. Surti U. Genetic concepts and techniques. In: Szulman A, Buchsbaum H, eds. Gestational trophoblastic disease. New York: Springer-Verlag, 1987:111–21 (Buchsbaum HJ, ed. Clinical perspectives in obstetrics and gynecology; Vol 7).

36. Surti U, Szulman AE, O'Brien S. Dispermic origin and clinical outcome of three complete hydatidiform moles with 46,XY karyotype. Am J Obstet Gynecol 1982; 144:84–7.

37. Surti U, Szulman AE, Wagner K, Leppert M, O'Brien S. Tetraploid partial hydatidiform moles: two cases with a triple paternal contribution and a 92,XXXY karyotype. Hum Genet 72:15–21.

38. Szulman AE. Complete hydatidiform mole: clinicopathologic features. In: Szulman AE, Buchsbaum HJ, eds. Gestational trophoblastic disease. New York: Springer-Verlag, 1987:27–36 (Buchsbaum HJ, ed. Clinical perspectives in obstetrics and gynecology, Vol 7).

39. Szulman AE. Partial hydatidiform mole. In: Szulman AE, Buchsbaum HJ, eds. Gestational trophoblastic disease. New York: Springer-Verlag, 1987:37–44 (Buchsbaum HJ, ed. Clinical perspectives in obstetrics and gynecology, Vol 7).

40. Szulman AE. Syndromes of hydatidiform moles. Partial vs. complete. J Reprod Med 1984;29:788–91.

41. Szulman AE, Ma HK, Wong LC, Hsu C. Residual trophoblastic disease in association with partial hydatidiform moles. Obstet Gynecol 1981; 57:392–4.

42. Szulman AE, Surti U. The clinicopathologic profile of the partial hydatidiform mole. Obstet Gynecol 1982; 59:597–602.

43. Szulman AE, Surti U. The syndromes of hydatidiform mole. I. Cytogenetic and morphologic correlations. Am J Obstet Gynecol 1978;131:665–71.

44. Szulman AE, Surti U. The syndromes of hydatidiform mole. II. Morphologic evolution of the complete and partial mole. Am J Obstet Gynecol 1978;132:20–7.

45. Takeuchi S. Nature of invasive mole and its rational management. Semin Oncol 1982;9:181–6.

46. Vassilakos P, Riotton G, Kajii T. Hydatidiform mole: two entities. Am J Obstet Gynecol 1977;127:167–70.

47. Vejerslev LO, Fisher RA, Surti U, Walke N. Hydatidiform mole: cytogenetically unusual cases and their implications for the present classification [erratum; Am J Obstet Gynecol 1988;159:537]. Am J Obstet Gynecol 1987;157:180–4.

48. Wake T, Seki T, Fujita H, et al. Malignant potential of homozygous and heterozygous complete moles. Cancer Res 1984;44:1226–30.

49. Wake N, Takagi N, Sasaki M. Androgenesis as a cause of hydatidiform mole. J Natl Cancer Inst 1978;60: 51–7.

50. Wallace DC, Surti U, Adams CW, Szulman AE. Complete moles have paternal chromosomes but maternal mitochondrial DNA. Hum Genet 1982;61:145–7.

51. Wong LC, Ma HK. The syndrome of partial mole. Arch Gynecol 1984; 234:161–6.

Choriocarcinoma

52. Aozasa K, Ito H, Kohro T, Ha K, Nakamura M, Okada A. Choriocarcinoma in infant and mother. Acta Pathol Jpn 1981;31:317–22.

53. Bagshawe KD. Risk and prognostic factors in trophoblastic neoplasia. Cancer 1976;38:1373–85.

54. Berkowitz RS, Goldstein DP, Bernstein MR. Choriocarcinoma following term gestation. Gynecol Oncol 1984;17:52–7.

55. Brewer JI, Mazur MT. Gestational choriocarcinoma. Its origin in the placenta during seemingly normal pregnancy. Am J Surg Pathol 1981;5:267–77.

56. Brewer JI, Smith RT, Pratt GB. Choriocarcinoma. Absolute 5 year survival rates of 122 patients treated by hysterectomy. Am J Obstet Gynecol 1963;85:841–3.

57. Carlson JA Jr, Day TG Jr, Kuhns JG, Howell RS Jr, Masterson BJ. Endoarterial pulmonary metastasis of malignant trophoblast associated with a term intrauterine pregnancy. Gynecol Oncol 1984;17:241–8.

58. Civantos F, Rywlin AM. Carcinoma with trophoblastic differentiation and secretion of chorionic gonadotrophins. Cancer 1972;29:789–98.

59. Daamen CB, Bloem GW, Westerbeek AJ. Chorionepithelioma in mother and child. J Obstet Gynecol Br Commonw 1961;68:144–9.

60. Davis JR, Surwit EA, Garay JP, Fortier KJ. Sex assignment in gestational trophoblastic neoplasia. Am J Obstet Gynecol 1984;148:722–5.

61. Deligdisch L, Driscoll SG, Goldstein DP. Gestational trophoblastic neoplasms: morphologic correlates of therapeutic response. Am J Obstet Gynecol 1978;130:801–6.

62. Deligdisch L, Waxman J. Metastatic gestational trophoblastic neoplasm. A study of two cases in unusual clinical settings and review of the literature. Gynecol Oncol 1984;19:323–8.

63. Dougherty CM, Cunningham C, Mickal A. Choriocarcinoma with metastasis in a postmenopausal woman. Am J Obstet Gynecol 1978;132:700–1.

64. Driscoll SG. Choriocarcinoma. An "incidental finding" within a term placenta. Obstet Gynecol 1963;21:96–101.

65. Duncan DA, Mazur MT. Trophoblastic tumors: ultrastructural comparison of choriocarcinoma and placental-site trophoblastic tumor. Hum Pathol 1989;20:370–81.

66. Elston CW, Bagshawe KD. The diagnosis of trophoblastic tumours from uterine curettings. J Clin Pathol 1972;25:111–8.

67. Ertungealp E, Axelrod J, Stanek A, Boyce J, Sedlis A. Skin metastases from malignant gestational trophoblastic disease: report of two cases. Am J Obstet Gynecol 1982;143:843–6.

68. Greene JB, McCue SA. Choriocarcinoma with cerebral metastases coexistent with a first pregnancy. Am J Obstet Gynecol 1978;131:253–4.

69. Guvener S, Kazancigil A, Erez S. Long latent development of trophoblastic disease. Am J Obstet Gynecol 1972;114:679–84.

70. Hammond CB, Borchert LG, Tyrey L, Creasman WT, Parker RT. Treatment of metastatic trophoblastic disease: good and poor prognosis. Am J Obstet Gynecol 1973;115:451–7.

71. Hammond CB, Hertz R, Ross GT, Lipsett MB, Odell WD. Diagnostic problems of choriocarcinoma and related trophoblastic neoplasms. Obstet Gynecol 1967;29:224–9.

72. Heaton GE, Matthews TH, Christopherson WM. Malignant trophoblastic tumors with massive hemorrhage presenting as liver primary. A report of two cases. Am J Surg Pathol 1986;10:342–7.

73. Hertig AT, Mansell H. Tumors of the female sex organs. Part I. Hydatidiform mole and choriocarcinoma. Atlas of Tumor Pathology. Sect 9, 1st Series, Fascicle 33. Washington, D.C.: Armed Forces Institute of Pathology, 1956.

74. Heyderman E, Chapman DV, Richardson TC, Calvert I, Rosen SW. Human chorionic gonadotropin and human placental lactogen in extragonadal tumors. An immunoperoxidase study of ten non-germ cell neoplasms. Cancer 1985;56:2674–82.

75. Hou PC, Pang SC. Chorionepithelioma: an analytical study of 28 necropsied cases with special reference to the possibility of spontaneous retrogression. J Pathol Bacteriol 1956;72:95–104.

76. Kubosawa H, Nagao K, Kondo Y, Ishige H, Inaba N. Coexistence of adenocarcinoma and choriocarcinoma in the sigmoid colon. Cancer 1984;54:866–8.

77. Lathrop JC, Wachtel TJ, Meissner GF. Uterine choriocarcinoma fourteen years following bilateral tubal ligation. Obstet Gynecol 1978;51:477–88.

78. Libshitz HI, Baber CE, Hammond CB. The pulmonary metastases of choriocarcinoma. Obstet Gynecol 1977;49:412–6.

79. Lurain JR, Brewer JI, Torok EE, Halpern B. Gestational trophoblastic disease: treatment results at the Brewer Trophoblastic Disease Center. Obstet Gynecol 1982;60:354–60.

80. Mazur MT. Metastatic gestational choriocarcinoma. Unusual pathologic variant following therapy. Cancer 1989;63:1370–7.

81. Mazur MT, Lurain JR, Brewer JI. Fatal gestational choriocarcinoma. Cancer 1982;50:1833–46.

82. Mittal KK, Kachru RB, Brewer JI. The HLA and ABO antigens in trophoblastic disease. Tissue Antigens 1975;6:57–69.

83. Nisula BC, Tahadouros GS. Thyroid function in gestational trophoblastic neoplasia: evidence that the thyrotropic activity of chorionic gonadotropin mediates the thyrotoxicosis of choriocarcinoma. Am J Obstet Gynecol 1990;138:77–85.

84. Novak E, Seah CS. Choriocarcinoma of the uterus; study of 74 cases from the Mathieu Memorial Chorionepithelioma Registry. Am J Obstet Gynecol 1954;-67:933–61.

85. Obe JA, Rosen N, Koss LG. Primary choriocarcinoma of the urinary bladder. Report of a case with probable epithelial origin. Cancer 1983;52:1405–9.

86. Ober WB, Edgcomb JH, Price EB Jr. The pathology of choriocarcinoma. Ann NY Acad Sci 1971;172:299–426

87. Ober WB, Maier RC. Gestational choriocarcinoma of the fallopian tube. Diagn Gynecol Obstet 1981;3:213–31.

88. Olive DL, Lurain JR, Brewer JI. Choriocarcinoma associated with term gestation. Am J Obstet Gynecol 1984;148:711–6.

89. Park WW, Lees JC. Choriocarcinoma. Arch Pathol 1950;73:205–41.

90. Saigo PE, Rosen PP. Mammary carcinoma with "choriocarcinomatous" features. Am J Surg Pathol 1981;5:773–8.

91. Sasaki K, Hata H, Nakano R. ABO blood group in patients with malignant trophoblastic disease. Gynecol Obstet Invest 1985;20:23–6.

92. Savage J, Subby W, Okagaki T. Adenocarcinoma of the endometrium with trophoblastic differentiation and metastases as choriocarcinoma: a case report. Gynecol Oncol 1987;26:257–62.

93. Surwit EA, Alberts DS, Christian CD, Graham VE. Poor-prognosis gestational trophoblastic disease: an update. Obstet Gynecol 1984;64:21–6.

94. Tanimura A, Natsuyama H, Kawano M, Tanimura Y, Tanaka T, Kitazono M. Primary choriocarcinoma of the lung. Hum Pathol 1985;16:1281–4.

95. Tsao MS, Schraufnagel D, Wang NS. Pulmonary metastasis of choriocarcinoma with a miliary roentgenographic pattern [Letter]. Arch Pathol Lab Med 1981;105:557–8.

96. Tsuji K, Yagi S, Nakano R. Increased risk of malignant transformation of hydatidiform moles in older gravidas: a cytogenetic study. Obstet Gynecol 1981;58:351–5.

97. Van Der Werf AJ, Broeders GH, Vooys GP, Mastboom JL. Metastatic choriocarcinoma as a complication of pregnancy. Obstet Gynecol 1970;35:78–88.

98. Vogler C, Schmidt WA, Edwards CL. Primary ovarian nongestational choriocarcinoma. Report of a case in a young woman of childbearing age. Diagn Gynecol Obstet 1981;3:331–6.

99. Wake N, Tanaka K, Chapman V, Matsui S, Sandberg AA. Chromosomes and cellular origin of choriocarcinoma. Cancer Res 1981;41:3137–43.

100. Yamashita K, Nakamura T, Shimizu T. Absence of major histocompatibility complex antigens in choriocarcinoma. Am J Obstet Gynecol 984;150:896–7.

Placental Site Trophoblastic Tumor

101. Eckstein RP, Paradinas FJ, Bagshawe KD. Placental site trophoblastic tumour (trophoblastic pseudotumour). Histopathology 1982;6:211–26.

102. Eckstein RP, Russell P, Friedlander ML, Tattersall MH, Bradfield A. Metastasizing placental site trophoblastic tumor: a case study. Hum Pathol 1985;16:632–6.

103. Finkler NJ, Berkowitz RS, Driscoll SG, Goldstein DP, Bernstein MR. Clinical experience with placental site trophoblastic tumors at the New England Trophoblastic Disease Center. Obstet Gynecol 1988;71:854–7.

104. Gloor E, Dialdas J, Hurlimann J, Ribolzi J, Barrelet L. Placental site trophoblastic tumor (trophoblastic pseudotumor) of the uterus with metastases and fatal outcome. Clinical and autopsy outcome of a case. Am J Surg Pathol 1983;7:483–6.

105. Gloor E, Hurlimann J. Trophoblastic pseudotumor of the uterus: clinicopathologic report with immunohistochemical and ultrastructural studies. Am J Surg Pathol 1981;5:5–13.

106. Hopkins M, Nunez C, Murphy JR, Wentz WB. Malignant placental site trophoblastic tumor. Obstet Gynecol 1985;66(Suppl):95S–100S.

107. Kurman RJ, Main CS, Chen HC. Intermediate trophoblast: a distinctive form of trophoblast with specific morphological, biochemical and functional features. Placenta 1984;5:349–69.

108. Kurman RJ, Scully RE, Norris HJ. Trophoblastic pseudotumor of the uterus: an exaggerated form of "syncytial endometritis" simulating a malignant tumor. Cancer 1976;38:1214–26.

109. Nagelberg SB, Rosen SW. Clinical and laboratory investigation of a virilized woman with placental site trophoblastic tumor. Obstet Gynecol 1985;65:527–34.

110. Nickels J, Risberg B, Melander S. Trophoblastic pseudotumor of the uterus. Acta Pathol Microbiol Scand [A] 1978;86:14–6.

111. Twiggs LB, Okagaki T, Philips GL, Stroemer JR, Adcock LL. Trophoblastic pseudotumor—evidence of malignant disease potential. Gynecol Oncol 1981; 12:238–48.

112. Young RE, Kurman RJ, Scully RE. Proliferations and tumors of intermediate trophoblast of the placental site. Semin Diagn Pathol 1988;5:223–37.

113. Young RE, Scully RE, McCluskey RT. A distinctive glomerular lesion complicating placental site trophoblastic tumor. Hum Pathol 1985;16:35–42.

Exaggerated Placental Site and Placental Site Nodule

114. Carinelli SG, Vendola N, Zanottif, Benzi G. Placental site nodules. [Abstract]. Pathol Res Pract 1989;185:30.

115. Ewing J. Chorioma. Surg Gynecol Obstet 1910;10:366–92.

116. Young RH, Kurman RJ, Scully RE. Placental site nodules and plaques. A clinicopathologic analysis of 20 cases. Am J Surg Pathol 1990;14:1001–9.

GENERAL ASPECTS OF CLINICAL MANAGEMENT AND STAGING

Since the demonstration in 1956 that systemic chemotherapy could cure metastatic choriocarcinoma, enormous progress has been made in the clinical management of this disease (8). Initially, all patients were managed in the same way, with a single chemotherapeutic agent. In the early 1970s, it became apparent that certain patients using this regimen were at a high risk of failure. In an effort to improve survival, certain clinical criteria were selected to identify patients at high risk and to whom multiagent chemotherapy was administered at the outset of treatment (5). This led to the development of a clinical classification and staging system that was related to treatment planning but not based solely on the histologic diagnosis. In addition to the advances in systemic chemotherapy, the development of sensitive assays for the detection of hCG (11) in blood or urine specimens led to the introduction of monitoring of the tumor during treatment by serial measurement of serum hCG levels.

Staging. There are currently two widely used staging systems for patients with gestational trophoblastic disease, both of which are based on an anatomic classification proposed by the International Federation of Obstetrics and Gynecology (Table 16). The older of the two staging systems is a clinical classification (Table 17), and the more recent system is a prognostic scoring system proposed by the World Health Organization (Table 18) (13).

Clinical Management. The most common presenting symptom of gestational trophoblastic disease is uterine bleeding that follows an abortion, a term pregnancy, or the evacuation of a mole. Other less common clinical signs and symptoms that follow evacuation of a mole include 1) subinvolution of the uterus; 2) acute massive intraperitoneal bleeding, usually signaling uterine perforation; or 3) persistently enlarged ovarian lutein cysts (7).

The diagnosis of malignant gestational trophoblastic disease is based on a histologic diagnosis of residual molar disease after evacuation of a hydatidiform mole, of choriocarcinoma or placental site trophoblastic tumor, or a plateau or rise in successive serum hCG levels after evacuation of a mole. After the diagnosis has been made, a number of clinical tests are performed to determine whether the patient has nonmetastatic or metastatic disease. These include chest X rays; CT scanning of the head, chest, and liver; kidney and liver function tests; and hematologic assessment. Although desirable, histologic diagnosis may not always be feasible. On the basis of these studies, the disease is classified as either nonmetastatic or metastatic.

Nonmetastatic Gestational Trophoblastic Disease. Treatment of nonmetastatic disease is single-agent systemic chemotherapy, usually methotrexate or actinomycin D. To reduce toxicity, many centers now use methotrexate and folinic acid rescue. Treatment is monitored by the serum hCG level. Because hCG becomes undetectable in the serum when a tumor load of only 1000 trophoblastic cells remains (3), it has become common practice to continue treatment just beyond an undetectable hCG level. Hysterectomy is performed in approximately 10 percent of women with nonmetastatic disease, but this does not obviate chemotherapy and serum hCG monitoring. Essentially all patients with nonmetastatic disease are curable.

Metastatic Gestational Trophoblastic Disease. Included in this category are all patients who have evidence of extrauterine disease after a complete metastatic workup. In an effort to provide the most effective chemotherapy for

Table 16

ANATOMIC CLASSIFICATION OF GESTATIONAL TROPHOBLASTIC DISEASE *

Stage	Definition
I	Confined to uterus
II	Metastases to pelvis and vagina
III	Metastases to lung
IV	Distant metastases

* As proposed by the International Federation of Obstetrics and Gynecology.

Table 17

CLINICAL CLASSIFICATION OF MALIGNANT TROPHOBLASTIC DISEASE

I. Nonmetastatic GTD *

II. Metastatic GTD

  A. Good prognosis

    1. Urinary hCG * less than 100,000 IU/24-h urine or less than 40,000 mIU/ml serum

    2. Symptoms present for less than 4 months

    3. No brain or liver metastases

    4. No prior chemotherapy

    5. Pregnancy event is not term delivery (i.e., mole, ectopic, or spontaneous abortion)

  B. Poor prognosis

    1. Urinary hCG greater than 100,000 IU/24-h urine or ? 40,000 mIU/ml serum

    2. Symptoms present for over 4 months

    3. Brain or liver metastases

    4. Prior chemotherapeutic failure

    5. Antecedent term pregnancy

* GTD = gestational trophoblastic disease; hCG = human chorionic gonadotropin.

women with metastasis, they have been divided into low-risk and high-risk groups. High-risk patients have one or more of the following features: 1) a pretreatment hCG titer greater than 40,000 mIU/ml in the serum or greater than 100,000 mIU/ml in a 24-hour urine specimen, 2) symptoms present for more than 4 months, 3) brain or liver metastases, 4) an antecedent term pregnancy, or 5) prior chemotherapeutic failure. Gestational trophoblastic disease after a term gestation has a worse prognosis due to delay in treatment and the greater probability of metastases beyond the lungs and vagina.

Approximately one half of all patients with metastatic disease are in the low-risk group and have been shown to have nearly 100 percent survival with single-agent chemotherapy (6). Women in the low-risk group are treated with either methotrexate or actinomycin D and, if resistance develops, are treated with triple chemotherapy such as methotrexate, actinomycin D, and cyclophosphamide (MAC) (7). On the other hand, the high-risk patients require initial treatment with multiagent systemic chemo-therapy, usually MAC. Patients in the high-risk group who are treated in this manner have a reported survival of 70 percent (2,9). In 1980, a subset of high-risk patients, specifically those with long-standing disease, previous chemotherapy, and liver metastasis were reported to respond poorly to initial treatment with MAC chemotherapy (10). Identification of this ultra–high-risk subset depended on inclusion of patients with three or more of the high-risk factors shown in Table 17 or with a poor prognostic score in the World Health Organization system (Table 18). In an effort to simplify the latter, some investigators have deleted certain factors such as the ABO type, making it more acceptable for routine use (12). In one study, all patients with a score of 7 or less who received initial MAC chemotherapy survived, compared to only 46 percent of those with a score of 8 or more ($P = 0.0004$) (4). These women may benefit from the use of new multiagent regimens, including etoposide (VP-16), methotrexate, actinomycin D alternating with cyclophosphamide, and oncovin (EMA-C0). Analyses of

Table 18
GESTATIONAL TROPHOBLASTIC DISEASE PROGNOSTIC SCORE *

	0	1	2	4
Age (years)	<39	>39		
Antecedent pregnancy	Mole	Abortion	Term pregnancy	
Interval (months)	4	4–6	7–12	>12
Pretreatment hCG [†] (log)	<3	<4	<5	<5
ABO group (female x male)		O x A	B	
		A x O	AB	
Largest tumor (cm)		3–5	5	
Site of metastasis		Spleen, kidney	GI tract, [†] liver	Brain
Number of metastases identified		1–4	4–8	>8
Previous chemotherapy failed			Single drug	2 or more

* <4, Low risk; 5–7, middle risk; >7, high risk.

† hCG = human chorionic gonadotropin, GI tract = gastrointestinal tract.

patients treated with these regimens have shown a sustained remission rate of 80 percent (2,10). Similar to patients with low-risk metastatic disease, some patients with high-risk metastatic disease may benefit from surgical intervention. For example, hysterectomy is appropriate for patients with no evidence of residual metastatic disease but who continue to have an elevated hCG titer due to persistent disease in the uterus. Similarly, thoracotomy for extrauterine disease apparently localized to the lungs may be beneficial (1).

REFERENCES

1. Bagshawe KD. Treatment of high-risk choriocarcinoma. J Reprod Med 1984;29:813–20.
2. DuBeshter B, Berkowitz RS, Goldstein DP, Cramer DW, Bernstein MR. Metastatic gestational trophoblastic disease: experience of the New England Trophoblastic Disease Center, 1965 to 1985. Obstet Gynecol 1987;69:390–5.
3. Goldstein DP, Berkowitz RS. Gestational trophoblastic neoplasms. Clinical principles of diagnosis and management. Philadelphia: WB Saunders, 1982.
4. Gordon AN, Gershenson DM, Copeland LJ, Stringer CA, Morris M, Wharton JT. High-risk metastatic gestational trophoblastic disease: further stratification into two clinical entities. Gynecol Oncol 1989;34:54–6.
5. Hammond CB, Borchert LG, Tyrey L, Creasman WT, Parker RT. Treatment of metastatic trophoblastic disease: good and poor prognosis. Am J Obstet Gynecol 1973;115:451–7.
6. Jones WB. Current management of low-risk metastatic gestational trophoblastic disease. J Reprod Med 1987;32:653–6.
7. Kohorn EI. Nonmetastatic gestational trophoblastic neoplasia. Controversies in definition and management. J Reprod Med 1987;32:644–51.
8. Li MC, Hertz R, Spencer DB. Effects of methotrexate therapy upon choriocarcinoma and chorioadenoma. Proc Soc Exp Biol Med 1956;93:361–6.
9. Surwit EA. Management of high-risk gestational trophoblastic disease. J Reprod Med 1987;32:657–62.
10. Surwit EA, Hammond CB. Recurrent gestational trophoblastic disease. Gynecol Oncol 1981;12:177–85.
11. Vaitukaitis JL, Braunstein GD, Ross GT. A radioimmunoassay which specifically measures human chorionic gonadotropin in the presence of human luteinizing hormone. Am J Obstet Gynecol 1972;113:751–8.
12. Wong LC, Choo YC, Ma HK. Primary and etoposide therapy in gestational trophoblastic disease. An update. Cancer 1986;58:14–7.
13. World Health Organization Scientific Group. Gestational Trophoblastic Disease, Technical Report Series 692. Geneva: World Health Organization, 1983:1–81.

INDEX

✧ ✧ ✧